P9-AFA-570

Get Programming with

HASKELL

Will Kurt

MANNING
Shelter Island

For online information and ordering of this and other Manning books, please visit www.manning.com. The publisher offers discounts on this book when ordered in quantity. For more information, please contact

Special Sales Department
Manning Publications Co.
20 Baldwin Road
PO Box 761
Shelter Island, NY 11964
Email: orders@manning.com

Development editor: Dan Maharry
Senior technical development editor: Al Sherer
Technical development editor: Palak Mathur
Review editor: Aleksandar Dragosavljević
Project editor: David Novak
Copyeditor: Sharon Wilkey
Proofreader: Melody Dolab
Technical proofreader: Vitaly Bragilevsky
Typesetter: Dottie Marsico
Cover designer: Monica Kamsvaag

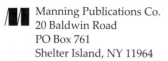

Manning Publications Co.
20 Baldwin Road
PO Box 761
Shelter Island, NY 11964

ISBN 9781617293764
Printed in the United States of America
1 2 3 4 5 6 7 8 9 10 – EBM – 23 22 21 20 19 18

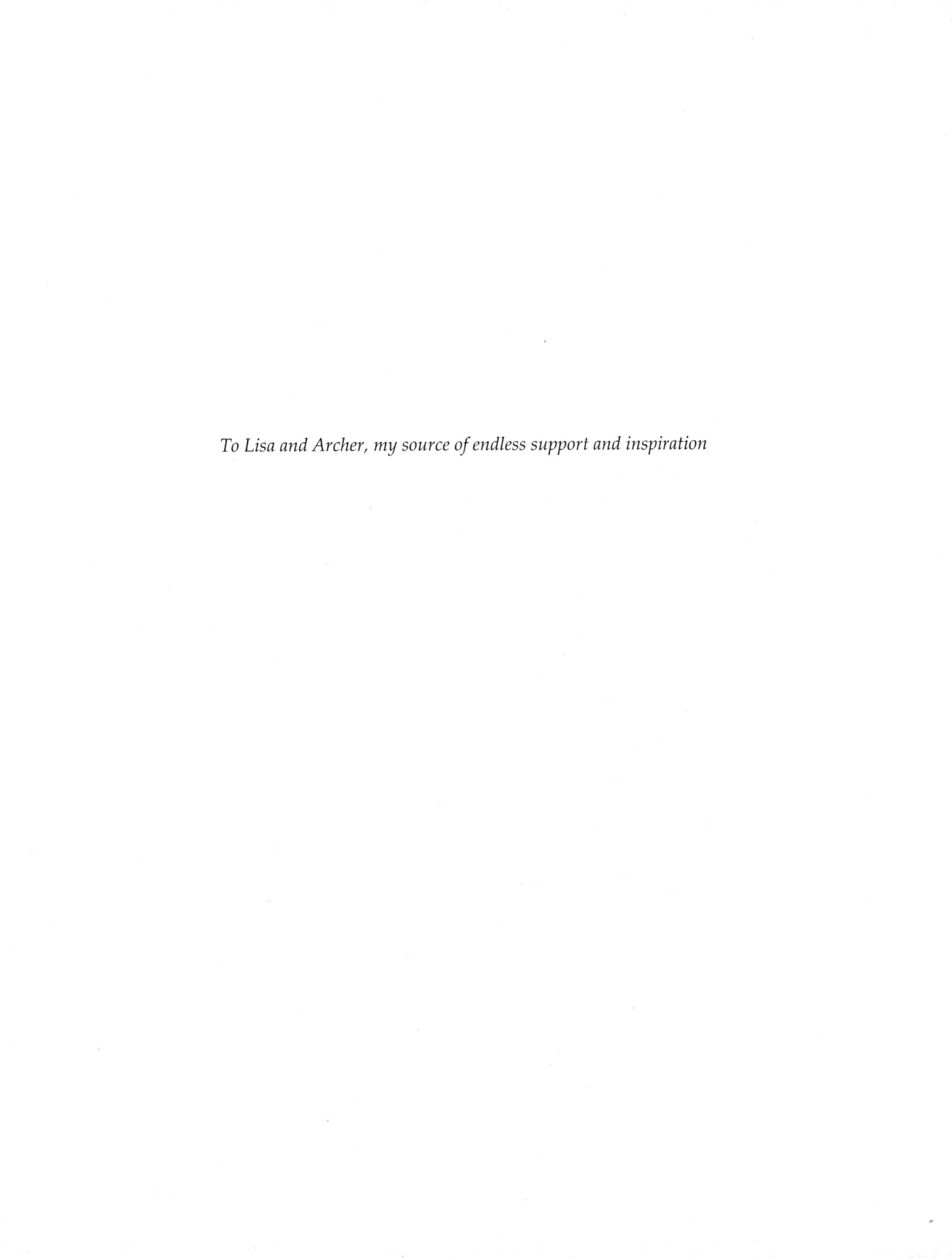

To Lisa and Archer, my source of endless support and inspiration

Contents

Preface

When I was first approached with the idea of writing *Get Programming with Haskell*, I was unsure of whether I should. At the time, my primary interest was in writing about probability topics on my blog, Count Bayesie. Though I had experience teaching both Haskell and functional programming in general, it had been a while, and I was frankly a bit rusty. My active interest in data science, probability, and machine learning were somewhat borne out of a personal frustration with Haskell. Sure, the language was beautiful and powerful, but in a few ugly lines of R and some linear algebra, I could perform sophisticated analysis and build models to predict the future; in Haskell I/O is nontrivial! I was hardly the evangelist to write a Haskell book.

Then I recalled a quote from J.D. Salinger in *Seymour: An Introduction*, where he describes the trick to writing:

> *Ask yourself, as a reader, what piece of writing in all the world ... would [you] most want to read if [you] had [your] heart's choice. The next step is terrible, but so simple I can hardly believe it as I write it. You just sit down shamelessly and write the thing yourself.*

I realized this is exactly why I needed to write *Get Programming with Haskell*. There are a fair number of good Haskell books out there, but none scratched my particular itch for learning Haskell. I've always wanted to read a book that shows you how to solve practical problems that are often a real pain in Haskell. I don't particularly care to see large, industrial-strength programs, but rather fun experiments that let you explore the world with this impressive programming language. I've also always wanted to read a Haskell book that's reasonably short and that, when I'm finished, enables me to feel comfortable doing all sorts of fun weekend projects in Haskell. It was with this realization that the Haskell book I wanted to read didn't yet exist that I decided that writing *Get Programming with Haskell* would be a good idea.

Now that I've finished writing (and reading) this book, I'm thrilled with how much fun I've had. Haskell is an endlessly interesting language that always offers more to teach. It's a difficult language to learn, but that's part of the fun. Nearly every topic in this book is likely something you haven't seen done quite the same way before (unless you're an experienced Haskeller). The joy of Haskell is opening yourself up to a rich learning experience. If you rush to master Haskell, you'll be in for an awful time. If, however, you take the time to explore, to be a beginner again, you'll find it endlessly rewarding.

Acknowledgments

Writing a book is an enormous undertaking, and the author is just one of many people essential to making sure the project is a success. The first people I have to thank are those who supported me both emotionally and intellectually during this great adventure. My wife, Lisa, and son, Archer, have been incredibly patient with my long hours of work and endlessly encouraging of me all along the way. I also have to thank my dear friends Dr. Richard Kelley and Xavier Bengoechea, who were a constant source of feedback, support, and intellectual stimulation. This book never would have happened if it weren't for my graduate advisor, Dr. Fred Harris, giving me the amazing opportunity to teach Haskell to a group of excited undergraduates. Additionally, I want to thank my fellow coworkers at Quick Sprout: Steve Cox, Ian Main, and Hiten Shah, who endured my rambling endlessly about Haskell for the last year.

It's difficult to overstate how much the incredible team at Manning has contributed to this book; more people have helped than can be named in this space. This book would have been a shadow of what it has become without the support of my editor, Dan Maharry. Dan has been essential to pushing every good thought I have into a much better one. I also must give Erin Twohey credit for being the person who first came up with the crazy idea that I should write a Haskell book. My technical editor, Palak Mathur, did a great job of ensuring that the technical content of the book was easy to follow and understand. I also want to thank Vitaly Bragilevsk for providing valuable feedback for improving the code in this book, and Sharon Wilkey for her patient copyediting. Finally, I'd like to recognize the reviewers who took the time to read and comment on the book: Alexander A. Myltsev, Arnaud Bailly, Carlos Aya, Claudio Rodriguez, German Gonzalez-Morris, Hemanth Kapila, James Anaipakos, Kai Gellien, Makarand Deshpande, Mikkel Arentoft, Nikita Dyumin, Peter Hampton, Richard Tobias, Sergio Martinez, Victor Tatai, Vitaly Bragilevsky, and Yuri Klayman.

About this book

The aim of *Get Programming with Haskell* is to give you a thorough-enough introduction to the Haskell programming language that you can write nontrivial, practical programs when you finish it. Many other Haskell books focus heavily on the academic foundations of Haskell but often leave readers a bit bewildered when it comes to accomplishing tasks that would be mundane in other languages. At the end of this book, you should have a solid sense of what makes Haskell interesting as a programming language, and should also be comfortable making larger applications that work with I/O, generate random numbers, work with databases, and generally accomplish the same things you can in whatever language you're most comfortable in.

Who should read this book

This book is for anyone with existing programming experience who wants to take their programming skills and understanding of programming languages to the next level. You can come to your own conclusions about how practical Haskell is, but there are two great and practical reasons to learn it.

First and foremost, even if you never touch Haskell again, learning to be a competent Haskell programmer will make you a better programmer in general. Haskell forces you to write safe and functional code, and to model your problems carefully. Learning to think in Haskell will make you reason better about abstraction and stop potential bugs in code in any language. I have yet to meet a software developer who was proficient in Haskell who was not also an above-average programmer.

The second benefit of learning Haskell is that it provides a crash course in understanding programming language theory. You can't learn enough Haskell to write nontrivial programs and not come away knowing a fair bit about functional programming, lazy evaluation, and sophisticated type systems. This background in programming language theory is not merely beneficial for the academically curious, but serves a great pragmatic purpose as well. Language features from Haskell are constantly making their way into new programming languages and as new features in existing languages. Knowing Haskell and its features well will give you a leg up in understanding what's coming over the horizon in programming for years to come.

How this book is organized

The structure of *Get Programming with Haskell* might be different from many other programming books you've read before. Rather than lengthy chapters, the book is divided into short, easy-to-digest lessons. The lessons are grouped into seven units that cover a common topic. Except for the last unit, all units end with a capstone feature. These capstone exercises combine everything covered in the unit to create a larger code example. All lessons contain Quick Check exercises, easy-to-answer questions that ensure you're keeping up. At the end of each lesson, we also provide a few longer exercises (all of the answers to these are in the back of the book). The units cover the following content:

- *Unit 1*—This unit sets the foundations for functional programming in general, as well as covering the basics of many of the unique features of working with Haskell. After reading this unit, you'll be familiar enough with the basics of functional programming that you could start learning any other functional programming language and find the material familiar.
- *Unit 2*—Here you start looking at Haskell's powerful type system. This unit covers basic types such as `Int`, `Char`, and `Boolean`, and how to make your own data types in Haskell by using these. You'll also begin looking at Haskell's type class system, which allows you to use the same function for a variety of types.
- *Unit 3*—Now that you've covered the basics of types in Haskell, you can move to more-abstract types and type classes that make Haskell so powerful. You'll see how Haskell allows you to combine types in ways that aren't possible in most other programming languages. You'll learn about the `Monoid` and `Semigroup` type classes, in addition to seeing how the `Maybe` type can remove an entire class of errors from your programs.
- *Unit 4*—Finally, you've learned enough Haskell to discuss I/O. This unit covers all of the basics of performing I/O in Haskell and what makes it unique (and sometimes challenging). By the end of this unit, you'll be comfortable writing command-line tools, reading and writing text files, working with Unicode data, and manipulating binary data.

- *Unit 5*—By this point in the book, you've seen several types that create a *context* for other types. `Maybe` types are a context for possibly missing values, and `IO` types are values that have the context of being used in I/O. In this unit, you'll take a deep dive into a family of type classes that are essential for working with values in a context: `Functor`, `Applicative`, and `Monad`. Though they have intimidating names, they provide a relatively straightforward role: using any function in the various contexts that you use frequently. Although these concepts are abstract, they also allow you to find a single way to work with `Maybe` types, `IO` types, and even lists.
- *Unit 6*—With one of the most challenging topics in the book behind you, it's time to start thinking about writing real-world code. The first thing you need is to make sure your code is organized. This unit starts with a lesson on Haskell's module system. You'll then spend the rest of the unit learning about stack, a powerful tool for creating and maintaining Haskell projects.
- *Unit 7*—We conclude this book by looking at some of the missing pieces for working with Haskell in the real world. This unit begins with an overview of handling errors in Haskell, which is different from many other languages. After that, you'll look at three practical tasks in Haskell: using HTTP to make requests to a REST API, parsing JSON data by using the Aeson library, and putting together a database-backed application. You'll end the book by looking at a problem you usually don't think about using Haskell for: efficient, stateful, array-based algorithms.

The most difficult part of learning (and teaching) Haskell is that you need to cover a fairly large number of topics before you can comfortably perform even basic I/O. If your aim is to understand and use Haskell, I recommend that you read each unit in succession. But the intention of this book is for you to be able to stop at a few places in the book and still retain something of value. Unit 1 is designed to provide you with a solid foundation for any functional programming language. Whether it's Clojure, Scala, F#, Racket, or Common Lisp, all of them share the core features discussed in unit 1. If you already have a background in functional programming, you can feel free to skim unit 1, although you should pay close attention to the lessons on partial application and lazy evaluation. At the end of unit 4, you should know enough Haskell to play around on weekend projects. After unit 5, you should be fairly comfortable moving on to more-advanced topics on your own. Units 6 and 7 are primarily focused on using Haskell for practical projects.

About the code

This book contains many code samples. The code in this book is presented in a `fixed-width font like this` to separate it from ordinary text. Many code samples are annotated using numbers to explain each section of the code. More-complicated code examples include arrows pointing out each section and explaining it in more detail. When writing Haskell, you'll make heavy use of the REPL to interact with your code. These sections will be different than normal code sections as they'll have the text `GHCi>` indicating where the user inputs code. There are also occasional references to the command line, in which case `$` is used to indicate where a user is to input commands.

There are many exercises throughout the book. The exercises take the form of quick checks, which can be answered quickly, and lesson exercises that take more time and thought. The code solutions for the quick checks are at the end of each lesson, and the code for the lesson exercises is in the appendix at the end of the book.

Book forum

Purchase of *Get Programming with Haskell* includes free access to a private web forum run by Manning Publications where you can make comments about the book, ask technical questions, and receive help from the author and from other users. To access the forum, go to https://forums.manning.com/forums/get-programming-with-haskell. You can also learn more about Manning's forums and the rules of conduct at https://forums.manning.com/forums/about.

Manning's commitment to our readers is to provide a venue where a meaningful dialogue between individual readers and between readers and the author can take place. It is not a commitment to any specific amount of participation on the part of the author, whose contribution to the forum remains voluntary (and unpaid). We suggest you try asking the author some challenging questions lest his interest stray! The forum and the archives of previous discussions will be accessible from the publisher's website as long as the book is in print.

About the author

Will Kurt works as a data scientist at Bombora. With a formal background in both computer science (MS) and English literature (BA), he is fascinated with explaining complex technical topics as clearly and generally as possible. He has taught a course section on Haskell at the University of Nevada, Reno, and given workshops on functional programming. He also blogs about probability at CountBayesie.com.

LESSON 1

GETTING STARTED WITH HASKELL

After reading lesson 1, you'll be able to

- Install tools for Haskell development
- Use GHC and GHCi
- Use tips for writing Haskell programs

1.1 Welcome to Haskell

Before you dive into learning Haskell, you need to become familiar with the basic tools you'll be using on your journey. This lesson walks you through getting started with Haskell. The lesson starts with downloading the basics to write, compile, and run Haskell programs. You'll then look at example code and start thinking about how to write code in Haskell. After this lesson, you'll be ready to dive in!

1.1.1 The Haskell Platform

The worst part of learning a new programming language is getting your development environment set up for the first time. Fortunately, and somewhat surprisingly, this isn't a problem at all with Haskell. The Haskell community has put together a single, easily installable package of useful tools referred to as the *Haskell Platform*. The Haskell Platform is the "batteries included" model of packaging a programming language.

The Haskell Platform includes the following:

- The Glasgow Haskell Compiler (GHC)
- An interactive interpreter (GHCi)
- The stack tool for managing Haskell projects
- A bunch of useful Haskell packages

The Haskell Platform can be downloaded from www.haskell.org/downloads#platform. From there, follow the directions for installing on your OS of choice. This book uses Haskell version 8.0.1 or higher.

1.1.2 Text editors

Now that you have the Haskell Platform installed, you're probably curious about which editor you should use. Haskell is a language that strongly encourages you to *think before you hack*. As a result, Haskell programs tend to be extremely terse. There's little that an editor can do for you, other than manage indentation and provide helpful syntax highlighting. Many Haskell developers use Emacs with `haskell-mode`. But if you're not already familiar with Emacs (or don't like to work with it), it's certainly not worth the work to learn Emacs in addition to Haskell. My recommendation is that you look for a Haskell plugin for whatever editor you use the most. A bare-bones text editor, such as Pico or Notepad++, will work just fine for this book, and most full-fledged IDEs have Haskell plugins.

1.2 The Glasgow Haskell Compiler

Haskell is a compiled language, and the Glasgow Haskell Compiler is the reason Haskell is as powerful as it is. The job of the compiler is to transform human-readable source code into machine-readable binary. At the end compilation, you're left with an executable binary file. This is different from when you run Ruby, for example, in which another program reads in your source code and interprets it on the fly (this is accomplished with an *interpreter*). The main benefit of a compiler over an interpreter is that because the compiler transforms code in advance, it can perform analysis and optimization of the code you've written. Because of some other design features of Haskell, namely its powerful type system, there's an adage that *if it compiles, it works*. Though you'll use GHC often, never take it for granted. It's an amazing piece of software in its own right.

To invoke GHC, open a terminal and type in `ghc`:

```
$ ghc
```

In this text, whenever you come across a $ sign, it means you're typing into a command prompt. Of course, with no file to compile, GHC will complain. To get started, you'll make a simple file called hello.hs. In your text editor of choice, create a new file named hello.hs and enter the following code.

Listing 1.1 hello.hs a Hello World program

```
--hello.hs my first Haskell file!        <-- A commented line with the name of your file
main = do                                <-- The start of your 'main' function
  print "Hello World!"                   <-- The main function prints out "Hello World"
```

At this point, don't worry too much about what's happening in any of the code in this section. Your real aim here is to learn the tools you need so that they don't get in the way while you're learning Haskell.

Now that you have a sample file, you can run GHC again, this time passing in your hello.hs file as an argument:

```
$ ghc hello.hs
[1 of 1] Compiling Main
Linking hello ...
```

If the compilation was successful, GHC will have created three files:

- hello (hello.exe on Windows)
- hello.hi
- hello.o

Starting out, the most important file is hello, which is your binary executable. Because this file is a binary executable, you can simply run the file:

```
$ ./hello
"Hello World!"
```

Notice that the default behavior of the compiled program is to execute the logic in `main`. By default, all Haskell programs you're compiling need to have a `main`, which plays a similar role to the `Main` method in Java/C++/C# or `__main__` in Python.

Like most command-line tools, GHC supports a wide range of optional flags. For example, if you want to compile hello.hs into an executable named helloworld, you can use the `-o` flag:

```
$ghc hello.hs -o helloword
[1 of 1] Compiling Main
Linking helloworld ....
```

For a more complete listing of compiler options, call `ghc --help` (no filename argument is required).

Quick check 1.1 Copy the code for hello.hs and compile your own executable named testprogram.

1.3 Interacting with Haskell—GHCi

One of the most useful tools for writing Haskell programs is GHCi, an interactive interface for GHC. Just like GHC, GHCi is started with a simple command: `ghci`. When you start GHCi, you'll be greeted with a new prompt:

```
$ ghci
GHCi>
```

This book indicates when you're using GHCi by using `GHCi>` for lines you input and a blank for lines that are output by GHCi. The first thing to learn about any program you start from the command line is how to get out of it! For GHCi, you use the `:q` command to exit:

```
$ ghci
GHCi> :q
Leaving GHCi.
```

Working with GHCi is much like working with interpreters in most interpreted programming languages such as Python and Ruby. It can be used as a simple calculator:

```
GHCi> 1 + 1
2
```

You can also write code on the fly in GHCi:

```
GHCi> x = 2 + 2
GHCi> x
4
```

QC 1.1 answer Simply copy the code to a file and then run this in the same directory as the file:

```
ghc hello.hs -o testprogram
```

Prior to version 8 of GHCi, function and variable definitions needed to be prefaced with a `let` keyword. This is no longer necessary, but many Haskell examples on the web and in older books still include it:

```
GHCi> let f x = x + x
GHCi> f 2
4
```

The most important use of GHCi is interacting with programs that you're writing. There are two ways to load an existing file into GHCi. The first is to pass the filename as an argument to `ghci`:

```
$ ghci hello.hs
[1 of 1] Compiling Main
Ok, modules loaded: Main.
```

The other is to use the `:l` (or `:load`) command in the interactive session:

```
$ ghci
GHCi> :l hello.hs
[1 of 1] Compiling Main
Ok, modules loaded: Main.
```

In either of these cases, you can then call functions you've written:

```
GHCi> :l hello.hs
GHCi> main
"Hello World!"
```

Unlike compiling files in GHC, your files don't need a `main` in order to be loaded into GHCi. Anytime you load a file, you'll overwrite existing definitions of functions and variables. You can continually load your file as you work on it and make changes. Haskell is rather unique in having strong compiler support as well as a natural and easy-to-use interactive environment. If you're coming from an interpreted language such as Python, Ruby, or JavaScript, you'll feel right at home using GHCi. If you're familiar with compiled languages such as Java, C#, or C++, you'll likely be surprised that you're working with a compiled language when writing Haskell.

Quick check 1.2 Edit your Hello World script to say Hello <Name> with your name. Reload this into GHCi and test it out.

1.4 Writing and working with Haskell code

One of the most frustrating issues for newcomers to Haskell is that basic I/O in Haskell is a fairly advanced topic. Often when new to a language, it's a common pattern to print output along the way to make sure you understand how a program works. In Haskell, this type of ad hoc debugging is usually impossible. It's easy to get a bug in a Haskell program, along with a fairly sophisticated error, and be at an absolute loss as to how to proceed.

Compounding this problem is that Haskell's wonderful compiler is also strict about the correctness of your code. If you're used to writing a program, running it, and quickly fixing any errors you made, Haskell will frustrate you. Haskell strongly rewards taking time and thinking through problems before running programs. After you gain experience with Haskell, I'm certain that these frustrations will become some of your favorite features of the language. The flipside of being obsessed with correctness during compilation is that programs will work, and work as expected far more often than you're likely used to.

The trick to writing Haskell code with minimal frustration is to write code in little bits, and play with each bit interactively as it's written. To demonstrate this, you'll take a messy Haskell program and clean it up so it's easy to understand each piece. For this example, you'll write a command-line app that will draft *thank-you* emails to readers from authors. Here's the first, poorly written, version of the program.

QC 1.2 answer Edit your file so that it has your name:

```
main = do
  print "Hello Will!"
```

In GHCi, load your file:

```
GHCi> :l hello.hs
GHCi> main
Hello Will!
```

Listing 1.2 A messy version of first_prog.hs

```
messyMain :: IO()
messyMain = do
   print "Who is the email for?"
   recipient <- getLine
   print "What is the Title?"
   title <- getLine
   print "Who is the Author?"
   author <- getLine
   print ("Dear " ++ recipient ++ ",\n" ++
     "Thanks for buying " ++ title  ++ "\nthanks,\n" ++
     author )
```

The key issue is that this code is in one big monolithic function named `messyMain`. The advice that it's good practice to write modular code is fairly universal in software, but in Haskell it's essential for writing code that you can understand and troubleshoot. Despite being messy, this program does work. If you changed the name of `messyMain` to `main`, you could compile and run this program. But you can also load this code into GHCi as it is, assuming that you're in the same directory as your first_prog.hs:

```
$ghci
GHCi> :l first_prog.hs
[1 of 1] Compiling Main             ( first_prog.hs, interpreted )
Ok, modules loaded: Main.
```

If you get the `Ok` from GHCi, you know that your code compiled and works just fine! Notice that GHCi doesn't care if you have a `main` function. This is great, as you can still interact with files that don't have a `main`. Now you can take your code for a test drive:

```
GHCi> messyMain
"Who is the email for?"
Happy Reader
"What is the Title?"
Learn Haskell
"Who is the Author?"
Will Kurt
"Dear Happy Reader,\nThanks for buying Learn Haskell\nthanks,\nWill Kurt"
```

Everything works fine, but it'd be much easier to work with if this code was broken up a bit. Your primary goal is to create an email, but it's easy to see that the email consists of tying together three parts: the recipient section, the body, and the signature. You'll start by pulling out these parts into their own functions. The following code is written into your first_prog.hs file. Nearly all of the functions and values defined in this book can be assumed to be written into a file you're currently working with. You'll start with just the `toPart` function:

```
toPart recipient = "Dear" ++ recipient ++ ",\n"
```

In this example, you could easily write these three functions together, but it's often worth it to work slowly and test each function as you go. To test this out, you'll load your file again in GHCi:

```
GHCi> :l "first_prog.hs"
[1 of 1] Compiling Main             ( first_prog.hs, interpreted )
Ok, modules loaded: Main.
GHCi> toPart "Happy Reader"
"DearHappy Reader,\n"
GHCi> toPart "Bob Smith"
"DearBob Smith,\n"
```

This pattern of writing code in an editor and then loading and reloading it into GHCi will be your primary means of working with code throughout the book. To avoid repetition, the `:l "first_prog.hs"` will be assumed rather than explicitly written from here on.

Now that you've loaded this into GHCi, you see there's a slight error, a missing space between *Dear* and the recipient's name. Let's see how to fix this.

Listing 1.3 Corrected `toPart` function

```
toPart recipient = "Dear " ++ recipient ++ ",\n"
```

And back to GHCi:

```
GHCi> toPart "Jane Doe"
"Dear Jane Doe,\n"
```

Everything looks good. Now to define your two other functions. This time you'll write them both at the same time. While following along, it's still a good idea to write code one function at a time, load it into GHCi, and make sure it all works before moving on.

Listing 1.4 Defining the `bodyPart` and `fromPart` functions

```
bodyPart bookTitle = "Thanks for buying " ++ bookTitle ++ ".\n"
fromPart author = "Thanks,\n"++author
```

You can test these out as well:

```
GHCi> bodyPart "Learn Haskell"
"Thanks for buying Learn Haskell.\n"
GHCi> fromPart "Will Kurt"
"Thanks,\nWill Kurt"
```

Everything is looking good! Now you need a function to tie it all together.

Listing 1.5 Defining the `createEmail` function

```
createEmail recipient bookTitle author = toPart recipient ++
                                         bodyPart bookTitle ++
                                         fromPart author
```

Notice the alignment of the three function calls. Haskell makes limited use of significant whitespace (but nothing as intense as Python). Assume that any formatting in this text is intentional; if sections of code are lined up, it's for a reason. Most editors can handle this automatically with a Haskell plugin.

With all your functions written, you can test `createEmail`:

```
GHCi> createEmail "Happy Reader" "Learn Haskell" "Will Kurt"
"Dear Happy Reader,\nThanks for buying Learn Haskell.\nThanks,\nWill Kurt"
```

Your functions each work as expected. Now you can put them all together in your `main`.

Listing 1.6 Improved first_prog.hs with a cleaned-up `main`

```
main = do
   print "Who is the email for?"
   recipient <- getLine
   print "What is the Title?"
   title <- getLine
   print "Who is the Author?"
   author <- getLine
   print (createEmail recipient title author)
```

You should be all set to compile, but it's always a good idea to test in GHCi first:

```
GHCi> main
"Who is the email for?"
  Happy Reader
"What is the Title?"
```

```
  Learn Haskell
"Who is the Author?"
  Will Kurt
"Dear Happy Reader,\nThanks for buying Learn Haskell.\nThanks,\nWill Kurt"
```

It looks like all your pieces are working together, and you were able to play with them each individually to make sure they worked as expected. Finally, you can compile your program:

```
$ ghc first_prog.hs
[1 of 1] Compiling Main             ( first_prog.hs, first_prog.o )
Linking first_prog ...
$ ./first_prog
"Who is the email for?"
Happy Reader
"What is the Title?"
Learn Haskell
"Who is the Author?"
Will Kurt
"Dear Happy Reader,\nThanks for buying Learn Haskell.\nThanks,\nWill Kurt"
```

You've just finished your first successful Haskell program. With your basic workflow understood, you can now dive into the amazing world of Haskell!

Summary

In this lesson, our objective was to get you started with Haskell. You started by installing the Haskell Platform, which bundles together the tools you'll be using through this book. These tools include GHC, Haskell's compiler; GHCi, the interactive interpreter for Haskell; and stack, a build tool you'll use later in the book. The rest of this lesson covered the basics of writing, refactoring, interacting with, and compiling Haskell programs. Let's see if you got this.

Q1.1 In GHCi, find out what 2^{123} is.

Q1.2 Modify the text in each of the functions in first_prog.hs, test them out in GHCi while you do this, and, finally, compile a new version of your email templating program so that the executable is named *email*.

1

Foundations of functional programming

There are two major ways to understand the act of programming. The first, and historically more common, is the view that the programmer provides a sequence of instructions to a computer in order to make it behave a certain way. This model of programming ties the programmer to the design of a particular tool for programming, namely a computer. In this type of programming, the computer is a device that takes input, accesses memory, sends instructions to a processing unit, and finally delivers output to the user. This model of a computer is called *von Neumann architecture*, after the famous mathematician and physicist John von Neumann.

The programming language that best embodies this way of thinking about programs is C. A C program takes in data from the standard input controlled by the operating system, stores and retrieves necessary values in physical memory that frequently must be manually managed, requires the handling of pointers to a specific block of memory, and finally returns all output through the standard output controlled by the OS. When writing C programs, programmers must understand as much about the problem at hand as the physical architecture of the computer in front of them.

But a computer built with von Neumann architecture isn't the only way to perform computation. Humans perform a wide variety of computations that have nothing to do with thinking of memory allocation and instruction sets: sorting books on a shelf, solving a derivative of a function in calculus, giving directions to friends, and so forth. When we write C code, we're programming to a specific implementation of computation. John Backus, who led the team that created Fortran, asked in his Turing Award lecture, "Can programming be liberated from the von Neumann style?"

This question leads to the second way to understand programming, which is the subject of the first unit in this book. *Functional programming* attempts to liberate programming from the von Neumann style. The foundations of functional programming are abstract, mathematical notions of computation that transcend a specific implementation. This leads to a method of programming that often solves problems simply by describing them. By focusing on computation, not computers, functional programming allows the programmer access to powerful abstractions that can make many challenging problems much easier to solve.

The price of this is that getting started can be much more difficult. Ideas in functional programming are often abstract, and we must start by building the idea of programming up from first principles. Many concepts need to be learned before we can build useful programs. When working through this first unit, remember that you're learning to program in a way that transcends programming a computer.

Just as C is the nearly perfect embodiment of the von Neumann style of programming, Haskell is the purest functional programming language you can learn. As a language, Haskell commits fully to Backus's dream and doesn't allow you to stray back to more-familiar styles of programming. This makes learning Haskell more difficult than many other languages, but learning Haskell makes it impossible for you to not gain deep insights into functional programming as you go. By the end of this unit, you'll have a strong enough foundation in functional programming to understand the basics of all other functional programming languages, as well as being prepared for your journey to learn Haskell.

FUNCTIONS AND FUNCTIONAL PROGRAMMING

After reading lesson 2, you'll be able to

- Understand the general idea of functional programming
- Define simple functions in Haskell
- Declare variables in Haskell
- Explain the benefits of functional programming

The first topic you need to understand when learning Haskell is, what is functional programming? Functional programming has a reputation for being a challenging topic to master. Although this is undoubtedly true, the foundations of functional programming are surprisingly straightforward. The first thing you need to learn is what it means to have a *function* in a functional programming language. You likely already have a good idea of what using a function means. In this lesson, you'll see the simple rules that functions must obey in Haskell that not only make your code easier to reason about, but also lead to entirely new ways of thinking about programming.

Consider this You and your friends are out getting pizza. On the menu are three sizes of pizza pie with three different prices:

1. 18 inches for $20
2. 16 inches for $15
3. 12 inches for $10

You want to know which choice gives you the most pizza for your dollar. You want to write a function that will give you the dollar-per-square-inch cost of the pizza.

2.1 Functions

What *exactly* is a function? This is an important question to ask and understand if you're going to be exploring functional programming. The behavior of functions in Haskell comes directly from mathematics. In math, we often say things like $f(x) = y$, meaning there's some function f that takes a parameter x and maps to a value y. In mathematics, every x can map to one and only one y. If $f(2) = 2{,}000{,}000$ for a given function f, it can never be the case that $f(2) = 2{,}000{,}001$.

The thoughtful reader may ask, "What about the square-root function? 4 has two roots, 2 and –2, so how can sqrt x be a true function when it clearly points to two ys!" The key thing to realize is that x and y don't have to be the same thing. We can say that sqrt x is the positive root, so both x and y are positive real numbers, which resolves this issue. But we can also have sqrt x be a function from a positive real number to pairs of real numbers. In this case, each x maps to exactly one pair.

In Haskell, functions work exactly as they do in mathematics. Figure 2.1 shows a function named `simple`.

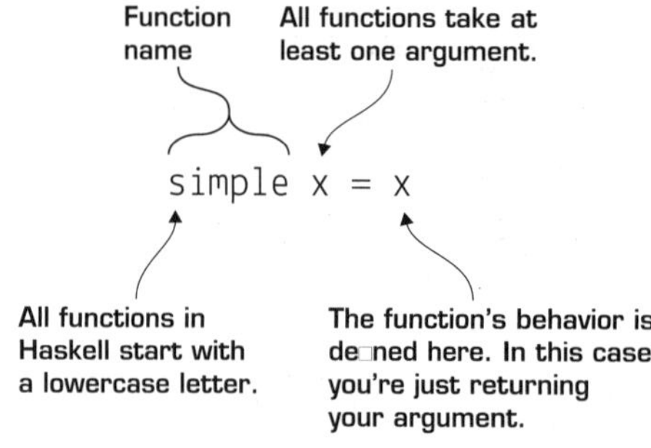
Function name
All functions take at least one argument.
simple x = x
All functions in Haskell start with a lowercase letter.
The function's behavior is de ned here. In this case you're just returning your argument.

Figure 2.1 Defining a simple function

The simple function takes a single argument x and then returns this argument untouched. Notice that unlike many other programming languages, in Haskell you don't need to specify that you're returning a value. In Haskell, functions must return a value, so there's never a need to make this explicit. You can load your simple function into GHCi and see how it behaves. To load a function, all you have to do is have it in a file and use :load <filename> in GHCi:

```
GHCi> simple^2
2
GHCi> simple "dog"
"dog"
```

> **NOTE** In this section, we're using GHCi—Haskell's Interactive Read-Eval-Print Loop (REPL)—to run commands and get results.

All functions in Haskell follow three rules that force them to behave like functions in math:

- All functions must take an argument.
- All functions must return a value.
- Anytime a function is called with the same argument, it must return the same value.

The third rule is part of the basic mathematical definition of a function. When the rule that the same argument must always produce the same result is applied to function in a programming language, it's called *referential transparency*.

2.2 Functional programming

If functions are just mappings from a bunch of *x*s (that's the plural of *x*—"exes") to a bunch of *y*s (that's the plural of *y*—"whys") what do they have to do with programming? In the 1930s, a mathematician named Alonzo Church attempted to create a system of logic that used only functions and variables (*x*s and *y*s). This system of logic is called *lambda calculus*. In lambda calculus, you represent everything as functions: true and false are functions, and even all the integers can be represented as functions.

Church's goal was initially to resolve some problems in the mathematical field of set theory. Unfortunately, lambda calculus didn't solve these problems, but something much more interesting came out of Church's work. It turns out that lambda calculus allows for a universal model of computation, equivalent to a Turing machine!

What is a Turing machine?

A Turing machine is an abstract model of a computer developed by the famous computer scientist Alan Turing. From a theoretical standpoint, the Turing machine is useful because it allows you to reason about what can and can't be computed, not just on a digital computer, but any possible computer. This model also allows computer scientists to show equivalence between computing systems if they can each simulate a Turing machine. You can use this to show, for example, that there's nothing that you can compute in Java that you can't also compute in assembly language.

This discovery of the relationship between lambda calculus and computing is called the *Church-Turing thesis* (for more information, see www.alanturing.net/turing_archive/pages/reference%20articles/The%20Turing-Church%20Thesis.html). The wonderful thing about this discovery is that you have a mathematically sound model for programming!

Most programming languages that you use are marvelous pieces of engineering but provide little assurance about how programs will behave. With a mathematical foundation, Haskell is able to remove entire classes of bugs and errors from the code you write. Cutting-edge research in programming languages is experimenting with ways to mathematically prove that programs will do exactly what you expect. Additionally, the nonmathematical nature of most programming language designs means the abstractions you can use are limited by engineering decisions in the language. If you could program math, you'd be able to both prove things about your code and have access to the nearly limitless abstractions that mathematics allows. This is the aim of functional programming: to bring the power of mathematics to the programmer in a usable way.

2.3 The value of functional programming in practice

This mathematical model for programming has a variety of practical implications. Because of the simple rules that all functions must take and return values, and must always return the same value for the same argument, Haskell is a *safe* programming language. Programs are safe when they always behave exactly the way you expect them to and you can easily reason about their behavior. A safe programming language is one that forces your programs to behave as expected.

Let's look at code that isn't safe and violates our simple rules for functions. Suppose you're reading through a new code base and you come across lines of code that look like the following.

Listing 2.1 Hidden state in function calls

```
tick()
if(timeToReset){
  reset()
}
```

This code clearly isn't Haskell, because both `tick` and `reset` violate the rules we established. Neither function takes any arguments nor returns any value. The question is, then, what are these functions doing, and how is this different from functions in Haskell? It's not a long shot to suppose that `tick` is incrementing a counter and that `reset` restores that counter to its starting value. Even if we're not exactly right, this reasoning gives us insight into our question. If you aren't passing an argument to a function, you must be accessing a value in your environment, and if you aren't returning a value, you must also be changing a value in your environment. When you change a value in your programming environment, you're changing the program's *state*. Changing state creates *side effects* in your code, and these side effects can make code hard to reason about and therefore unsafe.

It's likely that both `tick` and `reset` are accessing a *global variable* (a variable reachable from anywhere in the program), which in any programming language is considered poor design. But side effects make it hard to reason about even the simplest, well-written code. To see this, you'll look at a collection of values, `myList`, and reverse it by using built-in functionality. The following code is valid Python, Ruby, and JavaScript; see if you can figure out what it does.

Listing 2.2 Confusing behavior in standard libraries

```
myList = [1,2,3]
myList.reverse()
newList = myList.reverse()
```

Now what do you expect the value of `newList` to be? Because this is a valid program in Ruby, Python, and JavaScript, it seems reasonable to assume that the value of `newList` should be the same. Here are the answers for all three languages:

```
Ruby -> [3,2,1]
Python -> None
JavaScript -> [1,2,3]
```

Three completely different answers for the exact same code in three languages! Python and JavaScript both have side effects that occur when `reverse` is called. Because the side effects of calling `reverse` are different for each language and aren't made visible to the programmer, both languages give different answers. The Ruby code here behaves like Haskell, without side effects. Here you see the value of referential transparency. With Haskell, you can always see which effects each function has. When you called `reset` and `tick` earlier, the changes they made were invisible to you. Without looking at the source code, you have no way of knowing exactly which or even how many other values they're using and changing. Haskell doesn't allow functions to have side effects, which explains why all Haskell functions must take an argument and return a value. If Haskell functions didn't always return a value, they'd have to change a hidden state in the program; otherwise, they'd be useless. If they didn't take an argument, they'd have to access a hidden one, which would mean they're no longer transparent.

This small property of Haskell's functions leads to code that's dramatically easier to predict. Even in Ruby, the programmer is allowed to use side effects. When using another programmer's code, you still can't assume anything about what's happening when you call a function or method. Because Haskell doesn't allow this, you can look at any code, written by any programmer, and reason about its behavior.

Quick check 2.1 Many languages use the ++ operator to increment a value; for example, x++ increments x. Do you think Haskell has an operator or function that works this way?

2.3.1 Variables

Variables in Haskell are straightforward. Here you're assigning `2` to the variable `x`.

Listing 2.3 Defining your first variable

```
x = 2
```

The only catch with variables in Haskell is that they're not really variable at all! If you were to try to compile the following bit of Haskell, you'd get an error, as shown in the next listing.

QC 2.1 answer The ++ operator used in languages such as C++ couldn't exist in Haskell because it violates our mathematical rules for functions. The most obvious rule is that each time you call ++ on a variable, the result is different.

Listing 2.4 Variables aren't variable!

```
x = 2
x = 3
```

Won't compile because it changes the value of x

A better way to think about variables in Haskell is as definitions. Once again, you see mathematical thinking replace the way you typically think about code. The problem is that in most programming languages, variable reassignment is essential to solving many problems. The inability to change variables is also related to referential transparency. This may seem like a strict rule to follow, but the reward is that you always know that after calling a function, the world remains the same.

Quick check 2.2 Even languages that don't have a ++ operator allow for a += operator, often also used for incrementing a value. For example, `x += 2` increments `x` by 2. You can think of += as a function that follows our rules: it takes a value and returns a value. Does this mean += can exist in Haskell?

The key benefit of variables in programming is to clarify your code and avoid repetition. For example, suppose you want a function called `calcChange`. This function takes two arguments: how much is owed and how much is given. If you're given enough money, you return the difference. But if you aren't given enough money, you don't want to give negative dollars; you'll return 0. Here's one way to write this.

Listing 2.5 `calcChange` v.1

```
calcChange owed given = if given - owed > 0
                        then given - owed
                        else 0
```

Two things are wrong with this function:

- Even for a tiny function, it's hard to read. Each time you see the expression `given - owed`, you have to reason about what's happening. For anything more complicated than subtraction, this would be unpleasant.
- You're repeating your computation! Subtraction is a cheap operation, but if this had been a costlier operation, you'd be needlessly wasting resources.

QC 2.2 answer Although the += operator returns and takes an argument, just like ++, every time you call +=, you get a different result.

Haskell solves these problems by using a special `where` clause. Here's the previous function written with a `where` clause.

Listing 2.6 calcChange v.2

```
calcChange owed given = if change > 0
                        then change
                        else 0
  where change = given - owed
```

given – owed is computed only once and assigned to change.

The first thing that should strike you as interesting is that a `where` clause reverses the normal order used to write variables. In most programming languages, variables are declared before they're used. This convention in most programming languages is partially the byproduct of being able to change state. Variable order matters because you can always reassign the value of something after you've assigned it. In Haskell, because of referential transparency, this isn't an issue. There's also a readability gain with the Haskell approach: if you read the algorithm, the intention is clear right away.

Quick check 2.3 Fill in the missing part of the following `where` clause:

```
doublePlusTwo x = doubleX + 2
    where doubleX = ________
```

2.3.2 Variables that are variable

Because change is an inevitable part of life, sometimes it makes sense to have variables that can be reassigned. One of these cases occurs when working in the Haskell REPL, GHCi. When working in GHCi, you're allowed to reassign variables. Here's an example:

```
GHCi> x = 7
GHCi> x
7
GHCi> x  = [1,2,3]
GHCi> x
[1,2,3]
```

QC 2.3 answer

```
doublePlusTwo x = doubleX + 2
  where doubleX = x*2
```

Prior to version 8 of GHC, variables in GHCi needed to be prefaced with the `let` keyword to mark them as different from other variables in Haskell. You can still define variables by using `let` in GHCi if you like:

```
GHCi> let x = 7
GHCi> x
7
```

It's also worth noting that one-line functions can be defined in the same way:

```
GHCi> let f x = x^2
GHCi> f 8
64
```

In a few other special contexts in Haskell, you'll see `let` used in this way. It can be confusing, but this difference is primarily to make real-world tasks less frustrating.

It's important to acknowledge that being able to change the definition of variables in GHCi is a special case. Although Haskell may be strict, having to restart GHCi every time you wanted to experiment with a different variable would be frustrating.

Quick check 2.4 What's the final value of the `x` variable in the following code?

```
GHCi> let x = simple simple
GHCi> let x = 6
```

Summary

In this lesson, our objective was to introduce you to functional programming and writing basic functions in Haskell. You saw that functional programming puts restrictions on the behavior of a function. These restrictions are as follows:

- A function must always take an argument.
- A function must always return a value.
- Calling the same function with the same argument must always return the same result.

QC 2.4 answer Because you can reassign values, the final value of `x` is 6.

These three rules have profound consequences for the way you write programs in Haskell. The major benefit of writing code in this style is that your programs are much easier to reason about, and behave predictably. Let's see if you got this.

Q2.1 You used Haskell's `if then else` expression to write `calcChange`. In Haskell, all `if` statements must include an `else` component. Given our three rules for functions, why can't you have an `if` statement all by itself?

Q2.2 Write functions named `inc`, `double`, and `square` that increment, double, and square an argument `n`, respectively.

Q2.3 Write a function that takes a value `n`. If `n` is even, the function returns `n - 2`, and if the number is odd, the function returns `3 × n + 1`. To check whether the number is even, you can use either Haskell's `even` function or `mod` (Haskell's modulo function).

LAMBDA FUNCTIONS AND LEXICAL SCOPE

After reading lesson 3, you'll be able to

- Write lambda functions in Haskell
- Use lambda functions for ad hoc function definitions
- Understand lexical scope
- Create scope with a lambda function

In this lesson, you're going to continue your journey into understanding functional programming and Haskell by learning about one of the most foundational concepts in all of functional programming: the lambda function. On the surface, a *lambda function*—which is a function with no name—seems almost too simple to be interesting. But lambda functions provide incredible theoretical benefits as well as a surprising amount of real-world usefulness.

Consider this You're messing around in GHCi and want to quickly calculate the difference between the square of the sum of three values and the sum of the squares of three values: 4, 10, 22. You could write this out by hand:

```
GHCi> (4 + 10 + 22)^2 - (4^2 + 10^2 + 22^2)
```

But this makes it easy to have a typo that causes your expression to create an error. Additionally, it's difficult to change these values if you want to edit this item from your GHCi command history (press the up arrow in GHCi to get the previous item). Is there a way to make this a bit cleaner without having to explicitly define a function?

3.1 Lambda functions

One of the most foundational concepts in functional programming is a function without a name, called a *lambda function* (hence lambda calculus). Lambda functions are often referred to using the lowercase Greek letter λ. Another common name for a lambda function is an *anonymous function*. You can use a lambda function to redefine your simple function from lesson 2, only without a name. To do this, you use Haskell's lambda syntax, shown in figure 3.1.

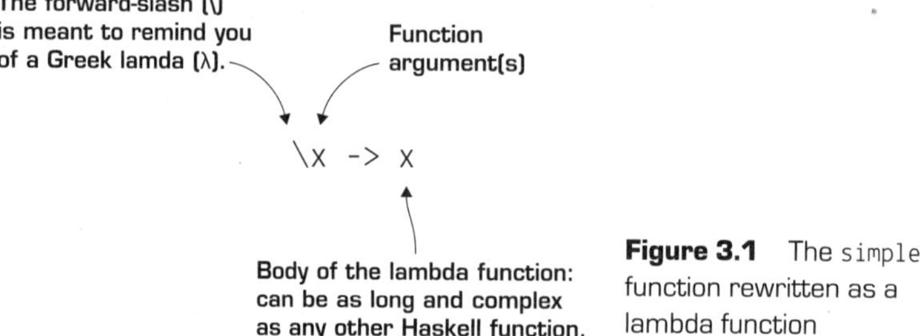

Figure 3.1 The `simple` function rewritten as a lambda function

Lambda functions are the minimum possible function: they take a value and return a value, and that's all. You can't paste this anonymous function you just wrote into GHCi or a Haskell program, because it's just an expression that by itself does nothing. To bring life to a lambda function, you must use it for something. The easiest thing you can do is pass an argument to it:

```
GHCi> (\x -> x) 4
4
```

```
GHCi> (\x -> x) "hi"
hi
GHCi> (\x -> x) [1,2,3]
[1,2,3]
```

Notice that each time you use your lambda expression, you have to redefine it. This makes sense, because you have no name to call it by! Lambda functions are useful but are designed to exist for only a short while. In general, if a named function will do the job, it's better to use one.

Quick check 3.1 Write a lambda function that doubles its argument, and pass in a few numbers as arguments.

3.2 Writing your own where clause

A recurring theme in functional programming is that there's little you can't build from scratch if you want to. Therefore, after you're experienced in functional programming, you'll typically have a deep understanding of the way programs work. To demonstrate how powerful lambda functions can be, you'll conduct an experiment by removing Haskell's `where` clause and seeing whether you can rebuild it from nothing. It's worth taking in what this means. So far, `where` is the only way you know of, inside a function, to store a variable.

It turns out the lambda function on its own is powerful enough to create variables from nothing. To start, you'll look at a function that uses a `where` statement. For this function, you'll take two numbers and return whichever is greater: the sum of the square of the values (`x^2 + y^2`) or the square of the sum (`(x + y)^2`). Here's our version with `where`.

QC 3.1 answer

```
GHCi> (\x -> x*2) 2
4
GHCi> (\x -> x*2) 4
8
```

Listing 3.1 `sumSquareOrSquareSum` **v.1**

```
sumSquareOrSquareSum x y = if sumSquare > squareSum
                           then sumSquare
                           else squareSum
  where sumSquare = x^2 + y^2
        squareSum = (x+y)^2
```

In `sumSquareOrSquareSum`, you're using `where` to both make your code easier to read and reduce computation (though, technically, Haskell will eliminate many cases of duplicate function calls even without variables). Without a `where`, you could just replace the variables, but then you're doubling computation and the code is ugly, as you can see here:

```
sumSquareOrSquareSum x y = if (x^2 + y^2) > ((x+y)^2)
                           then (x^2 + y^2)
                           else (x+y)^2
```

Your function is relatively trivial, but without `where` or some sort of variable, it's hideous! One solution to not having variables is to split your function into two steps. You'll start with a function named `body` that handles the main comparison part of `sumSquareOrSquareSum`, and then your new `sumSquareOrSquareSum` can compute `sumSquare` and `squareSum` and pass them to `body`. Here's the code for `body`:

```
body sumSquare squareSum = if sumSquare > squareSum
                           then sumSquare
                           else squareSum
```

Then `sumSquareOrSquareSum` has to compute `sumSquare` and `squareSum` and pass them on to `body`:

```
sumSquareOrSquareSum x y = body (x^2 + y^2) ((x+y)^2)
```

This solves the problem but adds a lot of work, and you need to define a new, intermediary function `body`. This is such a simple function that it'd be nice if you didn't need an in-between step. Because you want to somehow get rid of the named `body` function, this is a perfect job for a lambda function! First let's look at the lambda function for `body`:

```
body = (\sumSquare squareSum ->
         if sumSquare > squareSum
         then sumSquare
         else squareSum)
```

Now if you substitute this lambda function for `body` in your preceding definition of `sumSquareOrSquareSum`, you get the expression in figure 3.2.

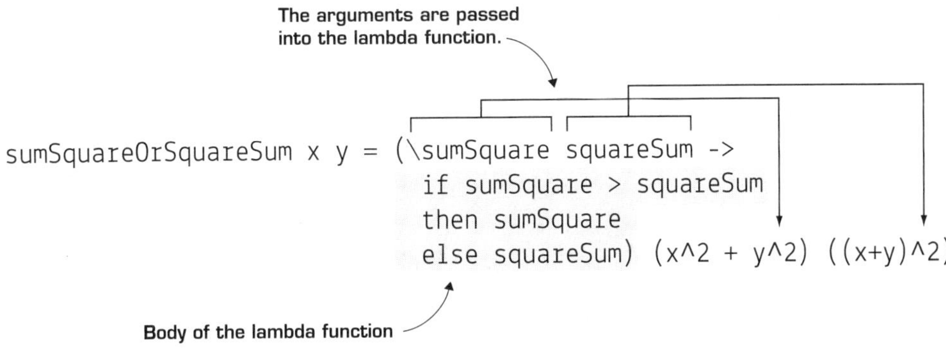
The arguments are passed into the lambda function.
sumSquareOrSquareSum x y = (\sumSquare squareSum ->
if sumSquare > squareSum
then sumSquare
else squareSum) (x^2 + y^2) ((x+y)^2)
Body of the lambda function

Figure 3.2 How `sumSquareOrSquareSum` works using a lambda function

This still isn't as pretty as a `where` clause (which is why Haskell has one in the first place) but much nicer than what you had before. More important, you've implemented the idea of variables from scratch!

Quick check 3.2 Rewrite the following function to use a lambda function in place of `where`:

```
doubleDouble x = dubs*2
where dubs = x*2
```

3.3 From lambda to let: making your own variable variables!

Although the lambda function is messier than the original `where`, it's also more powerful! The `where` statement makes everything much easier to understand, but it's also syntactically wrapped up in your function. There's no way to just pull out a `where` section. This clearly isn't the case with your lambda expression. You pasted it into place and could just as easily pull it out. Your lambda function is an *expression*, a self-contained chunk of code, all on its own.

Haskell has an alternative to `where` clauses called `let` expressions. A `let` expression allows you to combine the readability of a `where` clause with the power of your lambda function. Figure 3.3 shows the `sumSquareOrSquareSum` function using `let`.

QC 3.2 answer

```
doubleDouble x = (\dubs -> dubs*2) (x*2)
```

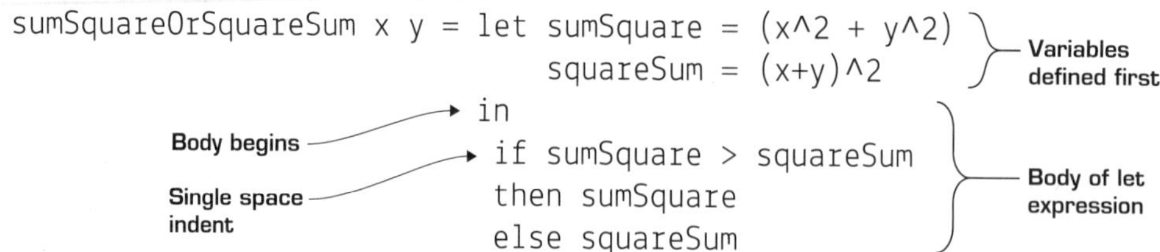

Figure 3.3 The `sumSquareOrSquareSum` function rewritten to use a `let` expression

Whether you choose to use `let` or `where` is a matter of style the vast majority of the time in Haskell.

At this point, it should be clear that lambda functions, all by themselves, can be immensely powerful. To drive this point home, you can also do something that Haskell won't normally let you do: overwrite variables! For this example, you're going to use a `let` expression instead of the raw lambda expression for readability. In functional programming, it rarely makes sense to overwrite a variable on purpose, but to show it can be done, the next listing shows a function `overwrite` that takes a variable `x` and then overwrites its value three times.

Listing 3.2 The `overwrite` function

```
overwrite x = let x = 2
              in
               let x = 3
               in
                let x = 4
                in
                 x
```

This, by itself, is a useless function, but it should remind you of the way to redefine variables in GHCi:

```
GHCi> let x = 2
GHCi> x
2
GHCi> let x = 3
GHCi> x
3
```

The `overwrite` function provides insight into how GHCi can allow you to redefine variables and still not be "cheating" regarding the rules of functional programming.

Quick check 3.3 Redefine `overwrite` by using only lambdas.

And there you have it. If you want to, you can use an unnamed function to allow you to redefine variables just as you would in any other programming language.

3.4 Practical lambda functions and lexical scope

These `let` and `where` examples of using a lambda function may initially seem academic and contrived, but they're the basis of one of the most important design patterns in JavaScript. JavaScript has strong support for lambda functions; the equivalent of `\x -> x` in JavaScript is as follows:

```
function(x){
  return x;
}
```

Originally, JavaScript wasn't designed to do more than add a little flair to websites. Therefore, unfortunate design flaws have made large, complex code bases difficult to manage. One of the biggest flaws is that JavaScript has no implementation of namespaces or modules. If you need to define a `length` function in your code, you'd better hope that you aren't accidently overwriting another `length` function written in one of the many other libraries you're using. On top of this, JavaScript makes it extremely easy to accidentally declare global variables. To demonstrate this, you'll start with the function `libraryAdd`, which you'll pretend is in a third-party library:

```
var libraryAdd = function(a,b){
   c = a + b;     <- Oops! You forgot to use JavaScript's
                     var keyword, accidentally creating a
                     global variable.
   return c;
}
```

QC 3.3 answer

```
overwrite x = (\x ->
               (\x ->
                 (\x -> x) 4
                )3
               )2
```

This simple function has a huge problem: the variable c has accidentally been declared a global variable! How dangerous can this be? Here's an example of how this can cause problems:

```
var a = 2;
var b = 3;
var c = a + b;
var d = libraryAdd(10,20);
console.log(c);
```

Internally, this function accesses a global variable c, but you have no way of knowing that.

The value of this is 30, not 5!

You did everything right, but after calling libraryAdd, the variable c is now 30! This occurs because there are no namespaces in JavaScript, so when libraryAdd assigns a value to c, it keeps looking until it finds one or creates a new global variable. Unfortunately, var c is what it finds. Unless you dig deep into someone else's JavaScript code, you'll never be able to figure out this bug!

To solve this problem, JavaScript developers used a lambda function. By wrapping your code in a lambda function and then immediately calling that function, you can keep your code safe. This pattern is called an *immediately invoked function expression* (IIFE). Using IIFE, your code now looks like this:

```
(function(){
 var a = 2;
 var b = 3;
 var c = a + b;
 var d = libraryAdd(10,20);
 console.log(c);
})()
```

Defining a lambda function

This dangerous function can't hurt you now.

The correct value of 5

It's great that you have a solution! IIFE works on exactly the same principles as our example of replacing a where statement. Whenever you create a new function, named or not, you create a new *scope*, which is the context in which a variable is defined. When a variable is used, the program looks at the nearest scope; if the definition of the variable isn't there, it goes to the next one up. This particular type of variable lookup is called *lexical scope*. Both Haskell and JavaScript use lexical scoping, which is why IIFE and your lambda function variables behave in a similar fashion. Figure 3.4 shows an example of a variable definition and three function definitions that use lexical scope to change their values.

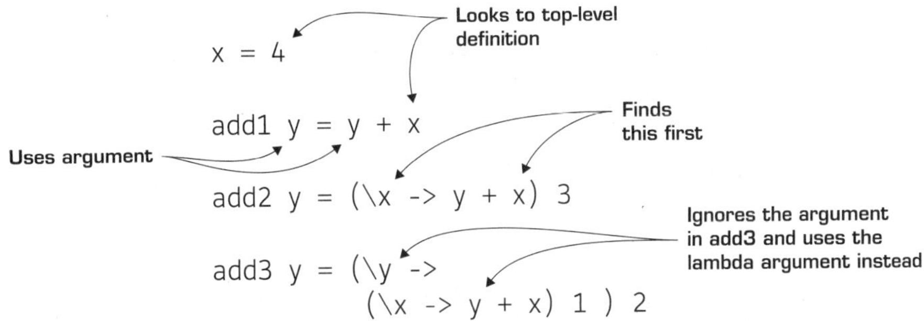

Figure 3.4 Lexical scope with `add1`, `add2`, and `add3`

And you can see how different the results are when calling all three functions with the same argument:

```
GHCi> add1 1
5
GHCi> add2 1
4
GHCi> add3 1
3
```

Being able to use unnamed functions to create scope on the fly is an essential tool for doing much more powerful things with lambda functions, which you'll explore in lesson 5.

Summary

In this lesson, our objective was to teach you about lambda functions. Lambda functions are a simple idea: a function with no name. But they're foundational for functional programming. Aside from their role as a theoretical corner store of functional programming, they provide practical benefits. The most obvious benefit is that lambda functions allow you to easily write functions on the fly. The even more powerful feature of lambda functions is that they allow you to create scope as needed. Let's see if you got this.

Q3.1 Practice writing lambda functions by rewriting each function in lesson 3 as a lambda expression.

Q3.2 Using a `let` expression and a lambda function aren't exactly the same thing under the hood. For example, the following code will cause an error if you try to run it:

```
counter x = let x = x + 1
            in
             let x = x + 1
             in
              x
```

To prove that `let` and lambda aren't identical, rewrite the `counter` function exactly as it is here, but use nested lambdas instead of `let`.

(*Hint*: Start at the end.)

FIRST-CLASS FUNCTIONS

After reading lesson 4, you'll be able to

- Understand the definition of first-class functions
- Use functions as arguments to other functions
- Abstract computation out of a function
- Return functions as values

Although functional programming has long had the reputation of being overly academic, nearly all of the key features of functional programming languages are starting to appear in many other more mainstream programming languages. The most widespread of these features is that of *first-class functions*. These are functions that can be passed around like any other values. A decade ago, this idea was shocking to many programmers, but today the majority of programming languages support and frequently use this concept. If you've ever assigned an event handler in JavaScript or passed custom sort logic into a sort method in a language such as Python, you've already used first-class functions.

Consider this Suppose you want to create a website that compares prices of various items on other sites such as Amazon and eBay. You already have a function that returns the URL of the item you need, but you need to write code for each site that determines how to extract the price from the page. One solution is to make a custom function for each site:

```
getAmazonPrice url
getEbayPrice url
getWalmartPrice url
```

This would be fine, except all of these functions share a lot of logic (for example, parsing a string price such as $1,999.99 into a numeric type such as 1999.99). Is there a way to entirely separate the logic that extracts the price from the HTML and pass that into a common `getPrice` function?

4.1 Functions as arguments

The concept of first-class functions is that functions are no different from any other data used in a program. Functions can be used as arguments and returned as values from other functions. This is a deceptively powerful feature for a programming language to have. It allows you to abstract out any repetitive computation from your code, and ultimately allows you to write functions that write other functions.

Suppose you have a function `ifEveninc` that increments a number `n` if it's even; otherwise, it returns the number unchanged, as the next listing shows.

Listing 4.1 `ifEvenInc`

```
ifEvenInc n = if even n
              then n + 1
              else n
```

Later you find out that you need two more functions, `ifEvenDouble` and `ifEvenSquare`, which double and square even numbers, respectively, as shown next. These are easy functions to write, given that you know how to write `ifEveninc`.

Listing 4.2 `ifEvenDouble` and `ifEvenSquare`

```
ifEvenDouble n = if even n
                 then n * 2
                 else n

ifEvenSquare n = if even n
                 then n^2
                 else n
```

Although these functions are easy to write, all three are nearly identical. The only difference is in the behavior of incrementing, doubling, and squaring. What you've discovered here is a general pattern of computation that you can abstract away. The key thing you need to do this is the ability to pass a function as an argument to perform the desired behavior.

Let's demonstrate this with the function `ifEven`, which takes a function and a number as arguments. If that number is even, `ifEven` applies a function to that number.

Listing 4.3 `ifEven`

```
ifEven myFunction x = if even x
                      then myFunction x
                      else x
```

You can also abstract out your incrementing, doubling, and squaring behavior into three separate functions:

```
inc n = n + 1
double n = n*2
square n = n^2
```

Let's see how to re-create the previous definitions by using the power of first-class functions:

```
ifEvenInc n = ifEven inc n
ifEvenDouble n = ifEven double n
ifEvenSquare n = ifEven square n
```

Now you can easily handle adding new functions such as `ifEvenCube` or `ifEvenNegate`.

Function and operator precedence

In this lesson, you've already seen examples of functions and operators. For example, `inc` is a function and `+` is an operator. An important part of writing Haskell code is that functions are always evaluated before operators. What does this mean? Take this example in GHCi:

```
GHCi> 1 + 2 * 3
7
```

As in most programming languages, `*` has a higher precedence than `+`, so you multiply 2 and 3 and then add 1, giving you 7. Now let's look what happens when you replace `1 +` with `inc`:

```
GHCi> inc 2 * 3
9
```

This result is different because functions always have precedence over operators. This means that `inc 2` is evaluated first and then the result is multiplied by 3. This is true even for multi-argument functions:

```
GHCi> add x y = x + y
GHCi> add 1 2 * 3
9
```

The key benefit is that this enables you to avoid using a large number of unnecessary parentheses in your code.

4.1.1 Lambda functions as arguments

Naming functions is generally a good idea, but you can also use lambda functions to quickly add code to pass into a function. If you want to double the value, you can quickly put together a lambda function for this:

```
GHCi> ifEven (\x -> x*2) 6
12
```

Although named functions are preferred, many times you'll want to pass in simple functionality.

Quick check 4.1 Write a lambda function for cubing `x` and pass it to `ifEven`.

4.1.2 Example—custom sorting

A practical use of passing functions into other functions is for sorting. Suppose you have a list of first and last names. In this example, each name is represented as a tuple. A *tuple* is a type that's like a list, but it can contain multiple types and is of a fixed size. Here's an example of a name in a tuple:

```
author = ("Will","Kurt")
```

Tuples of two items (a *pair*) have two useful functions, `fst` and `snd`, which access the first and second elements of the tuple, respectively:

```
GHCi> fst author
"Will"
GHCi> snd author
"Kurt"
```

Now suppose you have a list of names you want to sort. Here's a set of names represented as a list of tuples.

Listing 4.4 names

```
names = [("Ian", "Curtis"),
         ("Bernard","Sumner"),
         ("Peter", "Hook"),
         ("Stephen","Morris")]
```

You want to sort names. Thankfully, Haskell does have a built-in `sort` function. To use it, you first need to `import` the `Data.List` module. To do this is fairly straightforward; you need to add the following declaration to the top of whatever file you're working in:

```
import Data.List
```

QC 4.1 answer

```
GHCi> ifEven (\x -> x^3) 4
```

Alternatively, *you can import into GHCi*. If you load a file with `names` and your import, you can see that Haskell's `sort` takes a good guess at how to sort these tuples:

```
GHCi> sort names
[("Bernard","Sumner"),("Ian", "Curtis"),("Peter", "Hook"),
➥("Stephen","Morris")]
```

Not bad, given Haskell has no idea what you're trying to do! Unfortunately, you usually don't want to sort by first name. To solve this, you can use Haskell's `sortBy` function, which is included in the `Data.List` module. You need to supply `sortBy` with another function that will compare two of your tuple names. After you explain how to compare two elements, the rest is taken care of. For this, you write a function `compareLastNames`. This function takes two arguments, `name1` and `name2`, and returns `GT`, `LT`, or `EQ`. `GT`, `LT`, and `EQ` are special values representing *greater than*, *less than*, and *equal*. In many programming languages, you'd return `True` or `False`, or `1`, `-1`, or `0`.

Listing 4.5 `compareLastNames`

```
compareLastNames name1 name2 = if lastName1 > lastName2
                               then GT
                               else if lastName1 < lastName2
                                    then LT
                                    else EQ
  where lastName1 = snd name1
        lastName2 = snd name2
```

Now you can go back to GHCi and use `sortBy` with your custom sorting:

```
GHCi> sortBy compareLastNames names
[("Ian", "Curtis"),("Peter", "Hook"),("Stephen","Morris),
➥("Bernard","Sumner")]
```

Much better! JavaScript, Ruby, and Python all support a similar use of first-class functions for custom sorting, so this technique is likely familiar to many programmers.

Quick check 4.2 In `compareLastNames`, you didn't handle the case of having two last names that are the same but with different first names. Modify the `compareLastNamesfunction` to compare first names and use it to fix `compareLastNames`.

4.2 Returning functions

We've talked a fair bit about passing functions as arguments, but this is only half of what it means to have first-class functions as values. Functions also return values, so for truly first-class functions, it makes sense that functions must sometimes return other functions. As always, the question should be, why would I ever want to return a function? One good reason is that you want to dispatch certain functions based on other parameters.

Suppose you create a Secret Society of Contemporary Alchemists and you need to send newsletters to members at various regional post office boxes. There are offices in three cities: San Francisco, Reno, and New York. Here are the office addresses:

- PO Box 1234, San Francisco, CA, 94111
- PO Box 789, New York, NY, 10013
- PO Box 456, Reno, NV, 89523

QC 4.2 answer

```
compareLastNames name1 name2 = if lastName1 > lastName2
                               then GT
                               else if lastName1 < lastName2
                                    then LT
                                    else if firstName1 > firstName2
                                         then GT
                                         else if firstName1 < firstName2
                                              then LT
                                              else EQ
  where lastName1 = snd name1
        lastName2 = snd name2
        firstName1 = fst name1
        firstName2 = fst name2
```

You need to build a function that will take a name tuple (as you used before in the sorting example) and an office location and then put together the mailing address for you. A first pass at this function might look like the following. The only other thing we need to introduce that you haven't seen yet is the ++ operator used to concatenate strings (and lists).

Listing 4.6 addressLetter v.1

```
addressLetter name location = nameText ++ " - " ++location
  where nameText = (fst name) ++ " " ++ (snd name)
```

To use this function, you have to pass a name tuple and the full address:

```
GHCi> addressLetter ("Bob","Smith") "PO Box 1234 - San Francisco, CA, 94111"
"Bob Smith - PO Box 1234 - San Francisco, CA, 94111"
```

This is a fine solution. You also could easily use variables to keep track of the addresses, and that would make errors much less likely (and save typing). You're all set to send out your newsletters!

After the first round of newsletters, you get some complaints and requests from the regional offices:

- San Francisco added a new address for members with last names starting with the letter *L* or later in the alphabet: PO Box 1010, San Francisco, CA, 94109.
- New York wants the name followed by a colon rather than a hyphen, for mystical reasons they won't share.
- Reno wants only last names to be used for greater secrecy.

It's clear that now you need a different function for each office.

Listing 4.7 sfOffice, nyOffice, renoOffice

```
sfOffice name = if lastName < "L"
                then nameText
                     ++ " - PO Box 1234 - San Francisco, CA, 94111"
                else nameText
                     ++ " - PO Box 1010 - San Francisco, CA, 94109"
  where lastName = snd name
        nameText = (fst name) ++ " " ++ lastName

nyOffice name = nameText ++ ": PO Box 789 - New York, NY, 10013"
  where nameText = (fst name) ++ " " ++ (snd name)
```

```
renoOffice name = nameText ++ " - PO Box 456 - Reno, NV 89523"
  where nameText = snd name
```

The question now is, how should you use these three functions with `addressLetter`? You could rewrite `addressLetter` to take a function rather than a location as an argument. The trouble with this is that the `addressLetter` function is going to be part of a larger web application, and you'd like to pass in a string parameter for the location. What you'd really like is another function that will take a location string and dispatch the right function for you. You'll build a new function called `getLocationFunction` that will take a single string and dispatch the correct function. Rather than a bunch of nested `if then else` expressions, you'll use Haskell's `case` expression.

Listing 4.8 `getLocationFunction`

```
getLocationFunction location = case location of    -- case looks at the value of location.
  "ny" -> nyOffice          -- If location is ny, returns nyOffice
  "sf" -> sfOffice          -- If location is sf, returns sfOffice
  "reno" -> renoOffice      -- If location is reno, returns renoOffice
  _ -> (\name -> (fst name) ++ " " ++ (snd name))   -- If it's anything else (_ is a wildcard), returns a generic solution
```

This `case` expression should seem straightforward, except for that underscore (_) at the end. You want to capture the situation in which a string other than one of the official locations is passed in. In Haskell, _ is used frequently as a wildcard. This is covered in much more depth in the next lesson. In this case, if the user of your code passes in an invalid location, you put together a quick lambda function that will make the name tuple into a string. Now you have a single function that will return the function you need when you need it. Finally, you can rewrite `addressLetter`, as shown next.

Listing 4.9 `addressLetter` v.2

```
addressLetter name location = locationFunction name
  where locationFunction = getLocationFunction location
```

In GHCi, you can test that your function performs as expected:

```
GHCi> addressLetter ("Bob","Smith") "ny"
"Bob Smith: PO Box 789 - New York, NY, 10013"
```

```
GHCi> addressLetter ("Bob","Jones") "ny"
"Bob Jones: PO Box 789 - New York, NY, 10013"
GHCi> addressLetter ("Samantha","Smith") "sf"
"Samantha Smith - PO Box 1010 - San Francisco, CA, 94109"
GHCi> addressLetter ("Bob","Smith") "reno"
"Smith - PO Box 456 - Reno, NV 89523"
GHCi> addressLetter ("Bob","Smith") "la"
"Bob Smith"
```

Now that you've separated each function needed for generating addresses, you can easily add new rules as they come in from each office. In this example, returning functions as values helped tremendously to make your code easier to understand and extend. This is a simple use of returning functions as values; all you've done is automate the way functions can move around.

Summary

In this lesson, our objective was to explain first-class functions. First-class functions allow you to pass functions in as arguments as well as return them as values. First-class functions are an incredibly powerful tool, because they allow you to abstract out computation from your functions. The power of first-class functions is evidenced by their wide adoption in most modern programming languages. Let's see if you got this.

Q4.1 Anything that can be compared in Haskell (for example, `[Char]`, which you use for the names in your name tuples) can be compared with a function called `compare`. The `compare` function returns `GT`, `LT`, or `EQ`. Rewrite `compareLastNames` by using compare.

Q4.2 Define a new location function for Washington, DC and add it to `getLocationFunction`. In the DC function, everyone's names must be followed by *Esq*.

CLOSURES AND PARTIAL APPLICATION

After reading lesson 5, you'll be able to

- Capture values in a lambda expression
- Use closures to create new functions
- Simplify this process with partial application

In this lesson, you'll learn the final key element of functional programming: closures. *Closures* are the logical consequence of having lambda functions and first-class functions. By combining these lambda functions and first-class functions to create closures, you can dynamically create functions. This turns out to be an incredibly powerful abstraction, though the one that takes the most getting used to. Haskell makes closures much easier to work with by allowing for partial application. By the end of the lesson, you'll see how partial application makes otherwise confusing closures much easier to work with.

Consider this In the preceding lesson, you learned how to pass in programming logic to other functions because of first-class functions. For example, you might have a `getPrice` function that takes a URL and a website-specific price-extraction function:

```
getPrice amazonExtractor url
```

Although this is useful, what happens if you need to extract items from 1,000 URLs, but all using `amazonExtractor`? Is there a way to capture this argument on the fly so you have to pass in only the `url` parameter for future calls?

5.1 Closures—creating functions with functions

In lesson 4, you defined a function named ifEven (listing 4.3). By using a function as an argument to ifEven, you were able to abstract out a pattern of computation. You then created the functions ifEvenInc, ifEvenDouble, and ifEvenSquare.

Listing 5.1 ifEvenInc, ifEvenDouble, ifEvenSquare

```
ifEvenInc n = ifEven inc n
ifEvenDouble n = ifEven double n
ifEvenSquare n = ifEven square n
```

Using functions as arguments helped to clean up your code. But you'll notice you're still repeating a programming pattern! Each of these definitions is identical except for the function you're passing to ifEven. What you want is a function that builds ifEvenX functions. To solve this, you can build a new function that returns functions, called genIfEven, as shown in figure 5.1.

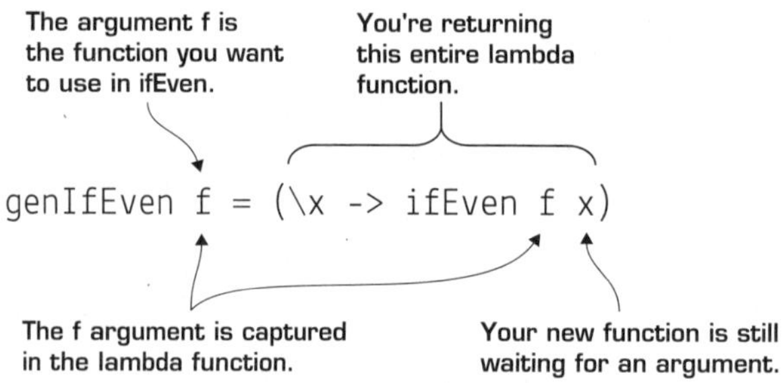

Figure 5.1 The genIfEven function lets you build ifEvenX functions simply.

Now you're passing in a function and returning a lambda function. The function f that you passed in is captured inside the lambda function! When you capture a value inside a lambda function, this is referred to as a *closure*.

Even in this small example, it can be difficult to understand exactly what's happening. To see this better, let's see how to create your ifEvenInc function by using genIfEven, as shown in figure 5.2.

```
ifEvenInc = genIfEven inc

(\x -> ifEven f x)

(\x -> ifEven inc x)

ifEvenInc = (\x -> ifEven inc x)
```

Figure 5.2 `ifEvenInc` with closure

Now let's move on to a real-world example of using closures to help build URLs to use with an API.

Quick check 5.1 Write a function `genIfXEven` that creates a closure with `x` and returns a new function that allows the user to pass in a function to apply to `x` if `x` is even.

5.2 Example: Generating URLs for an API

One of the most common ways to get data is to make calls to a RESTful API by using an HTTP request. The simplest type of request is a `GET` request, in which all of the parameters you need to send to another server are encoded in the URL. In this example, the data you need for each request is as follows:

- The hostname
- The name of the resource you're requesting
- The ID of the resource
- Your API key

Figure 5.3 shows an example URL.

QC 5.1 answer

```
ifEven f x = if even x
             then f x
             else x

genIfXEven x = (\f -> ifEven f x)
```

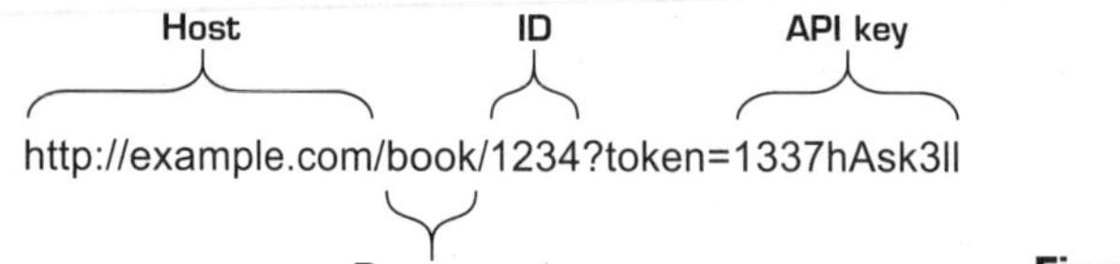

Figure 5.3 Parts of a URL

Building a URL from these parts is straightforward. Here's your basic `getRequestURL` builder.

Listing 5.2 `getRequestUrl`

```
getRequestURL host apiKey resource id = host ++
                                        "/" ++
                                        resource ++
                                        "/" ++
                                        id ++
                                        "?token=" ++
                                        apiKey
```

One thing that might strike you as odd about this function is that the order of your arguments isn't the same as the order you use them or that they appear in the URL itself. *Anytime you might want to use a closure (which in Haskell is pretty much anytime), you want to order your arguments from most to least general.* In this case, each host can have multiple API keys, each API key is going to use different resources, and each resource is going to have many IDs associated with it. The same is true when you define `ifEven`; the function you pass will work with a huge range of inputs, so it's more general and should appear first in the argument list.

Now that you have the basic request-generating function down, you can see how it works:

```
GHCi> getRequestURL "http://example.com" "1337hAsk3ll" "book" "1234"
"http://example.com/book/1234?token=1337hAsk3ll"
```

Great! This is a nice, general solution, and because your team as a whole will be querying many hosts, it's important not to be too specific. Nearly every programmer on the team will be focusing on data from just a few hosts. It seems silly, not to mention error-prone, to have programmers manually type in http://example.com every time they need to make a request. What you need is a function that everyone can use to generate a request URL builder just for them. The answer to this is a closure. Your generator will look like figure 5.4.

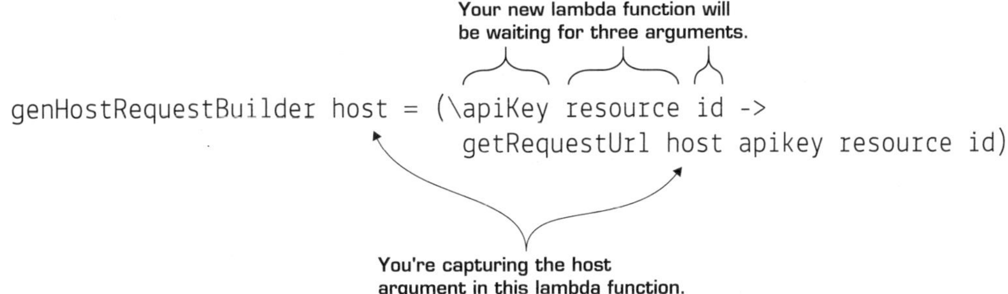

Figure 5.4 Capturing the host value in a closure

Listing 5.3 exampleUrlBuilder v.1

```
exampleUrlBuilder = genHostRequestBuilder "http://example.com"
```

When you pass the value `example.com`, you create a new, unnamed function that captures the host and needs only the three remaining arguments. When you define `exampleUrlBuilder`, you give a name to the anonymous function. Anytime you have a new URL that you want to make requests to, you now have an easy way to create a custom function for this. Load this function into GHCi and see how it simplifies your code:

```
GHCi> exampleUrlBuilder "1337hAsk3ll" "book" "1234"
"http://example.com/book/1234?token=1337hAsk3ll"
```

It's clear you run into the same problem again when you look at `apiKey`. Passing your API key in each time you call `exampleUrlBuilder` is still tedious because you'll likely be using only one or two API keys. Of course, you can use another closure to fix this! This time, you'll have to pass both your `exampleUrlBuilder` function and your `apiKey` to your generator.

Listing 5.4 genApiRequestBuilder

```
genApiRequestBuilder hostBuilder apiKey = (\resource id ->
                                             hostBuilder apiKey resource id)
```

What's interesting here is that you're combining both functions as arguments and functions as return values. Inside your closure is a copy of the specific function that you're going to need, as well as the API key you need to capture. Finally, you can build a function that makes creating a request URL much easier.

Listing 5.5 `myExampleUrlBuilder` v.1

```
myExampleUrlBuilder = genApiRequestBuilder exampleUrlBuilder "1337hAsk3ll"
```

And you can use this to quickly create URLs for different resource/ID combos:

```
GHCi> myExampleUrlBuilder "book" "1234"
"http://example.com/book/1234?token=1337hAsk3ll"
```

Quick check 5.2 Write a version of `genApiRequestBuilder` that also takes the resource as an argument.

5.2.1 Partial application: making closures simple

Closures are both powerful and useful. But the use of a lambda function to create the closure makes reading and reasoning about them more difficult than it should be. Additionally, all the closures you've written so far follow a nearly identical pattern: provide some of the parameters that a function takes and create a new function awaiting the rest. Suppose you have a function `add4` that takes four variables and adds them:

```
add4 a b c d = a + b + c + d
```

Now you want to create a function `addXto3`, which takes an argument `x` and then returns a closure awaiting the remaining three arguments:

```
addXto3 x = (\b c d ->
              add4 x b c d)
```

The explicit lambda makes it relatively hard to reason about what's happening. What if you want to make an `addXYto2`?

```
addXYto2 x y = (\c d ->
                 add4 x y c d)
```

With four arguments to manage visually, even this trivial function isn't easy to understand. Lambda functions are powerful and useful, but can definitely clutter up otherwise neat function definitions.

QC 5.2 answer

```
genApiRequestBuilder hostBuilder apiKey resource = (\id ->
                                                     hostBuilder apiKey
                                                     resource id)
```

Haskell has an interesting feature that addresses this problem. What happens if you call `add4` with fewer than four arguments? This answer seems obvious: it should throw an error. This *isn't* what Haskell does. You can define a `mystery` value in GHCi by using `Add4` and one argument:

```
GHCi> mystery = add4 3
```

If you run this code, you'll find that it doesn't cause an error. Haskell has created a brand new function for you:

```
GHCi> mystery 2 3 4
12
GHCi> mystery 5 6 7
21
```

This `mystery` function adds 3 to the three remaining arguments you pass to it. When you call any function with fewer than the required number of parameters in Haskell, you get a new function that's waiting for the remaining parameters. This language feature is called *partial application*. The mystery function is the same thing as if you wrote `addXto3` and then passed in the argument `3` to it. Not only has partial application saved you from using a lambda function, but you don't even need to define the awkwardly named `addXto3`! You can also easily re-create the behavior of `addXYto2`:

```
GHCi> anotherMystery = add4 2 3
GHCi> anotherMystery 1 2
8
GHCi> anotherMystery 4 5
14
```

If you find using closures confusing so far, you're in luck! Thanks to partial application, you rarely have to write or think explicitly about closures in Haskell. All of the work of `genHostRequestBuilder` and `genApiRequestBuilder` is built in and can be replaced by leaving out the arguments you don't need.

Listing 5.6 `exampleUrlBuilder` v.2 and `myExampleUrlBuilder` v.2

```
exampleUrlBuilder = getRequestUrl "http://example.com"
myExampleUrlBuilder = exampleUrlBuilder "1337hAsk3ll"
```

In some cases in Haskell, you'll still want to use lambda functions to create a closure, but using partial application is far more common. Figure 5.5 shows the process of partial application.

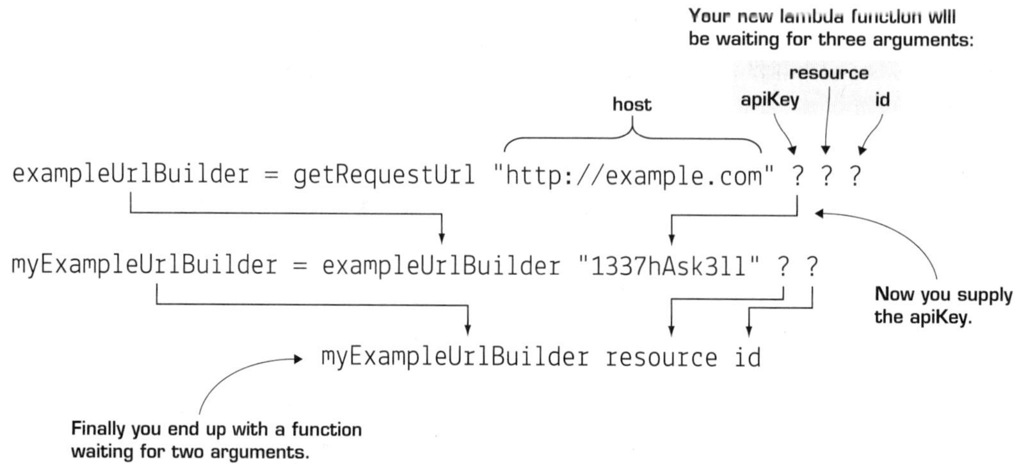

Figure 5.5 Visualizing partial application

> **Quick check 5.3** Make a builder function that's specifically for http://example.com, the 1337hAsk3ll API key, and the book resource. That's a function that requires only the ID of a specific book and then generates the full URL.

5.3 Putting it all together

Partial application is also the reason we created the rule that arguments should be ordered from most to least general. When you use partial application, the arguments are applied first to last. You violated this rule when you defined your `addressLetter` function in lesson 4 (listing 4.6):

```
addressLetter name location = locationFunction name
  where locationFunction = getLocationFunction location
```

In `addressLetter`, the `name` argument comes before the `location` argument. It makes much more sense that you'd want to create a function `addressLetterNY` that's waiting for a name,

QC 5.3 answer

```
exampleBuilder = getRequestUrl "http://example.com" "1337hAsk3ll" "books"
```

rather than an `addressLetterBobSmith` that will write letters to all the Bob Smiths of the world. Rather than rewriting your function, which might not always be possible if you're using functions from another library, you can fix this by creating a partial-application-friendly version, as follows.

Listing 5.7 `addressLetterV2`

```
addressLetterV2 location name = addressLetter name location
```

This is a fine solution for the one-time case of fixing your `addressLetter` function. What if you inherited a code base in which many library functions had this same error in the case of two arguments? It'd be nice to find a general solution to this problem rather than individually writing out each case. Combining all the things you've learned so far, you can do this in a simple function. You want to make a function called `flipBinaryArgs` that will take a function, flip the order of its arguments, and then return it otherwise untouched. To do this, you need a lambda function, first-class functions, and a closure. You can put all these together in a single line of Haskell, as shown in figure 5.6.

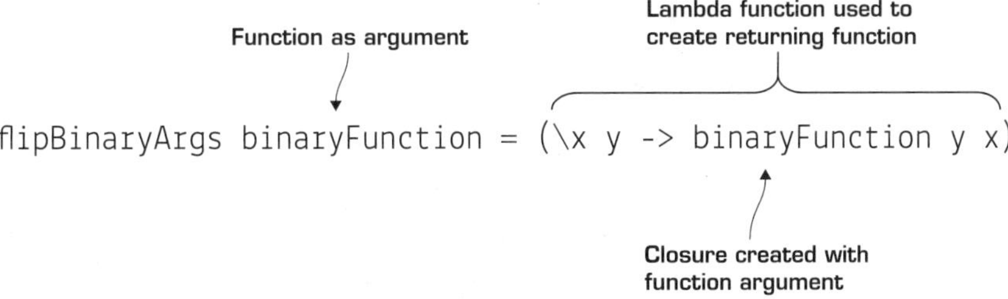

Figure 5.6 The `flipBinaryArgs` function

Now you can rewrite `addressLetterV2` by using `flipBinaryArgs`, and then create an `addressLetterNY`:

```
addressLetterV2 = flipBinaryArgs addressLetter
addressLetterNY = addressLetterV2 "ny"
```

And you can test this out in GHCi:

```
GHCi> addressLetterNY ("Bob","Smith")
Bob Smith: PO Box 789 - New York, NY, 10013
```

Your `flipBinaryArgs` function is useful for more than fixing code that didn't follow our generalization guidelines. Plenty of binary functions have a natural order, such as division. A useful trick in Haskell is that any infix operator (such as +, /, -, *) can be used as a prefix function by putting parentheses around it:

```
GHCi> 2 + 3
5
GHCi> (+) 2 3
5
GHCi> 10 / 2
5.0
GHCi> (/) 10 2
5.0
```

In division and subtraction, the order of arguments is important. Despite there being a natural order for the arguments, it's easy to understand that you might want to create a closure around the second argument. In these cases, you can use `flipBinaryArgs` to help you. Because `flipBinaryArgs` is such a useful function, there's an existing function named `flip` that behaves the same.

> **Quick check 5.4** Use `flip` and partial application to create a function called `subtract2` that removes 2 from whatever number is passed in to it.

Summary

In this lesson, our objective was to teach the important idea of a closure in functional programming. With lambda functions, first-class functions, and closures, you have all you need to perform functional programming. Closures combine lambda functions and first-class functions to give you amazing power. With closures, you can easily create new functions on the fly. You also learned how partial application makes working with closures much easier. After you're used to using partial application, you may sometimes forget you're working with closures at all! Let's see if you got this.

Q5.1 Now that you know about partial application, you no longer need to use `genIfEvenX`. Redefine `ifEvenInc`, `ifEvenDouble`, and `ifEvenSquare` by using `ifEven` and partial application.

QC 5.4 answer

```
subtract2 = flip (-) 2
```

Q5.2 Even if Haskell didn't have partial application, you could hack together some approximations. Following a similar pattern to `flipBinaryArgs` (figure 5.6), write a function `binaryPartialApplication` that takes a binary function and one argument and returns a new function waiting for the missing argument.

LESSON 6

LISTS

After reading lesson 6, you'll be able to

- Identify the parts that make up a list
- Know how to build lists
- Understand the role of lists in functional programming
- Use common functions on a list
- Learn the basics of lazy evaluation

In many ways, an array is the fundamental data structure for programming in C. If you properly understand arrays in C, you necessarily understand how memory allocation works, how data is stored on a computer, and the basics of pointers and pointer arithmetic. For Haskell (and functional programming in general), the fundamental data structure is a list. Even as you approach some of the more advanced topics in this book, such as functors and monads, the simple list will still be the most useful example.

This lesson provides a proper introduction to this surprisingly important data structure. You'll learn the basics of taking lists apart and putting them back together, as well as learning some of the essential functions for a list that Haskell provides. Finally, you'll take a peek at another unique feature of Haskell: lazy evaluation. Lazy evaluation is so powerful that it allows you to represent and work with lists that are infinitely long! If you get stuck on a topic in Haskell, it's almost always helpful to turn back to lists to see if they can give you some insight.

Consider this You work for a company that has 10,000 employees, and some of them want to play on an after-work softball team. The company has five teams, named after colors, which you want to use to assign employees:

```
teams = ["red","yellow","orange","blue","purple"]
```

You have a list of employees and you want to match them to the correct team as evenly as possible. What's a simple way that you can use Haskell's list functions to perform this task?

6.1 The anatomy of a list

Lists are the single most important data structure in functional programming. One of the key reasons is that lists are inherently recursive. A list is either an empty list or an element followed by another list. Taking apart and building lists are fundamental tools for many techniques in functional programming.

When taking apart a list, the main pieces are the `head`, the `tail`, and the end (represented by `[]`). The `head` is just the first element in a list:

```
GHCi> head [1,2,3]
1
GHCi> head [[1,2],[3,4],[5,6]]
[1,2]
```

The `tail` is the rest of the list left over, after the head:

```
GHCi> tail [1,2,3]
[2,3]
GHCi> tail [3]
[]
```

The `tail` of a list with just one element is `[]`, which marks the end of the list. This end of the list is just an empty list. But an empty list is different from other lists, as it has neither a head nor a tail. Calling `head` or `tail` on `[]` will result in an error. If you look at the head and tail, you can start to see the recursive nature of working with lists: a head is an element, and a tail is another list. You can visualize this by imagining tearing the first item off a grocery list, as in figure 6.1.

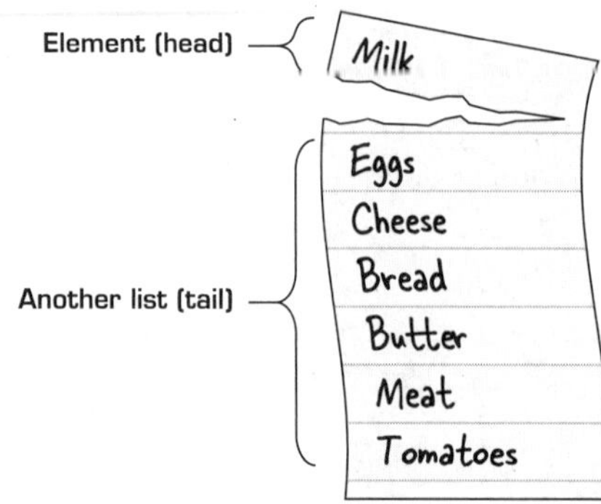

Figure 6.1 A list is made up of the head element and the tail list.

You can break a list into pieces, but this does you little good if you can't put them back together again! In functional programming, building lists is just as important as breaking them down. To build a list, you need just one function and the infix operator (:), which is called *cons*. This term is short for *construct* and has its origins in Lisp. We'll refer to this operation as *consing*, because : looks a bit odd in a sentence.

To make a list, you need to take a value and cons it with another list. The simplest way to make a list is to cons a value with the empty list:

```
GHCi> 1:[]
[1]
```

Under the hood, all lists in Haskell are represented as a bunch of consing operations, and the [...] notation is *syntactic sugar* (a feature of the programming language syntax designed solely to make things easier to read):

```
GHCi> 1:2:3:4:[]
[1,2,3,4]
GHCi> (1,2):(3,4):(5,6):[]
[(1,2),(3,4),(5,6)]
```

Notice that all of these lists end with the empty list []. By definition, a list is always a value consed with another list (which can also be an empty list). You could attach the value to the front of an existing list if you wanted:

```
GHCi> 1:[2,3,4]
[1,2,3,4]
```

It's worth noting that the strings you've seen so far are themselves syntactic sugar for lists of characters (denoted by single quotes rather than double quotes):

```
GHCi>['h','e','l','l','o']
"hello"
GHCi> 'h':'e':'l':'l':'o':[]
"hello"
```

An important thing to remember is that in Haskell every element of the list must be the same type. For example, you can cons the letter `'h'` to the string `"ello"` because `"ello"` is just a list of characters and `'h'` (single quotes) is a character:

```
GHCi> 'h':"ello"
"hello"
```

But you can't cons `"h"` (double quotes) to `"ello"` because `"h"` is a list of one character and the values inside `"ello"` are individual characters. This becomes more obvious when you remove the syntactic sugar.

Listing 6.1 Consing characters and strings

```
GHCi> "h":"ello"                     <-- Error!
GHCi> ['h']:['e','l','l','o']        <-- Same code with one layer of sugar removed
GHCi>  'h':[]:'e':'l':'l':'o':[]     <-- Completely desugared
```

If you do want to combine two lists, you need to concatenate them by using `++`. You saw this in lesson 3 with concatenating text, but given that strings are just lists, it will work on any list:

```
GHCi> "h" ++ "ello"
"hello"
GHCi> [1] ++ [2,3,4]
[1,2,3,4]
```

Consing is important to understand because it's an essential part of writing recursive functions on lists. Nearly all sequential operations in functional programing involve building lists, breaking them apart, or a combination of the two.

6.2 Lists and lazy evaluation

Because lists are so important in Haskell, there are many ways to quickly generate ranges of data. Here are some examples:

```
GHCi> [1 .. 10]                  <-- Generates a list of numbers
[1,2,3,4,5,6,7,8,9,10]               from 1 through 10
```

```
GHCi> [1,3 .. 10]
[1,3,5,7,9]
```

Adding the next step, 3, generates odd numbers.

```
GHCi> [1, 1.5 .. 5]
[1.0,1.5,2.0,2.5,3.0,3.5,4.0,4.5,5.0]
```

Generates a list in increments of 0.5

```
GHCi> [1,0 .. -10]
[1,0,-1,-2,-3,-4,-5,-6,-7,-8,-9,-10]
```

Generates a decrementing list

These are useful but not particularly interesting. Many programing languages have a `range` function that works in a similar manner. What happens if you forget to put an upper bound to your range?

```
GHCi> [1 .. ]
[1,2,3,4,5,6,7,8,9,10,11,12 ..
```

An unending list is generated! This is cool but quickly clogs up the terminal and doesn't seem particularly useful. What's interesting is that you can assign this list to a variable and even use it in a function:

```
simple x = x
longList = [1 .. ]
stillLongList = simple longList
```

What's shocking is that this code compiles just fine. You defined an infinite list and then used it in a function. Why didn't Haskell get stuck trying to evaluate an infinitely long list? Haskell uses a special form of evaluation called *lazy evaluation*. In lazy evaluation, no code is evaluated until it's needed. In the case of `longList`, none of the values in the list were needed for computation.

Lazy evaluation has advantages and disadvantages. It's easy to see some of the advantages. First, you get the computational benefit that any code you don't absolutely need is never computed. Another benefit is that you can define and use interesting structures such as an infinite list. This can be useful for plenty of practical problems. The disadvantages of lazy evaluation are less obvious. The biggest one is that it's much harder to reason about the code's performance. In this trivial example, it's easy to see that any argument passed to `simple` won't be evaluated, but even a bit more complexity makes this less obvious. An even bigger problem is that you can easily build up large collections of unevaluated functions that would be much cheaper to store as values.

Quick check 6.1 True or false: You can compile and run a program with the variable `backwardsInfinity = reverse [1..]`.

6.3 Common functions on lists

Because lists are so important, a wide range of useful functions are built into Haskell's standard library module, called `Prelude`. So far, you've seen `head`, `tail`, `:` and `++`, which allow you to take apart lists and put them back together. There are many other useful functions on lists that will come up so frequently when writing Haskell that it's worth familiarizing yourself with them.

6.3.1 The !! operator

If you want to access a particular element of a list by its index, you can use the `!!` operator. The `!!` operator takes a list and a number, returning the element at that location in the list. Lists in Haskell are indexed starting at 0. If you try to access a value beyond the end of the list, you'll get an error:

```
GHCi> [1,2,3] !! 0
1
GHCi> "puppies" !! 4
'i'
GHCi> [1..10] !! 11
*** Exception: Prelude.!!: index too large
```

As mentioned in lesson 5, any infix operator (an operator that's placed between two values, such as `+`) can also be used like a prefix function by wrapping it in parentheses:

```
GHCi> (!!) [1,2,3] 0
1
```

Using prefix notation can often make things such as partial application easier. Prefix notation is also useful for using operators as arguments to other functions. You can still

QC 6.1 answer True. Even though you're reversing an infinite list, you're never calling this code, so the infinite list is never evaluated. If you loaded this code into GHCi and typed the following

```
GHCi> backwardsInfinity
```

you'd have a problem, as the program would need to evaluate this argument to print it out.

use partial application with an infix operator; you just need to wrap the expression in parentheses:

```
GHCi> paExample1 = (!!) "dog"
GHCi> paExample1 2
'g'
GHCi> paExample2 = ("dog" !!)
GHCi> paExample2 2
'g'
```

Notice that in `paExample2` you see how partial application works with infix binary operators. To perform partial application on a binary operator, called a *section*, you need to wrap the expression in parentheses. If you include only the argument on the right, the function will be waiting for the leftmost argument; if you include only the argument on the left, you get a function waiting for the argument on the right. Here's `paExample3`, which creates partial application of the right argument:

```
GHCi> paExample3 = (!! 2)
GHCi> paExample3 "dog"
'g'
```

The important thing to remember about sections is that the parentheses aren't optional.

6.3.2 length

The `length` function is obvious; it gives you the length of the list!

```
GHCi> length [1..20]
20
GHCi> length [(10,20),(1,2),(15,16)]
3
GHCi> length "quicksand"
9
```

6.3.3 reverse

As expected, `reverse` reverses the list:

```
GHCi> reverse [1,2,3]
[3,2,1]
GHCi> reverse "cheese"
"eseehc"
```

You can use `reverse` to make a basic palindrome checker, as shown in the next listing.

Listing 6.2 `isPalindrome`

```
isPalindrome word = word == reverse word
```

```
GHCi> isPalindrome "cheese"
False
GHCi> isPalindrome "racecar"
True
GHCi> isPalindrome [1,2,3]
False
GHCi> isPalindome [1,2,1]
True
```

6.3.4 elem

The `elem` function takes a value and a list and checks whether the value is in the list:

```
GHCi> elem 13 [0,13 .. 100]
True
GHCi> elem 'p' "cheese"
False
```

`elem` is a function that you may want to treat as an infix operator for readability. Any binary function can be treated as an infix operator by wrapping it in back-quotes (`). For example, the function `respond` returns a different response depending on whether a string has an exclamation mark, as follows.

Listing 6.3 `respond`

```
respond phrase = if '!' `elem` phrase
                 then "wow!"
                 else "uh.. okay"
```

```
GHCi> respond "hello"
"uh.. okay"
GHCi> respond "hello!"
"wow!"
```

Whether infix `elem` adds much readability is certainly debatable, but in the real world you'll frequently come across infix forms of binary functions.

6.3.5 take and drop

The `take` function takes a number and a list as arguments and then returns the first *n* elements of the list:

```
GHCi> take 5 [2,4..100]
[2,4,6,8,10]
GHCi> take 3 "wonderful"
"won"
```

If you ask for more values then a list has, `take` gives you what it can, with no error:

```
GHCi> take 1000000 [1]
[1]
```

`take` works best by being combined with other functions on lists. For example, you can combine `take` with `reverse` to get the last *n* elements of a list.

Listing 6.4 takeLast

```
takeLast n aList = reverse (take n (reverse aList))
GHCi> takeLast 10 [1..100]
[91,92,93,94,95,96,97,98,99,100]
```

The `drop` function is similar to `take`, except it removes the first `n` elements of a list:

```
GHCi> drop 2 [1,2,3,4,5]
[3,4,5]
GHCi> drop 5 "very awesome"
"awesome"
```

6.3.6 zip

You use `zip` when you want to combine two lists into tuple pairs. The arguments to `zip` are two lists. If one list happens to be longer, zip will stop whenever one of the two lists is empty:

```
GHCi> zip [1,2,3] [2,4,6]
[(1,2),(2,4),(3,6)]
GHCi> zip "dog" "rabbit"
[('d','r'),('o','a'),('g','b')]
GHCi> zip ['a' .. 'f'] [1 .. ]
[('a',1),('b',2),('c',3),('d',4),('e',5),('f',6)]
```

6.3.7 cycle

The `cycle` function is particularly interesting, because it uses lazy evaluation to create an infinite list. Given a list, `cycle` repeats that list endlessly. This may seem somewhat useless but comes in handy in a surprising number of situations. For example, it's common in numerical computing to need a list of *n* ones. With `cycle`, this function is trivial to make.

Listing 6.5 ones

```
ones n = take n (cycle [1])
```

```
GHCi> ones 2
[1,1]
GHCi> ones 4
[1,1,1,1]
```

`cycle` can be extremely useful for dividing members of a list into groups. Imagine you want to divide a list of files and put them on *n* number of servers, or similarly spilt up employees onto *n* teams. The general solution is to create a new function, `assignToGroups`, that takes a number of groups and a list, and then cycles through the groups, assigning members to them.

Listing 6.6 assignToGroups

```
assignToGroups n aList = zip groups aList
  where groups = cycle [1..n]
```

```
GHCi> assignToGroups 3 ["file1.txt","file2.txt","file3.txt"
                       ,"file4.txt","file5.txt","file6.txt","file7.txt"
                       ,"file8.txt"]
```

```
[(1,"file1.txt"),(2,"file2.txt"),(3,"file3.txt"),(1,"file4.txt"),
➥(2,"file5.txt"),(3,"file6.txt"),(1,"file7.txt"),(2,"file8.txt")]
```

```
GHCi> assignToGroups 2 ["Bob","Kathy","Sue","Joan","Jim","Mike"]
[(1,"Bob"),(2,"Kathy"),(1,"Sue"),(2,"Joan"),(1,"Jim"),(2,"Mike")]
```

These functions are just some of the more common of a wide range of list functions that Haskell offers. Not all of the functions on lists are included in the standard `Prelude` module. All list functions, including those automatically included in `Prelude`, are in the `Data.List` module. An exhaustive list of `Data.List` functions can be found online in the standard Haskell documentation (https://hackage.haskell.org/package/basedocs/Data-List.html).

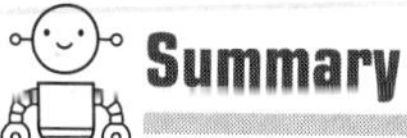

Summary

In this lesson, our objective was to go over the basic structure of a list. You learned that a list is made up of a `head` and a `tail` that are consed together. We also went over many of the most common functions on a list. Let's see if you got this.

Q6.1 Haskell has a function called `repeat` that takes a value and repeats it infinitely. Using the functions you've learned so far, implement your own version of `repeat`.

Q6.2 Write a function `subseq` that takes three arguments: a start position, an end position, and a list. The function should return the subsequence between the start and end. For example:

```
GHCi> subseq 2 5 [1 .. 10]
[3,4,5]
GHCi> subseq 2 7 "a puppy"
"puppy"
```

Q6.3 Write a function `inFirstHalf` that returns `True` if an element is in the first half of a list, and otherwise returns `False`.

LESSON 7

RULES FOR RECURSION AND PATTERN MATCHING

After reading lesson 7, you'll be able to

- Understand the definition of a recursive function
- Learn the rules for writing recursive functions
- Walk through examples of recursive function definitions
- Use basic pattern matching to solve recursive problems

One of the first challenges of writing practical code in a functional language is that because you don't have state changes, you also don't have common looping functions that rely on changing state, such as `for`, `while`, and `until` loops. All iteration problems have to be solved through recursion. For many programmers, this is a terrifying thought, as recursion typically brings up memories of headache-inducing problem solving. Thankfully, you can use a few simple rules to make recursion much easier. Additionally, just as Haskell offers partial application to make closures easier to work with, Haskell provides a feature called *pattern matching* to make recursion much saner to reason about.

Consider this In the preceding lesson, you learned the function `take`, which allows you to take n elements from a list:

```
take 3 [1,2,3,4]
[1,2,3]
```

How would you write your own version of `take` in Haskell?

7.1 Recursion

In general, something is *recursive* if it's defined in terms of itself. This normally leads to headaches, as programmers often imagine unwinding an infinite loop of a recursive definition. Recursion doesn't need to induce headaches, and is often a lot more natural than other forms of iteration in programing. Lists are a recursive data structure defined as an empty list, or an element and another list. No headaches or mystical acts of mental gymnastics are required to work with lists. Recursive functions are just functions that use themselves in their own definition. This, legitimately, sounds confusing.

But if you think of recursive functions as defining recursive processes, recursion becomes fairly mundane. Nearly every human activity is a recursive process! Take washing the dishes. If there are no dishes in the sink, you're done washing, but if there is a dish, you grab it, clean it, and put it on the rack. To continue washing dishes, you repeat until you're finished.

Quick check 7.1 Write down something mundane you do daily as a recursive process.

QC 7.1 answer

When writing a lesson for this book, I write the lesson and then then do the following:

1. Get edits from the editor.
2. Accept or reject those changes and make my own edits.
3. Submit the lesson to the editor.
4. If the editor is happy, I'm finished!

Otherwise, go back to step 1.

7.2 Rules for recursion

The trouble with recursion comes when you write down recursive processes. Even in the case of a list or a dishwashing algorithm, writing these from scratch seems much trickier than just being comfortable with what they are. The secret to writing recursive functions is to *not think about the recursion*! Thinking about recursion too much leads to headaches. The way to solve recursive functions is by following this simple set of rules:

1. Identify the end goal(s).
2. Determine what happens when a goal is reached.
3. List all alternate possibilities.
4. Determine your "rinse and repeat" process.
5. Ensure that each alternative moves you toward your goal.

7.2.1 Rule 1: Identify the end goal(s)

Generally, recursive processes come to an end. What does this end look like? For a list, the end of the process is the empty list; for washing dishes, it's an empty sink. After you recognize that something is a recursive process, the first step to solving it is figuring out when you know you're finished. Sometimes there's more than one goal. A telemarketer might have to call 100 people or make 5 sales before calling it a day. In this case, the goal is either 100 people have been called, or 5 sales have been made.

7.2.2 Rule 2: Determine what happens when a goal is reached

For each goal you establish in rule 1, you need to figure out what the result will be. In the case of washing dishes, the result is that you're finished washing the dishes. With functions, you need to return a value, so you have to determine what value should be returned at the end state. A typical problem programmers face is trying to think of the goal state in terms of being the end of a long recursive process. This is usually unnecessary and overly complicated. Often the answer is obvious when you ask the question, "What happens if I call my function on the goal state value?" For example, the end state of the Fibonacci sequence is to arrive at 1; by definition, fib 1 = 1. A more mundane example is determining the number of books you have by counting the number on each shelf. The goal state is to have no more shelves to count; the number of books on no shelves is 0.

7.2.3 Rule 3: List all alternate possibilities

If you aren't at your goal state, what do you have? This sounds like it can be a lot of work, but most of the time you have only one or two alternatives to being in the goal state. If you don't have an empty list, you have a list with something in it. If the sink isn't empty, you have a sink with dishes. For the telemarketer making calls, if you still haven't called 100 people or made 5 sales, you have two possibilities. You can call and make a sale, or call and not make a sale.

7.2.4 Rule 4: Determine your "Rinse and Repeat"

This rule is nearly identical to rule 2, except you have to repeat your process. Don't overthink or try to unwind the recursion. For a list, you might take the element and look at the tail. For washing dishes, you wash a dish, put it up to dry, and look in the sink again. The telemarketer either makes the call, records the sale, and repeats, or records that the call was made (no sale) and repeats.

7.2.5 Rule 5: Ensure that each alterative moves you toward the goal

This is a big one! For every process you list in rule 4, you need to ask yourself, "Does this move me closer to the goal?" If you keep taking the tail of a list, you'll get the empty list. If you keep removing dishes from the sink, you'll have an empty sink. Recording either sales or calls will eventually cause the counts for each to reach their goal. But suppose you want to flip a coin until you get heads. The goal is getting a head: if you get heads, you stop. The alternate is getting tails: if you get tails, you flip again. But flipping again doesn't ensure that you'll ever get heads. Statistically, you should arrive there, so in practice this would be fine, but this is a potentially dangerous function to run (imagine if instead of a coin, you used something with a small chance of success).

7.3 Your first recursive function: greatest common divisor

To introduce recursion, you'll start with one of the oldest numeric algorithms in existence: Euclid's algorithm. This algorithm is a remarkably simple method for computing the greatest common divisor (GCD) of two numbers. In case you've forgotten, the greatest common divisor of two numbers is the largest number that evenly divides them both. For example, the GCD for 20 and 16 is 4, because 4 is the largest number that divides evenly into both 20 and 16. For 10 and 100, the GCD is 10. Euclid outlined the algorithm in his book *Elements* (written in about 300 BC). Here's the basic rundown:

1. You start with two numbers, a and b.
2. If you divide a by b and the remainder is 0, clearly b is the GCD.
3. Otherwise, you change the value of a by assigning it the value of b (b becomes the new a). You also change the value of b to be the remainder you obtained in step 2 (the new b is the remainder of the original a divided by the original b).
4. Then repeat until a/b has no remainder.

Let's work through one example:

1. a = 20, b = 16
2. a/b = 20/16 = 1 remainder 4
3. a = 16, b = 4
4. a/b = 4 remainder 0
5. GCD = b = 4

To implement this algorithm in code, you want to start with the goal condition (rule 1). The goal is to have no remainder for a/b. In code, you use the modulus function to express this idea. In Haskell, your goal is expressed as follows:

```
a `mod` b == 0
```

The next question to answer is what do you return when you reach the goal state (rule 2)? If a/b has no remainder, b must divide a evenly; therefore, b is the GCD. This gives you the entire goal behavior:

```
if a `mod` b == 0
then b ....
```

Next you need to figure out all the ways that you can move closer to your goal if your goal isn't met (rule 3). For this problem, there's only one alternative: the remainder isn't 0. If the remainder isn't 0, you repeat the algorithm with b being the new a and the new b being the remainder: `a `mod` b` (rule 4):

```
else gcd b (a `mod` b)
```

Now you can put all of this into your recursive implementation of Euclid's algorithm, as shown next.

Listing 7.1 myGCD

```
myGCD a b = if remainder == 0
            then b
            else myGCD b remainder
  where remainder = a `mod` b
```

Finally, you make sure you're moving toward your goal (rule 5). Using the remainder, you're always going to be shrinking your new b; in the worst case (both numbers are prime), you'll eventually get to 1 for a and b. This confirms that your algorithm must terminate. By following the rules for creating recursive functions, you've avoided having to think too much about endlessly spiraling recursion!

Quick check 7.2 For the myGCD function, does it matter if a > b or a < b?

In our myGCD example, only two possible things can happen: either the goal is met, or the process is repeated. This fits nicely into an if then else expression. It's easy to imagine that as you come across more-complicated functions, you might get larger and larger if then else statements or use case. Haskell has an amazing feature called *pattern matching* that allows you to peek at the values passed as arguments and behave accordingly. As an example, let's make a function sayAmount that returns "one" for 1, "two" for 2, and for everything else returns a bunch. First, let's see how to implement this by using case rather than pattern matching in the function definition.

Listing 7.2 sayAmount v.1

```
sayAmount n = case n of
  1 -> "one"
  2 -> "two"
  n -> "a bunch"
```

The pattern matching version of this looks like three separate definitions, each for one of the possible arguments.

Listing 7.3 sayAmount v.2

```
sayAmount 1 = "one"
sayAmount 2 = "two"
sayAmount n = "a bunch"
```

QC 7.2 answer It doesn't matter, and adds only one extra step, if a < b. For example, 20 `mod` 50 is 20, so the next call would be myGCD 50 20, which is just one more step than calling myGCD 50 20 to begin with.

Pattern matching, just like `case`, looks at the options in order, so if you'd placed `sayAmount n` first in your list, calling `sayAmount` would always return "`a bunch`".

The important thing to realize about pattern matching is that it can look only at arguments, but it can't do any computation on them when matching. For example, with pattern matching, you can't check to see whether `n` is less than 0. Even with this restriction, pattern matching is powerful. You can use pattern matching to check whether a list is empty by matching against `[]`:

```
isEmpty [] = True
isEmpty aList = False
```

In Haskell, it's standard practice to use `_` as a wildcard for values you don't use. In `isEmpty`, you don't use the `aList` parameter, so standard practice is to write it as follows:

```
isEmpty [] = True
isEmpty _ = False
```

You can do even more-sophisticated pattern matching on lists. A popular convention in Haskell is to use the single `x` to represent a single value, and the variable `xs` to represent a list of values (though we'll frequently ignore this convention for readability). You could define your own version of `head` as follows:

```
myHead (x:xs) = x
```

To better understand what Haskell is doing as far as pattern matching is concerned, take a look at figure 7.1 to see how Haskell views a list argument as a pattern.

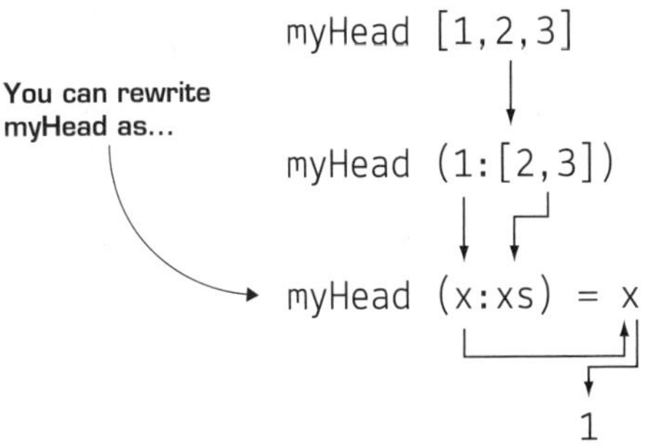

Figure 7.1 Visualizing pattern-matching internals for `myHead`

Like the real version of `head` in Haskell, you don't have a way to handle the case of an empty list, which has no head. You can use Haskell's `error` function to throw an error in this case.

Listing 7.4 myHead

```
myHead (x:xs) = x
myHead [] = error "No head for empty list"
```

Because you want to think of recursion as merely a list of goals and alternative cases, pattern matching becomes valuable in writing recursive code without getting a migraine. The trick is thinking in patterns. Whenever you write recursive functions, you can split up the definitions so that you're concerned only with the goal state, always defined first, and then all the possible alternatives one at a time. This often leads to shorter function definitions, but even more important, it makes it easier to reason about each step. Pattern matching is a wonderful way to alleviate the pain and symptoms of recursion.

Quick check 7.3

Fill in this definition of `myTail` by using pattern matching, and make sure to use _ where the value isn't needed:

```
myTail (<fill in this>) = xs
```

Summary

In this lesson, our objective was to teach you how to reason about writing recursive functions. When you're inexperienced in writing recursive functions, the problem often can appear much more challenging than it needs to. Here are the general rules for recursion that should help when you get stuck:

1. Identify the end goal(s).
2. Determine what happens when a goal is reached.
3. List all alternate possibilities.
4. Determine your "rinse and repeat" process.
5. Ensure that each alternative moves you toward the goal.

Let's see if you got this.

QC 7.3 answer

```
myTail (_:xs) = xs
```

Q7.1 The `tail` function in Haskell returns an error when called on an empty list. Modify `myTail` so that it does handle the case of an empty list by returning the empty list.

Q7.2 Rewrite `myGCD` by using pattern matching.

LESSON 8

WRITING RECURSIVE FUNCTIONS

After reading lesson 8, you'll be able to

- See common patterns of applying rules of recursion
- Understand how to use recursion on lists
- Learn to time functions in GHCi
- Reason about the edge cases of our five rules of recursion

The best way to get better at recursion is to practice, practice, practice! In this lesson, we'll walk through a variety of recursive functions to help you apply the rules of recursion presented in the preceding lesson. As you do this, you'll start to see that a few patterns repeat when solving recursive problems. Because Haskell doesn't allow you to "cheat" by using stateful iteration, nearly all the code you write in Haskell will involve some recursion (though often this is abstracted away). This will lead you to quickly becoming comfortable writing recursive functions and solving problems in a recursive style.

Consider this In the preceding lesson, you were asked to consider writing a `take` function on your own. This time, consider the `drop` function:

```
drop 3 [1,2,3,4]
[4]
```

Write your own version of `drop` and consider how this function is both similar to and different from `take`.

8.1 Review: Rules of recursion

In the preceding lesson, you learned about the rules for writing recursive functions. Here they are again for easy reference:

1. Identify the end goal(s).
2. Determine what happens when a goal is reached.
3. List all alternate possibilities.
4. Determine your "rinse and repeat" process.
5. Ensure that each alternative moves you toward the goal.

To get a better feel for these rules, you'll walk through a wide range of examples in this lesson. You'll also make heavy use of pattern matching in order to solve problems recursively as easily as possible.

8.2 Recursion on lists

In lesson 6, we talked about how important lists are to functional programming and discussed a few of the functions included in Haskell's `Prelude` that make working with lists easier. Now you'll revisit a few of those functions, but this time you'll write them from scratch. This will demonstrate how to think recursively to solve real problems, as well as giving a deeper sense of how these essential functions in Haskell work.

8.2.1 Implementing length

Calculating the length of a list is one of the simplest and most straightforward examples of a recursive function on a list. Using pattern matching, decomposing our problem is easy.

For our goal state, you have the empty list (rule 1). The majority of recursive functions on a list have the empty list as their goal state. What do you do when you get to that goal (rule 2)? Well, the length of an empty list is 0, because there's nothing in it. Now you have your goal state described:

```
myLength [] = 0
```

Next you have to consider any alternate cases (rule 3). There's only one option, which is a nonempty list. When you encounter a nonempty list, you know that you've seen one element. To get the length of this nonempty list, you add 1 to the length of the `tail` of the list (rule 4):

```
myLength xs = 1 + length (tail xs)
```

Before declaring yourself finished, you have to think about whether this step moves you toward your goal (rule 5). Clearly, if you keep taking the `tail` of a (noninfinite) list, you'll eventually reach `[]`. No other alternative possibilities are left, and each of your nongoal states moves you toward your goal, so you're finished!

Listing 8.1 myLength

```
myLength [] = 0
myLength xs = 1 + myLength (tail xs)
```

Quick check 8.1 Use pattern matching to rewrite `myLength` without needing to explicitly call `tail`.

8.2.2 Implementing take

The `take` function is interesting for two reasons: `take` uses two arguments, `n` and a list, and it turns out `take` has two goal states! As is almost always the case, `take` terminates on the empty list `[]`. As mentioned earlier, unlike `tail` and `head`, `take` has no problem with the empty list, and will return as many items as it can. The other condition when `take` can be finished occurs when `n = 0`. In either case, you end up doing the same thing. Taking `n` elements from an empty list is `[]`, and taking 0 elements of any list is `[]`. So you end up with this:

```
myTake _ [] = []
myTake 0 _ = []
```

QC 8.1 answer

```
myLength [] = 0
myLength (x:xs) = 1 + myLength xs
```

The only case that isn't the goal occurs when both n is greater than 0 and the list is nonempty. In your length function, you had to worry only about taking apart your list, but with myTake, you're going to return a list so you have to build one as you go. What is your new list built from? Let's think about this with take 3 [1,2,3,4,5]:

1 You want the first element, 1, and then cons that along with take 2 [2,3,4,5].
2 Then you want the next element, 2, and cons it with take 1 [3,4,5].
3 Then you want 3 and cons it with take 0 [4,5].
4 At 0 you've reached a goal, so return [].
5 This leads to 1:2:3:[], which is [1,2,3].

In code, the process is as follows:

```
myTake n (x:xs) = x:rest
  where rest = myTake (n - 1) xs
```

Finally, you ask the question, "Does the recursive call move you closer to your goal?" In this case, it's yes on both counts. Reducing n eventually leads to 0, and taking the tail of the list eventually leads to [].

Listing 8.2 myTake

```
myTake _ [] = []
myTake 0 _ = []
myTake n (x:xs) = x:rest
  where rest = myTake (n - 1) xs
```

8.2.3 Implementing cycle

The cycle function is the most interesting of the list functions to implement, and also one that you can write in few languages other than Haskell. In cycle, you take a list and repeat it forever. This is possible only because of lazy evaluation, which few languages other than Haskell possess. Even more interesting from the viewpoint of our rules is that cycle has no goal state. Thankfully, recursion without goal states, even in Haskell, is fairly rare. Nonetheless, if you understand this example, you have a strong understanding of both recursion and lazy evaluation.

Once again, you'll be building a list. To start, you'll build a noninfinite version of the list. The basic behavior you want is to return your exact list, only with the first element at the end:

```
finiteCycle (first:rest) = first:rest ++ [first]
```

The `finiteCycle` function doesn't really cycle; it returns your original list with one element at the end. To cycle this, you need to repeat the cycle behavior for the `rest:[first]` section.

Listing 8.3 `myCycle`

```
myCycle (first:rest) = first:myCycle (rest++[first])
```

Even with our rules as a guide, often recursion can cause quite a headache. The key to solving recursive problems is to take your time, work through the goals, and reason through the processes. The benefit of recursive problems is that their solutions are often just a few lines of code. With practice, you'll also come to see that there are only a few patterns of recursion.

8.3 Pathological recursion: Ackerman function and the Collatz conjecture

In this section, you'll look at two interesting functions from mathematics that demonstrate some of the limits of our five rules for recursion.

8.3.1 The Ackermann function

The *Ackermann function* takes two arguments, m and n. When referring to the mathematical definition of the function, you'll use A(m, n) to save space. The Ackermann function follows these three rules:

- If m = 0, return n + 1.
- If n = 0, then A(m – 1, 1).
- If both m != 0 and n != 0, then A(m –1, A(m, n – 1)).

Now let's see how to implement this in Haskell by using our rules. First, your goal state occurs when m is `0`, and when you're in your goal state, you return `n + 1`. Using pattern matching, this is easy to implement (rules 1 and 2):

```
ackermann 0 n = n + 1
```

Now you have only two alternatives: n can be `0`, and both m and n are nonzero. The definition of the function also tells you what to do in these cases (rules 3 and 4):

```
ackermann m 0 = ackermann (m-1) 1
ackermann m n = ackermann (m-1) (ackermann m (n-1))
```

Finally, are you moving toward your goal in these two alternates (rule 5)? In the case of n = 0, yes, because if you keep decreasing m, you'll eventually get to m = 0. The same goes for your final case. Even though you have two calls to `ackermann`, the first m is decreasing to 0, and the n in the second call is decreasing toward 0 as well, which brings you to your goal!

Everything is perfect until you run the code. You can load this function into GHCi, and this time you can use `:set +s` to time your function calls:

```
GHCi> :set +s
GHCi> ackermann 3 3
61
(0.01 secs)
GHCi> ackermann 3 8
2045
(3.15 secs)
GHCi> ackermann 3 9
4093
(12.97 secs)
```

Because your recursive call is making nested calls to itself, its runtime cost quickly starts to explode! Even though you followed the rules for recursion, you end up getting into serious trouble with the Ackermann function.

8.3.2 The Collatz conjecture

The *Collatz conjecture* is an addictively fascinating problem in mathematics. The Collatz conjecture involves defining a recursive process given a starting number *n*:

- If n is 1, you're finished.
- If n is even, repeat with n/2.
- If n is odd, repeat with n × 3 + 1.

Let's write a function `collatz` that implements this process. The only issue is that as described, `collatz` would always return 1. To spice things up a bit, you'll record how long it takes to reach 1. So, for example, for `collatz 5`, you go through the following path:

```
5 -> 16 -> 8 -> 4 -> 2 -> 1
```

In this case, you'd expect `collatz 5` to be `6`.

Now to write your code. First, you establish your goal (rule 1): this is simply the case that n is 1. What do you do when you get to your goal (rule 2)? You'll want to return 1 because we consider this to be one step. You can use pattern matching to make this step easy to describe:

```
collatz 1 = 1
```

Next you have to list your alternatives (rule 3). In this case, you have two alternatives: n isn't 1 and is even, or n isn't 1 and is odd. Because you're comparing, which requires computation, you can't use pattern matching for both of these cases:

```
collatz n = if even n
            then ....
            else ...
```

You're nearly finished! The next step is to describe what happens in your alternate cases (rule 4). This is easy, because they're described clearly in the conjecture. Don't forget that you also want to keep track of how long your path is. This means you have to add 1 to your next call to `collatz`.

Listing 8.4 `collatz`

```
collatz 1 = 1
collatz n = if even n
            then 1 + collatz (n `div` 2)
            else 1 + collatz (n*3 + 1)
```

And your function is all done. This is a fun function to play with:

```
GHCi> collatz 9
20
GHCi> collatz 999
50
GHCi> collatz 92
18
GHCi> collatz 91
93
GHCi> map collatz [100 .. 120]
[26,26,26,88,13,39,13,101,114,114,114,70,21,13,34,34,21,21,34,34,21]
```

But you forgot to confirm that the recursion in each of your alternate states leads you closer to your goal (rule 5). Your first alternate case, of n being even, is no problem. When n is even, you're dividing it in half; if you keep doing this, you'll eventually reach 1. But in the odd case of $n \times 3 + 1$, it doesn't look like you're moving closer. It's possible, even likely, that increasing an odd number in this way, combined with the way you decrease even numbers, always leads to 1. Unfortunately, you don't know. Nobody knows! The Collatz conjecture is the supposition that your `collatz` function always terminates, but there's no proof that this is true. If you happen to find a number that locks up GHCi, make a note of it; it could lead to a famous mathematical paper!

This `collatz` function violates our rules in an interesting way. This doesn't necessarily mean you should throw the function away. You can test it for large ranges of values (figure 8.1), so if you needed to use this function in software, it's likely okay to use. Nonetheless, it's important to see that rule 5 *is* violated, as this can be extremely dangerous, leading to functions that never terminate.

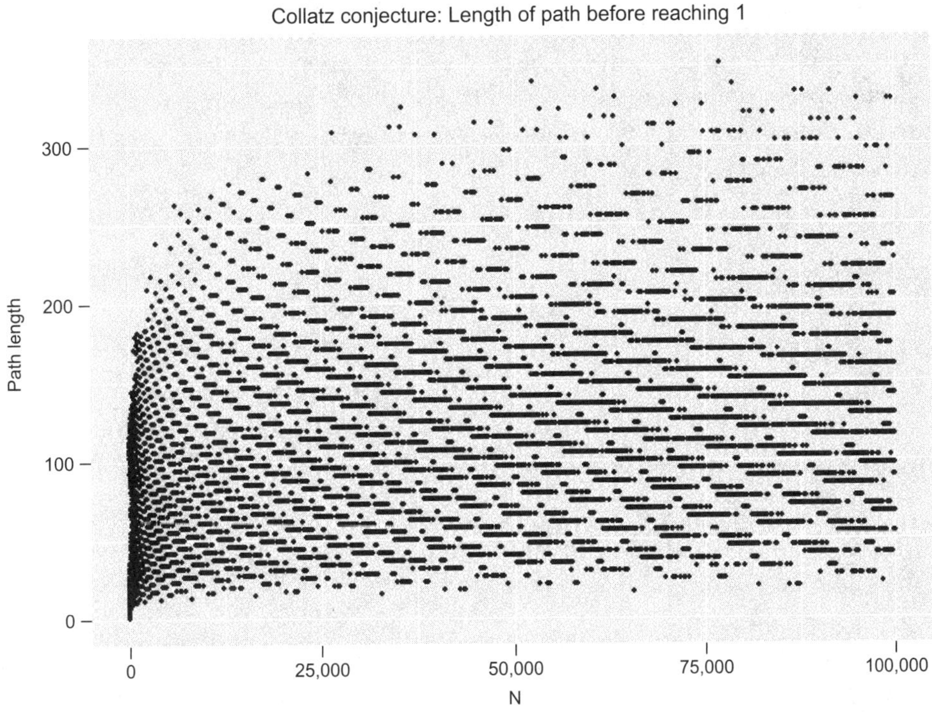

Figure 8.1 Visualizing `collatz` path lengths

Summary

In this lesson, our objective was to reinforce the rules of recursion you learned in the preceding lesson. With practice, and keeping the rules of recursion in mind, writing recursive code becomes much more natural. You also learned that edge cases exist: your code can pass the rules of recursion but still be risky to run, and it can fail to pass the rules but for all practical purposes work fine. Let's see if you got this.

Q8.1 Implement your own version of `reverse`, which reverses a list.

Q8.2 Calculating Fibonacci numbers is perhaps the single most common example of a recursive function. The most straightforward definition is as follows:

```
fib 0 = 0
fib 1 = 1
fib n = fib (n-1) + fib (n-2)
```

Like the Ackermann function, this implementation quickly explodes due to the mutually recursive calls. But unlike the Ackermann function, there's a much more efficient way to compute the *n*th Fibonacci number. Write a function, `fastFib`, that can compute the 1,000th Fibonacci number nearly instantly. Hint: `fastFib` takes three arguments: `n1`, `n2`, and `counter`. To calculate the 1,000th Fibonacci number, you call `fastFib 1 1 1000` and for the 5th, you call `fastFib 1 1 5`.

LESSON 9

HIGHER-ORDER FUNCTIONS

After reading lesson 9, you'll be able to

- Understand higher-order functions
- Use `map`, `filter`, and `foldl` to avoid writing explicitly recursive functions
- Implement many higher-order functions yourself

In the preceding lesson, you saw a wide variety of recursive functions. Although practice makes writing recursive code easier, many functions share the exact same patterns of recursion. Therefore, you can abstract out this recursion into a small number of commonly used functions that don't require you to think about recursion explicitly. The practical answer to the challenge of writing recursive code is that you usually use these existing functions, which are part of a group of functions referred to as higher-order functions.

A *higher-order function* is technically *any function that takes another function as an argument*. Typically, when higher-order functions are mentioned, a specific group of them comes to mind, and nearly all of these are used to abstract away common patterns of recursion. In this lesson, you'll look at higher-order functions that make writing recursive functions much easier. The true cure for recursive headaches is abstraction!

Consider this Here are two functions, add3ToAll and mul3byAll, which add 3 to each member of a list and multiply 3 by each member of the list, respectively:

```
add3ToAll [] = []
add3ToAll (x:xs) = (3 + x):add3ToAll xs
mul3ByAll [] = []
mul3ByAll (x:xs) = (3 * x):mul3ByAll xs
```

Both functions are easy to write and understand, and they share nearly identical structures. Now imagine a function squareAll, which squares each element in a list. The squareAll function also shares this same basic structure. You can probably think of an endless variety of functions that share this exact same pattern. Can you think of how you'd use first-class functions to rewrite these examples by using a new function that takes in a function as an argument and a list and can be used to define both add3ByAll and mul3ByAll?

9.1 Using map

It's hard to overstate how important the map function is to functional programming and Haskell. The map function takes another function and a list as arguments and applies that function to each element in the list:

```
GHCi> map reverse ["dog","cat", "moose"]
["god","tac","esoom"]
GHCi> map head ["dog","cat", "moose"]
"dcm"
GHCi> map (take 4) ["pumpkin","pie","peanut butter"]
["pump","pie","pean"]
```

A common first impression most programmers have of map is that it's a cleaner version of a for loop. Compare these two approaches to adding the determiner a to a list of animal names in JavaScript (which supports both map and for loops), as shown in the following listing.

Listing 9.1 JavaScript map example

```
var animals = ["dog","cat","moose"]
//with a for loops
```

```
for(i = 0; i < animals.length; i++){
  animals[i] = "a " + animals[i]
}
//with map
var addAnA = function(s){return "a "+s}
animals = animals.map(addAnA)
```

Even in a language that doesn't enforce functional programming as strictly as Haskell, `map` has several advantages. For starters, because you're passing in a named function, you know exactly what's happening. Given this trivial example, that's not a big deal, but the body of a `for` loop can get complicated. If the function is well named, seeing what's happening in the code is easy. You can also decide that you later want to change the behavior of your map (say, using an `addAThe` function), and all you have to do is change an argument.

The readability of the code is additionally improved because `map` is a specific kind of iteration. You know that you'll get a new list back that's exactly the same size as the one you put in. This advantage may not be obvious when you're new to `map` and other higher-order functions on lists. As you become more literate in the idioms of functional programming, you'll begin thinking in terms of how you're transforming a list rather than the general form of iterating through values that a `for` loop represents.

9.2 Abstracting away recursion with map

The main reason that you use first-class functions, and therefore have higher-order functions, is so you can abstract out programming patterns. To make this clear, let's look at how `map` works. It turns out that `map` bears only a superficial resemblance to a `for` loop, and under the hood looks nothing at all like it. To figure out how `map` works, you'll take two simple tasks you could solve with `map` and then write them assuming `map` didn't exist (nor first-class functions, for that matter). You'll take your `addAnA` behavior from our JavaScript example and another function that squares a list of numbers, `squareAll`. For clarification, here's the `map` behavior you're trying to re-create:

```
GHCi> map ("a "++) ["train","plane","boat"]
["a train","a plane","a boat"]
GHCi> map (^2) [1,2,3]
[1,4,9]
```

You'll start with addAnA first. Once again, the first question you need to ask is, "What's your goal state?" Because you're going straight through the list, you'll be finished when you hit []. The next question is, "What do you do at the end?" You're trying to add a to each of the terms in the list, and there are no terms, so it's sensible to return the empty list. The other hint that you want to return an empty list is that you're building a list. If your recursive function returns a list, it must somehow end in the empty list. For your goal state, you get a simple definition:

```
addAnA [] = []
```

The only other possibility is that there's a nonempty list. In that case, you want to take the head of the list and apply addAnA to whatever is left:

```
addAnA (x:xs) = ("a " ++ x):addAnA xs
```

Do you meet your demand of moving closer to your goal? Yes, because you're taking the tail of your list, which will eventually lead you to the empty list.

The squareAll function follows a similar pattern. It ends at the empty list, and the only other option is for the argument to be a non-empty list. In the event of a nonempty list, you square the head and continue on your way:

```
squareAll [] = []
squareAll (x:xs) = x^2:squareAll xs
```

If you go ahead and remove the concatenating and squaring function, replacing them with an f for any function, you end up with the definition of map!

Listing 9.2 myMap

```
myMap f [] = []
myMap f (x:xs) = (f x):myMap f xs
```

If you didn't have map, you'd end up repeating this pattern of writing a recursive function over and over again. The literal recursion isn't particularly difficult, but would be much less pleasant to write and read frequently. If you find recursion challenging, the good news is that any pattern of recursion that has been used enough is abstracted out. In practice, you don't explicitly write out recursive functions that often. But because the common patterns of recursion are already higher-order functions, when you do come across a truly recursive problem, it typically requires careful thought.

9.3 Filtering a list

Another important higher-order function for working with lists is `filter`. The `filter` function looks and behaves similarly to `map`, taking a function and a list as arguments and returning a list. The difference is that the function passed to `filter` must be passed a function that returns `True` or `False`. The `filter` function works by keeping only the elements of the list that pass the test:

```
GHCi> filter even [1,2,3,4]
[2,4]
GHCi> filter (\(x:xs) -> x == 'a') ["apple","banana","avocado"]
["apple","avocado"]
```

The use of `filter` is straightforward, and it's a handy tool to have. The most interesting thing about `filter` is the pattern of recursion it abstracts out. As with `map`, the goal of `filter` is an empty list. What makes `filter` different is that there are two possible alternatives: a nonempty list in which the first element passes, and a nonempty list in which the first element doesn't pass. The only difference is that when the test fails, the element isn't recursively consed to the list.

Listing 9.3 `myFilter`

```
myFilter test [] = []
myFilter test (x:xs) = if test x
                       then x:myFilter test xs
                       else myFilter test xs
```

- See whether the head of the list passes the test.
- If it does pass, cons it with filtering the rest of the list.
- Otherwise, continue filtering the rest of the list.

Quick check 9.1 Implement `remove`, which removes elements that pass the test.

QC 9.1 answer

```
remove test [] = []
remove test (x:xs) = if test x
                     then remove test xs
                     else x:remove test xs
```

9.4 Folding a list

The function `foldl` (the `l` stands for *left*, which we'll explain soon) takes a list and reduces it to a single value. The function takes three arguments: a binary function, an initial value, and a list. The most common use of `foldl` is to sum a list:

```
GHCi> foldl (+) 0 [1,2,3,4]
10
```

`foldl` is probably the least obvious of the higher-order functions we've covered. The way `foldl` works is to apply the binary argument to the initial value and the head of the list. The result of this function is now the new initial value. Figure 9.1 shows the process.

```
foldl (+) 0 [1,2,3,4]
0 + 1 = 1
foldl (+) 1 [2,3,4]
1 + 2 = 3
foldl (+) 3 [3,4]
3 + 3 = 6
foldl (+) 6 [4]
6 + 4 = 10
foldl (+) 10 [] = 10
```

Figure 9.1 Visualizing `foldl (+)`

> **Quick check 9.2** Write the function `myProduct`, which calculates the product of a list of numbers.

Fold is useful but definitely takes some practice to get used to. You can build a `concatAll` function that joins all strings in a list:

```
concatAll xs = foldl (++) "" xs
```

QC 9.2 answer

```
myProduct xs = foldl (*) 1 xs
```

It's common to use `foldl` and `map` together. For example, you can create `sumOfSquares`, which squares every value in a list and then takes the sum of it:

```
sumOfSquares xs = foldl (+) 0 (map (^2) xs)
```

Perhaps the most remarkable use of `foldl` is to reverse a list. To do this, you need a helper function named `rcons`, which will cons elements in the reverse order.

Listing 9.4 myReverse

```
rcons x y = y:x
myReverse xs = foldl rcons [] xs
```

This is another function worth visualizing to add clarity; see figure 9.2.

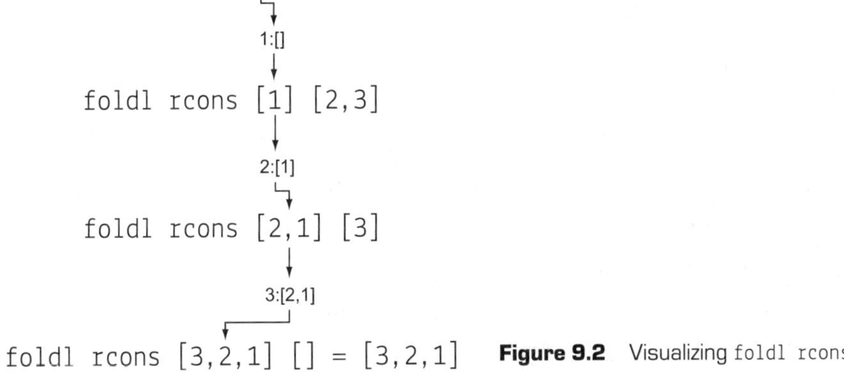

Figure 9.2 Visualizing `foldl rcons`

Note that in this case, the "single" value that `foldl` returns is another list!

Implementing `foldl` is a bit trickier than the other functions you've seen so far. Once again, your goal state is the empty list, `[]`. But what should you return? Because the initial value will get updated after each call to the binary function, it'll contain the final value in your computation. When you reach the end of the list, you return the current value for `init`:

```
myFoldl f init [] = init
```

You have only one other alternative: a nonempty list. For this, you pass your initial value and the head of your list to the binary function. This creates your new `init` value. Then you call `myFoldl` on the rest of the list by using this new value as your `init`.

Listing 9.5 myFoldl

```
myFoldl f init [] = init
myFoldl f init (x:xs) = myFoldl f newInit xs
  where newInit = f init x
```

Quick check 9.3 True or false: The nongoal step in `myFoldl` terminates.

The question that remains is, why *left* fold? It turns out that there's another way to solve this general problem of folding a list of values into a single value. The alterative to `foldl` is `foldr`; the `r` stands for *right*. If you look at the definition of `myFoldr`, you can see how it differs.

Listing 9.6 myFoldr

```
myFoldr f init [] = init
myFoldr f init (x:xs) = f x rightResult
  where rightResult = myFoldr f init xs
```

The reason we call it a *right* fold is that there are two arguments in a binary function: a left argument and a right argument. The left fold compacts the list into the left argument, and the right fold into the right argument.

Both performance and computational differences exist between `foldl` and `foldr`. At this stage in learning, it's important to know that these functions give different answers if the order of the application matters. For addition, the order doesn't matter, so these functions behave the same:

```
GHCi> foldl (+) 0 [1,2,3,4]
10
GHCi> foldr (+) 0 [1,2,3,4]
10
```

But for subtraction, order does matter:

```
GHCi> foldl (-) 0 [1,2,3,4]
-10
GHCi> foldr (-) 0 [1,2,3,4]
-2
```

QC 9.3 answer

True: because you're always recursing on the rest of the list, it must get smaller until it's empty (if it's not infinite).

When learning Haskell, `foldl` is preferable for folding lists because its behavior is more intuitive. Understanding the difference between `foldl` and `foldr` is a good sign that you've mastered recursion.

The many kinds of folds

The family of fold functions are, undoubtedly, the trickiest of the higher-order functions introduced here. There's another useful fold function named `foldl'` (note the tick mark) found in the `Data.List` module. Here's a list of advice for when to use each fold:

- `foldl` is the most intuitive behaving of the folds, but it usually has terrible performance and can't be used on infinite lists.
- `foldl'` is a nonlazy version of `foldl` that's often much more efficient.
- `foldr` is often more efficient than `foldl` and is the only fold that works on infinite lists.

When learning Haskell, there's no need to immediately master these various types of folds. You'll likely run into an issue with `foldl` as you write more-sophisticated Haskell code.

Summary

In this lesson, our objective was to introduce you to a family of functions that make working with recursion much easier. Many recursive problems can be solved with `map`, `filter`, and `foldl`. When encountering a recursive problem, the first question you should ask is whether you can solve it with one of these three functions. Let's see if you got this.

Q9.1 Use `filter` and `length` to re-create the `elem` function.

Q9.2 Your `isPalindrome` function from lesson 6 doesn't handle sentences with spaces or capitals. Use `map` and `filter` to make sure the phrase "A man a plan a canal Panama" is recognized as a palindrome.

Q9.3 In mathematics, the harmonic series is the sum of 1/1 + 1/2 + 1/3 + 1/4 .... Write a function `harmonic` that takes an argument `n` and calculates the sum of the series to `n`. Make sure to use lazy evaluation.

10 CAPSTONE: FUNCTIONAL OBJECT-ORIENTED PROGRAMMING WITH ROBOTS!

This capstone covers

- Using functional programming to create objects
- Creating example objects that interact with each other
- Representing state in a functional way

A common misconception is that object-oriented programming (OOP) and functional programming somehow stand in opposition. In reality, this couldn't be further from the truth. Many functional programming languages support some form of object-oriented programming, including Common Lisp, R, F#, OCaml, and Scala. In this unit, you explored the idea that functions can be used to perform any computation. So it makes perfect sense that by using the tools of functional programming, you can create a basic object-oriented programming system!

This is your first capstone exercise. In this exercise, you'll see how to use the tools of functional programming to replicate common design features found in OOP languages. You'll build a simple cup object and then move on to modeling fighting robots!

> **Think like a programmer**
> Haskell doesn't use objects, so why on earth should you spend time implementing OOP from scratch? The main reason is it allows you to understand the power of the functional tools you've been learning about so far. If you can understand how to build OOP by using closures, lambdas, and first-class functions, you've truly reached functional enlightenment.

10.1 An object with one property: a cup of coffee

Let's start with modeling a simple cup of coffee. You'll save all the code for this section in a cup.hs file. For this example, a cup has only one minimal property: the number of ounces of liquid currently in it. You need a way to store this value so you can access it later. This will act as your basic object. Fortunately, in lesson 5, you discovered a useful tool for capturing values inside a function: closures! You'll define a `cup` function that takes the number of fluid ounces in the cup and returns a closure storing that value:

```
cup flOz = \_ -> flOz
```

Because you have first-class functions, you can treat this value stored in a closure just like data. You can now pass your stored information around like an object. But clearly this isn't enough, as you can't do anything interesting with the fact that you've stored your ounces. What you want is to be able to apply a message to that internal value of the cup. You'll use a first-class function to pass a message to your object. This message can then act on the internal property of the object. Notice that you're going to be using a slightly different pattern of sending messages to the object rather than the common approach of calling methods. When calling methods, your object > action pattern looks like figure 10.1.

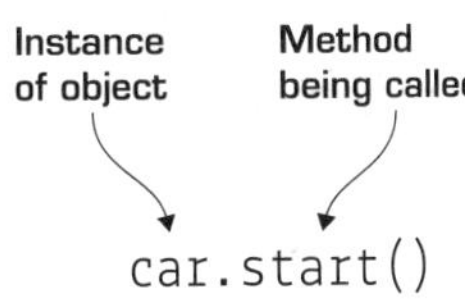

Figure 10.1 Method-calling approach to OOP

Your approach will invert this pattern by sending a message to an object, as shown in figure 10.2.

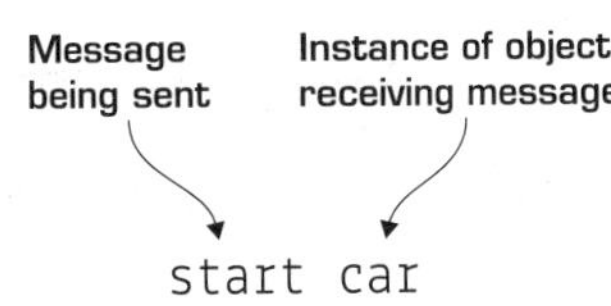

Figure 10.2 Message-passing approach to OOP (commonly used in functional programming languages)

This less common notation is used in the Common Lisp Object System (CLOS) as well as R's S3 object system.

10.1.1 Creating a constructor

The most common way to create an instance of an object is by using a special method called a *constructor*. The only thing you need to do to create a constructor for your object is to allow a way for you to send a message to your object. By adding a single named argument to your closure, you can add a way to pass messages in.

Listing 10.1 Constructor for a basic cup object

```
cup flOz = \message -> message flOz
```

Now you have a basic constructor that can make instances of your object. Note that you've done this using a lambda function, a closure, and first-class functions! In GHCi, you can create an instance of your cup object:

```
GHCi> aCup = cup 6
```

You can also define a 12-ounce coffee cup in a cup.hs file.

Listing 10.2 coffeeCup

```
coffeeCup = cup 12
```

10.1.2 Adding accessors to your object

You've stored your value in an object, but you need something useful for this object to do. Next you'll create simple messages to get and set values inside your object. First you want to be able to get the volume of coffee currently in the cup. You'll create a `getOz` message that takes a `cup` object and returns the number of fluid ounces (`flOz`) it has.

Listing 10.3 getOz message

```
getOz aCup = aCup (\flOz -> flOz)
```

To use this function, you pass this message into the object:

```
GHCi> getOz coffeeCup
12
```

Next you want to do something a little more complicated. The most useful thing to do with a cup is to drink from it! Drinking from a cup inherently changes the state of the object. But how in the world are you going to do this in Haskell!? Easy: you'll create a new object behind the scenes. Your message to set a value for fluid ounces needs to return a new instance of your object with the internal property appropriately modified.

Listing 10.4 Defining a `drink` message that updates state

```
drink aCup ozDrank = cup (flOz - ozDrank)
  where flOz = getOz aCup
```

Now you can sip some coffee in GHCi:

```
GHCi> afterASip = drink coffeeCup 1
GHCi> getOz afterASip
11
GHCi> afterTwoSips = drink afterASip 1
GHCi> getOz afterTwoSips
10
GHCi> afterGulp = drink afterTwoSips 4
GHCi> getOz afterGulp
6
```

This definition has one slight bug: you can drink more coffee than the cup can hold.

The only issue is that your drink message allows you to have negative values in your cup. You can rewrite `drink` so that the minimum amount of coffee in a cup is 0.

Listing 10.5 Improving the `drink` definition

```
drink aCup ozDrank = if ozDiff >= 0
                     then cup ozDiff
                     else cup 0
  where flOz = getOz aCup
        ozDiff = flOz - ozDrank
```

With this improvement, your cup can never have a coffee debt:

```
GHCi> afterBigGulp = drink coffeeCup 20
GHCi> getOz afterBigGulp
0
```

You'll add one more helper message to check whether the cup is empty.

Listing 10.6 Defining `isEmpty`

```
isEmpty aCup = getOz aCup == 0
```

Because you need to constantly keep track of the object's state, taking many drinks from the cup could make your code get a bit verbose. Luckily, `foldl` can save you here. In lesson 9, we discussed the fact that `foldl` is a higher-order function that takes a function, an initial value, and a list and reduces them to a single value. Here's a partial example of using `foldl` to take five drinks from the cup.

Listing 10.7 Using `foldl` to model taking many sips

```
afterManySips = foldl drink coffeeCup [1,1,1,1,1]
```

In GHCi, you can see that this works without you having to do as much bookkeeping:

```
GHCi> getOz afterManySips
7
```

10.2 A more complex object: let's build fighting robots!

So far, you've modeled the basics of an object. You've been able to capture information about an object by using a constructor. Then you've interacted with that object by using accessors. With the basics of representing an object behind you, you can build something more exciting. Let's put together some fighting robots!

Your robot will have some basic properties:

- A name
- An attack strength
- A number of hit points

You need something a little more sophisticated to handle these three attributes. You could pass in three values to your closure, but that's going to make working with them confusing. Instead, you'll use a tuple of values that represent the attributes of your robot. For example, `("Bob",10,100)` is a robot named Bob that has an attack of 10 and has 100 hit points for his life.

Rather than sending a message to a single value, you'll send a message to this collection of attributes. Notice that you'll use pattern matching on our tuple argument to make the values easier to read and understand.

Listing 10.8 A `robot` constructor

```
robot (name,attack,hp)  = \message -> message (name,attack,hp)
```

All objects can be viewed as a collection of attributes that you send messages to. In the next unit, you'll look at Haskell's type system, which allows a much more powerful method of abstracting out data. Even then, the idea of a tuple serving as a minimum viable data structure will persist.

You can create an instance of your robot like this:

```
killerRobot = robot ("Kill3r",25,200)
```

To make this object useful, you'll have to add a few accessors so you can work with these values more easily. You'll start by making a helper function that allows you to easily access various parts of your tuple by name. These work just like `fst` and `snd` do for a tuple of two values (as used in lesson 4).

Listing 10.9 `name`, `attack`, **and** `hp` **helper functions**

```
name (n,_,_) = n
attack (_,a,_) = a
hp (_,_,hp) = hp
```

With these helper functions, you can easily implement your getters.

Listing 10.10 `getName`, `getAttack`, **and** `getHP` **accessors**

```
getName aRobot = aRobot name
getAttack aRobot = aRobot attack
getHP aRobot = aRobot hp
```

Having these accessors means you no longer have to worry about remembering the order of the values in your tuple:

```
GHCi> getAttack killerRobot
25
GHCi> getHP killerRobot
200
```

Because you have a more complicated object this time, you'll also want to write some setters that allow you to set the properties. Each of these cases will have to return a new instance of your robot.

Listing 10.11 setName, setAttack, and setHP accessors

```
setName aRobot newName = aRobot (\(n,a,h) -> robot (newName,a,h))
setAttack aRobot newAttack = aRobot (\(n,a,h) -> robot (n,newAttack,h))
setHP aRobot newHP = aRobot (\(n,a,h) -> robot (n,a,newHP))
```

Notice that now you not only can set values, but also can emulate the behavior of prototype-based object-oriented programming, because you never change state.

Prototype-based OOP

Prototype-based object-oriented languages, such as JavaScript, create instances of objects by modifying a prototypical object, rather than using classes. Prototypes in JavaScript are often a source of much confusion. Here you can see how cloning an object and modifying it to create a new object is a natural result of using functional programming. In Haskell, you can create new objects by modifying copies of old, existing ones:

```
nicerRobot = setName killerRobot "kitty"
gentlerRobot = setAttack killerRobot 5
softerRobot = setHP killerRobot 50
```

One more nice function would be to print all your robot's stats. You'll define a `printRobot` message that works much like a `toString` method in other languages.

Listing 10.12 Defining a printRobot message

```
printRobot aRobot = aRobot (\(n,a,h) -> n ++
                                        " attack:" ++ (show a) ++
                                        " hp:"++ (show h))
```

This makes inspecting your objects in GHCi much easier:

```
GHCi> printRobot killerRobot
"Kill3r attack:25 hp:200"
GHCi> printRobot nicerRobot
"kitty attack:25 hp:200"
GHCi> printRobot gentlerRobot
"Kill3r attack:5 hp:200"
GHCi> printRobot softerRobot
"Kill3r attack:25 hp:50"
```

10.2.1 Sending messages between objects

The most interesting part about fighting robots is the fighting! First you need a send a damage message to a robot. This will work just like your drink message did in the cup example (listings 10.4 and 10.5). In this case, you need to get all of your attributes rather than just `flOz`.

Listing 10.13 Completing the `damage` function

```
damage aRobot attackDamage = aRobot (\(n,a,h) ->
                                      robot (n,a,h-attackDamage))
```

With the damage message, you can tell a robot that it has taken damage:

```
GHCi> afterHit = damage killerRobot 90
GHCi> getHP afterHit
110
```

Now it's time to fight! This is your first case of having one object interact with another, so you're doing some real OOP now. Your fight message is going to be the mainstream OOP equivalent of the following:

```
robotOne.fight(robotTwo)
```

Your fight message applies damage from the attacker to the defender; additionally, you want to prevent a robot with no life from attacking.

Listing 10.14 The definition of `fight`

```
fight aRobot defender = damage defender attack
  where attack = if getHP aRobot > 10
                 then getAttack aRobot
                 else 0
```

Next you need a contender to fight your `killerRobot`:

```
gentleGiant = robot ("Mr. Friendly", 10, 300)
```

Let's go for a three-round fight:

```
gentleGiantRound1 = fight killerRobot gentleGiant
killerRobotRound1 = fight gentleGiant killerRobot
gentleGiantRound2 = fight killerRobotRound1 gentleGiantRound1
killerRobotRound2 = fight gentleGiantRound1 killerRobotRound1
```

```
gentleGiantRound3 = fight killerRobotRound2 gentleGiantRound2
killerRobotRound3 = fight gentleGiantRound2 killerRobotRound2
```

After this fight, you can see how they both did:

```
GHCi> printRobot gentleGiantRound3
"Mr. Friendly attack:10 hp:225"
GHCi> printRobot killerRobotRound3
"Kill3r attack:25 hp:170"
```

10.3 Why stateless programming matters

So far, you've been able to create a reasonable approximation of an OOP system. You've ended up having to do some extra bookkeeping to explicitly keep track of state after each round. Although this solution works, wouldn't it be easier if you could have mutable state to solve these problems? Hidden state would make this code cleaner, but major problems can easily arise with hidden state. Let's look at another fight to see the real costs of having hidden state:

```
fastRobot = robot ("speedy", 15, 40)
slowRobot = robot ("slowpoke",20,30)
```

Now you'll have another three-round fight.

Listing 10.15 Three-round robot fight with simultaneous attacks

```
fastRobotRound1 = fight slowRobot fastRobot
slowRobotRound1 = fight fastRobot slowRobot
fastRobotRound2 = fight slowRobotRound1 fastRobotRound1
slowRobotRound2 = fight fastRobotRound1 slowRobotRound1
fastRobotRound3 = fight slowRobotRound2 fastRobotRound2
slowRobotRound3 = fight fastRobotRound2 slowRobotRound2
```

And you can check out the results in GHCi:

```
GHCi> printRobot fastRobotRound3
"speedy attack:15 hp:0"
GHCi> printRobot slowRobotRound3
"slowpoke attack:20 hp:0"
```

Who should win? Because of the way you changed your values, each robot attacks at the exact same time. Looking at the names of the robots, the behavior you want is for the fast robot to win. The fast robot should land the fatal blow before the slow robot, and the slow robot shouldn't be able to attack.

Because you have absolute control over how to handle state, you can change this easily.

Listing 10.16 Changing the priority of attacks

```
slowRobotRound1 = fight fastRobot slowRobot
fastRobotRound1 = fight slowRobotRound1 fastRobot
slowRobotRound2 = fight fastRobotRound1 slowRobotRound1
fastRobotRound2 = fight fastRobotRound1 slowRobotRound1
slowRobotRound3 = fight fastRobotRound2 slowRobotRound2
fastRobotRound3 = fight slowRobotRound3 fastRobotRound2
```

In this example, you can make sure that the slow-robot version that's attacking is the one that's updated after the faster robot strikes first:

```
GHCi> printRobot fastRobotRound3
"speedy attack:15 hp:20"
GHCi> printRobot slowRobotRound3
"slowpoke attack:20 hp:-15"
```

As expected, your `fastRobot` wins this match.

Because you don't have state in functional programming, you have complete control over the way computation happens. Compare this with stateful OOP. Here's one round using objects storing state:

```
fastRobot.fight(slowRobot)
slowRobot.fight(fastRobot)
```

But say your code is executed this way:

```
slowRobot.fight(fastRobot)
fastRobot.fight(slowRobot)
```

Then you'd get completely different results!

In the case of sequentially executed code, this is no problem at all. But suppose you're using asynchronous, concurrent, or parallel code. You may have no control over when these operations execute! Furthermore, controlling the priority of fights would be much more difficult, if you wanted to ensure that `fastRobot` always got in the first punch.

As a mental exercise, sketch out how to ensure that `fastRobot` does damage to `slowRobot` first, even if you don't know which of `fastRobot.fight` and `slowRobot.fight` will execute first.

Now think about how much extra code you'd need in order to solve this for a three-round fight, if it's possible that round 3 code could execute before round 1 or round 2. If you've ever written low-level parallel code, you're likely already aware of how difficult managing state in this environment can be.

Believe it or not, Haskell also has solved the problem of round 3 happening before round 2. This may be a surprise, but Haskell doesn't care about the order of these functions! You can rearrange the previous code any way you like and get the exact same results!

Listing 10.17 Order has no importance in execution of Haskell code

```
fastRobotRound3 = fight slowRobotRound3 fastRobotRound2
fastRobotRound2 = fight slowRobotRound2 fastRobotRound1
fastRobotRound1 = fight slowRobotRound1 fastRobot
slowRobotRound2 = fight fastRobotRound1 slowRobotRound1
slowRobotRound3 = fight fastRobotRound2 slowRobotRound2
slowRobotRound1 = fight fastRobot slowRobot
```

The results in GHCi are the same:

```
GHCi> printRobot fastRobotRound3
"speedy attack:15 hp:20"
GHCi> printRobot slowRobotRound3
"slowpoke attack:20 hp:-15"
```

Any bugs that might come up because of the order in which the functions have been written are much less common in Haskell. Because you can control exactly when and how state is modeled, there are no mysteries at all in how the code is executed. We have deliberately made this code more verbose than it needs to be so that it's easier to understand how much control you have over state. This robot fight could happen in any order, and the results are the same.

10.4 Types—objects and so much more!

Haskell isn't an object-oriented language. All of the functionality built here from scratch already exists in a much more powerful form, using Haskell's type system. Many of the ideas used in this section will come up again, but rather than hacking together objects, you'll be creating types. Haskell's types can replicate all the behavior you've modeled here, but give you the added benefit that Haskell's compiler can reason much more deeply about types than your ad hoc objects. Because of this ability to reason about types, code created using a powerful type system tends to be much more robust and predictable. The advantages you've seen from using functional programming are magnified tremendously when you combine them with Haskell's type system.

Summary

In this capstone, you

- Saw that object-oriented programming and functional programming aren't inherently at odds
- Represented OOP by using the tools of functional programming covered in this unit
- Used closures to represent objects created with lambda functions
- Sent messages to objects by using first-class functions
- Managed state in a functional way, allowing you to be more exact in controlling program execution

Extending the exercise

Here are some ideas for simple exercises you can do to extend this capstone on your own:

- Use `map` on a list of `robot` objects to get the life of each robot in the list.
- Write a `threeRoundFight` function that takes two robots and has them fight for three rounds, returning the winner. To avoid having so many different variables for robot state, use a series of nested lambda functions so you can just overwrite `robotA` and `robotB`.
- Create a list of three robots. Then create a fourth robot. Use partial application to create a closure for the `fight` method so the fourth robot can fight all three robots at once, using `map`. Finally, use `map` to get the remaining life from the rest of the robots.

Introducing types

Nearly every programming language supports some idea of types. Types are important because they define the kinds of computation allowed on certain data. Take, for example, the text `"hello"` and the number `6`. Say you want to do something like add them together:

```
"hello" + 6
```

Even someone with no prior programming experience would find this question interesting, because it's not clear what to do. The two most obvious answers are to

- Throw an error
- Combine these values in the most reasonable way: `"hello6"`

To arrive at either option, you need a way to keep track of the type of your data, as well as the type of data your computation is expecting. Typically, we call the value of `"hello"` a `String`, and the value of `6` an `Int`. Regardless of your choice of programming language, you need to know the types you're dealing with so you can either throw an error when they don't match or do some sort of automatic conversion by knowing how to transform types. Even if you don't think about types much in your programming language of choice, they are an important part of programming.

Languages such as Ruby, Python, and JavaScript use *dynamic typing*. In a dynamic type system, all the decisions like the one we made with `"hello"` and `6` happen during runtime. The benefit of dynamic typing for the programmer is a generally more flexible language and no need to manually keep track of types. The danger of dynamic typing is that errors happen only at runtime. For example, say you have the following expression in Python:

```
def call_on_xmas():
  "santa gets a "+10
```

This code will cause an error because Python requires 10 to be converted to a string before adding it to the string literal. As you can guess by the function name, this function won't be called until Christmas! If this mistake snuck into a production system, it could mean a frustrating Christmas debugging a rare problem. The solution has been to incorporate extensive unit testing to ensure that bugs like this can't slip in. This somewhat negates the benefit of not having to annotate types as you code.

Languages such as Java, C++, and C# use *static typing*. With static typing, problems such as `"hello" + 6` are resolved during compilation. If a type error occurs, the program won't compile. The obvious benefit of static typing is that an entire class of bugs can't make it into running programs. The downside, traditionally, is that statically typed languages require the programmer to add many type annotations. Type signatures are required for every function/method, and all variables must have their type declared.

Haskell is a statically typed programming language, but it certainly doesn't look like a statically typed language in the examples you've seen so far. All of your variables and functions have made no references to types at all. This is because Haskell makes heavy use of *type inference*. The Haskell compiler is smart, and can figure out what types you're using based on the way the functions and variables are used.

Haskell's type system is extremely powerful, and is at least as fundamental to making Haskell unique as its adherence to pure functional programming. In this unit, you'll be introduced to the basics of Haskell's type system. You'll learn how to model data and define your own types and type classes.

LESSON 11

TYPE BASICS

After reading lesson 11, you'll be able to

- Understand basic types in Haskell, including `Int`, `String`, and `Double`
- Read type signatures for functions
- Use simple type variables

This lesson introduces one of the most powerful aspects of Haskell: its robust type system. The fundamentals of functional programming covered in the preceding lessons are shared by all functional programming languages from Lisp to Scala. It's Haskell's type system that sets it apart from other programming languages. Our introduction in this lesson starts with the basics of Haskell's type system.

Consider this You need to create a simple function for taking the average of a list of numbers. The most obvious solution is to take the sum of the list and divide it by the length of the list:

```
myAverage aList = sum aList / length aList
```

But this simple definition doesn't work. How can you write a function to compute the mean of a list of numbers?

11.1 Types in Haskell

It may come as a bit of a surprise that Haskell is a statically typed language. Other common statically typed languages include C++, C#, and Java. In these and most other statically typed languages, the programmer is burdened with keeping track of type annotations. So far in Haskell, you haven't had to write down any information about the type you're using for any of your values. It turns out this is because Haskell has done it for you! Haskell uses *type inference* to automatically determine the types of all values at compile time based on the way they're used! You don't have to rely on Haskell to determine your types for you. Figure 11.1 shows a variable that you'll give the `Int` type.

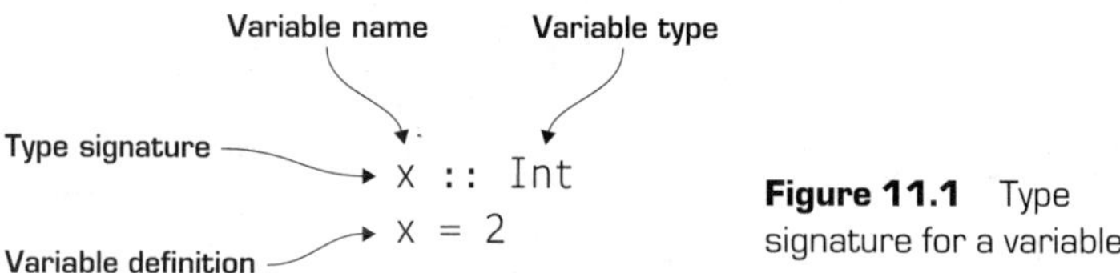

Figure 11.1 Type signature for a variable

All types in Haskell start with a capital letter to distinguish them from functions (which all start with a lowercase letter or _). The `Int` type is one of the most ubiquitous and traditional types in programming. `Int` represents how the computer is to interpret a number represented by a fixed number of bits, often 32 or 64 bits. Because you're describing numbers with a fixed number of bits, you're limited by a maximum and minimum value that a number can take on. For example, if you load `x` in GHCi, you can do some simple operations to show the limits of this type:

```
x :: Int
x = 2
```

```
GHCi> x*2000
4000
GHCi> x^2000
0
```

As you can see, Haskell handles exceeding the bounds of the `Int` by returning `0`. This property of having limited maximum and minimum values is referred to as being *bounded*. You'll learn more about bounded types in lesson 13.

The `Int` type is a traditional way of viewing types in programming. `Int` is a label that tells the computer how to read and understand physical memory. In Haskell, types are more abstract. They provide a way of understanding how values behave and how to organize data. For example, the `Integer` type more closely resembles the typical Haskell way of thinking about types. Let's see how to define a new variable `y` as an `Integer`.

Listing 11.1 `Integer` type

```
y :: Integer
y = 2
```

You can clearly see the difference between these two types by repeating your calculations from before:

```
GHCi> y*2000
4000
GHCi> y^2000
114813069527425452423283320117768198402231770208869520047764273682576626l3
923703138566594863165062699184459646389874627734471189608630553314259313561
666531853912998914531228000068877914824004487142892699006348624478161546364
638836394731702604046635397090499655816239880894462960562331164953616422197
033268134416890898445850560237948480791405890093477650042900271670662583052
200813223628129176126788331720659899539641812702177985840404215985318325154
088943390209192055495778358967203916008195721663058275538042558372601552834
878641943205450891527578388262517543552880082284277081796545376218485114902
9376
```

As you can see, the `Integer` type fits more closely with the mathematical sense of what an integer is: any whole number. Unlike the `Int` type, the `Integer` type isn't bounded by memory limitations framed in terms of bytes.

Haskell supports all the types that you're likely familiar with in other languages. Here are some examples.

Listing 11.2 Common types `Char`, `Double`, and `Bool`

```
letter :: Char
letter = 'a'

interestRate :: Double
interestRate = 0.375

isFun :: Bool
isFun = True
```

Another important type is `List`. Here are a few examples.

Listing 11.3 List types

```
values :: [Int]
values = [1,2,3]

testScores :: [Double]
testScores = [0.99,0.7,0.8]

letters :: [Char]
letters = ['a','b','c']
```

A list of characters is the same as a string:

```
GHCi> letters == "abc"
True
```

To make things easier, Haskell allows you to use `String` as a type synonym for `[Char]`. Both of these type signatures mean exactly the same thing to Haskell:

```
aPet :: [Char]
aPet = "cat"

anotherPet :: String
anotherPet = "dog"
```

Another important type is a `Tuple`. You used tuples briefly in lesson 4. When you weren't thinking about types, tuples didn't seem too different from a list, but they're quite a bit more sophisticated. Two main differences are that each tuple is of a specific length, and tuples can contain multiple types. A list of type `[Char]` is a string of any size, whereas a tuple of type `(Char)` is a tuple of *exactly* one character. Here are some more tuple examples.

Listing 11.4 Tuple types

```
ageAndHeight ::(Int,Int)
ageAndHeight = (34,74)

firstLastMiddle :: (String,String,Char)
firstLastMiddle = ("Oscar","Grouch",'D')

streetAddress :: (Int,String)
streetAddress = (123,"Happy St.")
```

Tuples are useful for modeling simple data types quickly.

11.2 Function types

Functions also have type signatures. In Haskell an -> is used to separate arguments and return values. The type signature for `double` looks like figure 11.2.

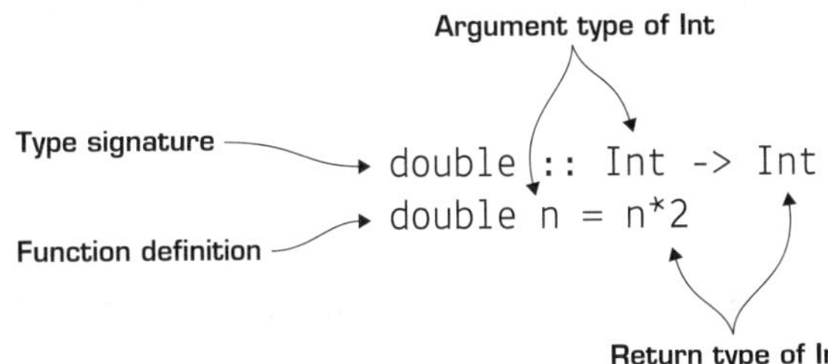

Figure 11.2 Defining the `double` function by using a type signature

You could easily have chosen `Integer`, `Double`, or any other number of types for your argument. In lesson 12, you'll look at type classes that allow you to generalize numbers better.

Taking in an `Int` and returning an `Int` works for doubling a number, but it doesn't work for halving a number. If you want to write a function `half` and you want to take in an `Int`, you need to return a `Double`. Your type signature will look like the following.

Listing 11.5 Converting from one type to another with `half`

```
half :: Int -> Double
```

Now you need to define your function, and a first guess would be this:

```
half n = n/2          <—— Incorrect code!
```

But this results in an error. The problem is that you're trying to divide a whole number `Int` in half, and such a thing is nonsensical because you've already declared that you're going to return a `Double`. You need to convert your value from an `Int` into a `Double`. Most programming languages have the idea of casting a variable from one type to another. Casting forces a value to be represented as a different type. Because of this, casting variables often feels like hammering a square peg through a round hole. Haskell has no convention for casting types and instead relies on functions that properly transform values from one type to another. In this case, you can use Haskell's `fromIntegral` function:

```
half n = (fromIntegral n) / 2
```

Here you've transformed `n` from an `Int` into a more general number. A good question now might be, "Why don't you have to call `fromIntegral` on 2?" In many programming languages, if you want to treat a literal number as a `Double`, you need to add a decimal to it. In both Python and Ruby, `5/2` is `2` and `5/2.0` is `2.5`. Haskell is both stricter and more flexible. It's stricter because Haskell never does the implicit type conversion that happens in Ruby and Python, and it's more flexible because in Haskell literal numbers are *polymorphic*: their type is determined from the compiler based on the way they're used. For example, if you want to use GHCi as a calculator, you'll find you rarely need to worry about type with numbers:

```
GHCi> 5/2
2.5
```

Quick check 11.1 Haskell has a function named `div` that does perform integer division (it returns only whole numbers). Write `halve`, which uses `div` instead, and include a type signature.

11.2.1 Functions for converting to and from strings

One of the most common type conversions is to convert values to and from strings. Haskell has two useful functions that achieve this: `show` and `read`. Lessons 12 and 13 detail how these work, but for now let's look at some examples in GHCi. The `show` function is straightforward:

```
GHCi> show 6
"6"
GHCi> show 'c'
"'c'"
GHCi>show 6.0
"6.0"
```

Quick check 11.2 Write a function `printDouble` that takes an `Int` and returns that value doubled as a string.

QC 11.1 answer

```
halve :: Integer -> Integer
halve value = value `div` 2
```

QC 11.2 answer

```
printDouble :: Int -> String
printDouble value = show (value*2)
```

The `read` function works by taking a string and converting it to another type. But this is a bit trickier than `show`. For example, without type signatures, what should Haskell do here?

```
z = read "6"
```

It's impossible to tell whether to use `Int`, `Integer`, or even `Double`. If you can't figure it out, there's absolutely no way that Haskell can. In this case, type inference can't save you. There are a few ways to fix this. If you use the value `z`, it's likely that Haskell will have enough info to figure out how to treat your value:

```
q = z / 2
```

Now Haskell has enough information to treat `z` like a `Double`, even though your `String` representation didn't have a decimal. Another solution is to explicitly use your type signature.

Listing 11.6 Example of reading values from strings: `anotherNumber`

```
anotherNumber :: Int
anotherNumber = read "6"
```

Even though you got through the first unit with no type signatures, it's generally a good idea to always use them. This is because in practice type signatures help you reason about the code you're writing. This little extra annotation lets Haskell know what you expect `read` to do and makes your own intentions clearer in the code. There's one more way to force Haskell to understand what type you want that comes up often in practice. You can always append the expected return type to the end of a function call. This happens most frequently in GHCi, but at other times it's helpful to specify an ambiguous return type:

```
GHCi> read "6" :: Int
6
GHCi> read "6" :: Double
6.0
```

11.2.2 Functions with multiple arguments

So far, most of your type signatures have been straightforward. One thing that frequently trips up newcomers to Haskell is the type signature for multi-argument functions. Suppose you want a function that takes a house number, street address, and town and makes a tuple representing an address. Figure 11.3 shows the type signature.

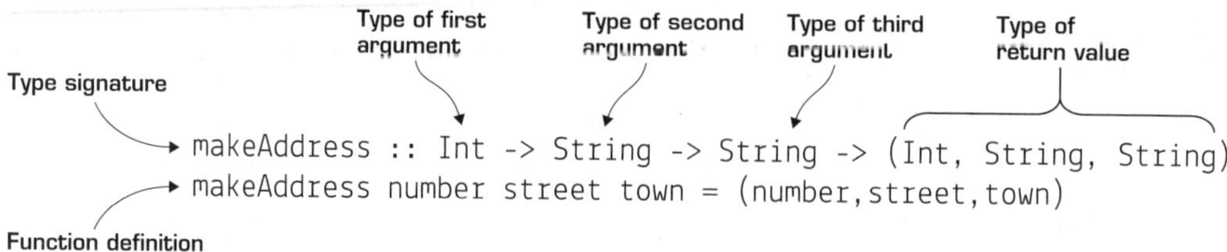

Figure 11.3 Type signature for multi-argument functions and definition `makeAddress`

What makes this confusing is that there's no clear separation between which types are for arguments and which are for return values. The easy way to remember is that the last type is always the return type. A good question is, why are type signatures this way? The reason is that behind the scenes in Haskell, all functions take only one argument. By rewriting `makeAddress` by using a series of nested lambda functions, as shown in figure 11.4, you can see a multi-argument function the way Haskell does.

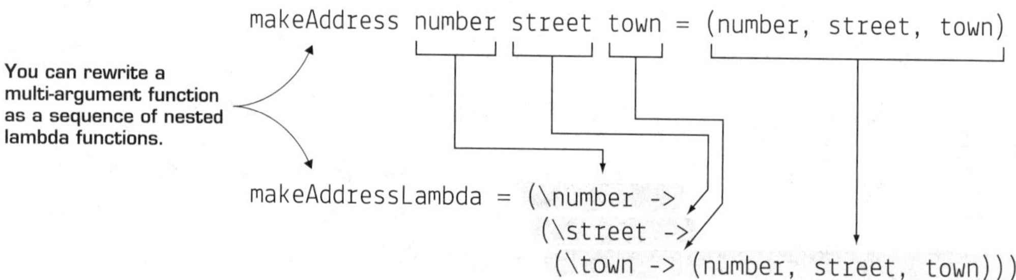

Figure 11.4 Desugaring the multi-argument `makeAddress` into a sequence of single-argument functions

You could then call this function like so:

```
GHCi> (((makeAddressLambda 123) "Happy St") "Haskell Town")
(123,"Happy St","Haskell Town")
```

In this format, each function returns a function waiting for the next. This might seem crazy until you realize this is how partial application works! You could apply arguments in exactly the same way with `makeAddress` and get the exact same results:

```
GHCi> (((makeAddress 123) "Happy St") "Haskell Town")
(123,"Happy St","Haskell Town")
```

It also turns out that because of the way Haskell evaluates arguments, you can call your desugared lambda version the way you would any ordinary function:

```
GHCi>makeAddressLambda 123 "Happy St" "Haskell Town"
(123,"Happy St","Haskell Town")
```

Quick check 11.3 As each argument is passed to `makeAddress`, write out the type signature of the returned function.

Hopefully, this helps to demystify multi-argument type signatures as well as partial application!

11.2.3 Types for first-class functions

As we mentioned in lesson 4, functions can take functions as arguments and return functions as values. To write these type signatures, you write the individual function values in parentheses. For example, you can rewrite `ifEven` with a type signature.

Listing 11.7 Type signatures for first-class functions: `ifEven`

```
ifEven :: (Int -> Int) -> Int -> Int
ifEven f n = if even n
             then f n
             else n
```

QC 11.3 answer Starting with our type original type signature:

```
makeAddress :: Int -> String -> String -> (Int,String,String)
```

And your type signatures is now as follows:

```
String -> String -> (Int,String,String)
```

Then pass in the first `String`:

```
((makeAddress 123) "Happy St")
```

And here's the type signature:

```
String -> (Int,String,String)
```

Finally, if you pass in all of your arguments, you get the type of the result:

```
(((makeAddress 123) "Happy St") "Haskell Town")
(Int,String,String)
```

11.3 Type variables

We've covered a bunch of common types and how they work in functions. But what about the `simple` function, which returns any value that's passed in to it? Really, `simple` could take any type of argument at all. Given what you know so far, you'd have to make a family of `simple` functions to work with every type.

Listing 11.8 `simpleInt` and

```
simpleInt :: Int -> Int
simpleInt n = n

simpleChar :: Char -> Char
simpleChar c = c
```

But this is ridiculous, and clearly not how Haskell works, because type inference was able to understand `simple`. To solve this problem, Haskell has *type variables*. Any lowercase letter in a type signature indicates that any type can be used in that place. The type definition for `simple` looks like the following.

Listing 11.9 Using type variables: `simple`

```
simple :: a -> a
simple x = x
```

Type variables are literally variables for types. Type variables work exactly like regular variables, but instead of representing a value, they represent a type. When you use a function that has a type variable in its signature, you can imagine Haskell substituting the variable that's needed, as shown in figure 11.5.

Type signatures can contain more than one type of variable. Even though the types can be any value, all types of the same variable name must be the same. Here's an example of a function that makes triples (tuples with three values).

Listing 11.10 Multiple type variables: `makeTriple`

```
makeTriple :: a -> b -> c -> (a,b,c)
makeTriple x y z = (x,y,z)
```

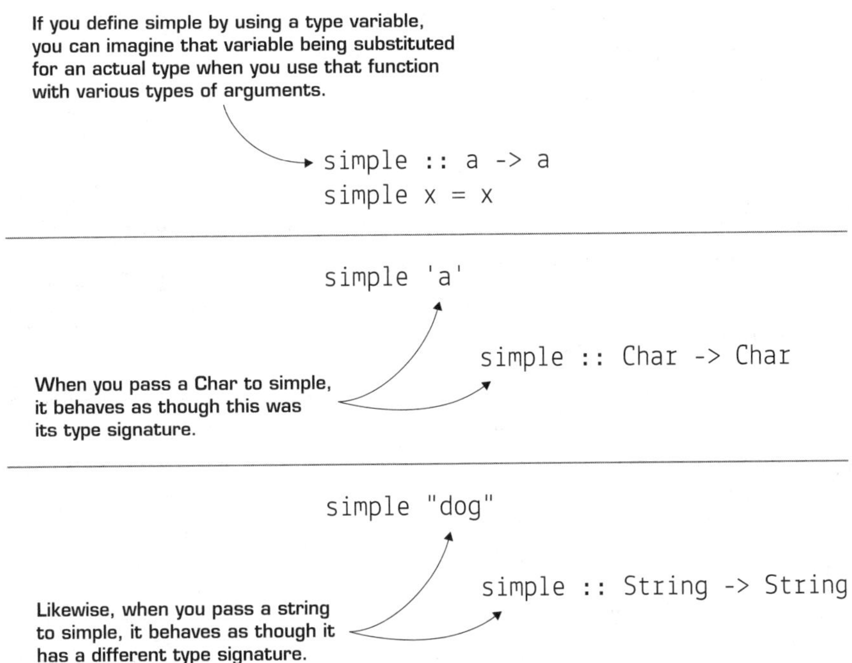

If you define simple by using a type variable, you can imagine that variable being substituted for an actual type when you use that function with various types of arguments.
simple :: a -> a
simple x = x
simple 'a'
simple :: Char -> Char
When you pass a Char to simple, it behaves as though this was its type signature.
simple "dog"
simple :: String -> String
Likewise, when you pass a string to simple, it behaves as though it has a different type signature.

Figure 11.5 Visualizing type variables taking on actual values

The reason for different names for type variables is the same as using different names for regular variables: they may contain different values. In the case of `makeTriple`, you can imagine a case in which you have a `String`, a `Char`, and another `String`:

```
nameTriple = makeTriple "Oscar" 'D' "Grouch"
```

In this example, you can imagine that the type signature that Haskell uses looks like this:

```
makeTriple :: String -> Char -> String -> (String, Char, String)
```

Notice that the definition of `makeTriple` and `makeAddress` are nearly identical. But they have different type signatures. Because of `makeTriple`'s use of type variables, `makeTriple` can be used for a more general class of problems than `makeAddress`. For example, you could use `makeTriple` to replace `makeAddress`. This doesn't render `makeAddress` useless. Because `makeAddress` has a more specific type signature, you can make more assumptions about how it behaves. Additionally, Haskell's type checker won't allow you to create an address where you accidently used a `String` for the number instead of an `Int`.

Just as with regular variables, using different names for type variables doesn't imply that the values represented by the variables must be different, only that they can be. Say you compare the type signatures of two unknown functions f1 and f2:

```
f1 :: a -> a
f2 :: a -> b
```

You know that f2 is a function that can produce a much wider range of possible values. The f1 function could behave only by changing a value and keeping it as the same type: Int -> Int, Char -> Char, and so forth. In contrast, f2 can represent a much broader range of possible behaviors: Int -> Char, Int -> Int, Int -> Bool, Char -> Int, Char -> Bool, and so forth.

Quick check 11.4 The type signature for map is as follows:

```
map :: (a -> b) -> [a] -> [b]
```

Why couldn't it be this?

```
map :: (a -> a) -> [a] -> [a]?
```

Hint: Fill in the type variables for myMap show [1,2,3,4].

Summary

In this lesson, our objective was to teach you the basics of Haskell's amazing type system. You saw that Haskell has many of the standard types that programmers are familiar with, such as Int, Char, Bool, and String. Despite Haskell's powerful type system, you were able to get this far in the book without explicitly using types because of Haskell's type inference, which allows Haskell to figure out the types you intend by how they're used. Even though Haskell can often handle your code without types, writing down type signatures turns out to be much more beneficial for the programmer. From this

QC 11.4 answer map:: (a -> a) -> [a] -> [a] would mean that map must always return the same type as it currently is.

In this case, you couldn't perform

```
map show [1,2,3,4]
```

because show returns a type String that isn't consistent with the original type. The real power of map isn't iteration, but transforming a list of one type into a list of another type.

point in the book onward, most of our discussion will typically come back to "thinking in types." Let's see if you got this.

Q11.1 What is the type signature for `filter`? How is it different from `map`?

Q11.2 In Haskell, both `tail` and `head` have an error when called on an empty list. You can write a version of `tail` that won't fail but instead return an empty list when called on an empty list. Can you write a version of `head` that returns an empty list when called on an empty list? To answer this, start by writing out the type signatures of both `head` and `tail`.

Q11.3 Recall `myFoldl` from lesson 9.

```
myFoldl f init [] = init
myFoldl f init (x:xs) = myFoldl f newInit xs
  where newInit = f init x
```

What's the type signature of this function? Note: `foldl` has a different type signature.

LESSON 12

CREATING YOUR OWN TYPES

After reading lesson 12, you'll be able to

- Define type synonyms to clarify code
- Create your own data type
- Build types from other types
- Work with complex types by using record syntax

In the preceding lesson, you learned how to use the basic types in Haskell. Now it's time to start creating some types of your own. Creating types in Haskell is more important than in most other programming languages, even statically typed ones, as nearly every problem you solve will come down to the types you're using. Even when using an existing type, you'll often want to rename it to make understanding your programs easier. For example, take a look at this type signature:

```
areaOfCircle :: Double -> Double
```

This is a perfectly fine type signature, but suppose you saw this instead:

```
areaOfCircle :: Diameter -> Area
```

With this alternate type signature, you know exactly what type of arguments your function expects as well as what the result means.

You'll also learn how to create more-complicated types of your own. Creating types for data in Haskell is as important as creating classes in object-oriented languages.

Consider this You want to write a function that operates on music albums. An album includes the following properties (and types): `artist` (`String`), `album title` (`String`), `year released` (`Int`) and a track listing (`[String]`). The only way you know how to store all this data right now is with a tuple. Unfortunately, this is a bit unwieldy and makes getting information out of the tuple tedious (because it requires pattern matching each attribute). Is there a better way to do this?

12.1 Using type synonyms

In lesson 11, we mentioned that in Haskell you can replace the `[Char]` type with `String`. From Haskell's perspective, these are two names for the same thing. When you have two names for the same type, it's referred to as a *type synonym*. Type synonyms are extremely useful, because they make reading type signatures much easier. You could have a function used for writing doctors' reports. The function `patientInfo` takes a first name, last name, age, and height and is used to create quick summaries of patients.

Listing 12.1 Defining the `patientInfo` function

```
patientInfo :: String -> String -> Int -> Int -> String
patientInfo fname lname age height = name ++ " " ++ ageHeight
 where name = lname ++ ", " ++ fname
       ageHeight = "(" ++ show age ++ "yrs. " ++ show height ++ "in.)"
```

You can use this function in GHCi:

```
GHCi> patientInfo "John" "Doe" 43 74
"Doe, John (43yrs. 74in.)"
GHCi> patientInfo "Jane" "Smith" 25 62
"Smith, Jane (25yrs. 62in.)"
```

If you assume that `patientInfo` is part of a larger application, it's likely that first name, last name, age, and height will be used frequently. Type signatures in Haskell are of much more benefit to the programmer than the compiler. You don't need to have a brand new type for each of these values, but quickly skimming a code base and seeing `String`s and `Int`s everywhere isn't helpful. Just as `String` is a type synonym for `[Char]`, you'd like to create type synonyms for some of the properties of your patients.

In Haskell, you can create new type synonyms by using the `type` keyword. Here's the code to create the type synonyms you'd like.

Listing 12.2 Type synonyms: `FirstName`, `LastName`, `Age`, and `Height`

```
type FirstName = String
type LastName = String
type Age = Int
type Height = Int
```

You can rewrite the original type signature now as follows:

```
patientInfo :: FirstName -> LastName -> Age -> Height -> String
```

Creating type synonyms isn't limited to one-to-one renaming of types. It's much more sensible to store patient names as a tuple. You can use a single type to represent the pair of a first and last name in a tuple as follows.

Listing 12.3 Type synonym: `PatientName`

```
type PatientName = (String,String)
```

And now you can create a few helper functions to get the first and last name of the patient.

Listing 12.4 Accessing `PatientName` values: `firstName` and `lastName`

```
firstName :: PatientName -> String
firstName patient = fst patient

lastName :: PatientName -> String
lastName patient = snd patient
```

And you can test your code in GHCi:

```
GHCi> firstName testPatient
"John"
GHCi> lastName testPatient
"Doe"
```

Quick check 12.1 Rewrite `patientInfo` to use your `patientName` type, reducing the total arguments needed to three instead of four.

12.2 Creating new types

Next you'll add the patient's sex, which can be either male or female. You could use a string for this, using the literal words `male` and `female`, or an `Int` or a `Bool`. In many other programming languages, this is likely the route you'd take. But none of these types seems like an ideal fit, and it's easy to imagine bugs that might arise from using these solutions. In Haskell, you should use the powerful type system to help you as much as you can. To do this, it's better to create a new type. Creating a new type can be done with the `data` keyword, as shown in figure 12.1.

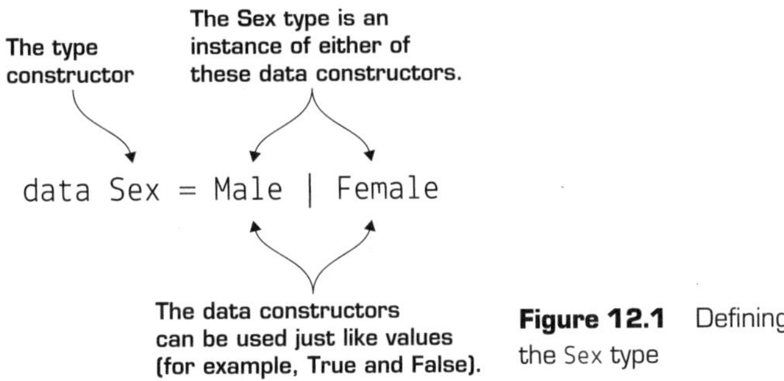

Figure 12.1 Defining the `Sex` type

In this new type, you define a few key pieces. The `data` keyword tells Haskell that you're defining a new type. The word `Sex` is the type constructor. In this case, the type constructor is the name of the type, but in later lessons you'll see that type constructors can take arguments. `Male` and `Female` are both data constructors. A *data constructor* is used to create a concrete instance of the type. By separating the data constructors with `|`, you're saying, "The `Sex` type can be either `Male` or an instance of `Female`."

QC 12.1 answer

```
patientInfoV2 :: PatientName -> Int -> Int -> String
patientInfoV2 (fname,lname) age height = name ++ " " ++ ageHeight
 where name = lname ++ ", " ++ fname
       ageHeight = "(" ++ show age ++ "yrs. " ++ show height ++ "in.)"
```

It turns out that `Bool` in Haskell is defined exactly the same way:

```
data Bool = True | False
```

Why not just use `Bool` as a type synonym? First, you have your own, more readable, data constructors. This makes things like pattern matching easier. Here's a function that returns a single character for the patients' sex.

Listing 12.5 Defining the `sexInitial` function

```
sexInitial :: Sex -> Char
sexInitial Male = 'M'
sexInitial Female = 'F'
```

If you had used a type synonym, you'd have to use `True` and `False` here, which would reduce readability. Even more important is that your compiler can now check to make sure you're always using the correct type. Any potential bug created by accidentally using a `Bool` in a way incompatible with your `Sex` type will now be caught.

Next you want to model the patient's blood type, which is more complicated than `Sex`. When you talk about blood types, you say things like, "He has AB positive" or "She's O negative." The AB and O part of a person's blood type is called their *ABO blood group*.

The ABO blood type can have four values: A, B, AB, or O. This refers to the family of antibodies in the blood. The *positive* or *negative* part refers to the person's Rhesus (Rh) group, which indicates the presence or absence of a particular antigen. A mismatch between antibodies and antigens can cause blood transfusions to provoke a deadly immune response.

To model blood type, you could replicate what you did with `Sex` and list a long range of data constructors (`APos | ANeg | BPos ...`). But given that you have two Rh blood types for each ABO blood type, you'd have eight possible constructors! A better solution is to start by modeling the Rh and ABO types separately.

`RhType` is going to look just like `Sex`.

Listing 12.6 Defining the type `RhType`

```
data RhType = Pos | Neg
```

`ABOType` is going to have four possible data constructors.

Listing 12.7 Defining the type `ABOType`

```
data ABOType = A | B | AB | O
```

Finally, you have to define your `BloodType`. You stated earlier that a `BloodType` is an `ABOType` and an `RhType`, so that's exactly how you'll define it, as shown in figure 12.2.

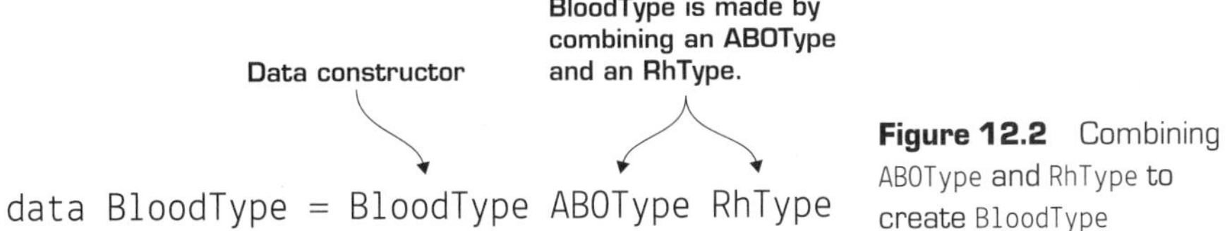
BloodType is made by combining an ABOType and an RhType.
Data constructor
data BloodType = BloodType ABOType RhType

Figure 12.2 Combining `ABOType` and `RhType` to create `BloodType`

Notice that in this case, the data constructor has the same name as your type constructor. It doesn't have to, but in this case it makes sense. You need this data constructor to combine your `ABOType` and `RhType`. You can read the data constructor as "A `BloodType` is an `ABOType` with an `RhType`."

Now you're able to create `BloodType` data:

```
patient1BT :: BloodType
patient1BT = BloodType A Pos

patient2BT :: BloodType
patient2BT = BloodType O Neg

patient3BT :: BloodType
patient3BT = BloodType AB Pos
```

It'd be nice to be able to print out these values. Lesson 13 covers a better way to do this, but for now let's write `showRh`, `showABO`, and `showBloodType`. Pattern matching with your new types will make this a breeze!

Listing 12.8 Displaying your types: showRh, showABO, showBloodType

```
showRh :: RhType -> String
showRh Pos = "+"
showRh Neg = "-"
showABO :: ABOType -> String
showABO A = "A"
showABO B = "B"
showABO AB = "AB"
showABO O = "O"
showBloodType :: BloodType -> String
showBloodType (BloodType abo rh)  = showABO abo ++ showRh rh
```

Notice that you're able to use pattern matching in the last step to easily extract the `ABOType` and `RhType` components of `BloodType`.

The most interesting question you can ask about blood type is whether one patient can be a donor for another. The rules for blood type matching are as follows:

- A can donate to A and AB.
- B can donate to B and AB.
- AB can donate only to AB.
- O can donate to anybody.

(Note: We won't worry about Rh compatibility for this example.)

You need a function `canDonateTo` to determine whether one `BloodType` can donate to another.

Listing 12.9 Defining the `canDonateTo` function

```
canDonateTo :: BloodType -> BloodType -> Bool
canDonateTo (BloodType O _) _ = True          <------ Universal donor
canDonateTo _ (BloodType AB _) = True         <------ Universal receiver
canDonateTo (BloodType A _) (BloodType A _) = True
canDonateTo (BloodType B _) (BloodType B _) = True
canDonateTo _ _ = False --otherwise
```

Here are some examples in GHCi:

```
GHCi> canDonateTo patient1BT patient2BT
False
GHCi> canDonateTo patient2BT patient1BT
True
GHCi> canDonateTo patient2BT patient3BT
True
GHCi> canDonateTo patient1BT patient3BT
True
GHCi> canDonateTo patient3BT patient1BT
False
```

At this point, it might be nice to refactor your names a bit. Another great feature would be to model an optional middle name. Right now you have a `PatientName` type synonym, which is a tuple with only first and last names. You can combine what you learned for your Sex type and your BloodType type to create a more robust Name type. You'll add a type synonym for MiddleName and use that to build out a more sophisticated type for names.

Listing 12.10 Support different names: MiddleName and Name

```
type MiddleName = String
data Name = Name FirstName LastName
          | NameWithMiddle FirstName MiddleName LastName
```

You can read this definition of Name as follows: a Name is either a first and last name, or a name with a middle name included. You can use pattern matching to create a showName function that works with either constructor.

Listing 12.11 Displaying multiple constructors: showName

```
showName :: Name -> String
showName (Name f l) = f ++ " " ++ l
showName (NameWithMiddle f m l) = f ++ " " ++ m ++ " " ++ l
```

Now to create a couple of examples:

```
name1 = Name "Jerome" "Salinger"
name2 = NameWithMiddle "Jerome" "David" "Salinger"
```

And you can see how these behave in GHCi:

```
GHCi> showName name1
"Jerome Salinger"
GHCi> showName name2
"Jerome David Salinger"
```

Now you have a much more flexible Name type.

12.3 Using record syntax

At the beginning of this lesson, you passed four arguments to your patientInfo function:

```
patientInfo :: String -> String -> Int -> Int -> String
patientInfo fname lname age height = name ++ " " ++ ageHeight
 where name = lname ++ ", " ++ fname
       ageHeight = "(" ++ show age ++ "yrs. " ++ show height ++ "in.)"
```

What you were trying to capture in defining that function was the idea of passing in a patient, but you didn't have the tools to model that information compactly in Haskell. Now that you've learned more about types, you should be able to create a `Patient` type that contains all this information and more. This will save you from having to pass in a confusing and large number of arguments every time you want to perform a task involving patient information in general.

The first step in modeling a patient should be to list all the features you want to keep track of along with the type that should represent them:

- Name: `Name`
- Sex: `Sex`
- Age (years): `Int`
- Height (inches): `Int`
- Weight (pounds): `Int`
- Blood type: `BloodType`

You can now use the `data` keyword to create a new type that represents this information just as you did for blood type.

Listing 12.12 `Patient` v.1

```
data Patient = Patient Name Sex Int Int Int BloodType
```

Here you have a compact representation of all six attributes of a patient. This is great, as you can perform all sorts of computations on a patient without having to worry about passing in a large list of arguments. Let's create your first example patient:

```
johnDoe :: Patient
johnDoe = Patient (Name "John" "Doe") Male 30 74 200 (BloodType AB Pos)
```

Quick check 12.2 Create a Jane Elizabeth Smith patient by using whatever reasonable values you like.

QC 12.2 answer

```
janeESmith :: Patient
janeESmith = Patient (NameWithMiddle "Jane" "Elizabeth" "Smith")
                     Female 28 62 140
```

Creating new data in this way worked great for Sex and BloodType, but it definitely feels awkward for data with so many properties. You could solve some of this with type synonyms from earlier. But even if the type definition of Patient was easier to read, you aren't always going to have the type signature handy. Look away from the page for a second and try to remember the order of the values. It's easy to imagine more values that you could add to the patient definition, which would only make this harder.

This representation of patients has one more annoying issue. It's reasonable to want to get each value of the patient individually. You can accomplish this by writing a bunch of functions to get each value by using pattern matching.

Listing 12.13 getName, getAge, getBloodType

```
getName :: Patient -> Name
getName (Patient n _ _ _ _ _) = n

getAge :: Patient -> Int
getAge (Patient  _ _ a _ _ _) = a

getBloodType :: Patient -> BloodType
getBloodType (Patient _ _ _ _ _ bt) = bt
```

Pattern matching makes these getters wonderfully easy to write, but having to write out all six of them seems annoying. Imagine that your final definition of a Patient ends up being 12 values used to define the type! It's going to be a lot of work just to get started, which seems unHaskell-like. Fortunately, Haskell has a great solution to this problem. You can define data types such as Patient by using *record syntax*. Defining a new data type by using record syntax makes it much easier to understand which types represent which properties of the data type.

Listing 12.14 Patient v.2 (with record syntax)

```
data Patient = Patient { name :: Name
                       , sex :: Sex
                       , age :: Int
                       , height :: Int
                       , weight :: Int
                       , bloodType :: BloodType }
```

The first victory for record syntax is that your type definition is much easier to read and understand now. The next big win for record syntax is that creating data for your `Patient` type is much easier. You can set each field by name, and order no longer matters!

```
jackieSmith :: Patient
jackieSmith = Patient {name = Name "Jackie" "Smith"
                      , age = 43
                      , sex = Female
                      , height = 62
                      , weight = 115
                      , bloodType = BloodType O Neg }
```

In addition, you don't have to write your getters; each field in the record syntax automatically creates a function to access that value from the record:

```
GHCi> height jackieSmith
62
GHCi> showBloodType (bloodType jackieSmith)
"O-"
```

Quick check 12.3 Show Jackie Smith's name.

You can also set values in record syntax by passing the new value in curly brackets to your data. Suppose you have to update Jackie Smith's age because of her birthday. Here's how you could do this using record syntax.

Listing 12.15 Updating `jackieSmith` by using record syntax

```
jackieSmithUpdated = jackieSmith { age = 44 }
```

Because you're still in a purely functional world, a new `Patient` type will be created and must be assigned to a variable to be useful.

QC 12.3 answer

```
showName (name jackieSmith)
```

Summary

In this lesson, our objective was to teach you the basics of creating types. You started with type synonyms, which allow you to provide alternate names for existing types. Type synonyms make it much easier to understand your code just by reading the type signature. Next you learned how to make your own original types by combining existing types with the `data` keyword. Finally, you learned how record syntax can make it easier to create accessors for your types. Let's see if you got this.

Q12.1 Write a function similar to `canDonateTo` that takes two patients as arguments rather than two `BloodType`s.

Q12.2 Implement a `patientSummary` function that uses your final `Patient` type. `patientSummary` should output a string that looks like this:

```
**************
Patient Name: Smith, John
Sex: Male
Age: 46
Height: 72 in.
Weight: 210 lbs.
Blood Type: AB+
**************
```

If you need to, feel free to create useful helper functions.

LESSON

TYPE CLASSES

After reading lesson 13, you'll be able to

- Understand the basics of type classes
- Read type class definitions
- Use common type classes: `Num`, `Show`, `Eq`, `Ord`, and `Bounded`

In this lesson, you're going to look an important abstraction in Haskell's type system: type classes. Type classes allow you to group types based on shared behavior. At first glance, type classes are similar to interfaces in most object-oriented programming languages. A type class states which functions a type must support in the same way that an interface specifies which methods a class must support. But type classes play a much more important role in Haskell than interfaces do in languages such as Java and C#. The major difference is that as you dive deeper into Haskell, you'll see that type classes typically require you to think in increasingly more powerful forms of abstraction. In many ways, type classes are the heart of Haskell programming.

Consider this You've written the function `inc` to increment a value a few times as a sample function. But how can you write an incrementing function that works with the wide range of possible numbers you've seen? Frustratingly enough, in unit 1, without specifying types, you could do this. How can you write the type signature of an `inc` function that works on all numbers?

13.1 Further exploring types

At this point, you've seen quite a few type signatures and even built some nontrivial types of your own. One of the best ways to learn about various Haskell types is to use the `:t` (or more verbose `:type`) command in GHCi to inspect the type of function you find in the wild. When you first wrote `simple`, you did so without a type signature:

```
simple x = x
```

If you wanted to know what type this function was, you could load it into GHCi and use `:t`:

```
GHCi> :t simple
simple :: t -> t
```

You could do the same thing for the lambda version of `simple`:

```
GHCi> :t (\x -> x)
(\x -> x) :: r -> r
```

Quick check 13.1 Find the type of the following:

```
aList = ["cat","dog","mouse"]
```

If you start exploring types this way, you'll almost immediately come across some things you haven't seen yet. Take, for example, something as simple as addition:

```
GHCi> :t (+)
(+) :: Num a => a -> a -> a
```

With all the time you've spent so far looking at types, something as simple as addition trips you up! The big mystery is the `Num a =>` part.

13.2 Type classes

What you've encountered here is your first type class! *Type classes* in Haskell are a way of describing groups of types that all behave in the same way. If you're familiar with Java or C#, type classes may remind you of interfaces. When you see `Num a`, the best way

QC 13.1 answer

```
aList = ["cat","dog","mouse"]
GHCi> :t aList
aList :: [[Char]]
```

to understand that statement is to say that there's some type `a` of class `Num`. But what does it mean to be part of type class `Num`? `Num` is a type class generalizing the idea of a number. All things of class `Num` must have a function (+) defined on them. There are other functions in the type class as well. One of the most valuable GHCi tools is `:info`, which provides information about types and type classes. If you use `:info` on `Num`, you get the following (partial) output.

Listing 13.1 `Num` type class definition

```
GHCi> :info Num
class Num a where
   (+) :: a -> a -> a
   (-) :: a -> a -> a
   (*) :: a -> a -> a
   negate :: a -> a
   abs :: a -> a
   signum :: a -> a
```

What `:info` is showing is the definition of the type class. The definition is a list of functions that all members of the class must implement, along with the type signatures of those functions. The family of functions that describe a number is `+`, `-`, `*`, `negate`, `abs`, and `signum` (gives the sign of a number). Each type signature shows the same type variable `a` for all arguments and the output. None of these functions can return a different type than it takes as an argument. For example, you can't add two `Int`s and get a `Double`.

Quick check 13.2 Why isn't division included in the list of functions needed for a `Num`?

13.3 The benefits of type classes

Why do you need type classes at all? So far in Haskell, each function you've defined works for only one specific set of types. Without type classes, you'd need a different name for each function that adds a different type of value. You do have type variables, but they're too flexible. For example, say you define `myAdd` with the following type signature:

```
myAdd :: a -> a -> a
```

QC 13.2 answer Because division with (/) isn't defined on all cases of `Num`.

Then you'd need the ability to manually check that you were adding only the types it makes sense to add (which isn't possible in Haskell).

Type classes also allow you to define functions on a variety of types that you can't even think of. Suppose you want to write an `addThenDouble` function like the following.

Listing 13.2 Using type classes: `addThenDouble`

```
addThenDouble :: Num a => a -> a -> a
addThenDouble x y = (x + y)*2
```

Because you use the `Num` type class, this code will automatically work not only on `Int` and `Double`, but also on anything that another programmer has written and implemented the `Num` type class for. If you end up interacting with a Roman Numerals library, as long as the author has implemented the `Num` type class, this function will still work!

13.4 Defining a type class

The output you got from GHCi for `Num` is the literal definition of the type class. Type class definitions have the structure illustrated in figure 13.1.

In the definition of `Num`, you see plenty of type variables. Nearly all functions required in any type class definition will be expressed in terms of type variables, because by definition you're describing an entire class of types. When you define a type class, you're doing so precisely because you don't want your functions to be tied to a single type. One way of thinking of type classes is as a constraint on the categories of types that a type variable can represent.

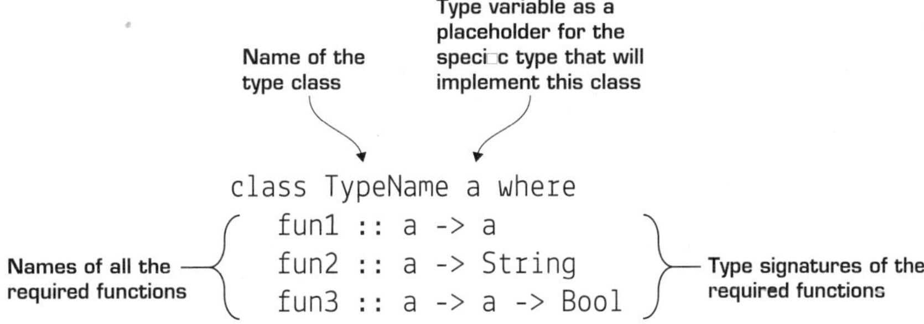

Figure 13.1 Structure of a type class definition

To help solidify the idea, you'll write a simple type class of your own. Because you're learning Haskell, a great type class to have is `Describable`. Any type that's an instance of your `Describable` type class can describe itself to you in plain English. So you require only one function, which is `describe`. For whatever type you have, if it's `Describable`, calling `describe` on an instance of the type will tell you all about it. For example, if `Bool` were `Describable`, you'd expect this:

```
GHCi> describe True
"A member of the Bool class, True is opposite of False"
GHCi> describe False
"A member of the Bool class, False is the opposite of True"
```

And if you wanted to describe an `Int`, you might expect this:

```
GHCi> describe (6 :: Int) "A member of the Int class, the number after 5 and
before 7"
```

At this point, you won't worry about implementing a type class (you'll do that in the next lesson)—only defining it. You know that you require only one function, which is `describe`. The only other thing you need to worry about is the type signature of that function. In each case, the argument for the function is whatever type has implemented your type class, and the result is always a string. So you need to use a type variable for the first type and a string for the return value. You can put this all together and define your type class as follows.

Listing 13.3 Defining your own type class: `Describable`

```
class Describable a where
   describe :: a -> String
```

And that's it! If you wanted to, you could build a much larger group of tools that use this type class to provide automatic documentation for your code, or generate tutorials for you.

13.5 Common type classes

Haskell defines many type classes for your convenience, which you'll learn about in the course of this book. In this section, you'll look at four more of the most basic: `Ord`, `Eq`, `Bounded`, and `Show`.

13.6 The Ord and Eq type classes

Let's look at another easy operator, *greater than* (>):

```
GHCi> :t (>)
(>) :: Ord a => a -> a -> Bool
```

Here's a new type class, `Ord`! This type signature says, "Take any two of the same types that implement `Ord`, and return a Boolean." `Ord` represents all of the things in the universe that can be compared and ordered. Numbers can be compared, but so can strings and many other things. Here's the list of functions that `Ord` defines.

Listing 13.4 `Ord` type class requires `Eq` type class

```
class Eq a => Ord a where
  compare :: a -> a -> Ordering
  (<) :: a -> a -> Bool
  (<=) :: a -> a -> Bool
  (>) :: a -> a -> Bool
  (>=) :: a -> a -> Bool
  max :: a -> a -> a
  min :: a -> a -> a
```

Of course, Haskell has to make things complicated. Notice that right in the class definition there's another type class! In this case, it's the type class `Eq`. Before you can understand `Ord`, you should look at `Eq`.

Listing 13.5 `Eq` type class generalizes the idea of equality

```
class Eq a where
  (==) :: a -> a -> Bool
  (/=) :: a -> a -> Bool
```

The `Eq` type class needs only two functions: `==` and `/=`. If you can tell that two types are equal or not equal, that type belongs in the `Eq` type class. This explains why the `Ord` type class includes the `Eq` type class in its definition. To say that something is ordered, clearly you need to be able to say that things of that type can be equal. But the inverse isn't true. We can describe many things by saying, "These two things are equal," but not "This is better than that one." You may love vanilla ice cream more than chocolate, and I might love chocolate more than vanilla. You and I can agree that two vanilla ice-cream cones are the same, but we can't agree on the order of a chocolate and vanilla cone. So if you created an `IceCream` type, you could implement `Eq`, but not `Ord`.

13.6.1 Bounded

In lesson 11, we mentioned the difference between the `Int` and `Integer` types. It turns out this difference is also captured by a type class. The `:info` command was useful for learning about type classes, but it's also helpful in learning about types. If you use `:info` on `Int`, you get a list of all the type classes that `Int` is a member of:

```
GHCi> :info Int
data Int = GHC.Types.I# GHC.Prim.Int#    -- Defined in 'GHC.Types'
instance Bounded Int -- Defined in 'GHC.Enum'
instance Enum Int -- Defined in 'GHC.Enum'
instance Eq Int -- Defined in 'GHC.Classes'
instance Integral Int -- Defined in 'GHC.Real'
instance Num Int -- Defined in 'GHC.Num'
instance Ord Int -- Defined in 'GHC.Classes'
instance Read Int -- Defined in 'GHC.Read'
instance Real Int -- Defined in 'GHC.Real'
instance Show Int -- Defined in 'GHC.Show'
```

You can do the same thing for the `Integer` type. If you did, you'd find there's a single difference between the two types. `Int` is an instance of the `Bounded` type class, and `Integer` isn't. Understanding the type classes involved in a type can go a long way toward helping you understand how a type behaves. `Bounded` is another simple type class (most are), which requires only two functions. Here's the definition of `Bounded`.

Listing 13.6 `Bounded` type class requires values but no functions

```
class Bounded a where
  minBound :: a
  maxBound :: a
```

Members of `Bounded` must provide a way to get their `upper` and `lower` bounds. What's interesting is that `minBound` and `maxBounds` aren't functions but values! They take no arguments but are just a value of whatever type they happen to be. Both `Char` and `Int` are members of the `Bounded` type class, so you never have to guess the upper and lower bounds for using these values:

```
GHCi> minBound :: Int
-9223372036854775808
GHCi> maxBound :: Int
9223372036854775807
GHCi> minBound :: Char
'\NUL'
GHCi> maxBound :: Char
'\1114111'
```

13.6.2 Show

We mentioned the functions show and read in lesson 11. Show and Read are incredibly useful type classes that make the show and read functions possible. Aside from two special cases for specific types, Show implements just one important function: show.

Listing 13.7 Show type class definition

```
class Show a where
  show :: a -> String
```

The show function turns a value into a String. Any type that implements Show can be printed. You've been making much heavier use of show than you might have realized. Every time a value is printed in GHCi, it's printed because it's a member of the Show type class. As a counter example, let's define your Icecream type but not implement show.

Listing 13.8 Defining the Icecream type

```
data Icecream = Chocolate | Vanilla
```

Icecream is nearly identical to Bool, but Bool implements Show. Look what happens when you type the constructors for these into GHCi:

```
GHCi> True
True
GHCi> False
False
GHCi> Chocolate
<interactive>:404:1:
No instance for (Show Icecream) arising from a use of 'print'
In a stmt of an interactive GHCi command: print it
```

You get an error because Haskell has no idea how to turn your data constructors into strings. Every value that you've seen printed in GHCi has happened because of the `Show` type class.

13.7 Deriving type classes

For your `Icecream` type class, it's a bit annoying that you have to implement `Show`. After all, `Icecream` is just like `Bool`, so why can't you have Haskell be smart about it and do what it does with `Bool`? In `Bool`, all that happens is that the data constructors are printed out. It just so happens that Haskell is rather smart! When you define a type, Haskell can do its best to automatically derive a type class. Here's the syntax for defining your `Icecream` type but deriving `Show`.

Listing 13.9 The `Icecream` type deriving the `Show` type class

```
data Icecream = Chocolate | Vanilla deriving (Show)
```

Now you can go back to GHCi, and everything works great:

```
GHCi> Chocolate
Chocolate
GHCi> Vanilla
Vanilla
```

Many of the more popular type classes have a reasonable default implementation. You can also add the `Eq` type class:

```
data Icecream = Chocolate | Vanilla deriving (Show, Eq, Ord)
```

And again you can use `GHCi` to show that you can see whether two flavors of `Icecream` are identical:

```
GHCi> Vanilla == Vanilla
True
GHCi> Chocolate == Vanilla
False
GHCi> Chocolate /= Vanilla
True
```

In the next lesson, you'll look more closely at how to implement your own type classes, as Haskell isn't always able to guess your true intentions.

Quick check 13.3 See which flavor Haskell thinks is superior by deriving the `Ord` type class.

Summary

In this lesson, our objective was to teach you the basics of type classes. All of the type classes we covered should seem familiar to users of object-oriented languages such as Java and C# that support interfaces. The type classes you saw make it easy to apply one function to a wide variety of types. This makes testing for equality, sorting data, and converting data to a string much easier. Additionally, you saw that Haskell is able to automatically implement type classes for you in some cases by using the `deriving` keyword. Let's see if you got this.

Q13.1 If you ran the `:info` examples, you likely noticed that the type `Word` has come up a few times. Without looking at external resources, use `:info` to explore `Word` and the relevant type classes to come up with your own explanation for the `Word` type. How is it different from `Int`?

Q13.2 One type class we didn't discuss is `Enum`. Use `:info` to look at the definition of this type class, as well as example members. Now consider `Int`, which is an instance of both `Enum` and `Bounded`. Given the following definition of `inc`:

```
inc :: Int -> Int
inc x = x + 1
```

and the `succ` function required by `Enum`, what's the difference between `inc` and `succ` for `Int`?

Q13.3 Write the following function that works just like `succ` on `Bounded` types but can be called an unlimited number of times without error. The function will work like `inc` in the preceding example but works on a wider range of types, including types that aren't members of `Num`:

```
cycleSucc :: (Bounded a, Enum a, ? a) => a -> a
cycleSucc n = ?
```

Your definition will include functions/values from `Bounded`, `Enum`, and the mystery type class. Make a note of where each of these three (or more) functions/values comes from.

QC 13.3 answer If you add `deriving Ord` to your definition of `Icecream`, Haskell defaults to the order of the data constructors for determining `Ord`. So `Vanilla` will be greater than `Chocolate`.

LESSON 14

USING TYPE CLASSES

After reading lesson 14, you'll be able to

- Implement your own type classes
- Understand polymorphism in Haskell
- Know when to use `deriving`
- Search for documentation with Hackage and Hoogle

In lesson 13, you got your first look at type classes, which are Haskell's way of grouping types by common behaviors they share. In this lesson, you'll take a deeper look at how to implement existing type classes. This will allow you to write new types that take advantage of a wide range of existing functions.

Consider this You have a data type consisting of data constructors for New England states:

```
data NewEngland = ME | VT | NH | MA | RI | CT
```

You want to be able to display them by their full name by using `Show`. You can easily display their abbreviations by deriving `show`, but there's no obvious way to create your own version of `show`. How can you make your `NewEngland` type display the full state name by using `show`?

14.1 A type in need of classes

You'll start by modeling a six-sided die. A good default implementation is a type similar to `Bool`, only with six values instead of two. You'll name your data constructors `S1` through `S6` to represent each of the six sides.

Listing 14.1 Defining the `SixSidedDie` data type

```
data SixSidedDie = S1 | S2 | S3 | S4 | S5 | S6
```

Next you want to implement some useful type classes. Perhaps the most important type class to implement is `Show`, because you'll nearly always want to have an easy way to display instances of your type, especially in GHCi. In lesson 13, we mentioned that you could add the `deriving` keyword to automatically create instances of a class. You could define `SixSidedDie` this way and call it a day.

Listing 14.2 The `SixSidedDie` type deriving `Show`

```
data SixSidedDie = S1 | S2 | S3 | S4 | S5 | S6 deriving (Show)
```

If you were to use this type in GHCi, you'd get a simple text version of your data constructors back when you type them:

```
GHCi> S1
S1
GHCi> S2
S2
GHCi> S3
S3
GHCi> S4
S4
```

This is a bit boring because you're just printing out your data constructors, which are more meaningful from an implementation standpoint than they are readable. Instead, let's print out the English word for each number.

14.2 Implementing Show

To do this, you have to implement your first type class, `Show`. There's only one function (or in the case of type classes, we call these *methods*) that you have to implement, `show`. Here's how to implement your type class.

Listing 14.3 Creating an instance of `Show` for `SixSidedDie`

```
instance Show SixSidedDie where
   show S1 = "one"
   show S2 = "two"
   show S3 = "three"
   show S4 = "four"
   show S5 = "five"
   show S6 = "six"
```

And that's it! Now you can return to GHCi and much more interesting output than you would with `deriving`:

```
GHCi> S1
one
GHCi> S2
two
GHCi> S6
six
```

Quick check 14.1 Rewrite this definition of `show` to print the numerals 1–6 instead.

QC 14.1 answer

```
data SixSidedDie = S1 | S2 | S3 | S4 | S5 | S6

instance Show SixSidedDie where
   show S1 = "I"
   show S2 = "II"
   show S3 = "III"
   show S4 = "IV"
   show S5 = "V"
   show S6 = "VI"
```

14.3 Type classes and polymorphism

One question that might come up is, why do you have to define show this way? Why do you need to declare an instance of a type class? Surprisingly, if you remove your early instance declaration, the following code will compile just fine.

Listing 14.4 Incorrect attempt to implement show for SixSidedDie

```
show :: SixSidedDie -> String
show S1 = "one"
show S2 = "two"
show S3 = "three"
show S4 = "four"
show S5 = "five"
show S6 = "six"
```

But if you load this code into GHCi, you get two problems. First, GHCi no longer can print your data constructors by default. Second, even if you manually use show, you get an error:

```
"Ambiguous occurrence 'show'"
```

You haven't learned about Haskell's module system yet, but the issue Haskell has is that the definition you just wrote for show is conflicting with another that's defined by the type class. You can see the real problem when you create a TwoSidedDie type and attempt to write show for it.

Listing 14.5 Demonstrating the need for polymorphism defining show for TwoSidedDie

```
data TwoSidedDie = One | Two

show :: TwoSidedDie -> String
show One = "one"
show Two = "two"
```

The error you get now is as follows:

```
Multiple declarations of 'show'
```

The problem is that by default you'd like to have more than one behavior for show, depending on the type you're using. What you're looking for here is called *polymorphism*. Polymorphism means that the same function behaves differently depending on the type of data it's working with. Polymorphism is important in object-oriented programming and equally so in Haskell. The OOP equivalent to `show` would be a `toString` method, one that's common among any classes that can be turned into a string. Type classes are the way you use polymorphism in Haskell, as shown in figure 14.1.

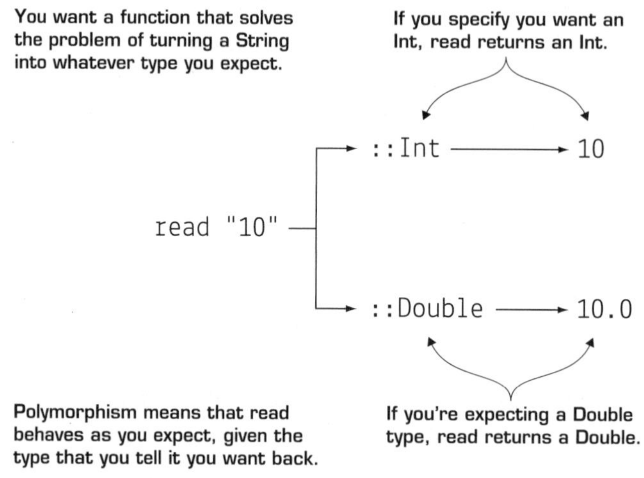

Figure 14.1 Visualizing polymorphism for `read`

 14.4 Default implementation and minimum complete definitions

Now that you can produce fun strings for your `SixSidedDie`, it'd be useful to determine that two dice are the same. This means that you have to implement the `Eq` class. This is also useful because `Eq` is the *superclass* of `Ord`. You touched on this relationship briefly in lesson 13 without giving it a name. To say that `Eq` is a superclass of `Ord` means that every instance of `Ord` must also be an instance of `Eq`. Ultimately, you'd like to compare `SixSidedDie` data constructors, which means implementing `Ord`, so first you need to implement `Eq`. Using the `:info` command in GHCi, you can bring up the class definition for `Eq`:

```
class Eq a where
  (==) :: a -> a -> Bool
  (/=) :: a -> a -> Bool
```

You have to implement only two methods: the Equals method `(==)` and the Not Equals method `(/=)`. Given how smart Haskell has been so far, this should seem like more work than makes sense. After all, if you know the definition of `(==)`, the definition of `(/=)` is *not* (==). Sure, there may be some exceptions to this, but it seems that in the vast majority of cases, if you know either one, then you can determine the other.

It turns out that Haskell is smart enough to figure this out. Type classes can have *default implementations* of methods. If you define (==), Haskell can figure out what (/=) means without any help.

Listing 14.6 Implementing an instance of Eq for SixSidedDie

```
instance Eq SixSidedDie where
   (==) S6 S6 = True
   (==) S5 S5 = True
   (==) S4 S4 = True
   (==) S3 S3 = True
   (==) S2 S2 = True
   (==) S1 S1 = True
   (==) _ _ = False
```

In GHCi, you'll see that (/=) works automatically!

```
GHCi> S6 == S6
True
GHCi> S6 == S5
False
GHCi> S5 == S6
False
GHCi> S5 /= S6
True
GHCi> S6 /= S6
False
```

This is useful, but how in the world are you supposed to know which methods you need to implement? The :info command is a great source of information right at your fingertips, but it isn't complete documentation. A source of more thorough information is *Hackage*, Haskell's centralized package library. Hackage can be found on the web at https://hackage.haskell.org. If you go to Eq's page on Hackage (https://hackage.haskell .org/package/base/docs/Data-Eq.html), you get much more info on Eq (probably more than you could ever want!). For our purposes, the most important part is a section called "Minimum complete definition." For Eq, you find the following:

```
(==) | (/=)
```

This is much more helpful! To implement the `Eq` type class, all you have to define is either `(==)` or `(/=)`. Just as in data declarations, | means *or*. If you provide either one of these options, Haskell can work out the rest for you.

> **Hackage and Hoogle**
> Although Hackage may be the central repository for Haskell information, you might find it a pain to search for specific types. To solve this, Hackage can be searched via a truly amazing interface called Hoogle. Hoogle can be found at www.haskell.org/hoogle. Hoogle allows you to search by types and type signatures. For example, if you search `a -> String`, you'll get results for `show` along with a variety of other functions. Hoogle alone is enough to make you love Haskell's type system.

> **Quick check 14.2** Use Hoogle to search for the `RealFrac` type class. What's its minimal complete definition?

14.5 Implementing Ord

One of the most important features of dice is that there's an order to their sides. `Ord` defines a handful of useful functions for comparing a type:

```
class Eq a => Ord a where
  compare :: a -> a -> Ordering
  (<) :: a -> a -> Bool
  (<=) :: a -> a -> Bool
  (>) :: a -> a -> Bool
  (>=) :: a -> a -> Bool
  max :: a -> a -> a
  min :: a -> a -> a
```

Luckily, on Hackage you can find that only the `compare` method needs to be implemented. The `compare` method takes two values of your type and returns `Ordering`. This is a type you

QC 14.2 answer Go to http://hackage.haskell.org/package/base/docs/Prelude.html#t:RealFrac. The minimal complete definition is `properFraction`.

saw briefly when you learned about `sort` in lesson 4. `Ordering` is just like `Bool`, except it has three data constructors. Here's its definition:

```
data Ordering = LT | EQ | GT
```

The following is a partial definition of `compare`.

Listing 14.7 Partial definition of `compare` for `SixSidedDie`

```
instance Ord SixSidedDie where
   compare S6 S6 = EQ
   compare S6 _ = GT
   compare _ S6 = LT
   compare S5 S5 = EQ
   compare S5 _ = GT
   compare _ S5 = LT
```

Even with clever uses of pattern matching, filling out this complete definition would be a lot of work. Imagine how large this definition would be for a 60-sided die!

Quick check 14.3 Write out the patterns for the case of `S4`.

14.6 To derive or not to derive?

So far, every class you've seen has been *derivable*, meaning that you can use the deriving keyword to automatically implement these for your new type definition. It's common for programming languages to offer default implementations for things such as an `.equals` method (which is often too minimal to be useful). The question is, how much should you rely on Haskell to derive your type classes versus doing it yourself?

QC 14.3 answer

```
compare S4 S4 = EQ

compare _ S4 = LT
```

Note: Because of pattern matching, the case of `compare S5 S4` and `compare S6 S4` will already be matched.

```
compare S4 _ = GT
```

Let's look at `Ord`. In this case, it's wiser to use `deriving (Ord)`, which works much better in cases of simple types. The default behavior when deriving `Ord` is to use the order that the data constructors are defined. For example, consider the following listing.

Listing 14.8 How deriving `Ord` is determined

```
data Test1 = AA | ZZ deriving (Eq, Ord)
data Test2 = ZZZ | AAA deriving (Eq, Ord)
```

In GHCi, you can see the following:

```
GHCi> AA < ZZ
True
GHCi> AA > ZZ
False
GHCi> AAA > ZZZ
True
GHCi> AAA < ZZZ
False
```

Quick check 14.4 Rewrite `SixSidedDie` to derive both `Eq` and `Ord`.

With `Ord`, using the `deriving` keyword saves you from writing a lot of unnecessary and potentially buggy code.

An even stronger case for using `deriving` when you can is `Enum`. The `Enum` type allows you to represent your dice sides as an enumerated list of constants. This is essentially what we think of when we think of a die, so it'll be useful. Here's the definition:

```
class Enum a where
  succ :: a -> a
  pred :: a -> a
  toEnum :: Int -> a
  fromEnum :: a -> Int
  enumFrom :: a -> [a]
```

QC 14.4 answer

```
data SixSidedDie = S1 | S2 | S3 | S4 | S5 | S6 deriving (Show,Eq,Ord)
```

```
enumFromThen :: a -> a -> [a]
enumFromTo :: a -> a -> [a]
enumFromThenTo :: a -> a -> a -> [a]
```

Once again, you're saved by having to implement only two methods: `toEnum` and `fromEnum`. These methods translate your `Enum` values to and from an `Int`. Here's the implementation.

Listing 14.9 Implementing `Enum` for `SixSidedDie` (errors with implementation)

```
instance Enum SixSidedDie where
   toEnum 0 = S1
   toEnum 1 = S2
   toEnum 2 = S3
   toEnum 3 = S4
   toEnum 4 = S5
   toEnum 5 = S6
   toEnum _ = error "No such value"

   fromEnum S1 = 0
   fromEnum S2 = 1
   fromEnum S3 = 2
   fromEnum S4 = 3
   fromEnum S5 = 4
   fromEnum S6 = 5
```

Now you can see some of the practical benefits of `Enum`. For starters, you can now generate lists of your `SixSidedDie` just as you can other values such as `Int` and `Char`:

```
GHCi> [S1 .. S6]
[one,two,three,four,five,six]
GHCi> [S2,S4 .. S6]
[two,four,six]
GHCi> [S4 .. S6]
[four,five,six]
```

This is great so far, but what happens when you create a list with no end?

```
GHCi> [S1 .. ]
[one,two,three,four,five,six,*** Exception: No such value
```

Yikes! You get an error because you didn't handle the case of having a missing value.

But if you had just derived your type class, this wouldn't be a problem:

```
data SixSidedDie = S1 | S2 | S3 | S4 | S5 | S6 deriving (Enum)
GHCi> [S1 .. ]
[one,two,three,four,five,six]
```

Haskell is pretty magical when it comes to deriving type classes. In general, if you don't have a good reason to implement your own, deriving is not only easier, but also often better.

14.7 Type classes for more-complex types

In lesson 4, we demonstrated that you can use first-class functions to properly order something like a tuple of names.

Listing 14.10 Using a type synonym for Name

```
type Name = (String,String)
names :: [Name]
names = [ ("Emil","Cioran")
        , ("Eugene","Thacker")
        , ("Friedrich","Nietzsche")]
```

As you may remember, you have a problem when these are sorted:

```
GHCi> import Data.List
GHCi> sort names
[("Emil","Cioran"),("Eugene","Thacker"),("Friedrich","Nietzsche")]
```

The good thing is that clearly your tuples automatically derive `Ord`, because they're sorted well. Unfortunately, they aren't sorted the way you'd like them to be, by last name and then first name. In lesson 4, you used a first-class function and passed it to `sortBy`, but that's annoying to do more than once. Clearly, you can implement your own custom `Ord` for `Name`.

Listing 14.11 Attempt to implement Ord for a type synonym

```
instance Ord Name where
   compare (f1,l1) (f2,l2) = compare (l1,f1) (l2,f2)
```

But when you try to load this code, you get an error! This is because to Haskell, `Name` is identical to `(String, String)`, and, as you've seen, Haskell already knows how to sort these. To solve these issues, you need create a new data type. You can do this by using the data as before.

Listing 14.12 Defining a new type Name using data

```
data Name = Name (String, String) deriving (Show, Eq)
```

Here the need for data constructors becomes clear. For Haskell, they're a way to note, "This tuple is special from the others." Now that you have this, you can implement your custom `Ord`.

Listing 14.13 Correct implementation of Ord for Name type

```
instance Ord Name where
   compare (Name (f1,l1)) (Name (f2,l2)) = compare (l1,f1) (l2,f2)
```

Notice that you're able to exploit the fact that Haskell derives `Ord` on the `(String, String)` tuple to make implementing your custom `compare` much easier:

```
names :: [Name]
names = [Name ("Emil","Cioran")
          , Name ("Eugene","Thacker")
          , Name ("Friedrich","Nietzsche")]
```

Now your names are sorted as expected:

```
GHCi> import Data.List
GHCi> sort names
[Name ("Emil","Cioran"),Name ("Friedrich","Nietzsche"),
➥Name ("Eugene","Thacker")]
```

Creating types with newtype

When looking at our type definition for `Name`, you find an interesting case in which you'd like to use a type synonym, but need to define a data type in order to make your type an instance of a type class. Haskell has a preferred method of doing this: using the `newtype` keyword. Here's an example of the definition of `Name` using `newtype`:

```
newtype Name = Name (String, String) deriving (Show, Eq)
```

In cases like this, `newtype` is often more efficient than using `data`. Any type that you can define with `newtype`, you can also define using data. But the opposite isn't true. Types defined with `newtype` can have only one type constructor and one type (in the case of `Name`, it's `Tuple`). In most cases, when you need a type constructor to make a type synonym more powerful, `newtype` is going to be the preferred method.

For simplicity, we'll stick to creating types with data throughout this book.

14.8 Type class roadmap

Figure 14.2 shows the type classes that are defined in Haskell's standard library. Arrows from one class to another indicate a superclass relationship. This unit has covered most of the basic type classes. In unit 3, you'll start exploring the more abstract type classes `Semigroup` and `Monoid`, and you'll start to see how different type classes can be from interfaces. In unit 5, you'll look at a family of type classes—`Functor`, `Applicative`, and `Monad`—that provide a way to model the context of a computation. Although this last group is particularly challenging to learn, it also allows for some of Haskell's most powerful abstractions.

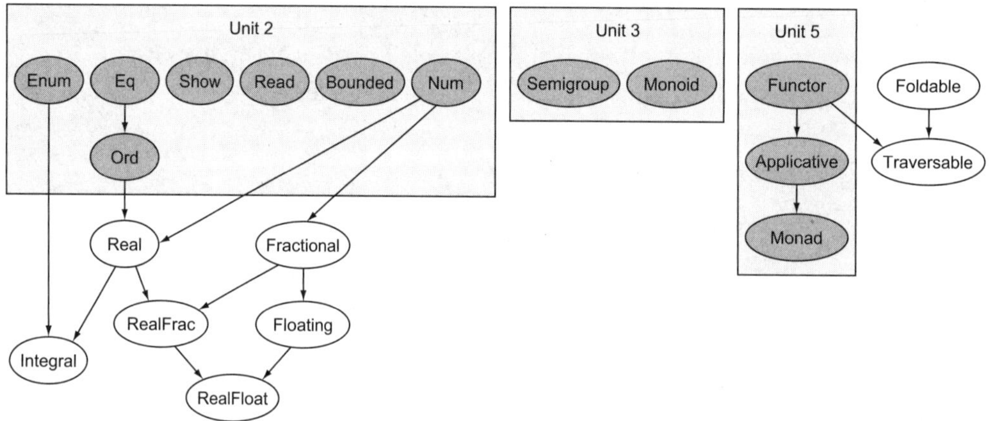

Figure 14.2 Type class road map

Summary

In this lesson, our objective was to dive deeper into Haskell's type classes. You learned how to read type class definitions as well as how to make types an instance of a type class beyond simply using the `deriving` keyword. You also learned when it's best to use `deriving` and when you should write your own instances of a type class. Let's see if you got this.

Q14.1 Note that `Enum` doesn't require either `Ord` or `Eq`, even though it maps types to `Int` values (which implement both `Ord` and `Eq`). Ignoring the fact that you can easily use `deriving` for `Eq` and `Ord`, use the derived implementation of `Enum` to make manually defining `Eq` and `Ord` much easier.

Q14.2 Define a five-sided die (`FiveSidedDie` type). Then define a type class named `Die` and at least one method that would be useful to have for a die. Also include superclasses you think make sense for a die. Finally, make your `FiveSidedDie` an instance of `Die`.

LESSON 15

CAPSTONE: SECRET MESSAGES!

This capstone covers

- Learning about the basics of cryptography
- Using basic types to model your data
- Making practical use of `Enum` and `Bounded`
- Writing and making instances of your own `Cipher` class

Everybody loves the idea of being able to communicate with a friend in secret. In this capstone, you're going to take your knowledge of types and type classes to build out a few example ciphers. A *cipher* in cryptography is a means of encoding a message so that others can't read it. Ciphers are the foundation of cryptography, but they're also just plain fun to play around with. You'll first look at an easy-to-implement and easy-to-break cipher, then you'll learn more about the basics of encrypting characters, and finally, you'll build an unbreakable cipher!

15.1 Ciphers for beginners: ROT13

Most people discover cryptography in elementary school, as they try to send secret messages to their friends. The typical way to encrypt text that most kids stumble upon is the ROT13 method. *ROT* is short for *rotation*, and the *13* refers to the number of letters you rotate a given letter by. The ROT13 approach works by translating each letter in a sentence up 13 letters. For example, *a* is the first letter in the alphabet, and 13 letters away is *n*. So *a* would be changed to *n* during the encoding.

Let's try sending a secret message by using ROT13 to make sure you understand it. You'll send the message *Jean-Paul likes Simone*. For this example, you'll treat capital letters like lowercase ones, and ignore spaces and any special characters. The best way to visualize ROT13 is as a decoder ring, like the one shown in figure 15.1.

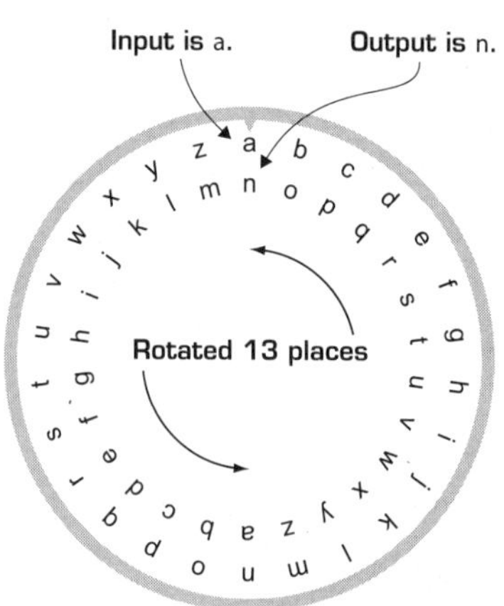

Figure 15.1 The best way to visualize ROT13 is as a decoder ring.

Using your decoder ring, you can translate your message. The letter *j* maps to *w*, *e* to *r*, and so forth. Finally, you end up with *Wrna-Cnhy yvxrf Fvzbar*.

The reason you specifically use 13 is that with 26 letters in the alphabet, applying ROT13 twice returns the original text. Performing ROT13 on *n* gives you back an *a*. Even more interesting is that ROT13 encoding *Wrna-Cnhy yvxrf Fvzbar* yields *Jean-Paul likes Simone*. This symmetry is common, and essential to most cryptography systems.

15.1.1 Implementing your own ROT cipher

Now that you've seen how ROT13 works, let's make a similar cipher for Haskell's `Char` type so that you can encode and decode strings. In the preceding example, you used 13 for your rotation because you had 26 characters and you wanted to rotate halfway around all the characters to encode your message. You already encountered a problem when you had to ignore both spaces and special characters in the sentence *Jean-Paul likes Simone*. Ideally, you could rotate over all *N* characters for any given character system. What you want is a generic `rotN` function that can rotate any alphabet system with *N* elements. Let's see how to create a simple four-letter alphabet that you can use to experiment with.

Listing 15.1 Defining a four-letter alphabet

```
data FourLetterAlphabet = L1 | L2 | L3 | L4 deriving (Show,Enum,Bounded)
```

It's important to notice the type classes you derive and why:

- You add `deriving Show` to your alphabet to make it easier to work with this type in GHCi.
- You add `deriving Enum` because this will allow you to automatically convert your data constructors to type `Int`. Being able to convert a letter into an `Int` allows you

to use simple math to rotate out letters. You can use fromEnum to convert your letters to Ints, and toEnum to take Ints and turn them back into letters.

- Finally, you add deriving Bounded because it provides maxBound and minBound values that will help you know how far you have to cycle.

Now that you have an alphabet class you can work with, let's think about how the cipher itself is going to work.

15.1.2 The rotN algorithm

Here's how your rotN function is going to work:

1. You pass in the size of your alphabet and a letter you want to rotate.
2. You use the div function to find the middle. Remember, div is different from / in that it divides Ints into whole-valued Ints: although 4 `div` 2 is 2, 5 `div` 2 is also 2. The result of your div function indicates how far you want to rotate your letter.
3. To rotate, you add half of your alphabet size to the Int value of your letter (as an Enum). Of course, for half of your Enum values, adding half the size of the alphabet will give you an Int outside the bounds of your enum. To solve this, you modulo your offset by the alphabet size.
4. Finally, you use toEnum to convert this Int representation of your letter back into an instance of the letter's type.

This rotN will work on any type that's both a member of Bounded and Enum.

Listing 15.2 A generic rotN function to work on any alphabet

```
rotN :: (Bounded a, Enum a) => Int -> a -> a
rotN alphabetSize c = toEnum rotation
 where halfAlphabet = n `div` 2
       offset = fromEnum c + halfAlphabet
       rotation =  offset `mod` alphabetSize
```

Finds the middle value of your alphabet

Uses the middle to find the offset of your character

Uses modulo arithmetic to make sure you're in the bounds of your Enum

You can try this with your FourLetterAlphabet in GHCi:

```
GHCi> rotN 4 L1
L3
GHCi> rotN 4 L2
L4
GHCi> rotN 4 L3
L1
GHCi> rotN 4 L4
L2
```

An interesting point to observe is that the `Bool` type is also a member of both `Enum` and `Bounded`, so your `rotN` function will also work to rotate `Bools`. Because of type classes, you can rotate any member of both `Enum` and `Bounded`.

Now you can use `rotN` to rotate `Chars`. The only thing you need to do is to figure out how many `Chars` there are. You can start by using the `maxBound` value required by the `Bounded` type class. By using `maxBound`, you can get the largest `Char` value. Then you can convert this to an `Int` by using the `fromEnum` function required by `Enum`. Here's the code to get the number of the largest `Char`.

Listing 15.3 Getting the number representing the largest `Char`

```
largestCharNumber :: Int
largestCharNumber  = fromEnum (maxBound :: Char)
```

Notice that you must add :: Char so maxBound knows which type you're using.

But the `Int` value for the lowest `Char` is 0 (you can get this using the same trick with (`minBound`). Because of this, the size of the `Char` alphabet is `largestCharNumber` + 1. If you look up the `Enum` type class on Hackage, you'll find that the definition does assume that `Enums` start at 0 and go to n–1 (recall that Hackage, https://hackage.haskell.org/, is the online source for full definitions of Haskell type classes). Because of this, it's generally safe for you to assume that the total number of items in any alphabet is always `maxBound` + 1. If you wanted to write a `Char`-specific `rotN` function, it would look like the following.

Listing 15.4 Rotating a single `Char`

```
rotChar :: Char -> Char
rotChar charToEncrypt = rotN sizeOfAlphabet charToEncrypt
 where sizeOfAlphabet = 1 + fromEnum (maxBound :: Char)
```

15.1.3 Rot encoding a string

So far, you have a method for rotating a single character for any type that's a member of both `Enum` and `Bounded`. But what you want is to encode and decode messages. Messages in any alphabet are just lists of letters. Suppose you have a message in your `FourLetterAlphabet` you'd like to send.

Listing 15.5 A message in your four-letter alphabet

```
message :: [FourLetterAlpha]
message = [L1,L3,L4,L1,L1,L2]
```

To encode this message, you want to apply the appropriate `rotN` function to each letter in this list. The best tool to apply a function to each item in a list is `map`! The following is an encoder for your four-letter alphabet.

Listing 15.6 Defining a `fourLetterEncoder` with `map`

```
fourLetterAlphabetEncoder :: [FourLetterAlphabet] -> [FourLetterAlphabet]
fourLetterEncoder vals = map rot4l vals
 where alphaSize = 1 + fromEnum (maxBound :: FourLetterAlphabet)
       rot4l = rotN alphaSize
```

Here's an example in GHCi of your new encoded message:

```
GHCi> fourLetterEncoder message
[L3,L1,L2,L3,L3,L4]
```

The next step is to `rotN` decode your message. As you may remember from the first section, the ROT13 cipher is symmetric: to decode an ROT13 message, you apply ROT13 to the message once again. It seems that you have an easy solution to your problem: you can apply the same `rotN` function. But this symmetry works only if your alphabet has an even number of letters.

15.1.4 The problem with decoded odd-sized alphabets

An issue arises when decoding odd-sized alphabets because you're doing integer division and always rounding down. As an illustration, here's a `ThreeLetterAlphabet` and a corresponding secret message and encoder.

Listing 15.7 A three-letter alphabet, message, and encoder

```
data ThreeLetterAlphabet = Alpha
                         | Beta
                         | Kappa deriving (Show,Enum,Bounded)

threeLetterMessage :: [ThreeLetterAlphabet]
threeLetterMessage = [Alpha,Alpha,Beta,Alpha,Kappa]

threeLetterEncoder :: [ThreeLetterAlphabet] -> [ThreeLetterAlphabet]
threeLetterEncoder vals =  map rot3l vals
 where alphaSize = 1 + fromEnum (maxBound :: ThreeLetterAlphabet)
       rot3l = rotN alphaSize
```

Now in GHCi, you can compare what happens when trying to encode and decode using the same function for each alphabet:

```
GHCi> fourLetterEncoder fourLetterMessage
[L3,L1,L2,L3,L3,L4]
GHCi> fourLetterEncoder (fourLetterEncoder fourLetterMessage)
[L1,L3,L4,L1,L1,L2]
GHCi> threeLetterMessage
[Alpha,Alpha,Beta,Alpha,Kappa]
GHCi> threeLetterEncoder threeLetterMessage
[Beta,Beta,Kappa,Beta,Alpha]
GHCi> threeLetterEncoder (threeLetterEncoder threeLetterMessage)
[Kappa,Kappa,Alpha,Kappa,Beta]
```

As you can see, in the case of an odd-numbered alphabet, your encoder isn't symmetric. To solve this, you can create a similar function to `rotN`, which adds 1 to the offset if the alphabet has an odd number of letters.

Listing 15.8 A `rotNdecoder` that works with odd-numbered alphabets

```
rotNdecoder :: (Bounded a, Enum a) => Int -> a -> a
rotNdecoder n c = toEnum rotation
 where halfN = n `div` 2
       offset = if even n
                then fromEnum c + halfN
                else 1 + fromEnum c + halfN
       rotation =  offset `mod` n
```

With `rotNdecoder`, you can build a much more robust decoder.

Listing 15.9 A working decoder for `ThreeLetterAlphabet`

```
threeLetterDecoder :: [ThreeLetterAlphabet] -> [ThreeLetterAlphabet]
threeLetterDecoder vals =  map rot3ldecoder vals
 where alphaSize = 1 + fromEnum (maxBound :: ThreeLetterAlphabet)
       rot3ldecoder = rotNdecoder alphaSize
```

In GHCi, you can see that this works:

```
GHCi> threeLetterMessage
[Alpha,Alpha,Beta,Alpha,Kappa]
```

```
GHCi> threeLetterEncoder threeLetterMessage
[Beta,Beta,Kappa,Beta,Alpha]
GHCi> threeLetterDecoder (threeLetterEncoder threeLetterMessage)
[Alpha,Alpha,Beta,Alpha,Kappa]
```

Finally, you can put this all together to create a robust `rotEncoder` and `rotDecoder` to decode strings. These will work even if a single extra `Char` is added or removed, making the number of `Char` letters odd.

Listing 15.10 Rotating strings with `rotEncoder` and `rotDecoder`

```
rotEncoder :: String -> String
rotEncoder text = map rotChar text
 where alphaSize = 1 + fromEnum (maxBound :: Char)
       rotChar = rotN alphaSize

rotDecoder :: String -> String
rotDecoder text =  map rotCharDecoder text
 where alphaSize = 1 + fromEnum (maxBound :: Char)
       rotCharDecoder = rotNdecoder alphaSize

threeLetterEncoder :: [ThreeLetterAlphabet] -> [ThreeLetterAlphabet]
threeLetterEncoder vals =  map rot3l vals
 where alphaSize = 1 + fromEnum (maxBound :: ThreeLetterAlphabet)
       rot3l = rotN alphaSize

threeLetterDecoder :: [ThreeLetterAlphabet] -> [ThreeLetterAlphabet]
threeLetterDecoder vals =  map rot3ldecoder vals
 where alphaSize = 1 + fromEnum (maxBound :: ThreeLetterAlphabet)
       rot3ldecoder = rotNdecoder alphaSize


fourLetterAlphabetEncoder :: [FourLetterAlphabet] -> [FourLetterAlphabet]
fourLetterEncoder vals = map rot4l vals
 where alphaSize = 1 + fromEnum (maxBound :: FourLetterAlphabet)
       rot4l = rotN alphaSize

fourLetterDecoder :: [FourLetterAlphabet] -> [FourLetterAlphabet]
fourLetterDecoder vals =  map rot4ldecoder vals
 where alphaSize = 1 + fromEnum (maxBound :: ThreeLetterAlphabet)
       rot4ldecoder = rotNdecoder alphaSize
```

In GHCi, you can explore encoding and decoding messages by rotating around all possible `Char` values:

```
GHCi> rotEncoder "hi"
"\557160\557161"
GHCi> rotDecoder(rotEncoder "hi")
"hi"
GHCi> rotEncoder "Jean-Paul likes Simone"
"\557130\557157\557153\55....
GHCi> rotDecoder (rotEncoder "Jean-Paul likes Simone")
"Jean-Paul likes Simone"
```

ROT13 is hardly a secure method of sending messages. Because each letter is always encoded exactly the same way, it's easy to find patterns that allow you to decode the encoded message. Next you'll look at a cryptographically stronger approach to sending secret messages.

15.2 XOR: The magic of cryptography!

Before you can implement a much stronger cipher, you need to learn a bit about cryptography. Thankfully, you only need to learn about one simple binary operator, `XOR`. `XOR` (short for *exclusive or*) is just like the typical logical `OR`, only it's false for the case where both values are true. Table 15.1 shows the values for `XOR`ing two Booleans.

Table 15.1 `XOR` Booleans

First value	Second value	Result
false	false	false
true	false	true
false	true	true
true	true	false

`XOR` is powerful in cryptography because it has two important properties. The first is that like ROT13, `XOR` is symmetric. `XOR`ing two lists of `Bool`s results in a new list of `Bool`s. `XOR`ing this new list with either one of the originals results in the other. Figure 15.2 is a visual example.

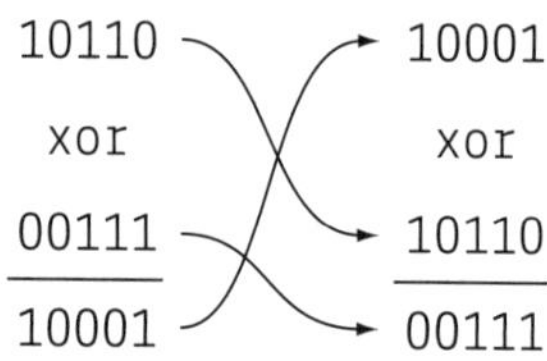

Figure 15.2 The symmetric nature of `XOR`

The other useful property of XOR is that given a uniform distribution of True and False values (or in practice a string of bits), no matter what the distribution of True and False values in your plain text, the output of the XOR will be a uniform distribution of True and False values. In practice, if you take a nonrandom string of values, such as text, and XOR it with a random one, the result will appear to the observer as random noise. This fixes a major problem with ROT13. Though the ROT13-encoded text is illegible on initial inspection, the patterns of characters in the output text are the same as the original and thus easy to decode. When properly XORing data, the output is indistinguishable from noise. You can best visualize this by comparing using rotN on an image to XORing it with noise (see figure 15.3). Assume that the gray pixels are False and the black ones are True.

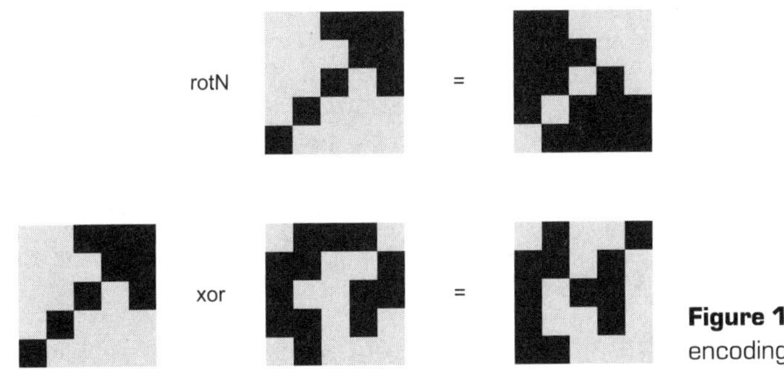

Figure 15.3 Comparing rotN encoding to XOR on an image

Let's define a simple xor function. You'll start by making a helper function named xorBool, which will operate on two Bools.

> **NOTE** Haskell's Data.Bool module does have an xor function that's identical to this xorBool function.

Listing 15.11 xorBool, a foundation for xor

```
xorBool :: Bool -> Bool -> Bool
xorBool value1 value2 = (value1 || value2) && (not (value1 && value2))
```

For your version of xor, your main goal is to easily XOR two lists of Bool values. Internally, in your final xor function, you'll want to work on pairs because it's easy to zip the two lists together and then map across the list of pairs. As a step toward this, you'll build an xorPair function that operates on a single pair of Booleans.

Listing 15.12 xorPair to xor pairs of Bools

```
xorPair :: (Bool,Bool) -> Bool
xorPair (v1,v2) = xorBool v1 v2
```

Finally, you can put this all together into an `xor` function that operates on two lists of Booleans.

Listing 15.13 Finally, your completed `xor` function

```
xor :: [Bool] -> [Bool] -> [Bool]
xor list1 list2 = map xorPair (zip list1 list2)
```

With your `xor` function in hand, the next thing you need to do is figure out how to `xor` two strings.

15.3 Representing values as bits

In cryptography, you don't think of lists of Booleans but rather streams of bits. To make reasoning about your code in the rest of this section easier, you'll create a useful type synonym, `Bits`.

> **NOTE** In unit 4, you'll look at how Haskell represents different values as bits, but for now you can create your own system to represent them.

Listing 15.14 `Bits` type synonym

```
type Bits = [Bool]
```

Your end goal is to encrypt strings of text, but to do that you need to translate them into bits. You can start by first converting `Int`s into bits because each `Char` can be converted into an `Int`. Given you have an `Int`, all you need to do is to transform a base 10 into a stream of bits, which is the binary equivalent.

You can convert a base 10 number into binary by recursively dividing a number by 2. If there's no remainder, you add `False` (or 0) to your list of bits and otherwise add a 1. You stop when the number is either 0 or 1. You'll define a function named `intToBits'` (note the apostrophe). You're adding the apostrophe to the name because this function will serve as a helper function for your final `intToBits` function.

Listing 15.15 `intToBits'` starting to convert an `Int` type to `Bits`

```
intToBits' :: Int -> Bits
intToBits' 0 = [False]
intToBits' 1 = [True]
intToBits' n = if (remainder == 0)
```

```
            then False : intToBits' nextVal
            else True : intToBits' nextVal
  where remainder = n `mod` 2
        nextVal = n `div` 2
```

If you try this on a few well-known powers of 2, you can see that this code has a small issue:

```
GHCi> intToBits' 2
[False,True]
GHCi> intToBits' 8
[False,False,False,True]
```

This algorithm works well, except your number is reversed! Your final version of this function, `intToBits` (with no `'`), will need to reverse the output of `intToBits'`. Additionally, you'd like all of your `Bit` lists to be the same size. Right now, `intToBits' 0` will return a list of a single `Bool`, whereas `intToBits maxBound` will return one with 63 `Bools`! To solve this, you'll make sure that you prepend extra `False` values so that the list is equal to the size of the length of the `e` converted to bits. For this example, you'll calculate `maxBits` first.

Listing 15.16 `maxBits` and your final `intToBits` function

```
maxBits :: Int
maxBits = length (intToBits' maxBound)

intToBits :: Int -> Bits
intToBits n = leadingFalses ++ reversedBits
  where reversedBits = reverse (intToBits' n)
        missingBits = maxBits - (length reversedBits)
        leadingFalses = take missingBits (cycle [False])
```

Finally, you can convert a single `Char` into `Bits`.

Listing 15.17 `charToBits` to convert `Chars` into `Bits`

```
charToBits :: Char -> Bits
charToBits char = intToBits (fromEnum char)
```

With `charToBits`, you have the basic tools to make more cryptographically secure secret messages! The only problem is that you'd like to be able to convert bits back into `Chars`. Fortunately, this isn't too complicated. You'll start with a function `bitsToInts`. You create a list of indices for each bit, and if the Bit is True, you add 2^index. To understand this, it's helpful to realize that binary 101 in decimal is 1*2^2 + 0*2^1 + 1*2^0. Because the only two values are 1 or 0, you take the sum of those nonzero powers. You could use an if then else expression here, but the more Haskellish approach is to use filter.

Listing 15.18 bitsToInt to go backward from Bits to an Int type

```
bitsToInt :: Bits -> Int
bitsToInt bits = sum (map (\x -> 2^(snd x)) trueLocations)
 where size = length bits
       indices = [size-1,size-2 .. 0]
       trueLocations = filter (\x -> fst x == True)
                       (zip bits indices)
```

You can verify that this function works in GHCi:

```
GHCi> bitsToInt (intToBits 32)
32
GHCi> bitsToInt (intToBits maxBound)
9223372036854775807
```

> **NOTE** There's a source of possible errors in your handling of converting integers to bits: you have no way to handle negative numbers. This is okay in this case, because you're using intToBits and its converse only as a means of working with Chars as Enums. All Char Enum values are between 0 and maxBound, so you should never encounter a negative number in practice. In lesson 38, you'll take a close look at issues like this.

The last function you need for working with bits is one to convert bitsToChar, which can be done with toEnum.

Listing 15.19 Completing the transformation by going back from bitsToChar

```
bitsToChar :: Bits -> Char
bitsToChar bits = toEnum (bitsToInt bits)
```

In GHCi, you can see that this works as well:

```
GHCi> bitsToChar (charToBits 'a')
'a'
GHCi> bitsToChar (charToBits maxBound)
'\1114111'
GHCi> bitsToChar (charToBits minBound)
'\NUL'
```

Now you can put all these pieces together to make a much more secure system of creating secret messages!

15.4 The one-time pad

With your xor function, you can go from the insecure ROT13 cipher to the unbreakable one-time pad! The *one-time pad* is an incredibly important tool in cryptography; if implemented correctly, it can't be cracked. Conceptually, the one-time pad is simple. You start with your plain text and another text at least as many characters long as your plain text. Then you take each character from the second text and xor it with a character from your plain text, one at a time. Traditionally, this second text was written on a pad of paper, hence the term *pad* in the cipher's name. The one-time pad is uncrackable as long as the pad is sufficiently random and, as indicated by the name, you use the pad only once.

15.4.1 Implementing your one-time pad

To implement your one-time pad, let's start with a sample pad.

Listing 15.20 A simple pad

```
myPad :: String
myPad = "Shhhhhh"
```

Next you have some plain text to encrypt.

Listing 15.21 Your plain text

```
myPlainText :: String
myPlainText = "Haskell"
```

To encrypt your myPlainText, you convert both your pad and your plain text to bits, and then xor the results.

Listing 15.22 applyOTP' for converting a string to bits with a one-time pad

```
applyOTP' :: String -> String -> [Bits]
applyOTP' pad plaintext =  map (\pair ->
                                (fst pair) `xor` (snd pair))
                           (zip padBits plaintextBits)
  where padBits =  map charToBits pad
        plaintextBits =  map charToBits plaintext
```

Of course, `applyOTP'` gives back only a list of bits. What you want is a string. Your final version of `applyOTP` will take the output of `applyOTP'` and map it into a string.

Listing 15.23 Finally, `applyOTP` to encode strings using a one-time pad

```
applyOTP :: String -> String -> String
applyOTP pad plaintext = map bitsToChar bitList
 where bitList = applyOTP' pad plaintext
```

With your final `applyOTP`, you can encrypt your plain text:

```
GHCi> applyOTP myPad myPlainText
"\ESC\t\ESC\ETX\r\EOT\EOT"
```

The first thing you should notice is why it's never a good idea to roll your own cryptography system! Clearly, your simple `XOR`-based one-time pad shows some patterns when you apply the same letters to each other. This is because your pad isn't a particularly good one, given how often letters are repeated in it. Remember that `xor` provides a uniformly random output, given one of the values being `xorBool` is also uniformly random. Clearly, your plain text isn't, and, unfortunately your pad also isn't random. If your pad was random, and an attacker didn't know the pad, your encrypted text would be uncrackable!

The interesting thing is that you can decode your text the same way you encoded it. By using partial application (applying fewer arguments to a function than required to get a function awaiting the remaining arguments, covered in lesson 5), you can create an encoder/decoder.

Listing 15.24 Partial application to create an `encoderDecoder`

```
encoderDecoder :: String -> String
encoderDecoder = applyOTP myPad
```

Your encoder/decoder will work with any text shorter than your pad:

```
GHCi> encoderDecoder "book"
"1\a\a\ETX"
GHCi> encoderDecoder "1\a\a\ETX"
"book"
```

With your one-time pad, you have a much better way to send encrypted messages than you started with using ROT13. The biggest constraints are that your pad is sufficiently random, and most important: you use it only one time!

15.5 A Cipher class

Now that you have two ciphers for encoding messages, it'd be a good idea to write a type class that captures the general behavior of encoding and decoding messages. This allows you to create a common interface for any new ciphers you may write, as well as making working with `rotEncode` and `applyOTP` easier. You'll create a type class `Cipher` that requires two methods: `encode` and `decode`.

Listing 15.25 A `Cipher` class to generalize your cipher operations

```
class Cipher a where
   encode :: a -> String -> String
   decode :: a -> String -> String
```

But what are the types for your ciphers? So far you don't have anything that looks like it would be a solid type, just some algorithms for transforming strings. You can start by making a simple type for your ROT13 cipher.

Listing 15.26 The `Rot` data type

```
data Rot = Rot
```

What good is a single type and data constructor? By using this simple type and implementing the `Cipher` class, you can specify ROTN encoding of your text by using the more generic `encode` and `decode` functions.

Listing 15.27 Making `Rot` an instance of `Cipher`

```
instance Cipher Rot where
   encode Rot text = rotEncoder text
   decode Rot text = rotDecoder text
```

To encode text using the ROT13 approach, you pass in the `Rot` data constructor and your text:

```
GHCi> encode Rot "Haskell"
"\557128\557153\557171\557163\557157\557164\557164"
GHCi> decode Rot "\557128\557153\557171\557163\557157\557164\557164"
"Haskell"
```

Next you need to make a type for your one-time pad. This is trickier because the one-time pad needs an extra argument. You can capture this extra argument in your definition of the type. You'll create a data type `OneTimePad`, which takes a `String`, which will serve as the pad.

Listing 15.28 The `OneTimePad` data type

```
data OneTimePad = OTP String
```

Then you make `OneTimePad` an instance of the `Cipher` class.

Listing 15.29 Making `OneTimePad` an instance of `Cipher`

```
instance Cipher OneTimePad where
   encode (OTP pad) text = applyOTP pad text
   decode (OTP pad) text = applyOTP pad text
```

You can test this if you create an instance of the `OneTimePad` data type. But what should you use for the pad? As long as it's longer than your plain text, you should be fine, but how can you get something long enough for any possible text you could input? You can solve this by using lazy evaluation to create an infinite list of all `Chars` cycling forever!

Listing 15.30 Using lazy evaluation to create a limitless pad

```
myOTP :: OneTimePad
myOTP = OTP (cycle [minBound .. maxBound])
```

Now you can encode and decode strings of any length:

```
GHCi> encode myOTP "Learn Haskell"
"Ldcqj%Nf{bog`"
GHCi> decode myOTP "Ldcqj%Nf{bog`"
"Learn Haskell"
GHCi> encode myOTP "this is a longer sentence, I hope it encodes"
"tikp$lu'i)fdbjk}0bw}`pxt}5:R<uqoE\SOHKW\EOT@HDGMOX"
GHCi> decode myOTP "tikp$lu'i)fdbjk}0bw}`pxt}5:R<uqoE\SOHKW\EOT@HDGMOX"
"this is a longer sentence, I hope it encodes"
```

With your `Cipher` class, you have a great interface for working with any sort of secret message system you can think up. But remember: never, ever, ever roll your own cryptography for practical use.

Summary

In this capstone, you

- Used some of the basic type classes, `Enum` and `Bounded`, to build your own generic `rotN` cipher.
- Learned how to use `XOR` in order to encrypt a stream of `Bools`.
- Used type synonyms to help you think of `[Bool]` as `Bits`. In the process of translating `Char` to `Bits`, and `Bits` to `Char`, you explored how different types work together and how to transform data in one type to another. You combined all this knowledge to create a powerful cryptographic tool, the one-time pad.
- Used a type class to create an interface for using different ciphers, and implemented the `Cipher` class for two types used to represent your different algorithms for encryption.

Extending the exercise

The problem with the one-time pad is the one-time pad itself. It has to be at least as long as the message you want to send, and you can use it only one time. The solution is to generate your own one-time pad from a "seed." How is this done? All you need is a pseudo-random number generator (PRNG). Given an initial seed value, a PRNG produces a random number. Then this next number can be used as the seed for the next number. By generating a stream of `Ints`, you can use `intToBits` to create all the necessary `xor` values you need. In this way, a PRNG can use a single number to transmit an effectively infinitely long one-time pad. Encrypting a message by using the output of a PRNG as the pad is called a *stream cipher*.

Here's the Haskell code for a simple PRNG. The specific algorithm is called a *linear congruential generator*.

Listing 15.31 A linear congruential PRNG

```
prng :: Int -> Int -> Int -> Int -> Int
prng a b maxNumber seed = (a*seed + b) `mod` maxNumber
```

The `a` and `b` parameters are initialization parameters that help determine the randomness, `maxNumber` determines the upper bound of the number that can be produced, and finally you have the seed. The following is an example of using partial application to create an example PRNG for numbers less than 100.

Listing 15.32 `examplePRNG`

```
examplePRNG :: Int -> Int
examplePRNG  = prng 1337 7 100
```

Here you're generating random numbers in GHCi:

```
GHCi> examplePRNG 12345
72
GHCi> examplePRNG 72
71
GHCi> examplePRNG 71
34
GHCi> examplePRNG 34
65
```

To explore this on your own, use the PRNG to create a `StreamCipher` type that can be an instance of the `Cipher` class. Remember: never use your own crypto in the real world! Assume that this should be used for passing notes only.

Programming in types

Types in Haskell constitute their own way of writing programs. Unit 1 introduced you to the general ideas of functional programming. If this was your first introduction to functional programming, you were likely presented with an entirely new way of thinking about writing code and solving problems. Haskell's type system is so powerful that it's best to approach it as a second programming language that works in conjunction with what you learned in unit 1.

But what does it mean to think about programming in types? When you look at the type signature of a function—say, `a -> b`—you can view this signature as a description of a transformation. Suppose you have a type signature `CoffeeBeans -> CoffeeGrounds`; what *function* could this possibly describe? Knowing no more than those two types, you could guess that this function is `grind`. What about `CoffeeGrounds -> Water -> Coffee`? Clearly, this is the `brew` function. Types in Haskell allow you to view programs as a series of transformations.

You can think of *transformations* as a more abstract level of thinking about functions. When solving problems in Haskell, you can approach them first as a sequence of abstract transformations. For example, say you have a large text document and you need to find all the numbers in that document and then add them all together. How are you going to solve this problem in Haskell? Let's start with knowing that a document can be represented as a `String`:

```
type Document = String
```

Then you need a function that will break your big `String` into pieces so you can search for numbers:

```
Document -> [String]
```

Next you need to search for numbers. This will take your list of `Strings` and a function to check whether a `String` is a number, and will return your numbers:

```
[String] -> (String -> Bool) -> [String]
```

Now you have your numbers, but they need to be converted from strings to numbers:

```
[String] -> [Integer]
```

Finally, you need to take a list of integers and transform it into a single integer:

```
[Integer] -> Integer
```

And you're finished! By thinking about the types of transformations that you're going to make, you've been able to design your overall program much the same way you design a single function.

Although this example has shown how types can allow you to design programs, you've only scratched the surface of what Haskell's type system has to offer. In this unit, you'll start exploring the more powerful features of types in Haskell. You'll combine types in ways not possible in other languages, see how types can take arguments of their own, and learn how the right types can eliminate entire classes of bugs from your code. The more Haskell you learn, the more you'll find yourself programming in types first and then using functions to hash out the details.

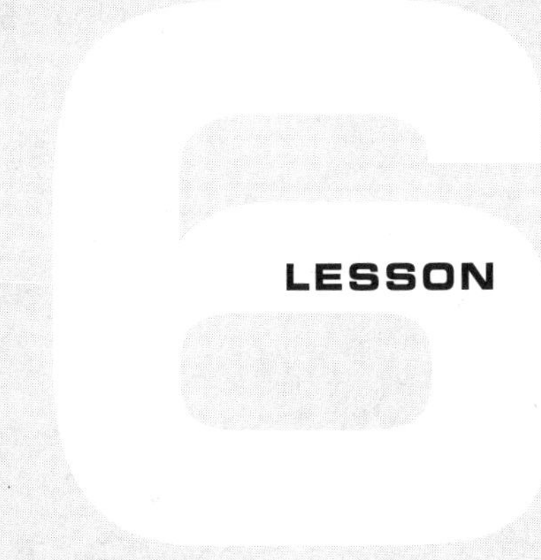

CREATING TYPES WITH "AND" AND "OR"

After reading lesson 16, you'll be able to

- Understand product types in various programming languages
- Use sum types to model problems in new ways
- Think beyond hierarchical program design

In this lesson, you'll take a closer look at some of the types we've already covered. You'll do this so you can learn more about what makes Haskell's types unique and how to design programs using types. Most of the types you've seen so far are algebraic data types. *Algebraic data types* are any types that can be made by combining other types. The key to understanding algebraic data types is knowing exactly how to combine other types. Thankfully, there are only two ways. You can combine multiple types with an *and* (for example, a name is a `String` *and* another `String`), or you can combine types with an *or* (for example, a `Bool` is a `True` data constructor *or* a `False` data constructor). Types that are made by combining other types with an *and* are called *product types*. Types combined using *or* are called *sum types*.

Consider this You're writing code to help manage the breakfast menu at a local diner. Breakfast specials are made up of selections of one or more sides, a meat choice, and the main meal. Here are the data types for these options:

```
data BreakfastSide = Toast | Biscuit | Homefries | Fruit deriving Show
data BreakfastMeat = Sausage | Bacon | Ham deriving Show
data BreakfastMain = Egg | Pancake | Waffle deriving Show
```

You want to create a `BreakfastSpecial` type representing specific combinations of these items that the customer can choose. Here are the options:

- Kids' breakfast—One main and one side
- Basic breakfast—One main, one meat, and one side
- The lumberjack!—Two mains, two meats, and three sides

How can you create a single type that allows for these, and only these, possible selections from your other breakfast types?

16.1 Product types—combining types with "and"

Product types are created by combining two or more existing types with *and*. Here are some common examples:

- A fraction can be defined as a numerator (`Integer`) *and* denominator (another `Integer`).
- A street address might be a number (`Int`) *and* a street name (`String`).
- A mailing address might be a street address *and* a city (`String`) *and* a state (`String`) *and* a zip code (`Int`).

Although the name *product type* might make this method of combining types sound sophisticated, this is the most common way in all programming languages to define types. Nearly all programming languages support product types. The simplest example is a struct from C. Here's an example in C of a struct for a book and an author.

Listing 16.1 C structs are product types—an example with a book and author

```
struct author_name {
 char *first_name;
```

```
  char *last_name;
};

struct book {
  author_name author;
  char *isbn;
  char *title;
  int  year_published;
  double price;
};
```

In this example, you can see that the `author_name` type is made by combining two `Strings` (for those unfamiliar, `char *` in C represents an array of characters). The `book` type is made by combining an `author_name`, two `Strings`, an `Int`, and a `Double`. Both `author_name` and `book` are made by combining other types with an *and*. C's structs are the predecessor to similar types in nearly every language, including classes and JSON. In Haskell, our book example would look like this.

Listing 16.2 C's `author_name` and `book` structs translated to Haskell

```
data AuthorName = AuthorName String String

data Book = Author String String Int
```

Preferably, you'd use record syntax (lesson 12) to write a version of `book` even more reminiscent of the C struct.

Listing 16.3 Using record syntax for `Book` to show the similarity to a C struct

```
data Book = Book {
     author  :: AuthorName
   , isbn    :: String
   , title   :: String
   , year    :: Int
   , price   :: Double}
```

`Book` and `AuthorName` are examples of product types and have an analog in nearly every modern programming language. What's fascinating is that in most programming languages, combining types with an *and* is the only way to make new types.

Quick check 16.1 Rewrite AuthorName by using record syntax.

16.1.1 The curse of product types: hierarchical design

Making new types only by combining existing types leads to an interesting model of designing software. Because of the restriction that you can expand an idea only by adding to it, you're constrained with top-down design, starting with the most abstract representation of a type you can imagine. This is the basis for designing software in terms of class hierarchies.

As an example, suppose you're writing Java and want to start modeling data for a bookstore. You start with the preceding Book example (assume that the Author class already exists).

Listing 16.4 A first pass at defining a Book class in Java

```
public class Book {
    Author author;
    String isbn;
    String title;
    int  yearPublished;
    double price;
}
```

This works great until you realize that you also want to sell vinyl records in the bookstore. Your default implementation of VinylRecord looks like this.

Listing 16.5 Expanding your selection by adding a Java class for VinylRecord

```
public class VinylRecord {
    String artist;
    String title;
    int  yearPublished;
    double price;
}
```

QC 16.1 answer

```
data AuthorName = AuthorName {
     firstName :: String
   , lastName  :: String
}
```

VinylRecord is similar to Book, but dissimilar enough that it causes trouble. For starters, you can't reuse your Author type, because not all artists have names; sometimes the artist is a band rather than an individual. You could use the Author type for *Elliott Smith* but not for *The Smiths*, for example. In traditional hierarchical design, there's no good answer to this issue regarding the Author and artist mismatch (in the next section, you'll see how to solve this in Haskell). Another problem is that vinyl records don't have an ISBN number.

The big problem is that you want a single type that represents both vinyl records and books so you can make a searchable inventory. Because you can compose types only by *and*, you need to develop an abstraction that describes everything that records and books have in common. You'll then implement only the differences in the separate classes. This is the fundamental idea behind *inheritance*. You'll next create the class StoreItem, which is a superclass of both VinylRecord and Book. Here's the refactored Java.

Listing 16.6 Creating a StoreItem superclass of Book and VinylRecord in Java

```
public class StoreItem {
    String title;
    int  yearPublished;
    double price;
}

public class Book extends StoreItem{
    Author author;
    String isbn;
}

public class VinylRecord extends StoreItem{
    String artist;
}
```

The solution works okay. You can now write all the rest of your code to work with StoreItems and then use conditional statements to handle Book and VinylRecord. But suppose you realize that you ordered a range of collectible toy figurines to sell as well. Here's the basic CollectibleToy class.

Listing 16.7 A CollectibleToy class in Java

```
public class CollectibleToy {
    String name;
```

```
    String description;
    double price;
}
```

To make everything work, you've completely refactored all of your code again! Now `StoreItem` can have only a `price` attribute, because it's the only value that all items share in common. The common attributes between `VinylRecord` and `Book` have to go back into those classes. Alternately, you could make a new class that inherits from `StoreItem` and is a superclass of `VinylRecord` and `Book`. What about `ColletibleToy`'s `name` attribute? Is that different from `title`? Maybe you should make an interface for all of your items instead! The point is that even in relatively simple cases, designing in strictly product types can quickly get complex.

In theory, creating object hierarchies is elegant and captures an abstraction about how everything in the world is interrelated. In practice, creating even trivial object hierarchies is riddled with design challenges. The root of all these challenges is that the only way to combine types in most languages is with an *and*. This forces you to start from extreme abstraction and move downward. Unfortunately, real life is full of strange edge cases that make this much more complicated than you'd typically want.

> **Quick check 16.2** Assume you have a `Car` type. How could you represent a `SportsCar` as a `Car` with a `Spoiler`? (Assume that you have a `Spoiler` type as well.)

16.2 Sum types—combining types with "or"

Sum types are a surprisingly powerful tool, given that they provide only the capability to combine two types with *or*. Here are examples of combining types with *or*:

- A die is either a 6-sided die or a 20-sided die or ....
- A paper is authored by either a person (`String`) or a group of people (`[String]`).
- A list is either an empty list (`[]`) or an item consed with another list (`a:[a]`).

The most straightforward sum type is `Bool`.

QC 16.2 answer

```
data SportsCar = SportsCar Car Spoiler
```

Listing 16.8 A common sum type: Bool

```
data Bool = False | True
```

An instance of `Bool` is either the `False` data constructor or the `True` data constructor. This can give the mistaken impression that sum types are just Haskell's way of creating enumerative types that exist in many other programming languages. But you've already seen a case in which sum types can be used for something more powerful, in lesson 12 when you defined two types of names.

Listing 16.9 Using a sum type to model names with and without middle names

```
type FirstName = String
type LastName = String
type MiddleName = String

data Name = Name FirstName LastName
   | NameWithMiddle FirstName MiddleName LastName
```

In this example, you can use two type constructors that can either be a `FirstName` consisting of two `Strings` *or* a `NameWithMiddle` consisting of three `Strings`. Here, using *or* between two types allows you to be expressive about what types mean. Adding *or* to the tools you can use to combine types opens up worlds of possibility in Haskell that aren't available in any other programming language without sum types. To see how powerful sum types can be, let's resolve some of the issues in the previous section.

An interesting place to start is the difference between author and artist. In our example, you need two types because you assume that the name of each book author can be represented as a first and last name, whereas an artist making records can be represented as a person's name or a band's name. Resolving this problem with product types alone is tricky. But with sum types, you can tackle this problem rather easily. You can start with a `Creator` type that's either an `Author` or an `Artist` (you'll define these next).

Listing 16.10 A Creator type that's either an Author or an Artist

```
data Creator = AuthorCreator Author | ArtistCreator Artist
```

You already have a `Name` type, so you can start by defining `Author` as a name.

Listing 16.11 Defining the Author type by using your existing Name type

```
data Author = Author Name
```

An artist is a bit trickier; as we already mentioned, `Artist` can be a person's name or a band's name. To solve this issue, you'll use another sum type!

Listing 16.12 An artist can be either a `Person` or a `Band`

```
data Artist = Person Name | Band String
```

This is a good solution, but what about some of those tricky edge cases that pop up in real life all the time? For example, what about authors such as H.P. Lovecraft? You could force yourself to use *Howard Phillips Lovecraft*, but why force yourself to be constrained by your data model? It should be flexible. You can easily fix this by adding another data constructor to `Name`.

Listing 16.13 Expanding your `Name` type to work with H.P. Lovecraft

```
data Name = Name FirstName LastName
    | NameWithMiddle FirstName MiddleName LastName
    | TwoInitialsWithLast Char Char LastName
```

Notice that `Artist`, `Author`, and as a result, `Creator` all depend on the definition of `Name`. But you had to change only the definition of `Name` itself and didn't need to worry at all about how any other types using `Name` are defined. At the same time, you still benefit from code reuse, as both `Artist` and `Author` types benefit from having `Name` defined in a single place. As an example of all of this, here's our H.P. Lovecraft `Creator` type.

Listing 16.14 Making a `Creator` type for H.P. Lovecraft

```
hpLovecraft :: Creator
hpLovecraft = AuthorCreator
                (Author
                  (TwoInitialsWithLast 'H' 'P' "Lovecraft"))
```

Although the data constructors in this example may be verbose, in practice you'd likely be using functions that would abstract out much of this. Now think of how this solution compares to one you could come up with using hierarchal design required by product types. From the hierarchical design standpoint, you'd need to have a `Name` superclass with only a last-name attribute (because this is the only property that all three types of name share). Then you'd need separate subclasses for each of the three data constructors you use. But even then, a name such as *Andrew W.K.*, with a last name as a `char`, would completely break that model. This is an easy fix with sum types.

Listing 16.15 Easily expanding Name to work with Andrew W.K.

```
data Name = Name FirstName LastName
    | NameWithMiddle FirstName MiddleName LastName
    | TwoInitialsWithLast Char Char LastName
    | FirstNameWithTwoInits FirstName Char Char
```

The only solution for the product-type-only view is to create a `Name` class with a growing list of fields that would be unused attributes:

```
public class Name {
    String firstName;
    String lastName;
    String middleName;
    char firstInitial;
    char middleInitial;
    char lastInitial;
}
```

This would require a lot of extra code to ensure that everything behaves correctly. Additionally, you have no guarantees about your `Name` being in a valid state. What if all these attributes had values? There's nothing a type checker in Java could do to ensure that a `Name` object met the constraints you've specified for names. In Haskell, you can know that only the explicit types you've defined can exist.

16.3 Putting together your bookstore

Now let's revisit our bookstore problem and see how thinking with sum types can help. With your powerful `Creator` type in hand, you can now rewrite `Book`.

Listing 16.16 The Book type using Creator

```
data Book = Book {
     author    :: Creator
   , isbn      :: String
   , bookTitle :: String
   , bookYear  :: Int
   , bookPrice :: Double
   }
```

You can also define your `VinylRecord` type.

Listing 16.17 The `VinylRecord` type

```
data VinylRecord = VinylRecord {
     artist        :: Creator
   , recordTitle   :: String
   , recordYear    :: Int
   , recordPrice   :: Double
   }
```

Why not just price?

The careful reader may notice that `Book` and `VinylRecord` have their own unique name for price. Why not make working with these types more consistent and use the name `price` rather than `bookPrice` and `recordPrice`? The issue here has nothing to do with the limitation of sum types but rather a limitation of Haskell's way of dealing with record syntax. You'll recall that without record syntax, you'd define your book type as follows:

```
data Book = Book Creator String String Int Double
```

Record syntax automates creating a function like this:

```
price :: Book -> Double
price (Book _ _ _ _ val) = val
```

The problem is that using the same name for a property of both a `Book` and a `VinylRecord` means defining conflicting functions!

This is incredibly annoying, and a failing of Haskell I have a hard time forgiving. We'll touch on workarounds later in the book. But if you think this is ridiculous, you're not alone.

Now you can trivially create a `StoreItem` type.

Listing 16.18 A `StoreItem` type is either a `Book` or a `VinylRecord`

```
data StoreItem = BookItem Book | RecordItem VinylRecord
```

But once again, we've forgotten about the `CollectibleToy`. Because of sum types, it's easy to add this data type and extend your `StoreItem` type to include it.

Listing 16.19 Adding a `CollectibleToy` type

```
data CollectibleToy = CollectibleToy {
     name :: String
   , descrption :: String
   , toyPrice :: Double
   }
```

Fixing `StoreItem` just means adding one more *or*.

Listing 16.20 Easily refactoring `StoreItem` to include `CollectibleToy`

```
data StoreItem = BookItem Book
  | RecordItem VinylRecord
  | ToyItem CollectibleToy
```

Finally, we'll demonstrate how to build functions that work on all of these types by writing a `price` function that gets the price of any item.

Listing 16.21 An example of using the `StoreItem` type with a `price` function

```
price :: StoreItem -> Double
price (BookItem book) = bookPrice book
price (RecordItem record) = recordPrice record
price (ToyItem toy) = toyPrice toy
```

Sum types allow you to be dramatically more expressive with your types while still providing convenient ways to create groups of similar types.

Quick check 16.3 Assume that `Creator` is an instance of `Show`. Write a `madeBy` function that has the type `StoreItem -> String` and does its best to determine who made the `StoreItem`.

QC 16.3 answer

```
madeBy :: StoreItem -> String
madeBy (BookItem book) = show (author book)
madeBy (RecordItem record) = show (artist record)
madeBy _ = "unknown"
```

Summary

In this lesson, our objective was to teach you about the two ways to create types from existing types. The first way is with product types. Product types work by combining types using *and*, bundling two or more types together to define a new type. Nearly every programming language supports product types, even if not by that name. The other way to combine types is with *or*. Sum types are much less common than product types. The problem with product types alone is that you're forced to think in hierarchical abstractions. Sum types are a powerful tool that allows you to be much more expressive in defining new types. Let's see if you got this.

Q16.1 To further complicate the items in your store, you eventually keep an inventory of free pamphlets. Pamphlets have a title, a description, and a contact field for the organization that provides the pamphlet. Create the `Pamphlet` type and add it to `StoreItem`. Additionally, modify the price so that it works with `Pamphlet`.

Q16.2 Create a `Shape` type that includes the following shapes: `Circle`, `Square`, and `Rectangle`. Then write a function to compute the perimeter of a `Shape` as well as its area.

17

LESSON

DESIGN BY COMPOSITION—SEMIGROUPS AND MONOIDS

After reading lesson 17, you'll be able to

- Create new functions with function composition
- Use `Semigroup` to mix colors
- Learn how to use guards in code
- Solve probability problems with `Monoid`

In the preceding lesson, you looked at how sum types allow you to think outside the typical hierarchical design patterns present in most programming languages. Another important way that Haskell diverges from traditional software design is with the idea of composability. *Composability* means that you create something new by combining two like things.

What does it mean to *combine* two things? Here are some examples: you can concatenate two lists and get a new list, you can combine two documents and get a new document, and you can mix two colors and get a new color. In many programming languages, each of these methods of combining types would have its own unique operator or function. In much the same way that nearly every programming language offers a standard way to convert a type to a string, Haskell offers a standard way to combine instances of the same type together.

Consider this So far, when you've combined multiple strings, you've used ++. This can get tedious for larger strings:

```
"this" ++ " " ++ "is" ++ " " ++ "a" ++ " " ++ "bit" ++ "much"
```

Is there a better way to solve this?

17.1 Intro to composability—combining functions

Before diving into combining types, let's look at something more fundamental: combining functions. A special higher-order function that's just a period (called *compose*) takes two functions as arguments. Using function composition is particularly helpful for combining functions on the fly in a readable way. Here are some examples of functions that can easily be expressed using function composition.

Listing 17.1 Examples of using function composition to create functions

```
myLast :: [a] -> a
myLast = head . reverse

myMin :: Ord a => [a] -> a
myMin = head . sort

myMax :: Ord a => [a] -> a
myMax = myLast . sort

myAll :: (a -> Bool) -> [a] -> Bool
myAll testFunc = (foldr (&&) True) . (map testFunc)
```

Using sort requires the Data.List module to be imported.

myAll tests that a property is true of all items in a list.

Quick check 17.1 Implement myAny by using function composition. myAny tests that a property is True for at least one value in the list.

QC 17.1 answer

```
myAny :: (a -> Bool) -> [a] -> Bool
myAny testFunc = (foldr (||) False) . (map testFunc)
```

Here's an example:

```
GHCi> myAny even [1,2,3]
True
```

In many cases where you'd use a lambda expression to create a quick function, function composition will be more efficient and easier to read.

17.2 Combining like types: Semigroups

To explore composability further, let's look at a remarkably simple type class called `Semigroup`. To do this, you need to import `Data.Semigroup` at the top of your file (Lesson17.hs for this lesson).

The `Semigroup` class has only one important method you need, the <> operator. You can think of <> as an operator for combining instances of the same type. You can trivially implement `Semigroup` for `Integer` by defining <> as +.

Listing 17.2 `Semigroup` for `Integer`

```
instance Semigroup Integer where
   (<>) x y = x + y
```

You use the "instance" keyword to make Integer an instance of the Semigroup type class.

You define the <> operator as simple addition.

This may seem all too trivial, but it's important to think about what this means. Here's the type signature for `(<>)`:

```
(<>) :: Semigroup a => a -> a -> a
```

This simple signature is the heart of the idea of composability; you can take two like things and combine them to get a new thing of the same type.

Quick check 17.2 Can you use `(/)` to make `Int` a `Semigroup`?

17.2.1 The Color Semigroup

Initially, it might seem like this concept would be useful only for mathematics, but we're all familiar with this idea from an early age. The most well-known example of this is

QC 17.2 answer No, because division doesn't always return an Int type, which violates the rule.

adding colors. As most children experience, we can combine basic colors to get a new color. For example:

- Blue and yellow make green.
- Red and yellow make orange.
- Blue and red make purple.

You can easily use types to represent this problem of mixing colors. First, you need a simple sum type of the colors.

Listing 17.3 Defining the `Color` type

```
data Color = Red |
   Yellow |
   Blue |
   Green |
   Purple |
   Orange |
   Brown deriving (Show,Eq)
```

Next you can implement `Semigroup` for your `Color` type.

Listing 17.4 Implementing `Semigroup` for `Color` v1

```
instance Semigroup Color where
   (<>) Red Blue = Purple
   (<>) Blue Red = Purple
   (<>) Yellow Blue = Green
   (<>) Blue Yellow = Green
   (<>) Yellow Red = Orange
   (<>) Red Yellow = Orange
   (<>) a b = if a == b
              then a
              else Brown
```

Now you can play with colors just as you did when you smeared your fingers in paint as a kid!

```
GHCi> Red <> Yellow
Orange
GHCi> Red <> Blue
```

```
Purple
GHCi> Green <> Purple
Brown
```

This works great, but you get an interesting problem when you add more than two colors. You want your color mixing to be associative. *Associative* means that the order in which you apply your <> operator doesn't matter. For numbers, this means that 1 + (2 + 3) = (1 + 2) + 3. As you can see, your colors clearly aren't associative:

```
GHCi> (Green <> Blue) <> Yellow
Brown
GHCi> Green <> (Blue <> Yellow)
Green
```

Not only does this rule about associativity make intuitive sense (mixing colors in any order should give you the same color), but this is formally required of the `Semigroup` type class. This can be one of the more confusing parts of the more advanced type classes we cover in this unit. Many of them have *type class laws* that require certain behavior. Unfortunately, the Haskell compiler can't enforce these. The best advice is to always carefully read the Hackage documentation (https://hackage.haskell.org/) whenever you implement a nontrivial type class on your own.

17.2.2 Making Color associative and using guards

You can fix this issue by making it so that if one color is used to make another, combining them yields the composite color. So purple plus red is still purple. You could approach this problem by listing out a large number of pattern-matching rules comparing each possibility. But this solution would be long. Instead, you'll use the Haskell feature called guards. *Guards* work much like pattern matching, but they allow you to do some computation on the arguments you're going to compare. Figure 17.1 shows an example of a function using guards.

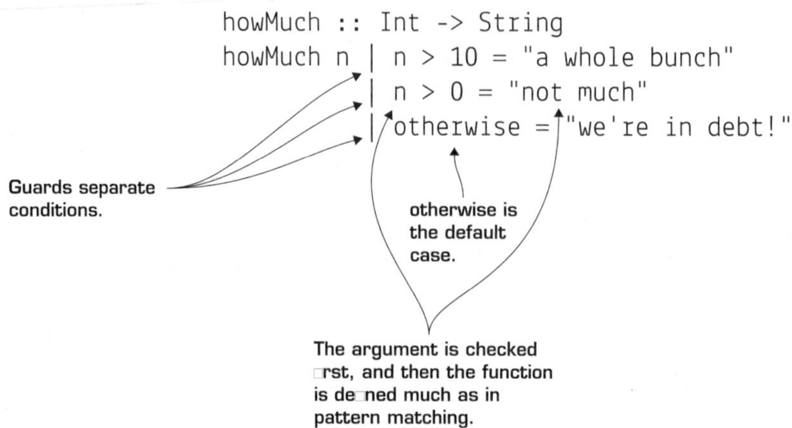

Figure 17.1 Using guards in howMuch

With an understanding of guards, you can rewrite your instance of `Semigroup` for `Color` so that you adhere to the type class laws for semigroups.

Listing 17.5 Reimplementing `Semigroup` for `Color` to support associativity

```
instance Semigroup Color where
   (<>) Red Blue = Purple
   (<>) Blue Red = Purple
   (<>) Yellow Blue = Green
   (<>) Blue Yellow = Green
   (<>) Yellow Red = Orange
   (<>) Red Yellow = Orange
   (<>) a b | a == b = a
            | all (`elem` [Red,Blue,Purple]) [a,b] = Purple
            | all (`elem` [Blue,Yellow,Green]) [a,b] = Green
            | all (`elem` [Red,Yellow,Orange]) [a,b] = Orange
            | otherwise = Brown
```

As you can see, now the problem is fixed:

```
GHCi> (Green <> Blue) <> Yellow
Green
GHCi> Green <> (Blue <> Yellow)
Green
```

Type class laws are important because any other code that uses an instance of a type class will assume that they're upheld.

Quick check 17.3 Does your implementation of `Semigroup` for `Integers` support associativity?

In the real world, there are many ways to make a new thing from two things of the same type. Imagine the following possibilities for composition:

- Combining two SQL queries to make a new SQL query
- Combining two snippets of HTML to make a new snippet of HTML
- Combining two shapes to make a new shape

17.3 Composing with identity: Monoids

Another type class that's similar to `Semigroup` is `Monoid`. The only major difference between `Semigroup` and `Monoid` is that `Monoid` requires an identity element for the type. An identity element means that `x <> id = x` (and `id <> x = x`). So for addition of integers, the identity element would be 0. But in its current state, your `Color` type doesn't have an identity element. Having an identity element might seem like a small detail, but it greatly increases the power of a type by allowing you to use a fold function to easily combine lists of the same type.

The `Monoid` type class is also interesting because it demonstrates an annoying problem in the evolution of Haskell type classes. Logically, you'd assume that the definition of `Monoid` would look like the following.

Listing 17.6 The rational definition of `Monoid`

```
class Semigroup a => Monoid a where
  identity :: a
```

QC 17.3 answer Yes, because addition of integers is associative: 1 + (2 + 3) = (1 + 2) + 3.

After all, Monoid should be a subclass of Semigroup because it's just Semigroup with identity. But Monoid predates Semigroup and isn't officially a subclass of Semigroup. Instead, the definition of Monoid is perplexing.

Listing 17.7 The actual definition of Monoid

```
class Monoid a where
  mempty :: a
  mappend :: a -> a -> a
  mconcat :: [a] -> a
```

Why mempty instead of identity? Why mappened instead of <>? These oddities in naming occur because the Monoid type class was added to Haskell before Semigroup. The most common Monoid is a list. The empty list is the identity for lists, and ++ (the append operator) is the <> operator for lists. The strange names of Monoid's methods are just m (for Monoid) tacked onto common list functions: empty, append, and concat. Here you can compare all three ways to do the same identity operation on a list:

```
GHCi [1,2,3] ++ []
[1,2,3]

GHCi [1,2,3] <> []
[1,2,3]

GHCi [1,2,3]  mappend  mempty
[1,2,3]
```

Notice that mappend has the exact same type signature as <>.

Quick check 17.4 If you implement mappend/<> for Integer as * instead of +, what will your mempty value be?

17.3.1 mconcat: Combining multiple Monoids at once

The easiest way to see how powerful identity is, is to explore the final method in the definition of Monoid: mconcat. The only required definitions in Monoid are mempty and mappend.

QC 17.4 answer

1, because x × 1 = x.

If you implement these two, you get `mconcat` for free. If you look at the type signature of `mconcat`, you get a good sense of what it does:

```
mconcat :: Monoid a => [a] -> a
```

The `mconcat` method takes a list of `Monoid`s and combines them, returning a single `Monoid`. The best way to understand `mconcat` is by taking a list of lists and seeing what happens when you apply `mconcat`. To make things easier, you'll use strings because those are just lists of `Char`s:

```
GHCi> mconcat ["does"," this"," make"," sense?"]
"does this make sense?"
```

The great thing about `mconcat` is that because you've defined `mempty` and `mappend`, Haskell can automatically infer `mconcat`! This is because the definition of `mconcat` relies only on `foldr` (lesson 9), `mappend`, and `mempty`. Here's the definition of `mconcat`:

```
mconcat = foldr mappend mempty
```

Any type class method can have a default implementation, provided the implementation needs only a general definition.

17.3.2 Monoid laws

Just like `Semigroup`, there are `Monoid` type class laws. There are four:

- The first is that `mappend mempty x` is `x`. Remembering that `mappend` is the same as `(++)`, and `mempty` is `[]` for lists, this intuitively means that
  ```
  [] ++ [1,2,3] = [1,2,3]
  ```
- The second is just the first with the order reversed: `mappend x mempty` is `x`. In list form this is
  ```
  [1,2,3] ++ [] = [1,2,3]
  ```
- The third is that `mappend x (mappend y z) = mappend (mappend x y) z`. This is just associativity, and again for lists this seems rather obvious:
  ```
  [1] ++ ([2] ++ [3]) = ([1] ++ [2]) ++ [3]
  ```
  Because this is a `Semigroup` law, then if `mappend` is already implemented as `<>`, this law can be assumed because it's required by the `Semigroup` laws.
- The fourth is just our definition of `mconcat`:
  ```
  mconcat = foldr mappend mempty
  ```

Note that the reason `mconcat` uses `foldr` instead of `foldl` is due to the way that `foldr` can work with infinite lists, whereas `foldl` will force the evaluation.

17.3.3 Practical Monoids—building probability tables

Now let's look at a more practical problem you can solve with monoids. You'd like to create probability tables for events and have an easy way to combine them. You'll start by looking at a simple table for a coin toss. You have only two events: getting heads or getting tails. Table 17.1 is your table.

Table 17.1 Probability of heads or tails

Event	Probability
Heads	0.5
Tails	0.5

You have a list of `String`s representing events and a list of `Double`s representing probabilities.

Listing 17.8 Type synonyms for `Events` and `Probs`

```
type Events = [String]
type Probs = [Double]
```

Your probability table is just a list of events paired with a list of probabilities.

Listing 17.9 `PTable` data type

```
data PTable = PTable Events Probs
```

Next you need a function to create a `PTable`. This function will be a basic constructor, but it'll also ensure that your probabilities sum to 1. This is easily achieved by dividing all the probabilities by the sum of the probabilities.

Listing 17.10 `createPTable` makes a `PTable` ensuring all probabilities sum to 1

```
createPTable :: Events -> Probs -> PTable
createPTable events probs = PTable events normalizedProbs
 where totalProbs = sum probs
       normalizedProbs = map (\x -> x/totalProbs) probs
```

You don't want to get too far without making `PTable` an instance of the `Show` type class. First you should make a simple function that prints a single row in your table.

Listing 17.11 `showPair` creates a `String` for a single event-probability pair

```
showPair :: String -> Double -> String
showPair event prob = mconcat [event,"|", show prob,"\n"]
```

Notice that you're able to use `mconcat` to easily combine this list of strings. Previously, you used the ++ operator to combine strings. It turns out that `mconcat` not only requires less typing, but also provides a preferable way to combine strings. This is because there are other text types in Haskell (discussed in unit 4) that support `mconcat`, but not ++.

To make `PTable` an instance of `Show`, all you have to do is use `zipWith` on your `showPair` function. This is the first time you've seen `zipWith`. This function works by zipping two lists together and applying a function to those lists. Here's an example adding two lists together:

```
GHCi> zipWith (+) [1,2,3] [4,5,6]
[5,7,9]
```

Now you can use `zipWith` to make your `PTable` an instance of `Show`.

Listing 17.12 Making `PTable` an instance of `Show`

```
instance Show PTable where
   show (PTable events probs) = mconcat pairs
     where pairs = zipWith showPair events probs
```

In GHCi, you can see that you have the basic setup you need:

```
GHCi> createPTable ["heads","tails"] [0.5,0.5]
heads|0.5
tails|0.5
```

What you want to be able to model using the `Monoid` type class is the combination of two (or more) `PTables`. For example, if you have two coins, you want an outcome like this:

```
heads-heads|0.25
heads-tails|0.25
tails-heads|0.25
tails-tails|0.25
```

This requires generating a combination of all events and all probabilities. This is called the *Cartesian product*. You'll start with a generic way to combine the Cartesian product of two lists with a function. The `cartCombine` function takes three arguments: a function for combining the two lists, and two lists.

Listing 17.13 The `cartCombine` function for the Cartesian product of lists

```
cartCombine :: (a -> b -> c) -> [a] -> [b] -> [c]
cartCombine func l1 l2 = zipWith func newL1 cycledL2
 where nToAdd = length l2
       repeatedL1 = map (take nToAdd . repeat) l1
       newL1 = mconcat repeatedL1
       cycledL2 = cycle l2
```

You need to repeat each element in the first list once for each element in the second.

Maps l1 and makes nToAdd copies of the element

The preceding line leaves you with a lists of lists, and you need to join them.

By cycling the second list, you can use zipWith to combine these two lists.

Then your functions for combining events and combining probabilities are specific cases of `cartCombine`.

Listing 17.14 `combineEvents` and `combineProbs`

```
combineEvents :: Events -> Events -> Events
combineEvents e1 e2 = cartCombine combiner e1 e2
 where combiner = (\x y -> mconcat [x,"-",y])

combineProbs :: Probs -> Probs -> Probs
combineProbs p1 p2 = cartCombine (*) p1 p2
```

When combining events, you hyphenate the event names.

To combine probabilities, you multiply them.

With your `combineEvent` and `combineProbs`, you can now make `PTable` an instance of `Semigroup`.

Listing 17.15 Making `PTable` an instance of `Semigroup`

```
instance Semigroup PTable where
   (<>) ptable1 (PTable [] []) = ptable1
   (<>) (PTable [] []) ptable2 = ptable2
   (<>) (PTable e1 p1) (PTable e2 p2) = createPTable newEvents newProbs
     where newEvents = combineEvents e1 e2
           newProbs = combineProbs p1 p2
```

You want to handle the special case of having an empty PTable.

Finally, you can implement the Monoid type class. For this class, you know that mappend and <> are the same. All you need to do is determine the identity, mempty element. In this case, it's PTable [] []. Here's your instance of Monoid for PTable.

Listing 17.16 Making PTable an instance of Monoid

```
instance Monoid PTable where
   mempty = PTable [] []
   mappend = (<>)
```

Don't forget: you gain the power of mconcat for free!

To see how all this works, let's see how to create two PTables. The first is a fair coin, and the other is a color spinner with different probabilities for each spinner.

Listing 17.17 Example PTables coin and spinner

```
coin :: PTable
coin = createPTable ["heads","tails"] [0.5,0.5]

spinner :: PTable
spinner = createPTable ["red","blue","green"] [0.1,0.2,0.7]
```

If you want to know the probability of getting tails on the coin and blue on the spinner, you can use your <> operator:

```
GHCi> coin <> spinner
heads-red|5.0e-2
heads-blue|0.1
heads-green|0.35
tails-red|5.0e-2
tails-blue|0.1
tails-green|0.35
```

For your output, you can see that there's a 0.1, or 10%, probability of flipping tails and spinning blue.

What about the probability of flipping heads three times in a row? You can use mconcat to make this easier:

```
GHCi> mconcat [coin,coin,coin]
heads-heads-heads|0.125
heads-heads-tails|0.125
```

```
heads-tails-heads|0.125
heads-tails-tails|0.125
tails-heads-heads|0.125
tails-heads-tails|0.125
tails-tails-heads|0.125
tails-tails-tails|0.125
```

In this case, each outcome has the same probability: 12.5%.

Initially, the idea of abstracting out "combining things" might seem a bit too abstract. Once you start seeing problems in terms of monoids, it's remarkable how frequently they appear every day. Monoids are a great demonstration of the power of thinking in types when writing code.

Summary

In this lesson, our objective was to introduce you to two interesting type classes in Haskell: `Semigroup` and `Monoid`. Though both classes have rather strange names, they provide a relatively simple role. `Monoid` and `Semigroup` allow you to combine two instances of a type into a new instance. This idea of abstraction through composition is an important one in Haskell. The only difference between `Monoid` and `Semigroup` is that `Monoid` requires you to specify an identity element. `Monoid` and `Semigroup` are also a great introduction to the abstract thinking typically involved in more-advanced type classes. Here you start to see the philosophical difference between type classes in Haskell and interfaces in most OOP languages. Let's see if you got this.

Q17.1 Your current implementation of `Color` doesn't contain an identity element. Modify the code in this unit so that `Color` does have an identity element, and then make `Color` an instance of `Monoid`.

Q17.2 If your `Events` and `Probs` types were data types and not just synonyms, you could make them instances of `Semigroup` and `Monoid`, where `combineEvents` and `combineProbs` were the `<>` operator in each case. Refactor these types and make instances of `Semigroup` and `Monoid`.

LESSON

PARAMETERIZED TYPES

After reading lesson 18, you'll be able to

- Use parameterized types to make generic data types
- Understand kinds of types
- Write code using the `Data.Map` type to look up values

In this unit so far, we've discussed how types can be added and multiplied, like data. Like functions, types can also take arguments. Types take arguments by using type variables in their definitions (so their arguments are always other types). Types defined using parameters are called *parameterized types*. Parameterized types perform an important role in Haskell, as they allow you to define generic data structures that work with a wide range of existing data.

Consider this Suppose you want to create a type representing a pair of two values of the same type. They could be a pair of `Double`s representing latitude and longitude, a pair of `Name`s representing a couple dating, or a pair of graph nodes representing an edge, for example. You don't want to use the existing `Tuple` type because you want to ensure that the elements in your pair are exactly the same type. How can you accomplish this?

18.1 Types that take arguments

If you're familiar with type generics in languages such as C# and Java, parameterized types will initially seem similar. Like generics in C# and Java, parameterized types allow you to create "containers" that can hold other types. For example, `List<String>` represents a `List` containing only strings, and `KeyValuePair<int, string>` represents a pair of values in which an `int` serves as a key to a `string`. Usually, you use generic types to constrain the types of values a `Container` type can take to make it easier to work with. In Haskell, the same is true.

The most basic parameterized type you could make is a `Box` that serves as a container for any other type. The `Box` type is the equivalent of your `simple` function, but for parameterized types (code from this lesson will go into a Lesson18.hs file). Figure 18.1 details the definition of `Box`.

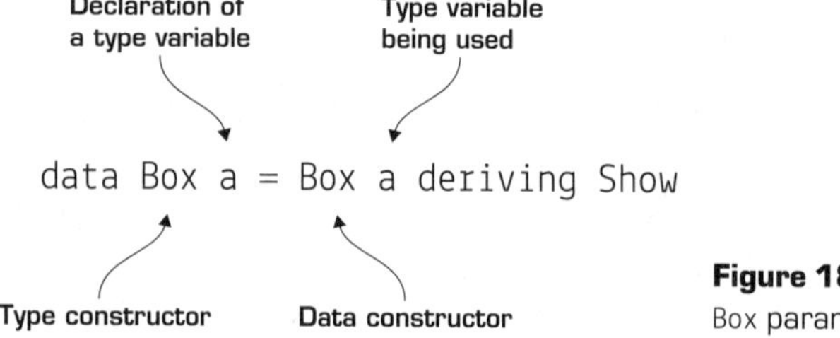

Figure 18.1 Definition of the Box parameterized type

The `Box` type is an abstract container that can hold any other type. As soon as you put a type inside `Box`, the `Box` type takes on a concrete value. You can use GHCi to explore some of these:

```
GHCi> n = 6 :: Int
GHCi> :t Box n
Box n :: Box Int
GHCi> word = "box"
GHCi> :t Box word
Box word :: Box [Char]
GHCi> f x = x
GHCi> :t Box f
Box f :: Box (t -> t)
GHCi> otherBox = Box n
GHCi> :t Box otherBox
Box otherBox :: Box (Box Int)
```

You can also make simple functions for your `Box`, such as `wrap` and `unwrap` to put items into or take them out of a box.

Listing 18.1 Defining the `wrap` and `unwrap` functions for `Box`

```
wrap :: a -> Box a
wrap x = Box x

unwrap :: Box a -> a
unwrap (Box x) = x
```

Notice that both of these functions don't know the concrete type of the box, but are still able to work with it.

Quick check 18.1 What's the type of `wrap (Box 'a')`?

18.1.1 A more useful parameterized type: Triple

Like the `simple` function, the `Box` type is a little too primitive to be of any use. A much more useful container is `Triple`, which we'll define as three values that are the same.

Listing 18.2 Defining the `Triple` type

```
data Triple a = Triple a a a deriving Show
```

It's worth noting that `Triple` *isn't* the same as a 3-tuple `(a,b,c)`. Tuples in Haskell can have different types as values. In this `Triple` type, all three values must be of the same type. There are many practical cases in which values have this property. For example, points in 3D space can be viewed as a `Triple` of type `Double`.

Listing 18.3 Defining a 3D point in space as a `Triple`

```
type Point3D = Triple Double

aPoint :: Point3D
aPoint = Triple 0.1 53.2 12.3
```

QC 18.1 answer

```
Box (Box Char)
```

People's names can be represented as a `Triple` of `Strings`.

Listing 18.4 Using a `Triple` to define a name data type

```
type FullName = Triple String

aPerson :: FullName
aPerson = Triple "Howard" "Phillips" "Lovecraft"
```

Likewise, initials are a `Triple` of `Char`.

Listing 18.5 Using a `Triple` to define `Initials`

```
type Initials = Triple Char

initials :: Initials
initials = Triple 'H' 'P' 'L'
```

Now that you have a model for homogenous `Triples`, you can write functions one time that work on all these cases. The first thing you can do is create a way to access each of the values in the `Triple`. It turns out that `fst` and `snd` are defined on only 2-tuples; in larger tuples, there's no way to access their values.

Listing 18.6 Assessors for the `Triple` type

```
first :: Triple a -> a
first (Triple x _ _) = x

second :: Triple a -> a
second (Triple _ x _ ) = x

third :: Triple a -> a
third (Triple _ _ x) = x
```

You can also easily turn your `Triple` into a list.

Listing 18.7 Defining a `toList` function on `Triple`

```
toList :: Triple a -> [a]
toList (Triple x y z) = [x,y,z]
```

Finally, you can make a simple tool to transform any `Triple` and keep it a `Triple` of the same type.

Listing 18.8 A function to transform Triples

```
transform :: (a -> a) -> Triple a -> Triple a
transform f (Triple x y z) = Triple (f x) (f y) (f z)
```

This type of transformation is useful for a variety of things. You can now move your third point in all directions by a constant value:

```
GHCi> transform (* 3) aPoint
Triple 0.30000000000000004 159.60000000000002 36.900000000000006
```

You can reverse all the letters in a person's name:

```
GHCi> transform reverse aPerson
Triple "drawoH" "spillihP" "tfarcevoL"
```

Or if you import `Data.Char`, you can make your initials lowercase:

```
GHCi> transform toLower initials
Triple 'h' 'p' 'l'
```

By combining this last transformation with `toList`, you can get a lowercase initial string:

```
GHCi> toList (transform toLower initials)
"hpl"
```

Quick check 18.2 What's the difference between `transform` and the `map` function for lists? (Hint: Look up the type signature of `map` again.)

18.1.2 Lists

The most common parameterized type is a `List`. The `List` type is interesting because it has a different constructor than most other types you've seen. As you know, you use brackets to construct a list and put values in them. This is for convenience but makes looking up information about lists more difficult than types that have a more typical

QC 18.2 answer The `transform` function doesn't allow you to change the type; that is, a function (`a -> b`). The `map` function for lists does allow this.

type constructor. In GHCi, you can get more info on the `List` type by using `:info []`. Figure 18.2 shows the formal definition of the `List` type.

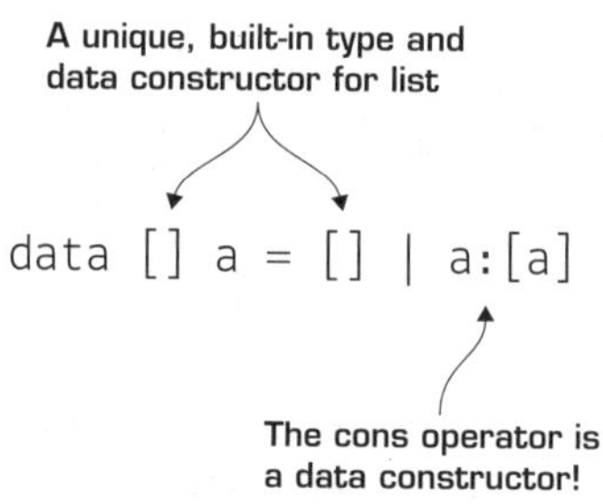
A unique, built-in type and data constructor for list
data [] a = [] | a:[a]
The cons operator is a data constructor!

Figure 18.2 The definition of a List

What's fascinating is that this is a complete and working implementation of a list! If you've ever written a linked list in another programming language, this should come as a surprise. To better understand this, you can reimplement a list on your own. The special usage of brackets around the type value is a built-in syntax for lists, one that you can't emulate. Likewise, you can't use the : cons data constructor either. For this definition, you'll use the terms `List`, `Cons`, and `Empty`. Here's the definition.

Listing 18.9 Defining your own list

```
data List a = Empty | Cons a (List a) deriving Show
```

Notice that the definition of `List` is recursive! In plain English, you can read this definition as follows: "A list of type `a` is either `Empty` or the consing of the value `a` with another list of type `a`." What may be hard to believe is that this type definition by itself is the complete definition of your `List` data structure! But here are lists that are identical.

Listing 18.10 Comparing your `List` to the built-in list

```
builtinEx1 :: [Int]
builtinEx1 = 1:2:3:[]

ourListEx1 :: List Int
ourListEx1 = Cons 1 (Cons 2 (Cons 3 Empty))

builtinEx2 :: [Char]
builtinEx2 = 'c':'a':'t':[]

ourListEx2 :: List Char
ourListEx2 = Cons 'c' (Cons 'a' (Cons 't' Empty))
```

As a final demonstration, you can implement `map` for your list.

Listing 18.11 Defining `ourMap` for your list

```
ourMap :: (a -> b) -> List a -> List b
ourMap _ Empty = Empty
ourMap func (Cons a rest)  = Cons (func a) (ourMap func rest)
```

And here's your code in GHCi:

```
GHCi> ourMap (*2) ourListEx1
Cons 2 (Cons 4 (Cons 6 Empty))
```

Now you know that next time you're in a job interview and you're asked to implement a linked list, your first question should be, "Can I do it in Haskell?"

18.2 Types with more than one parameter

Just like functions, types can also take more than one argument. The important thing to remember is that more than one type parameter means the type can be a container for more than one type. This is different from containing more than one value of the same type, as your `Triple` does.

18.2.1 Tuples

Tuples are the most ubiquitous multiparameter type in Haskell and the only multi-parameter type you've seen so far. Like lists, tuples use a built-in type constructor, `()`. If you want to use `:info` on a tuple, you have to use `()` with one comma inside for every n – 1 items in the tuple. For example, if you want the definition of a 2-tuple, you'd type `:info (,)` into GHCi. Here's the built-in definition.

Listing 18.12 Definition of a tuple

```
data (,) a b = (,) a b
```

Notice that the 2-tuple type definition includes two type variables. As we've mentioned before, this gives the tuple the useful capability to contain values of two types. In many dynamically typed languages such as Python, Ruby, and JavaScript, ordinary lists can contain multiple types. It's important to realize that Haskell's tuples aren't the same as lists in these other languages. The reason is that after you make your type, it takes on concrete values. This is best observed if you try to make lists of tuples. Suppose you have an inventory system that keeps track of items and their counts.

Listing 18.13 Exploring the types of tuples

```
itemCount1 :: (String,Int)
itemCount1 = ("Erasers",25)

itemCount2 :: (String,Int)
itemCount2 = ("Pencils",25)

itemCount3 :: (String,Int)
itemCount3 = ("Pens",13)
```

You can make a list of these items to keep track of your inventory.

Listing 18.14 Creating an item inventory

```
itemInventory :: [(String,Int)]
itemInventory = [itemCount1,itemCount2,itemCount3]
```

Notice that you specify the concrete type of your tuple: `(String,Int)`.

> **Quick check 18.3** What would happen if you tried to add `("Paper",12.4)` to your inventory?

18.2.2 Kinds: types of types

Another thing that Haskell's types have in common with functions and data is that they have their own types as well! The type of a type is called its *kind*. As you might expect, kinds are abstract. But they'll come up as you dive deeper into the more advanced types classes covered in unit 5 (`Functor`, `Applicative`, and `Monad`).

The *kind of a type* indicates the number of parameters the type takes, which are expressed using an asterisk (`*`). Types that take no parameters have a kind of `*`, types that take one parameter have the kind `* -> *`, types with two parameters have the kind `* -> * -> *`, and so forth.

QC 18.3 answer It would cause an error because the rest of your pairs are `(String,Int)`, and `("Paper",12.4)` would be a `(String,Double)`.

In GHCi, you use the `:kind` command to look up the kinds of any types you're unsure of (make sure to import Data.Map):

```
GHCi> :kind Int
Int :: *
GHCi> :kind Triple
Triple :: * -> *
GHCi> :kind []
[] :: * -> *
GHCi> :kind (,)
(,) :: * -> * -> *
GHCi> :kind Map.Map Map.Map :: * -> * -> *
```

It's worth pointing out that concrete types have a different kind than their nonconcrete equivalents:

```
GHCi> :kind [Int]
[Int] :: *
GHCi> :kind Triple Char
Triple Char :: *
```

Kinds may initially seem like abstract nonsense. But understanding kinds can be useful when trying to make instances of type classes such as `Functor` and `Monad` (which we cover in unit 5).

Quick check 18.4 What's the kind of `(,,)`?

18.2.3 Data.Map

Another useful parameterized type is Haskell's `Map` (not to be confused with the `map` function). To use `Map`, you first have to import `Data.Map`. Because the `Data.Map` module shares some functions with `Prelude`, you're going to do a qualified import. To perform a qualified import, add the details in figure 18.3 to the top of your file.

QC 18.4 answer

```
(a,b,c)
```

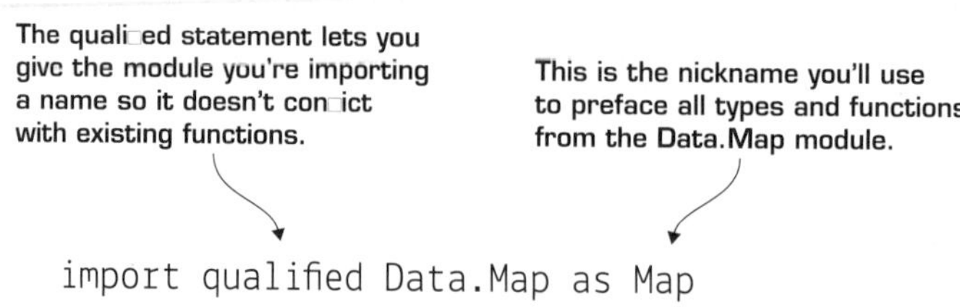
The quali ed statement lets you give the module you're importing a name so it doesn't con ict with existing functions.
This is the nickname you'll use to preface all types and functions from the Data.Map module.
import qualified Data.Map as Map

Figure 18.3 Using a qualified import

With your qualified import, every function and type from that module must be prefaced with `Map`. `Map` allows you to look up values by using keys. In many other languages, this data type is called `Dictionary`. The type parameters of `Map` are the types of the keys and values. Unlike `Lists` and `Tuples`, `Map`'s implementation is nontrivial. The best way to understand this type is through a concrete example.

Say you work at a mad scientist's laboratory and have a list of numbers that correspond to various organs used to create hideous monsters. You can start by making a quick sum type of relevant body parts.

Listing 18.15 The `Organ` data type

```
data Organ = Heart | Brain | Kidney | Spleen deriving (Show, Eq)
```

Suppose in your inventory you have the following organs. (Duplicates are okay; you can never have enough spleens!)

Listing 18.16 An example list of organs

```
organs :: [Organ]
organs = [Heart,Heart,Brain,Spleen,Spleen,Kidney]
```

Now each organ is placed in a numbered drawer so it can be retrieved at a later date. Each drawer has a number on it. Because the drawers are going to be used to look up items, each drawer number should be unique. Additionally, it's important that whatever ID you use, it must be of the class `Ord`. If the drawers have no order to them, it'll be difficult to look up your organ efficiently!

> **Maps and hash tables**
>
> Maps (or dictionaries) are similar to another data structure called a hash table. Both allow you to look up values with keys. The big difference between these two structures is the way the values are looked up. In a hash table, a function transforms your key into the index of an array where the value is stored. This allows for a fast lookup of items, but requires a large amount of memory to store in order to prevent collisions. A map looks up values by using a binary search tree. This is slower than a hash table but still fast. The map looks up values by searching the keys needed to have the property of being of class `Ord`, so you can compare two keys and efficiently find them in the tree.

Here's your list of IDs (not every drawer has an organ, so gaps exist).

Listing 18.17 A List of IDs to represent the locations of various organs

```
ids :: [Int]
ids = [2,7,13,14,21,24]
```

With the organs and the IDs, you have all the information you need to build a `Map`! This will serve as a catalog of your drawers so you can easily see which items are in which drawer.

The most common way to build a `Map` is with the `fromList` function. By using `:t` in GHCi, you can see that the type of `fromList` is as shown in figure 18.4.

Now you can see the type parameters for your map `Map`: `k` and `a`. What's interesting here is that your key type, `k`, must be of the class `Ord`. This restriction is due to the way keys are stored and looked up internally. The other thing to notice is that `fromList` expects a

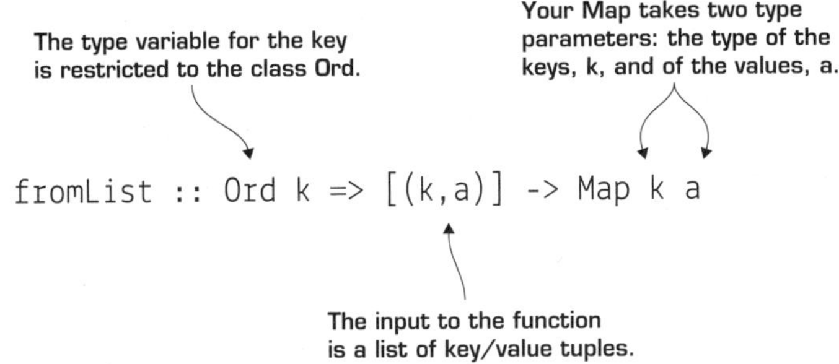
The type variable for the key is restricted to the class Ord.
Your Map takes two type parameters: the type of the keys, k, and of the values, a.
fromList :: Ord k => [(k,a)] -> Map k a
The input to the function is a list of key/value tuples.

Figure 18.4 The `fromList` function for building a `Map`

list of tuples, which represent pairs of keys and values. You could rewrite your two lists in the following way.

Listing 18.18 Pairs of organs and IDs v1

```
pairs = [(2,Heart),(7,Heart),(13,Brain) ...
```

But for sufficiently long lists, this would be a real pain! Instead, you can use the handy `zip` function from lesson 6. The `zip` function takes two lists and returns a list of pairs.

Listing 18.19 `organPairs` created using `zip`

```
organPairs :: [(Int,Organ)]
organPairs = zip ids organs
```

Now you have all the parts (get it!?) to put together your `organCatalog`.

Listing 18.20 Creating your `organCatalog`

```
organCatalog :: Map.Map Int Organ
organCatalog = Map.fromList organPairs
```

Finally, you can look up an item by using `Map.lookup`. When you do this in GHCi, you get an interesting result:

```
GHCi> Map.lookup 7 organCatalog
Just Heart
```

You get your `Heart` back as expected, but it's preceded by the data constructor `Just`. If you look at the type signature for `Map.lookup`, you get the answer.

Listing 18.21 The type signature for `Map.lookup`

```
Map.lookup :: Ord k => k -> Map.Map k a -> Maybe a
```

`Map.lookup` returns a new parameterized type: `Maybe`. `Maybe` is a simple but powerful type that's the subject of our next lesson!

Summary

In this lesson, our objective was to teach you about parameterized types. Parameterized types are types that take one or more arguments (like generics in most OOP languages). The most common instance of a parameterized type is `List`, which can contain elements of any type. Parameterized types can take any number of types as arguments. The number of types that a parameterized type takes as arguments defines its kind. `Map` is a parameterized type that takes two arguments: one for the type of its keys and another for the type of its values. Let's see if you got this.

Q18.1 For the types `Triple` and `Box`, implement a function similar to `map`, `tripleMap`, and `boxMap`.

Q18.2 Modify the `Organ` type so that it can be used as a key. Then build a `Map`, `organInventory`, of each organ to its count in the `organCatalog`.

LESSON

THE MAYBE TYPE: DEALING WITH MISSING VALUES

After reading lesson 19, you'll be able to

- Understand the `Maybe` type
- Use the `Maybe` type to handle missing values
- Design programs with `Maybe` types

Just as type classes can often be much more abstract than interfaces in OOP, parameterized types play a much larger role than generics do in most languages. This lesson introduces an important parameterized type: `Maybe`. Unlike `List` or `Map`, which represent containers for values, `Maybe` is the first of many types you'll see that represents a *context* for a value. `Maybe` types represent values that might be missing. In most languages, a missing value is represented by the `null` value. By using a context representing a value that might be missing, the `Maybe` type allows you to write much safer code. Because of the power of the `Maybe` type, errors related to `null` values are systematically removed from Haskell programs.

Consider this Suppose you have a simple Map that contains grocery items and indicates the number of them that you need to purchase:

```
groceries :: Map.Map String Int
groceries = Map.fromList [("Milk",1),("Candy bars",10),
➥("Cheese blocks",2)]
```

You accidentally look up MILK instead of Milk. What behavior should you expect from your Map, and how can you handle this type of mistake so that your programs can be sure to run safely even in the presence of missing values in your Map?

19.1 Introducing Maybe: solving missing values with types

At the end of lesson 18, you were working for a mad scientist organizing a collection of human organs. You used the Map type to store a list of organs for easy lookup. Let's continue exploring this exercise in a new file named Lesson19.hs. Here's the important code from the preceding lesson:

```
import qualified Data.Map as Map

data Organ = Heart | Brain | Kidney | Spleen deriving (Show, Eq)

organs :: [Organ]
organs = [Heart,Heart,Brain,Spleen,Spleen,Kidney]

ids :: [Int]
ids = [2,7,13,14,21,24]

organPairs :: [(Int,Organ)]
organPairs = zip ids organs

organCatalog :: Map.Map Int Organ
organCatalog = Map.fromList organPairs
```

Everything was going fine until you decided to use Map.lookup to look up an Organ in your Map. When doing this, you came across a strange new type, Maybe.

Maybe is a simple but powerful type. So far, all of our parameterized types have been viewed as containers. Maybe is different. Maybe is best understood as a type in a context. The context in this case is that the type contained might be missing. Here's its definition.

Listing 19.1 Definition of Maybe

```
data Maybe a = Nothing | Just a
```

Something of a Maybe type can be either Nothing, or Just something of type a. What in the world could this mean? Let's open up GHCi and see what happens:

```
GHCi> Map.lookup 13 organCatalog
Just Brain
```

When you look up an ID that's in the catalog, you get the data constructor Just and the value you expect for that ID. If you look up the type of this value, you get this:

```
Map.lookup 13 organCatalog :: Maybe Organ
```

In the definition of lookup, the return type is Maybe a. Now that you've used lookup, the return type is made concrete and the type is Maybe Organ. The Maybe Organ type means pretty much what it says: this data *might* be an instance of Organ. When would it not be? Let's see what happens when you ask for the value of an ID that you know has nothing in it:

```
GHCi> Map.lookup 6 organCatalog
Nothing
```

Quick check 19.1 What's the type of Nothing in the preceding example?

19.2 The problem with null

The organCatalog has no value at 6. In most programming languages, one of two things happens if you ask for a value that isn't in the dictionary. Either you get an error, or you get back a null value. Both of these responses have major issues.

QC 19.1 answer The type is Maybe Organ.

19.2.1 Handling missing values with errors

In the case of throwing an error, many languages don't require you to catch errors that might be thrown. If a program requests an ID not in the dictionary, the programmer must remember to catch the error, or the whole program could crash. Additionally, the error must be handled at the time the exception is thrown. This might not seem like a big issue, because it might be wise to always stop the error at its source. But suppose that you want to handle the case of a missing `Spleen` differently from a missing `Heart`. When the missing ID error is thrown, you might not have enough information to properly handle the different cases of having a missing value.

19.2.2 Returning null values

Returning `null` has arguably more problems. The biggest issue is that the programmer once again has to remember to check for null values whenever a value that can be null is going to be used. There's no way for the program to force the programmer to remember to check. Null values are also extremely prone to causing errors because they don't typically behave like the value your program is expecting. A simple call of `toString` can easily cause a null value to throw an error in a part of the program. If you're a Java or C# developer, the mere phrase *null pointer exception* should be argument enough that null values are tricky.

19.2.3 Using Maybe as a solution to missing values

`Maybe` solves all of these problems in a clever way. When a function returns a value of the `Maybe` type, the program can't use that value without dealing with the fact that the value is wrapped in a `Maybe`. Missing values can never cause an error in Haskell because `Maybe` makes it impossible to forget that a value might be null. At the same time, the programmer never has to worry about this until absolutely necessary. `Maybe` is used in all the typical places that `Null` values pop up, including these:

- Opening files that might not exist
- Reading from a database that could have null values
- Making a RESTful API request to a potentially missing resource

The best way to illustrate the magic of `Maybe` is with code. Let's say you're the assistant of the mad scientist. Periodically you need to do inventory to figure out what new body parts must be harvested. You can never remember which drawers have what in them, or even which have anything in them. The only way you can query all the drawers is to use every ID in the range of 1 to 50.

Listing 19.2 List of `possibleDrawers` in your `organCatalog`

```
possibleDrawers :: [Int]
possibleDrawers = [1 .. 50]
```

Next you need a function to get the contents of each drawer. The following maps this list of possible drawers with the `lookup` function.

Listing 19.3 Definition of `getDrawers`

```
getDrawerContents :: [Int] -> Map.Map Int Organ -> [Maybe Organ]
getDrawerContents ids catalog = map getContents ids
 where getContents = \id -> Map.lookup id catalog
```

With `getDrawerContents`, you're ready to search the catalog.

Listing 19.4 A list of `availableOrgans` that can contain missing values

```
availableOrgans :: [Maybe Organ]
availableOrgans = getDrawerContents possibleDrawers organCatalog
```

Had this been a programming language that threw exceptions on nulls, your program would already have blown up. Notice that your type is still a `List` of `Maybe Organ`. You've also avoided the issue with returning a special null value. No matter what you do with this list, until you deal explicitly with this possibility of missing values, you must keep this data a `Maybe` type.

The final thing that you need is to be able to get a count of a particular organ you're interested in. At this point, you do need to deal with the `Maybe`.

Listing 19.5 `countOrgan` function counts instances of an `Organ`

```
countOrgan :: Organ -> [Maybe Organ] -> Int
countOrgan organ available = length (filter
                                     (\x -> x == Just organ)
                                     available)
```

The interesting thing here is that you didn't even have to remove the organ from the `Maybe` context. `Maybe` implements `Eq`, so you can just compare two `Maybe Organs`. You not only didn't have to handle any errors, but because your computation never explicitly dealt with values that didn't exist, you also never had to worry about handling that case! Here's the final result in GHCi:

```
GHCi> countOrgan Brain availableOrgans
1
GHCi> countOrgan Heart availableOrgans
2
```

19.3 Computing with Maybe

It would be useful to be able to print your list of availableOrgans so you could at least see what you have. Both your Organ type and Maybe support Show so you can print it out in GHCi:

```
GHCi> show availableOrgans [Nothing,Just Heart,Nothing,Nothing,Nothing,
➥Nothing,Just Heart,Nothing,Nothing,Nothing...
```

Although you do get printing for free, this is ugly. The first thing you want to do is remove all the Nothing values. You can use filter and pattern matching to achieve this.

Listing 19.6 Definition of isSomething

```
isSomething :: Maybe Organ -> Bool
isSomething Nothing = False
isSomething (Just _) = True
```

And now you can filter your list to the organs that aren't missing.

Listing 19.7 Using isSomething with filter to clean [Maybe Organ]

```
justTheOrgans :: [Maybe Organ]
justTheOrgans = filter isSomething availableOrgans
```

In GHCi, you can see that you've made quite an improvement:

```
GHCi>justTheOrgans
[Just Heart,Just Heart,Just Brain,Just Spleen,Just Spleen,Just Kidney]
```

The problem is you still have these Just data constructors in front of everything. You can clean this up with pattern matching as well. You'll make the showOrgan function that will turn a Maybe Organ into a String. You'll add the Nothing pattern even though you won't need it because it's a good habit to always match all patterns just in case.

isJust and isNothing

The `Data.Maybe` module contains two functions, `isJust` and `isNothing`, that solve the general case of handling `Just` values. `isJust` is identical to the `isSomething` function but works on all `Maybe` types. With `Data.Maybe` imported, you could've solved this problem as follows:

```
justTheOrgans = filter isJust availableOrgans
```

Listing 19.8 Definition of showOrgan

```
showOrgan :: Maybe Organ -> String
showOrgan (Just organ) = show organ
showOrgan Nothing = ""
```

Here are a couple of examples in GHCi to get a feel for how this works:

```
GHCi> showOrgan (Just Heart)
"Heart"
GHCi> showOrgan Nothing
""
```

Now you can map your `showOrgan` function on `justTheOrgans`.

Listing 19.9 Using showOrgan with map

```
organList :: [String]
organList = map showOrgan justTheOrgans
```

As a final touch, you'll insert commas to make the list prettier. You can use the `intercalate` (a fancy word for *insert*) function in the `Data.List` module (so you'll need to add `import Data.List` to the top of your file):

```
cleanList :: String
cleanList = intercalate ", " organList
```

```
GHCi> cleanList
"Heart, Heart, Brain, Spleen, Spleen, Kidney"
```

Quick check 19.2 Write a function `numOrZero` that takes a `Maybe Int` and returns 0 if it's nothing, and otherwise returns the value.

19.4 Back to the lab! More-complex computation with Maybe

Suppose you need to do several things to a value in a `Maybe`. The mad scientist has a more interesting project. You'll be given a drawer ID. You need to retrieve an item from the drawer. Then you'll put the organ in the appropriate container (a vat, a cooler, or a bag). Finally, you'll put the container in the correct location. Here are the rules for containers and locations:

For containers:

- Brains go in a vat.
- Hearts go in a cooler.
- Spleens and kidneys go in a bag.

For locations:

- Vats and coolers go to the lab.
- Bags go to the kitchen.

You'll start by writing this out, assuming everything goes well and you don't have to worry about `Maybe` at all.

Listing 19.10 Defining key functions and data types for mad scientist request

```
data Container = Vat Organ | Cooler Organ | Bag Organ

instance Show Container where
   show (Vat organ) = show organ ++ " in a vat"
   show (Cooler organ) = show organ ++ " in a cooler"
   show (Bag organ) = show organ ++ " in a bag"
```

QC 19.2 answer

```
numOrZero :: Maybe Int -> Int
numOrZero Nothing = 0
numOrZero (Just n) = n
```

```
data Location = Lab | Kitchen | Bathroom deriving Show

organToContainer :: Organ -> Container
organToContainer Brain = Vat Brain
organToContainer Heart = Cooler Heart
organToContainer organ = Bag organ

placeInLocation :: Container -> (Location,Container)
placeInLocation (Vat a) = (Lab, Vat a)
placeInLocation (Cooler a) = (Lab, Cooler a)
placeInLocation (Bag a) = (Kitchen, Bag a)
```

A function, `process`, will handle taking an `Organ` and putting it in the proper container and location. Then a `report` function will take your container and location, and output a report for the mad scientist.

Listing 19.11 The core functions `process` and `report`

```
process :: Organ -> (Location, Container)
process organ =  placeInLocation (organToContainer organ)

report ::(Location,Container) -> String
report (location,container) = show container ++
                              " in the " ++
                              show location
```

These two functions are written *assuming that no organs are missing*. You can test how they work before you worry about working with the catalog:

```
GHCi> process Brain
(Lab,Brain in a vat)
GHCi> process Heart
(Lab,Heart in a cooler)
GHCi> process Spleen
(Kitchen,Spleen in a bag)
GHCi> process Kidney
(Kitchen,Kidney in a bag)
GHCi> report (process Brain)
"Brain in a vat in the Lab"
GHCi> report (process Spleen)
"Spleen in a bag in the Kitchen"
```

You still haven't handled getting your `Maybe Organ` out of the catalog. In Haskell, other types such as `Maybe` handle the many cases in software where things could go wrong. What you've done here with your `process` function is a common pattern in Haskell: you separate the parts of the code for which you need to worry about a problem (for example, missing values) from the ones that you don't. Unlike in most other languages, it's impossible for `Maybe` values to accidentally find their way into `process`. Imagine that you could write code that couldn't possibly have null values in it!

Now let's put this together so you can get data out of your catalog. What you want is something like the following function, except you still need to handle the case of `Maybe`.

Listing 19.12 Ideal definition of `processRequest` (won't compile)

```
processRequest :: Int -> Map.Map Int Organ -> String
processRequest id catalog = report (process organ)
 where organ = Map.lookup id catalog
```

The trouble is that your `organ` value is a `Maybe Organ` type and that `process` takes an `Organ`. To solve this given the tools you have now, you'll have to combine `report` and `process` into a function that handles the `Maybe Organ`.

Listing 19.13 `processAndReport` to handle the `Maybe Organ` data

```
processAndReport :: (Maybe Organ) -> String
processAndReport (Just organ) = report (process organ)
processAndReport  Nothing = "error, id not found"
```

You can now use this function to process the request.

Listing 19.14 `processRequest` with support for `Maybe Organ`

```
processRequest :: Int -> Map.Map Int Organ -> String
processRequest id catalog = processAndReport organ
 where organ = Map.lookup id catalog
```

This solution works out well, as you can see in GHCi the function handles both null and existing organs:

```
GHCi> processRequest 13 organCatalog
"Brain in a vat in the Lab"
GHCi> processRequest 12 organCatalog
"error, id not found"
```

There's one minor issue from a design perspective. Right now your `processRequest` function handles reporting when there's an error. Ideally, you'd like the `report` function to handle this. But to do that given your knowledge so far, you'd have to rewrite `process` to accept a `Maybe`. You'd be in a worse situation, because you'd no longer have the advantage of writing a processing function that you can guarantee doesn't have to worry about a missing value.

> **Quick check 19.3** How would you rewrite `report` so that it works with `Maybe (Location, Container)` and handles the case of the missing `Organ`?

Summary

In this lesson, our objective was to introduce you to one of Haskell's more interesting parameterized types: `Maybe`. The `Maybe` type allows you to model values that may be missing. `Maybe` achieves this by using two data constructors, `Just` and `Nothing`. Values represented by the `Nothing` data constructor are missing. Values represented by the `Just a` constructor can be safely accessed through pattern matching. `Maybe` is a great example of how powerful types make your code less erro- prone. Because of the `Maybe` type, the entire class of errors related to having null values is completely eliminated. Let's see if you got this.

Q19.1 Write a function `emptyDrawers` that takes the output of `getDrawerContents` and tells you the number of drawers that are empty.

Q19.2 Write a version of `map` that works for `Maybe` types, called `maybeMap`.

QC 19.3 answer

```
report :: Maybe (Location,Container) -> String
report Nothing = "container not found"
report (Just (location,container)) = show container ++
                                     " in the " ++
                                      show location
```

LESSON

CAPSTONE: TIME SERIES

This capstone covers

- Learning the basics of time-series analysis
- Combining multiple time series with `Monoid` and `Semigroup`
- Using `Map` to solve problems of duplicate values in a time series
- Avoiding errors involving missing values by using `Maybe`

In this capstone, you'll model time-series data by using tools you'll build in Haskell. Time-series data is, in theory, relatively simple: it's a series of values and dates for each piece of data. Figure 20.1 presents sales data from the Box & Jenkins data set that's commonly used to demonstrate a time series (the data used in this capstone is also a subset of the first 36 months of this same data).

Although conceptually easy to work with, in practice time-series data presents many interesting challenges. Often you're missing data, need to combine multiple incomplete data sets, and then need to perform analytics on this messy data, which often requires other transformations to make sense of. In this capstone, you'll use the techniques covered in this unit to make tools for working with time-series data. You'll explore how to combine multiple time series into one, take summary statistics (such as the average) of time-series data with missing values, and conclude by performing transformations on your data such as smoothing to eliminate noise.

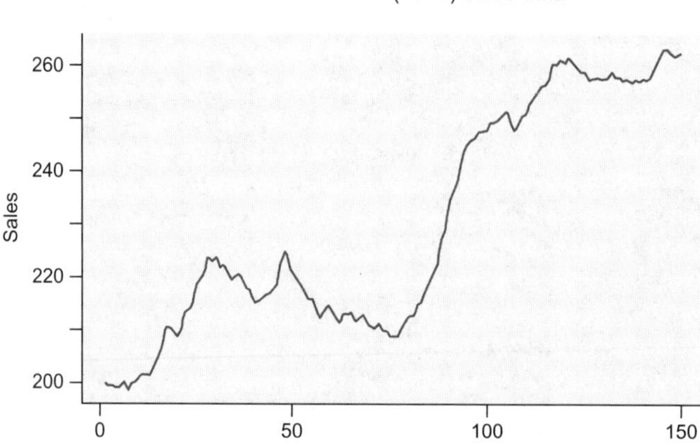

Figure 20.1 An example of time-series data for sales

All of the code for this section should live in a file named time_series.hs. The file should have the following imports at the top.

Listing 20.1 Imports for time_series.hs

```
import Data.List
import qualified Data.Map as Map
import Data.Semigroup
import Data.Maybe
```

With this file started, you're ready to begin!

20.1 Your data and the TS data type

Suppose you've started working at a new company and have been tasked with organizing its financial data. You have 36 months of (partial) financial data that you need to make sense of. The data is contained in four files, and no file has a complete set of data. Because we haven't covered working with files in Haskell yet, you'll assume that you've read in the data you have. You'll represent each file as lists of `(Int,Double)` tuples.

Listing 20.2 Your data

```
file1 :: [(Int,Double)]
file1 = [ (1, 200.1), (2,  199.5), (3, 199.4)
        , (4, 198.9), (5,  199.0), (6, 200.2)
        , (9, 200.3), (10, 201.2), (12, 202.9)]

file2 :: [(Int,Double)]
file2 = [(11, 201.6), (12, 201.5), (13, 201.5)
        ,(14, 203.5), (15, 204.9), (16, 207.1)
        ,(18, 210.5), (20, 208.8)]

file3 :: [(Int,Double)]
file3 = [(10, 201.2), (11, 201.6), (12, 201.5)
        ,(13, 201.5), (14, 203.5), (17, 210.5)
        ,(24, 215.1), (25, 218.7)]

file4 :: [(Int,Double)]
file4 = [(26, 219.8), (27, 220.5), (28, 223.8)
        ,(29, 222.8), (30, 223.8), (31, 221.7)
        ,(32, 222.3), (33, 220.8), (34, 219.4)
        ,(35, 220.1), (36, 220.6)]
```

When working with company data, it's common to find a similar pattern: you have your data split into multiple files, the data in the files is missing points, and there's overlap in the data as well. You want to be able to do the following:

- Stitch these files together easily
- Keep track of the missing data
- Perform analysis on the time series without having to worry about errors due to missing values

When stitching timelines together, you combine two timelines to make a new one. This is a familiar pattern that you saw when we discussed semigroups. You can solve the problem of stitching together individual time series by making your time series an instance of `Semigroup`. If you want to combine a list of time series elements, you'll also want to implement `Monoid` so you can use `mconcat`. For working with missing values, you can take advantage of your `Maybe` type. By using careful pattern matching on `Maybe` values, you can perform functions on your time-series data and handle the case of missing values.

20.1.1 Building a basic time-series type

First you need a basic type for your time series. To simplify things, consider that all of your dates are just Ints, which will be a relative index. Having 36 months, days, or milliseconds of data could be represented by the indices 1–36. For the values in the type series, you'll use a type parameter because you don't want to restrict the type of values you're going to allow in your time series. In this case, you want a type Double, but you could easily have a time series of Bools ("Did we meet the sales goal?") or a time series of Strings ("Who was the lead sales person?"). The type you use to represent the time series will be a parameterized type of kind * -> *, a parameterized type that takes only one argument. You also want to use a Maybe type for your values because having missing values is a common problem when working with any data. In data analytics, missing values are commonly referred to as having the value NA (for *not available*, as opposed to Null in software). Here's the definition of your TS type.

Listing 20.3 The definition of the TS data type

```
data TS a = TS [Int] [Maybe a]
```

Next you'll create a function that takes a list of times and a list of values and creates a TS type. As with the data in your files, you're assuming that the times might not be perfectly contiguous when you create a TS type. When you use createTS, you'll expand the timeline so that it's contiguous. Then you'll create a Map by using the existing times and values. You'll map over the completed list of times and look up the time in your Map. This will automatically create a Maybe a list of your values, where existing values will be Just a and NA values will be Nothing.

Listing 20.4 createTS to make an easier interface for creating TS types

You want to create your time series with a full timeline and a list of Maybe values; you assume the arguments may represent only a limited set of possible values.

The completeTimes are all the times from the minimum passed into the function up to the maximum.

```
createTS :: [Int] -> [a] -> TS a
createTS times values = TS completeTimes extendedValues
  where completeTimes = [minimum times .. maximum times]
        timeValueMap = Map.fromList (zip times values)
        extendedValues = map (\v -> Map.lookup v timeValueMap)
                             completeTimes
```

You'll create a simple Map of the times and values you know you have.

By mapping lookup over complete times, you'll get Just x values for all existing values and Nothing for all missing values. This takes care of filling in your complete set of values to match the complete timeline (even if some of those values are missing).

Your files aren't in quite the right format for your `createTS` function, so you'll make a helper function that will unzip the pairs.

Listing 20.5 `fileToTS` to easily convert your file data into TS types

```
fileToTS :: [(Int,a)] -> TS a
fileToTS tvPairs = createTS times values
   where (times, values) = unzip tvPairs
```

Before you go any further, it'd be nice to make a usable instance of `Show` for your `TS` object. First you'll create a function to show a time/value pair.

Listing 20.6 `showTVPair` to render time/value pairs readable

```
showTVPair :: Show a => Int -> (Maybe a) -> String
showTVPair time (Just value) = mconcat [show time,"|",show value,"\n"]
showTVPair time Nothing = mconcat [show time,"|NA\n"]
```

Now you can make an instance of `Show` by using `zipWith` and your `showTVPair` function.

Listing 20.7 Making `TS` an instance of `Show` by using `zipWith` and `showTVPair`

```
instance Show a => Show (TS a) where
   show (TS times values) = mconcat rows
     where rows = zipWith showTVPair times values
```

You can see your files as `TS` in GHCi:

```
GHCi> fileToTS file1
1|200.1
2|199.5
3|199.4
4|198.9
5|199.0
6|200.2
7|NA
8|NA
9|200.3
10|201.2
11|NA
12|202.9
```

Next you can convert all of your files to TS types.

Listing 20.8 Converting all your data files into TS types

```
ts1 :: TS Double
ts1 = fileToTS file1

ts2 :: TS Double
ts2 = fileToTS file2

ts3 :: TS Double
ts3 = fileToTS file3

ts4 :: TS Double
ts4 = fileToTS file4
```

Now you have all your file data converted to a basic TS type that you can also print to screen to make it easier to experiment with. Next you'll solve your first issue, which is using Semigroup and Monoid to simplify combining files.

20.2 Stitching together TS data with Semigroup and Monoid

With your basic time-series model done, you want to solve the problem of stitching together individual time series. Thinking about this problem in types, you want the following type signature:

```
TS a -> TS a -> TS a
```

You need a function that takes two TS types and returns just one. This type signature should remind you of a familiar pattern. If you look up the type of Semigroup's <> operator, you'll see that it's a generalization of the type signature you're looking for:

```
(<>) :: Semigroup a => a -> a -> a
```

This is a good sign that what you want to do is ultimately make TS an instance of Semigroup. Now you have to consider how you're going to combine two TS types.

Given that your TS type is basically two lists, it may be tempting to think you can append those two lists to make a new TS type. But you have two issues to solve that make this different from simply appending one list to another. The first is that data points aren't all bound by the range in an individual file; for example, file2 contains a value for date 11, but file1 includes a value for date 12. The other issue is that two time series might have conflicting values for a single date point. Files 1 and 2 both contain information on date 12, but they don't agree. You'll solve this problem by having the second file be the one that has priority.

You can use `Map` to solve both problems. You'll start by taking the time/value pairs in the first `TS` and use them to build them a `Map` of time/value pairs. You'll then insert the time/value pairs from the second `TS`. This will seamlessly combine the two sets of pairs and will handle the overwriting of duplicate values. Figure 20.2 shows how two time series would be combined.

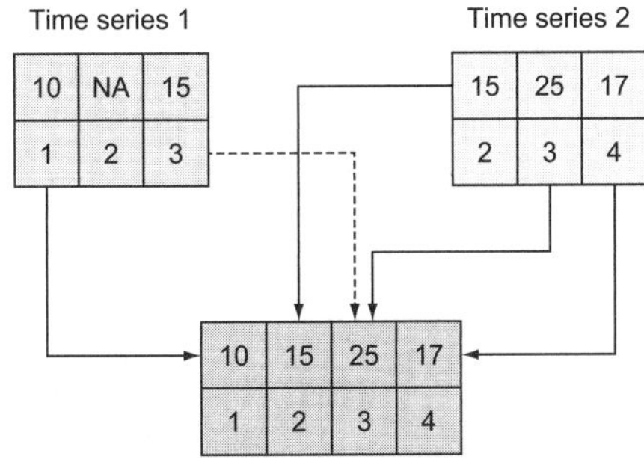

Figure 20.2 Combining two time series

The important thing to realize is that the `Map` to combine all the data from both time series will be of type `Map k v`, where `k` is the key type and `v` is the value type. But your values in the `TS` are `k` and `Maybe v`. You need one small helper function that will allow you to insert pairs of type `(k, Maybe v)` into a `Map` of type `k v`. The following is your `insertMaybePair` function.

Listing 20.9 `insertMaybePair`, a helper function for inserting `(k, Maybe v)` pairs

```
insertMaybePair :: Ord k => Map.Map k v -> (k, Maybe v) -> Map.Map k v
insertMaybePair myMap (_,Nothing) = myMap
insertMaybePair myMap (key,(Just value)) = Map.insert key value myMap
```

Because your map is of actual values, you can ignore the case when the Maybe value is missing by returning the original Map.

If you have an actual value, you grab it out of the Just context and insert it into your map.

With `insertMaybePair`, you have all the tools you need to combine two `TS` types into a new one. With this, you'll be able to seamlessly stitch together any two of your sets of data.

Listing 20.10 combineTS

```
combineTS :: TS a -> TS a -> TS a
combineTS (TS [] []) ts2 = ts2
combineTS ts1 (TS [] []) = ts1
combineTS (TS t1 v1) (TS t2 v2) = TS completeTimes combinedValues
   where bothTimes = mconcat [t1,t2]
         completeTimes = [minimum bothTimes .. maximum bothTimes]
         tvMap = foldl insertMaybePair Map.empty (zip t1 v1)
         updatedMap = foldl insertMaybePair tvMap (zip t2 v2)
         combinedValues = map (\v -> Map.lookup v updatedMap)
                              completeTimes
```

If one series is empty, return the nonempty one.

This indicates all the times in your two TS types. Duplicates may happen, but you use only the minimum and maximum values from the combined times.

You first insert all the values from ts1 into your Map. The zip function creates a list of time/value pairs, and you use foldl to insert them into the Map.

Finally, you create your list of Maybe values by looking up all the completed times.

Now you can make a complete timeline for both TS types.

Then you update that Map with the values from ts2. Inserting this way means duplicate values will automatically be overwritten by the values from ts2.

Here's how your `combineTS` function works: The first thing you need to do is solve the cases in which one (or both) of your `TS` types are empty. In this case, you return the non-empty one (or if both are empty, an empty one). If you have two nonempty `TS` types, you combine them by first combining all the times they cover. Using this, you can create a continuous timeline covering all the possible times. You then insert all of the existing values for the first `TS` type into a `Map` using `insertMaybePair` and folding over a list of value/time pairs created with `zip` and initializing the `foldl` function with an empty `Map`. After that, you insert the values of the second `TS` type the same way, only instead of using `foldl` with an empty `Map`, you use the `Map` created in the last step. By inserting the second after the first, you know that the second `TS` type will have the final say for any duplicates. Finally, you look up all the values in the `Map` from both `TS` types, which gives you a list of `Maybe` values just as in your `createTS` function.

And `combineTS` is all you need to implement a `Semigroup`! You could've put all of this logic directly into the definition of `(<>)`. Personally, I find it easier to debug a separate function.

To avoid duplication, it'd be better to paste the definition of `combineTS` as the definition of `(<>)`. But for this example, you'll define `(<>)` as `combineTS`.

Listing 20.11 Making TS an instance of Semigroup

```
instance Semigroup (TS a) where
   (<>) = combineTS
```

In GHCi, you can see that you can easily combine two time series now!

```
GHCi> ts1 <> ts2
1|200.1
2|199.5
3|199.4
4|198.9
5|199.0
6|200.2
7|NA
8|NA
9|200.3
10|201.2
11|201.6
12|201.5
13|201.5
14|203.5
15|204.9
16|207.1
17|NA
18|210.5
19|NA
20|208.8
```

With `TS` an instance of `Semigroup`, you can now combine time series, automatically filling missing values and overwriting the duplicate values.

20.2.1 Making TS an instance of Monoid

Being able to combine two or more `TS` types with `<>` is useful. But given that you have four unique files to combine, it'd be even nicer if you could combine a list of them.

Thinking in types again, you end up with this type signature to describe the behavior you want:

```
[TS a] -> TS a
```

Looking at this type signature should remind you of concatenating a list, which is done with the `mconcat` function. The type signature of `mconcat` generalizes this pattern:

```
mconcat :: Monoid a => [a] -> a
```

The only thing missing now is that your `TS` type isn't an instance of `Monoid`.

As always, after you have `Semigroup` implemented, all you need is to add the `mempty` (that is, the identity) element. Without an identity element, you can't automatically concatenate a list of `TS` types.

Listing 20.12 Making `TS` an instance of `Monoid`

```
instance Monoid (TS a) where
   mempty = TS [] []
   mappend = (<>)
```

Because you get `mconcat` for free with `Monoid`, you can easily combine lists of `TS`:

```
GHCi> mconcat [ts1,ts2]
1|200.1
2|199.5
3|199.4
4|198.9
5|199.0
6|200.2
7|NA
8|NA
9|200.3
10|201.2
11|201.6
12|201.5
13|201.5
14|203.5
15|204.9
16|207.1
17|NA
```

```
18|210.5
19|NA
20|208.8
```

Finally, you can stitch together all of your time series into a single time series that's as complete as possible from all of your files.

Listing 20.13 `tsAll` easily created using `mconcat`

```
tsAll :: TS Double
tsAll = mconcat [ts1,ts2,ts3,ts4]
```

Although it took a bit of work to get here, for all future time-series data you work with, you have a one-liner to safely combine separate files into a single `TS` type.

20.3 Performing calculations on your time series

Your time series data isn't helpful if you can't do basic analytics with it. The primary reason time series are used in analytics is to understand the general trends and changes over time to the value you're tracking. Even simple questions about a time series can be complicated because time-series data rarely represents a nice, neat straight line. To start analyzing your time-series data, you're going to look at simple summary statistics. A *summary statistic* is a small number of values that help summarize a more complex data set. The most common summary statistic for almost all data is the average. In this section, you'll look at calculating the average (mean) of your data, as well as finding when the highest and lowest values in your data happened and what they were.

The first thing you'll want to do is calculate the mean of the values in your time series. Your `meanTS` function will take a `TS` parameterized with a `Real` type and return the mean of the values in the `TS` as a `Double`. The `Real` type class allows you to use the `realToFrac` function to make it easier for you to divide types such as `Integer`. Your mean will have to return a `Maybe` type because in two instances there's no meaningful result: an empty time series and a time series in which all values are `Nothing`.

First you need a function to calculate the mean of a list.

Listing 20.14 `mean` to average a list of most number types

```
mean :: (Real a) => [a] -> Double
mean xs = total/count
```

```
  where total = (realToFrac . sum) xs
        count = (realToFrac . length) xs
```

Then you can move on to your `meanTS` function:

```
meanTS :: (Real a) => TS a -> Maybe Double
meanTS (TS _ []) = Nothing
meanTS (TS times values) = if all (== Nothing) values
                           then Nothing
                           else Just avg
   where justVals = filter isJust values
         cleanVals = map fromJust justVals
         avg = mean cleanVals
```

isJust requires the import of the Data.Maybe module, and tests whether a value "is Just."

fromJust, also in Data.Maybe, is the equivalent of (\(Just x) -> x).

In GHCi, you can inspect your mean sales over time:

```
GHCi> meanTS tsAll
Just 210.5966666666667
```

20.3.1 Calculating the min and max values for your time series

Knowing the minimum and maximum of your time series would also be useful. You don't want to know only the values that represent the min and max, but also the times they happened. Because `maxTS` and `minTS` are going to be nearly the same except for their comparators, you might as well make a generic `compareTS` function that takes a `(a -> a -> a)` function (a function like max that compares two values and returns the "winner"). Interestingly, your comparison type signature is exactly the same as your `Semigroup (<>)`. But type signatures aren't always enough to tell the entire story. Typically, you want to use `Semigroup` (and `Monoid`) to abstract away *combining* two types, rather than *comparing* them.

Again, you're stuck with the problem that you have a compare function of the type `(a -> a -> a)` but you're going to want to compare types `(Int, Maybe a)`. This is because you want to keep track of the value and the time the value happened. But all you care about is comparing the values. To make this easier, you'll write a `makeTSCompare` function that takes a comparing function `(a -> a -> a)` and transforms it into a function of type `((Int, Maybe a) -> (Int, Maybe a) -> (Int, Maybe a))`. You can transform any function such as `min` or `max` and it'll work with `(Int, Maybe a)` tuples!

Listing 20.15 `makeTSCompare` and useful type synonyms

```
type CompareFunc a = a -> a -> a
type TSCompareFunc a = (Int, Maybe a) -> (Int, Maybe a) -> (Int, Maybe a)

makeTSCompare :: Eq a => CompareFunc a -> TSCompareFunc a
makeTSCompare func = newFunc
 where newFunc (i1, Nothing) (i2, Nothing) = (i1, Nothing)
       newFunc (_, Nothing) (i, val) = (i,val)
       newFunc (i, val) (_, Nothing) = i,val)
       newFunc (i1,Just val1) (i2,Just  val2) =
                                      if func val1 val2 == val1
                                      then  (i1, Just val1)
                                      else  (i2, Just val2)
```

Here you're creating a newFunction to return.

Even though you're in a where, you can still do pattern matching.

These first three cases handle when one or both values are Nothing.

This last definition performs the behavior of the comparison function, only it returns the full tuple.

With `makeTSCompare`, you no longer have to think about using comparison functions such as `max` and `min`, or any other similar function. As an example, let's compare two time/value pairs in GHCi:

```
GHCi> makeTSCompare max (3,Just 200) (4,Just 10)
(3,Just 200)
```

Now you can build a generic `compareTS` function that lets you compare all values in a `TS` type.

Listing 20.16 `compareTS`, a generic means of applying comparison functions to `TS`

```
compareTS :: Eq a =>  (a -> a -> a) -> TS a -> Maybe (Int, Maybe a)
compareTS func (TS [] []) = Nothing
compareTS func (TS times values) = if all (== Nothing) values
                                   then Nothing
                                   else Just best
  where pairs = zip times values
        best = foldl (makeTSCompare func) (0, Nothing) pairs
```

`compareTS` allows you to trivially create other comparison functions for `TS`. Here are `max` and `min`.

Listing 20.17 Trivially creating `minTS` and `maxTS` using `compareTS`

```
minTS :: Ord a => TS a -> Maybe (Int, Maybe a)
minTS = compareTS min

maxTS :: Ord a => TS a -> Maybe (Int, Maybe a)
maxTS = compareTS max
```

Here are some examples in GHCi:

```
GHCi> minTS tsAll
Just (4,Just 198.9)
GHCi> maxTS ts1
Just (12,Just 202.9)
```

With a few basic summary statistics to work with, you can move on to more-advanced analysis of time-series data.

20.4 Transforming time series

Basic summary statistics can be helpful but are rarely enough to cover all the details you want to know about a time series. In the case of monthly sales data, you might want to make sure your company is growing. Because time-series data isn't a simple straight line, it can be surprisingly tricky to answer simple questions such as, "How fast are sales growing?" The most straightforward approach is to look not at the values of the time series itself, but at how the values change over time. Another problem is that time-series data is noisy. To reduce noise, you perform a task called *smoothing*, which attempts to remove noise from the data to make it easier to understand. Both of these tasks are a way of transforming your original data so that you can extract further insights from it.

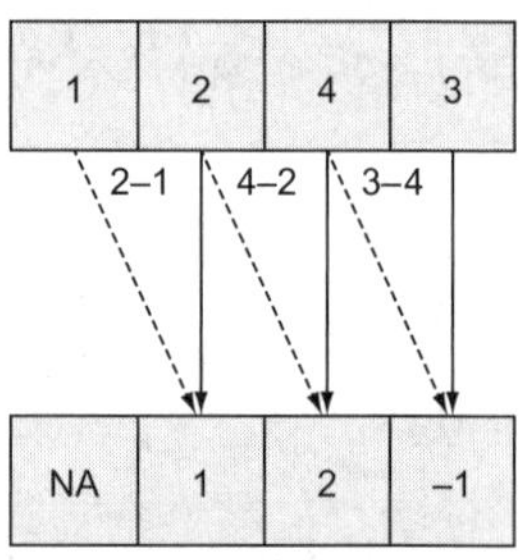

Figure 20.3 Visualizing the `diff` function

The first transformation you're going to look at is taking the `diff` of a `TS`. The `diff` indicates the change each day. Say, for example, you have the values shown in figure 20.3.

Notice that your list is one value shorter than before. This occurs because there's nothing to subtract from the first value. You'll have to make sure you add a `Nothing` value to the beginning of the resulting `TS` to reflect this. To enable you to see the effect that a `diff` transformation has on the time series, figure 20.4 shows the original sales data (from figure 20.1) with `diff` applied.

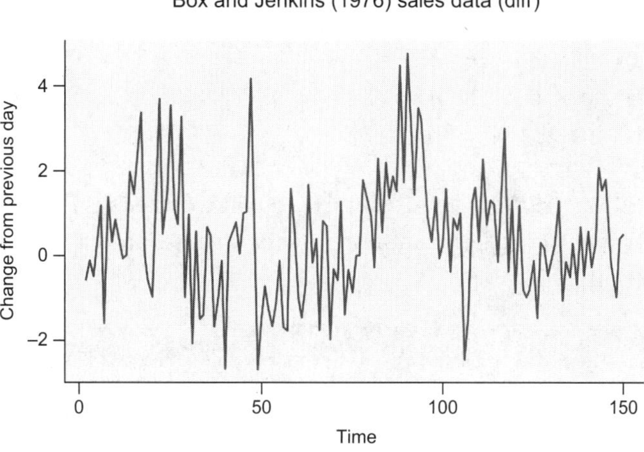

Figure 20.4 Sales time series with `diff` applied

In terms of types, the `diff` transformation can be cleanly expressed as follows:

```
TS a -> TS a
```

This isn't the perfect description of what you want your final result to be. Your `TS` type can take any parameter for the type of its values, but not all values can be subtracted from one another. Your transformation will be of any `Num` type because all `Num` types can be subtracted from each other:

```
Num a => TS a -> TS a
```

With your revised type signature, you're being more specific about exactly what type of transformation you're allowing.

You once again run into a problem: you're working with `Maybe` values when you want to perform an operation on the `Num a` type inside the `Maybe`. As you have before, you'll start with a `diffPair` function that takes two `Maybe a` values and subtracts them.

Listing 20.18 Type signature of diffPair

```
diffPair :: Num a => Maybe a -> Maybe a -> Maybe a
```

If either value is `Nothing`, you're going to return nothing; otherwise, you'll return the difference.

Listing 20.19 Definition of diffPair

```
diffPair Nothing _ = Nothing
diffPair _ Nothing = Nothing
diffPair (Just x) (Just y) = Just (x - y)
```

Now you can create `diffTS`. You can use `zipWith` to make this easy. The `zipWith` function works just like `zip`, but instead of combining the two values into a tuple, it combines them with a function.

Listing 20.20 diffTS to take the diff of a TS

```
diffTS :: Num a => TS a -> TS a
diffTS (TS [] []) = TS [] []
diffTS (TS times values) = TS times (Nothing:diffValues)
 where shiftValues = tail values
       diffValues = zipWith diffPair shiftValues values
```

With `diffTS`, you can see the mean change in your sales over time:

```
GHCi> meanTS (diffTS tsAll)
Just 0.6076923076923071
```

On average, your sales have grown about 0.6 each month. The great thing about this is that you can use these tools without worrying at all about missing values!

20.4.1 Moving average

Another important transformation of time-series data is smoothing. Many times data has noisy spikes, unexplainable drops, and other random noise that makes it harder to understand the data. Another issue is seasonality in the data. Suppose you have weekly data; do you expect sales to be as good on Sunday as on Tuesday? You don't want the seasonality of the data to affect how you understand it.

The best way to smooth is by taking a moving average. The *moving average* is similar to the diff, but rather than looking at just two numbers at a time, you're averaging over an entire window. A moving average takes a parameter *n* for the number of items it will smooth over. Here's an example of a moving average of 3 taken over these six numbers:

```
1,2,3,4,3,2
```

```
2.000000 3.000000 3.333333 3.000000
```

To visualize the effects of this smoothing, figure 20.5 shows the original time series (from figure 20.1) with a moving average of 12 applied.

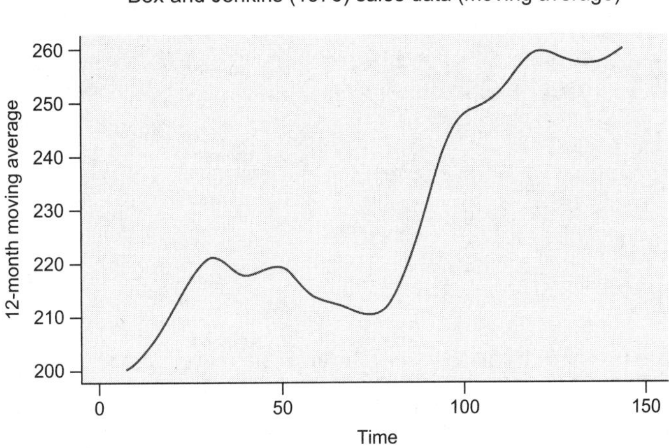

Figure 20.5 Sales time-series with a moving average of 12 applied

Notice that you end up missing *n*/2 values. For diff, you added a single `Nothing` at the beginning of your data, but for a moving average, you like to "center" the data, adding `NA` (or `Nothing`, in this case) values to both ends.

Your type signature of your `movingAverageTS` function is going to be more restrictive than your `diffTS` function. Because you know you'll be using your `mean` function to average numbers, you can look at its type signature to help figure out the final type signature for `movingAverageTS`:

```
mean :: (Real a) => [a] -> Double
```

Because `mean` will be doing most of the work for calculating your moving average, you know that your final type signature will involve transforming a `(Real a) => TS a` into one of type `TS Double`. You also need one more value for your type signature. You need to specify the number of values you want to smooth over. This means your final type signature should be as follows:

```
movingAverageTS :: (Real a) => TS a -> Int -> TS Double
```

With a better sense of your goal, you can start building out the functions that will get you there.

To make things easier to reason about, you'll abstract out just the part of the moving average function that has to work with a list of `[Maybe a]`, your values from the time series.

Listing 20.21 `meanMaybe`, which takes the mean of a list of `Maybe a` values

```
meanMaybe :: (Real a) => [Maybe a] -> Maybe Double
meanMaybe vals = if any (== Nothing) vals
                 then Nothing
                 else (Just avg)
  where avg = mean (map fromJust vals)
```

Now you can write the core logic to calculate your moving average.

Listing 20.22 `movingAvg` calculates the moving average of a `Maybe a` list

```
movingAvg :: (Real a) => [Maybe a] -> Int -> [Maybe Double]
movingAvg [] n = []
movingAvg vals n = if length nextVals == n
                   then meanMaybe nextVals:movingAvg restVals n
                   else []
   where nextVals = take n vals
         restVals = tail vals
```

With these two functions taking care of the work, the last thing you need to worry about is making sure your final `TS` is "centered." For this, you'll use integer division with `div` to give you a whole-number halfway point.

Listing 20.23 `maTS` for calculating the moving average of a `TS` with centering

```
movingAverageTS :: (Real a) => TS a -> Int -> TS Double
movingAverageTS (TS [] []) n= TS [] []
movingAverageTS (TS times values) n = TS times smoothedValues
 where ma = movingAvg values n
       nothings = replicate (n `div` 2) Nothing
       smoothedValues = mconcat [nothings,ma,nothings]
```

The replicate function creates a list of repeated values.

With `movingAverageTS`, you can smooth your `TS` data!

Summary

In this capstone, you

- Learned about common techniques you can apply to working with time-series data
- Created a `TS` type that handles the basics of a time series
- Used `Maybe` to model `NA` values in data
- Used the `Map` type to handle combining sets of values
- Combined `TS` types easily by using `Semigroup` and `Monoid` type classes
- Applied nontrivial computation in the context of a `Maybe`

Extending the exercise

If you'd like to continue this capstone on your own, there's no limit to the cool stuff you can do with a time series. Easy extensions to this project include the following:

- Use the median rather than the mean for smoothing.
- Create a function that calculates the `div` rather than the `diff` of data, capturing the percent change.
- Implement a function for calculating the standard deviation of a `TS` type.

If you still want more, the next most useful task is to add and subtract time series from each other. For each point in the timeline that two `TS` types have in common, you add or subtract the values as necessary.

IO in Haskell

So far in this book, you've seen many examples of the powerful things you can do with Haskell. A recurring theme of Haskell is that much of this power comes from simple things such as referential transparency and Haskell's type system. But there has been one glaring omission so far: I/O.

No matter what your program does, no matter what language it's written in, I/O is a hugely important part of software. It's the point where your code meets the real world. So why haven't you seen much Haskell involving I/O yet? The problem is that using I/O inherently requires you to change the world. Take, for example, getting user input from the command line. Each time you have a program that requests user input, you expect the result to be different. But in unit 1 we spent a great deal of time talking about how important it is that all functions take an argument, return a value, and always return the same value for the same argument. Another issue with I/O is that you're always changing the world, which means you're dealing with state. If you read a file and write to another, your programs would be useless if you didn't change the world somewhere along the way. But again, avoiding state is one of the key virtues of Haskell discussed in unit 1.

So how does Haskell solve this problem? As you might expect, Haskell does this by using types.

Haskell has a special parameterized type called `IO`. Any value in an `IO` context must stay in this context. This prevents code that's *pure* (meaning it upholds referential transparency and doesn't change state) and code that's necessarily impure from mixing.

To demonstrate this, you'll compare two similar mystery functions in both Java and Haskell. You'll start by taking a look at two nearly identical Java methods, called `mystery1` and `mystery2`.

Listing 1 Two Java methods with the same type signature, `mystery1` and `mystery2`

```
public class Example {

    public static int mystery1(int val1, int val2){
        int val3 = 3;
        return Math.pow(val1 + val2 + val3, 2);
    }

    public static int mystery2(int val1, int val2){
        int val3 = 3;
        System.out.print("Enter a number");
        try {
            Scanner in = new Scanner(System.in);
            val3 = in.nextInt();
        } catch (IOException e) {

            e.printStackTrace();
        }
        return Math.pow(val1 + val2 + val3,2);
    }
}
```

Here you have two static methods, `mystery1` and `mystery2`. Both do the same thing: they take in two values, add them with a mystery value, and square the result. What's most important is that these methods have identical type signatures in Java. But I don't think anyone would argue that these methods are remotely the same!

The `mystery1` method is predictable. Every time you enter two inputs, you'll get the exact same output. In Haskell terms, `mystery1` is a *pure function*. If you play around with this function enough, you'll eventually be able to figure out what it does.

The `mystery2` method, on the other hand, is a different method. Every time you call `mystery2`, many things can go wrong. Additionally, every time you call `mystery2`, you're likely to get a different answer. You may never be able to figure out what `mystery2` is doing. Now, in this example you could clearly tell the difference because `mystery2` will force a command prompt. But suppose `mystery2` just read from a random file on disk. You might never know what it was doing. The idea of mystery functions may seem contrived, but anytime you use legacy code or an external library, you're often dealing with mystery functions: you may easily understand them from their behavior, but have no way of knowing what they're doing.

Haskell solves this problem by forcing these two functions to be different types. Whenever a function uses `IO`, the results of that function are forever marked as coming from `IO`. Here are the two Java methods rewritten as Haskell functions.

Listing 2 `mystery1` and `mystery2` rewritten in Haskell

```
mystery1 :: Int -> Int -> Int
mystery1 val1 val2 = (val1 + val2 + val3)^2
 where val3 = 3

mystery2 :: Int -> Int -> IO Int
mystery2 val1 val2 = do
   putStrLn "Enter a number"
   val3Input <- getLine
   let val3 = read val3Input
   return ((val1 + val2 + val3)^2)
```

Why does this `IO` type make your code safer? `IO` makes it impossible to accidentally use values that have been tainted with I/O in other, pure functions. For example, addition is a pure function, so you can add the results of two calls to `mystery1`:

```
safeValue = (mystery1 2 4) + (mystery1 5 6)
```

But if you try to do the same thing, you'll get a compiler error:

```
unsafeValue = (mystery2 2 4) + (mystery2 2 4)
"No instance for (Num (IO Int)) arising from a use of '+'"
```

Although this certainly adds safety to your program, how in the world are you going to do things? In this unit, you'll focus on learning the Haskell tools that enable you to keep your pure code separated from I/O code and still make useful programs that interact with the real world. After this unit, you'll be able to use Haskell for a wide range of everyday, real-world programming problems that involve using I/O.

HELLO WORLD!—INTRODUCING IO TYPES

After reading lesson 21, you'll be able to

- Understand how Haskell handles I/O by using `IO` types
- Use do-notation to perform I/O
- Write pure programs that interact with the real world

In lesson 1, you saw a basic example of a Hello World program. In this lesson, you'll revisit a similar program to get a better sense of how I/O works in Haskell. Here's an example program using I/O that reads a name from the command line and prints out `"Hello <name>!"`.

Listing 21.1 A simple Hello World program

```
helloPerson :: String -> String
helloPerson name = "Hello" ++ " " ++ name ++ "!"

main :: IO ()
main = do
   putStrLn "Hello! What's your name?"
   name <- getLine
   let statement = helloPerson name
   putStrLn statement
```

Before you saw any Haskell, you likely could have read this program pretty well. Unfortunately, now that you know more about Haskell, this probably looks much more confusing! The `helloPerson` function should be straightforward, but everything starting with `main` is different from anything else you've seen so far. You should have the following questions:

- What in the world is the type `IO ()`?
- Why is there a `do` after `main`?
- Does `putStrLn` return a value?
- Why are some variables assigned with `<-` and others with `let`?

By the end of this lesson, you'll have a reasonable explanation of each of these things, and hopefully a much better understanding of the basics of `IO` in Haskell.

Quick check 21.1 Which line retrieves the user's input? What type do you assume that input is?

Consider this You can get a line of user input by using the `getLine` function. But each time `getLine` is called, it can clearly return a different result. How can this work, given one of the most important features of Haskell is always returning the same value for the same input?

21.1 IO types—dealing with an impure world

As is often the case with Haskell, if you're unsure of what's going on, it's best to look at the types! The first type you have to understand is the `IO` type. In the preceding unit, you ended by looking at the `Maybe` type. `Maybe` is a parameterized type (a type that takes another type as an argument) that represents a context when a value may be missing. `IO` in Haskell is a parameterized type that's similar to `Maybe`. The first thing they share in common is that they're parameterized types of the same kind. You can see this by looking at the kind of `IO` and of `Maybe`:

QC 21.1 answer The line using `getLine` receives the input. At this point, it's safe to assume that input is a `String` (at the end of the lesson, you'll know it's an `IO String`).

```
GHCi> :kind Maybe
Maybe :: * -> *
GHCi> :kind IO
IO :: * -> *
```

The other thing that `Maybe` and `IO` have in common is that (unlike `List` or `Map`) they describe a context for their parameters rather than a container. The context for the `IO` type is that the value has come from an input/output operation. Common examples of this include reading user input, printing to standard out, and reading a file.

With a `Maybe` type, you're creating a context for a single specific problem: sometimes a program's values might not be there. With `IO`, you're creating context for a wide range of issues that can happen with `IO`. Not only is `IO` prone to errors, but it's also inherently stateful (writing a file changes something) and also often impure (calling `getLine` many times could easily yield a different result each time if the user enters different input). Although these may be issues in I/O, they're also essential to the way I/O works. What good is a program that doesn't change the state of the world in some way? To keep Haskell code pure and predictable, you use the `IO` type to provide a context for data that may not behave the way all of the rest of your Haskell code does. `IO` actions aren't functions.

In your example code, you only see one `IO` type being declared, the type of your `main`:

```
main :: IO ()
```

At first `()` may seem like a special symbol, but in reality it's just a tuple of zero elements. In the past, we've found tuples representing pairs or triples to be useful, but how can a tuple of zero elements be useful? Here are some similar types with `Maybe` so you can see that `IO ()` is just `IO` parameterized with `()`, and can try to figure out why `()` might be useful:

```
GHCi> :type Just (1,2)
Just (1,2) :: (Num t, Num t1) => Maybe (t, t1)
GHCi> :type Just (1)
Just (1) :: Num a => Maybe a
GHCi> :type Just ()
Just () :: Maybe ()
```

For `Maybe`, being parameterized with `()` is useless. It can have only two values, `Just ()` and `Nothing`. But arguably, `Just ()` *is* `Nothing`. It turns out that representing nothing is exactly why you want to parameterize `IO` with an empty tuple.

You can understand this better by thinking about what happens when your `main` is run. Your last line of code is as follows:

```
putStrLn statement
```

As you know, this prints your statement. What type does `putStrLn` return? It has sent a message out into the world, but it's not clear that anything meaningful is going to come back. In a literal sense, `putStrLn` returns nothing at all. Because Haskell needs a type to associate with your `main`, but your `main` doesn't return anything, you use the `()` tuple to parameterize your `IO` type. Because `()` is essentially nothing, this is the best way to convey this concept to Haskell's type system.

Although you may have satisfied Haskell's type system, something else should be troubling you about your `main`. In the beginning of the book, we stressed three properties of functions that make functional programming so predictable and safe:

- All functions must take a value.
- All functions must return a value.
- Anytime the same argument is supplied, the same value must be returned (referential transparency).

Clearly, `main` doesn't return any meaningful value; it simply performs an *action*. It turns out that `main` *isn't* a function, because it breaks one of the fundamental rules of functions: it doesn't return a value. Because of this, we refer to `main` as an *IO action*. `IO` actions work much like functions except they violate at least one of the three rules we established for functions early in the book. Some IO actions return no value, some take no input, and others don't always return the same value given the same input.

21.1.1 Examples of IO actions

If `main` isn't a function, it should follow that neither is `putStrLn`. You can quickly clear this up by looking at `putStrLn`'s type:

```
putStrLn :: String -> IO ()
```

As you can see, the return type of `putStrLn` is `IO ()`. Like `main`, `putStrLn` is an IO action because it violates our rule that functions must return values.

The next confusing function should be `getLine`. Clearly, this works differently than any other function you've seen because it doesn't take an argument! Here's the type for `getLine`:

```
getLine :: IO String
```

Unlike `putStrLn`, which takes an argument and returns no value, `getLine` takes no value but returns a type `IO String`. This means `getLine` violates our rule that all functions must take an argument. Because `getLine` violates this rule of functions, it's also an IO action.

Now let's look at a more interesting case. If you import `System.Random`, you can use `randomRIO`, which takes a pair of values in a tuple that represents the minimum and maximum of a range and then generates a random number in that range. Here's a simple program called roll.hs that uses `randomRIO` and, when run, acts like rolling a die.

Listing 21.2 roll.hs program for simulating the roll of a die

```
import System.Random

minDie :: Int
minDie = 1

maxDie :: Int
maxDie = 6

main :: IO ()
main = do
  dieRoll <- randomRIO (minDie,maxDie)
  putStrLn (show dieRoll)
```

You can compile your program with GHC and "roll" your die:

```
$ ghc roll.hs
$ ./roll
2
```

What about `randomRIO`? It takes an argument (the min/max pair) and returns an argument (an `IO` type parameterized with the type of the pair), so is it a function? If you run your program more than once, you'll see the problem:

```
$ ./roll
4
$ ./roll
6
```

Each time you call `randomRIO`, you get a different result, even with the same argument. This violates the rule of referential transparency. So `randomRIO`, just like `getLine` and `putStrLn`, is an IO action.

Quick check 21.2 Is it okay if the last line in your `main` is `getLine`?

QC 21.2 answer No, because the type of `main` is `IO ()`, but the type of `getLine` is `IO String`

21.1.2 Keeping values in the context of IO

The interesting thing about `getLine` is that you have a useful return value of the type `IO String`. Just as a `Maybe String` means that you have a type that might be missing, `IO String` means that you have a type that comes from I/O. In lesson 19 we discussed the fact that a wide range of errors is caused by missing values that `Maybe` prevents from leaking into other code. Although null values cause a wide variety of errors, think of how many errors you've ever encountered caused by I/O!

Because I/O is so dangerous and unpredictable, after you have a value come from I/O, Haskell doesn't allow you to use that value outside of the context of the `IO` type. For example, if you fetch a random number using `randomRIO`, you can't use that value outside `main` or a similar `IO` action. You'll recall that with `Maybe` you could use pattern matching to take a value safely out of the context that it might be missing. This is because only one thing can go wrong with a `Maybe` type: the value is `Nothing`. With I/O, an endless variety of problems could occur. Because of this, after you're working with data in the context of `IO`, it must stay there. This initially may seem like a burden. After you're familiar with the way Haskell separates I/O logic from everything else, you'll likely want to replicate this in other programming languages (though you won't have a powerful type system to enforce it).

21.2 Do-notation

Not being able to escape the context of `IO` means that you need a convenient way to perform a sequence of computations within the context of `IO`. This is the purpose of the special `do` keyword. This *do-notation* allows you to treat `IO` types as if they were regular types. This also explains why some variables use `let` and others use `<-`. Variables assigned with `<-` allow you to act as though a type `IO a` is just of type `a`. You use `let` statements whenever you create variables that *aren't* `IO` types. Figure 21.1 shows the two lines in your `main` action that use `<-` and `let` so you can understand this better.

You know from earlier that `getLine` returns a type `IO String`. The type of `name` must be `IO String`. But you want to use `name` as an argument to `helloPerson`. Look at the type of `helloPerson` again:

```
helloPerson :: String -> String
```

You see that `helloPerson` works only with an ordinary `String`, not a type `IO String`. Do-notation allows you to assign an `IO String` variable by using `<-`, to act like it's an ordinary `String`, and then to pass it to functions that work with only regular `Strings`. Here's our

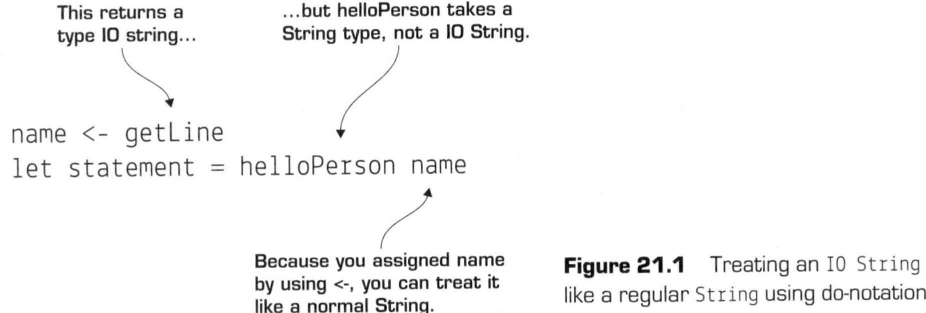
This returns a type IO string...
...but helloPerson takes a String type, not a IO String.
name <- getLine
let statement = helloPerson name
Because you assigned name by using <-, you can treat it like a normal String.

Figure 21.1 Treating an `IO String` like a regular `String` using do-notation

original program again, this time with annotations to highlight where you're using `IO` types and regular types.

Listing 21.3 Understanding do-notation in your Hello World program

```
helloPerson :: String -> String
helloPerson name = "Hello" ++ " " ++ name ++ "!"

main :: IO ()
main = do
   putStrLn "Hello! What's your name?"
   name <- getLine
   let statement = helloPerson name
   putStrLn statement
```

- getLine is an IO action and returns a type IO String.
- helloPerson is a function String -> String, but your IO String 'name' still works because of do-notation.
- putStrLn is an IO action that takes a normal String (not an IO String).

What makes this powerful is that you can blend functions that work with safe, non-`IO` values and use them seamlessly with data in an `IO` context.

> **Quick check 21.3** Could you simplify your code to combine `helloPerson` and `getLine` like this?
>
> ```
> let statement = helloPerson getLine
> ```

QC 21.3 answer No, because `getLine` is still of type `IO String`.

21.3 An example: command-line pizza cost calculator

To get a better sense of how do-notation works, let's try an extended example. You'll create a command-line tool that asks the user for the size and then the cost of two pizzas, and then tells the user which one is cheaper per square inch. Because you're using `IO` now, you can finally create a real, compiled program. You'll call this one pizza.hs. This program will ask you for the cost and size of two pizzas and tell you which one is the better deal in terms of cost per square inch. Here's what it'll look like to compile and run your program:

```
$ ghc pizza.hs
$ ./pizza
What is the size of pizza 1
12
What is the cost of pizza 1
15
What is the size of pizza 2
18
What is the cost of pizza 2
20
The 18.0 pizza is cheaper at 7.859503362562734e-2 per square inch
```

When designing programs that use I/O in Haskell, it's typical to write as much code as you can that doesn't use `IO` types. This makes reasoning about problems easier and allows you to easily test and experiment with pure functions. The more code you write that isn't in the `IO` context, the more code you know will never be vulnerable to I/O errors.

To get started, you'll need a function to calculate the cost of a pizza given its diameter. The first thing you need to do is calculate the area of a circle given its diameter. The area of a circle is equal to pi × radius^2, and the radius is half the diameter.

Listing 21.4 Calculating the area of a pizza given its diameter

```
areaGivenDiameter :: Double -> Double
areaGivenDiameter size = pi*(size/2)^2
```

You'll use size/cost pairs to more easily represent the pizza. You can use a type synonym for this.

Listing 21.5 `Pizza` type synonym

```
type Pizza = (Double,Double)
```

To calculate the cost per square inch, you divide the total cost by the area.

Listing 21.6 Calculating cost per inch

```
costPerInch :: Pizza -> Double
costPerInch (size, cost) = cost / areaGivenDiameter size
```

Next you'll compare two pizzas. The `comparePizzas` function will take two `Pizza` pairs and return the cheaper of the two.

Listing 21.7 Comparing two pizzas

```
comparePizzas :: Pizza -> Pizza -> Pizza
comparePizzas p1 p2 = if costP1 < costP2
                      then p1
                      else p2
   where costP1 = costPerInch p1
         costP2 = costPerInch p2
```

Finally, you want to print a statement to the user that indicates which pizza is cheaper and its price per square inch.

Listing 21.8 Describing a pizza

```
describePizza :: Pizza -> String
describePizza (size,cost) = "The " ++ show size ++ " pizza " ++
                            "is cheaper at " ++
                            show costSqInch ++
                            " per square inch"
   where costSqInch = costPerInch (size,cost)
```

Now all you have to do is tie this all together in a `main`. There's still one interesting problem to solve. `getLine` returns an `IO String`, but you need your values to be of type `Double`. To solve this, you can use `read`.

Listing 21.9 Putting all of your code together in `main`

```
main :: IO ()
main = do
   putStrLn "What is the size of pizza 1"
   size1 <- getLine
   putStrLn "What is the cost of pizza 1"
   cost1 <- getLine
   putStrLn "What is the size of pizza 2"
   size2 <-  getLine
   putStrLn "What is the cost of pizza 2"
   cost2 <- getLine
   let pizza1 = (read size1, read cost1)
   let pizza2 = (read size2, read cost2)
   let betterPizza = comparePizzas pizza1 pizza2
   putStrLn (describePizza betterPizza)
```

The key thing here is that you only worry about the parts of the program that must be done in the context of `IO`, which is mostly capturing and manipulating your input.

21.3.1 A peek at Monad—do-notation in Maybe

`IO` can use do-notation because it's a member of a powerful type class called `Monad`. We discuss `Monad` much more in unit 5. Do-notation has nothing to do with `IO` in particular and can be used by any member of `Monad` to perform computation in a context. The context for values in a `Maybe` is that they might not exist. The context for `IO` is that you're interacting with the real world and your data might not behave as it does in the rest of your Haskell program.

`Maybe` is also a member of the `Monad` type class and therefore can also use do-notation. Suppose that rather than getting your pizza values from user inputs, you had to retrieve these values from two `Maps`: one with sizes and one with costs. Here's a nearly identical program to the one you just wrote using `Maybe`. Rather than getting your info from a user, you'll look up the cost of a pizza by ID in a `costData Map`.

Listing 21.10 `costData Map` containing pizza cost info

```
costData :: Map.Map Int Double
costData = Map.fromList [(1,18.0),(2,16.0)]
```

Likewise, size is in another `Map`.

Listing 21.11 `sizeData` `Map` containing pizza size info

```
sizeData :: Map.Map Int Double
sizeData = Map.fromList [(1,20.0),(2,15.0)]
```

Now here's a `maybeMain` function that looks almost the same!

Listing 21.12 `maybeMain`: a version of your previous `main` using `Maybe` instead of `IO`

```
maybeMain :: Maybe String
maybeMain = do
   size1 <- Map.lookup 1 sizeData
   cost1 <- Map.lookup 1 costData
   size2 <- Map.lookup 2 sizeData
   cost2 <- Map.lookup 2 costData
   let pizza1 = (size1,cost1)
   let pizza2 = (size2,cost2)
   let betterPizza = comparePizzas pizza1 pizza2
   return  (describePizza betterPizza)
```

The only new thing you've added is the `return` function, which takes a value of a type and puts it back in the context of the do-notation. In this case, a `String` is returned as a `Maybe String`. You didn't need to do this in your `main` because `putStrLn` returns a type `IO ()`. In GHCi, you can see that this works out well:

```
GHCi> maybeMain
Just "The 20.0 pizza is cheaper at 5.729577951308232e-2 per square inch"
```

If you've heard of monads before and wondered what all the excitement is about, you may find this example underwhelming. But the `Monad` type class allows you to write general programs that can work in a wide range of contexts. Because of do-notation, you could write a different program, using all the same core functions as your original. In most other programming languages, you'd likely have to rewrite every function to translate it from one that used `IO` to one that worked with potentially null values in a dictionary. In unit 5, you'll dive much deeper into this topic. For now, it's perfectly okay to think of do-notation as a convenient way to perform IO actions in Haskell.

21.4 Summary

In this lesson, our object was to teach you how Haskell handles interacting with I/O. The trouble with I/O is that it requires all the features of functions that we removed earlier in the book. I/O often changes the state of the world, and likewise frequently causes values to return different results each time a function (or, more specifically, action) is called. Haskell handles this by ensuring that all I/O logic is contained in an `IO` type. Unlike the `Maybe` type, you can never remove values from an `IO` type after they're there. To make working with `IO` types easier, Haskell has a special do-notation that allows you to write code as though you weren't in the context of an `IO` type. Let's see if you got this.

Q21.1 Translate listing 21.1 (reproduced below) into code by using do-notation in a `Maybe`. Assume that all the user input is replaced with a `Map` with a value for the input. Ignore the first `putStrLn` and simply return the statement at the end.

```
helloPerson :: String -> String
helloPerson name = "Hello" ++ " " ++ name ++ "!"

main :: IO ()
main = do
   putStrLn "Hello! What's your name?"
   name <- getLine
   let statement = helloPerson name
   putStrLn statement
```

Q21.2 Create a program that asks the user to input a number and then returns the *n*th Fibonacci numbers (see lesson 8 for an example of computing Fibonacci numbers).

INTERACTING WITH THE COMMAND LINE AND LAZY I/O

After reading lesson 22, you'll be able to

- Access command-line arguments
- Use the traditional approach to interacting through I/O
- Write I/O code using lazy evaluation to make I/O easier

Often when people first learn about I/O and Haskell, they assume that I/O is somewhat of a challenge for Haskell because Haskell is all about pure programs and I/O is anything but pure. But there's another way to view I/O that makes it uniquely suited to Haskell, and somewhat clunky in other programming languages. Often when working with I/O in any language, we talk about *I/O streams*, but what is a stream? One good way to understand I/O streams is as a lazily evaluated list of characters. STDIN streams user input into a program until an eventual end is reached. But this end isn't always known (and in theory could never occur). This is exactly how to think about lists in Haskell when using lazy evaluation.

This view of I/O is used in nearly every programming language when reading from large files. Often it's impractical, or even impossible, to read a large file into memory before operating on it. But imagine that a given large file was simply some text assigned to a variable, and that variable was a lazy list. As you learned earlier, lazy evaluation allows you to operate on infinitely long lists. No matter how large your input is, you can handle it if you treat the problem like a large list.

In this lesson, you'll look at a simple problem and solve it in a few ways. All you want to do is create a program that reads in an arbitrarily long list of numbers entered by a user, and then adds them all up and returns the result to the user. Along the way, you'll learn both how to write traditional I/O and how to use lazy evaluation to come up with a much easier way to reason about the solution.

> **Consider this** You want to write a program that will let a user test whether words are palindromes. This is easy for a single word, but how can you let the user supply a continuous list of potential palindromes and keep checking as long as the user has words to check?

22.1 Interacting with the command line the nonlazy way

First let's design a command-line tool that reads a list of numbers entered by the user and adds them all up. You'll create a program called sum.hs. In the preceding lesson, you dealt with taking in user inputs and performing computations on them. The tricky thing this time is that you don't know how many items the user is going to enter in advance.

One way to solve this is to allow the user to enter a value as an argument to the program; for example:

```
$ ./sum 4
"enter your numbers"

 3
 5
 9
 25

"your total is 42"
```

To get arguments, you can use the `getArgs` function found in `System.Environment`. The type signature of `getArgs` is as follows:

```
getArgs :: IO [String]
```

So you get a list of `String`s in the context of `IO`. Here's an example of using `getArgs` in your `main`.

Listing 22.1 Getting command-line arguments by using `getArgs`

```
import System.Environment

main :: IO ()
main = do
 args <- getArgs
```

To get a feel for how `getArgs` works, it would be nice to print out all the `args` you have. Because you know that `args` is a list, you could use `map` to iterate over each value. But you have a problem, because you're working in the context of a `do` statement with an `IO` type. What you want is something like this.

Listing 22.2 Proposed solution to print your `args` (note: won't compile)

```
map putStrLn args
```

But `args` isn't an ordinary list, and `putStrLn` isn't an ordinary function. You can map over a list of values in `IO` with a special version of `map` that operates on `Lists` in the context of `IO` (technically, on any member of the `Monad` type class). For that, there's a special helper function called `mapM` (the `M` stands for *Monad*).

Listing 22.3 Next improvement: using `mapM` (still won't compile)

```
main :: IO ()
main = do
 args <- getArgs
 mapM putStrLn args
```

Now when you compile your program, you still end up getting an error:

```
Couldn't match type '[()]' with '()'
```

GHC is complaining because the type of `main` is supposed to be `IO ()`, but you'll recall that `map` always returns a list. The trouble is that you just want to iterate over `args` and perform an `IO` action. You don't care about the results, and don't want a list back at the end. To solve this, there's another function called `mapM_` (note the underscore). This works just like `mapM` but throws away the results. Typically, when a function ends with an underscore in Haskell, it indicates that you're throwing away the results. With this small refactor, you're ready to go:

```
main :: IO ()
main = do
 args <- getArgs
 mapM_ putStrLn args
```

You can try a few commands and see what you get:

```
$ ./sum
$ ./sum 2
2
$ ./sum 2 3 4 5
2
3
4
5
```

> **Quick check 22.1** Write a main that uses mapM to call getLine three times, and then use mapM_ to print out the values' input. (Hint: You'll need to throw away an argument when using mapM with getLine; use (_ -> ...) to achieve this.)

Now you can add the logic to capture your argument. You should also cover the case of a user failing to enter an argument. You'll treat that as 0 lines. Also note that you're using the print function for the first time. The print function is (putStrLn . show) and makes printing any type of value easier.

Listing 22.4 Using a command-line argument to determine how many lines to read

```
main :: IO ()
main = do
 args <- getArgs
 let linesToRead = if length args > 0
                   then read (head args)
                   else 0 :: Int
 print linesToRead
```

QC 22.1 answer

```
exampleMain :: IO ()
exampleMain = do
   vals <- mapM (\_ -> getLine) [1..3]
   mapM_ putStrLn vals
```

Now that you know how many lines you need, you need to repeatedly call `getLine`. Haskell has another useful function for iterating in this way called `replicateM`. The `replicateM` function takes a value for the number of times you want to repeat and an `IO` action and repeats the action as expected. You need to import `Control.Monad` to do this.

Listing 22.5 Reading a number of lines equal to the user's argument

```
import Control.Monad

main :: IO ()
main = do
 args <- getArgs
 let linesToRead = if length args > 0
                   then read (head args)
                   else 0
 numbers <- replicateM linesToRead getLine
 print "sum goes here"
```

Okay, you're almost there! Remember that `getLine` returns a `String` in the `IO` context. Before you can take the sum of all these arguments, you need to convert them to `Ints`, and then you can return the sum of this list.

Listing 22.6 The full content of your sum.hs program

```
import System.Environment
import Control.Monad

main :: IO ()
main = do
 args <- getArgs
 let linesToRead = if length args > 0
                   then read (head args)
                   else 0 :: Int
 numbers <- replicateM linesToRead getLine
 let ints = map read numbers :: [Int]
 print (sum ints)
```

That was a bit of work, but now you have a tool that lets users enter as many `ints` as they want, and you can add them up for them:

```
$ ./sum 2
4
59

$ ./sum 4
1
2
3
410
```

Even in this simple program, you've covered a number of the tools used to handle user inputs. Table 22.1 covers some useful functions for iterating in an `IO` type.

Table 22.1 Functions for iterating in an IO context

Function	Behavior
`mapM`	Takes an `IO` action and a regular list, performing the action on each item in the list, and returning a list in the `IO` context
`mapM_`	Same as `mapM`, but it throws away the values (note the underscore)
`replicateM`	Takes an `IO` action, an `Int` n, and then repeats the `IO` action n times, returning the results in an `IO` list
`replicateM_`	Same as `replicateM`, but it throws away the results

Next you'll look at how much easier this would be if you used lazy evaluation.

Quick check 22.2 Write your own version of `replicateM`, `myReplicateM`, that uses `mapM`. (Don't worry too much about the type signature.)

22.2 Interacting with lazy I/O

Your last program worked but had a few issues. First is that you require the user to input the specific number of lines needed. The user of your sum program needs to know this ahead of time. What if users are keeping a running tally of visitors to a museum, or

QC 22.2 answer

```
myReplicateM :: Monad m => Int -> m a -> m [a]
myReplicateM n func = mapM (\_ -> func) [1 .. n]
```

piping in the output of another program to yours? Recall that the primary purpose of having an `IO` type is to separate functions that absolutely must work in I/O with more general ones. Ideally, you want as much of your program logic outside your `main`. In this program, all your logic is wrapped up in `IO`, which indicates that you're not doing a good job of abstracting out your overall program. This is partially because so much I/O behavior is intermingled with what your program is supposed to be doing.

The root cause of this issue is that you're treating your I/O data as a sequence of values that you have to deal with immediately. An alternative is to think of the stream of data coming from the user in the same way you would any other list in Haskell. Rather than think of each piece of data as a discrete user interaction, you can treat the entire interaction as a list of characters coming from the user. If you treat your input as a list of `Chars`, it's much easier to design your program and forget all about the messy parts of I/O. To do this, you need just one special action: `getContents`. The `getContents` action lets you treat the I/O stream for STDIN as a list of characters.

You can use `getContents` with `mapM_` to see how strangely this can act. You'll be working with a new file named sum_lazy.hs for this section.

Listing 22.7 A simple `main` to explore lazy I/O

```
main :: IO ()
main = do
  userInput <- getContents
  mapM_ print userInput
```

The `getContents` action reads input until it gets an end-of-file signal. For a normal text file, this is the end of the file, but for user input you have to manually enter it (usually via Ctrl-D in most terminals). Before running this program, it's worth thinking about what's going to happen, given lazy evaluation. In a strict (nonlazy) language, you'd assume that you have to wait until you manually enter Ctrl-D before your input would be printed back to use. Let's see what happens in Haskell:

```
$ ./sum_lazy
hi
'h'
'i'
'\n'
what?
'w'
```

```
'h'
'a'
't'
'?'
'\n'
```

As you can see, because Haskell can handle lazy lists, it's able to process your text as soon as you enter it! This means you can handle continuous interaction in interesting ways.

> **Quick check 22.3** Use lazy I/O to write a program that reverses your input and prints it back to you.

22.2.1 Thinking of your problem as a lazy list

With getContents, you can rewrite your program, this time completely ignoring IO until later. All you need to do now is take a list of characters consisting of numbers and newline characters \n. Here's a sample list.

Listing 22.8 Sample data representing a string of input characters

```
sampleData = ['6','2','\n','2','1','\n']
```

If you can write a function that converts this into a list of Ints, you'll be all set! There's a useful function for Strings that you can use to make this easy. The lines function allows you to split a string by lines. Here's an example in GHCi with your sample data:

```
GHCi> lines sampleData
["62","21"]
```

The Data.List.Split module contains a more generic function than lines, splitOn, which splits a String based on another String. Data.List.Split isn't part of base Haskell, but is

QC 22.3 answer

```
reverser :: IO ()
reverser = do
   input <- getContents
   let reversed = reverse input
   putStrLn reversed
```

included in the Haskell Platform. If you aren't using the Haskell Platform, you may need to install it. The `splitOn` function is a useful one to know when processing text. Here's how lines could be written with `splitOn`.

Listing 22.9 Defining `myLines` with `splitOn` from `Data.List.Split`

```
myLines = splitOn "\n"
```

With lines, all you need is to map the `read` function over your new lists and you'll get your list of `Ints`. You'll create a `toInts` function to do this.

Listing 22.10 `toInts` function to convert your `Char` list into a list of `Ints`

```
toInts :: String -> [Int]
toInts = map read . lines
```

Making this function work with `IO` is remarkably easy. You apply it to your `userInput` you captured with `getContents`.

Listing 22.11 Your lazy solution to processing your numbers

```
main :: IO ()
main = do
  userInput <- getContents
  let numbers = toInts userInput
  print (sum numbers)
```

As you can see, your final `main` is much cleaner than your first version. Now you can compile your program and test it out:

```
$ ./sum_lazy
4
234
23
1
3
<ctrl-d>
265
```

This is much nicer than before, as your code is cleaner and users don't have to worry about how many numbers are in the list when they start. In this lesson, you've seen how to structure your program to work in a way similar to most other programming languages. You request data from the user, process that data, and then request more input from the user. In this model, you're performing *strict* I/O, meaning that you evaluate each piece of data as you get it. In many cases, if you treat the user input as a regular lazy list of `Chars`, you can abstract out nearly all of your non-I/O code much more easily. In the end, you have only one point where you need to treat your list as I/O: when you first receive it. This allows all the rest of your code to be written as code that operates on a normal list in Haskell.

Quick check 22.4 Write a program that returns the sum of the squares of the input.

Summary

In this lesson, our objective was to introduce you to the ways to write simple command-line interfaces in Haskell. The most familiar way is to treat I/O just like any other programming language. You can use do-notation to create a procedural list of `IO` actions, and build interactions with I/O this way. A more interesting approach, possible in few languages other than Haskell, is to take advantage of lazy evaluation. With lazy evaluation, you can think of the entire input stream as a lazily evaluated list of characters, `[Char]`. You can radically simplify your code by writing out pure functions as though they were just working on the type `[Char]`. Let's see if you got this.

Q22.1 Write a program, simple_calc.hs, that reads simple equations involving adding two numbers or multiplying two numbers. The program should solve the equation each user types into each line as each line is entered.

Q22.2 Write a program that allows a user to select a number between 1 and 5 and then prints a famous quote (quotes are of your choosing). After printing the quote, the program will ask whether the user would like another. If the user enters `n`, the program ends; otherwise, the user gets another quote. The program repeats until the user enters `n`. Try to use lazy evaluation and treat the user input as a list rather than recursively calling `main` at the end.

QC 22.4 answer

```
mainSumSquares :: IO ()
mainSumSquares = do
   userInput <- getContents
   let numbers = toInts userInput
   let squares = map (^2) numbers
   print (sum squares)
```

WORKING WITH TEXT AND UNICODE

After reading lesson 23, you'll be able to

- Use the `Text` type for more-efficient text processing
- Change Haskell's behavior with language extensions
- Program by using common text functions
- Use `Text` to properly handle Unicode text

So far in this book, you've made heavy use of the `String` type. In the preceding lesson, you saw that you can even view an I/O stream as a lazy list of type `Char`, or a `String`. `String` has been useful in helping you explore many topics in this book. Unfortunately, `String` has a huge problem: it can be woefully inefficient.

From a philosophical standpoint, nothing could be more perfect than representing one of the more important types in programing as one of the most foundational data structures in Haskell: a list. The problem is that a list isn't a great data structure to store data for heavy string processing. The details of Haskell performance are beyond the scope of this book, but it suffices to say that implementing `String`s as a linked list of characters is needlessly expensive in terms of both time and space.

In this lesson, you'll take a look at a new type, `Text`. You'll explore how to replace `String` with `Text` for more-efficient text processing. Then you'll learn about the functions common to both `String` and `Text` for processing text. Finally, you'll learn about how `Text` handles Unicode by building a function that can highlight search text, even in Sanskrit!

> **Consider this** In Haskell, `String` is a special case of a `List`. But in most programming languages, string types are stored much more efficiently as arrays. Is there a way in Haskell to use the tools you already know about for working with the `String` type, but still have the efficiency of an array-based implementation?

23.1 The Text type

For practical and commercial Haskell programming, the preferred type for working with text data is the type `Text`. The `Text` type can be found in the module `Data.Text`. In practice, `Data.Text` is almost always imported as a qualified import by using a single letter, usually `T`:

```
import qualified Data.Text as T
```

Unlike `String`, `Text` is implemented as an array under the hood. This makes many string operations faster and much more memory-efficient. Another major difference between `Text` and `String` is that `Text` *doesn't* use lazy evaluation. Lazy evaluation proved to be helpful in the preceding lesson, but in many real-world cases it can lead to performance headaches. If you do need lazy text, you can use `Data.Text.Lazy`, which has the same interface as `Data.Text`.

23.1.1 When to use Text vs. String

In the commercial Haskell community, `Data.Text` is strongly preferred over `String`. Some members of the Haskell community argue that the standard `Prelude` should be thrown out for anything practical due to the heavy dependency on `String`. While learning Haskell, `String` is useful for two reasons. First, as mentioned, many of the basic string utilities are baked into the standard `Prelude`. Second, lists are to Haskell what arrays are to C. Many concepts in Haskell are nicely demonstrated with lists, and strings are useful lists. For learning purposes, feel free to stick with `String`. But for anything beyond exercises, use `Data.Text` as much as possible. You'll continue to use `String` in many places in this book but will start to use `Data.Text` more often.

23.2 Using Data.Text

The first thing you need to do is learn how to use the `Text` type. `Data.Text` has two functions, `pack` and `unpack`, which can be used to convert `String -> Text` and `Text -> String`. Figuring out which function does what can easily be determined by their type signatures:

```
T.pack :: String -> T.Text
T.unpack :: T.Text -> String
```

Here are some examples of converting a `String` to `Text` and back again.

Listing 23.1 Converting back and forth between `String` and `Text` types

```
firstWord :: String
firstWord = "pessimism"

secondWord :: T.Text
secondWord = T.pack firstWord

thirdWord :: String
thirdWord = T.unpack secondWord
```

It's important to note that conversion isn't computationally cheap, because you have to traverse the entire string. Avoid converting back and forth between `Text` and `String`.

> **Quick check 23.1** Create `fourthWord` once again, making the `String` type `T.Text`.

23.2.1 OverloadedStrings and Haskell extensions

An annoying thing about `T.Text` is that this code throws an error.

Listing 23.2 The problem with using literal strings to define `Text`

```
myWord :: T.Text
myWord = "dog"
```

The error you get reads as follows:

```
Couldn't match expected type 'T.Text' with actual type '[Char]'
```

This error occurs because the literal `"dog"` is a `String`. This is particularly annoying because you don't have this problem with numeric types. Take, for example, these numbers.

QC 23.1 answer

```
fourthWord :: T.Text
fourthWord = T.pack thirdWord
```

Listing 23.3 The same numeric literal used in three types

```
myNum1 :: Int
myNum1 = 3

myNum2 :: Integer
myNum2 = 3

myNum3 :: Double
myNum3 = 3
```

This code will compile just fine even though you've used the same literal, `3`, for three different types.

Clearly this isn't a problem that you can solve with clever coding, no matter how powerful Haskell may be. To fix this issue, you need a way to fundamentally change how GHC reads your file. Surprisingly, an easy fix for this exists! GHC allows you to use *language extensions* to alter the way Haskell itself works. The specific extension you're going to use is called `OverloadedStrings`.

There are two ways to use a language extension. The first is by using it when compiling with GHC. To do this, use the flag `-X` followed by the extension name. For a program named text.hs, this looks like the following:

```
$ ghc text.hs -XOverloadedStrings
```

This can also be used as an argument to GHCi, to start an instance of GHCi by using the language extension.

The trouble is that someone who is using your code (and that someone could be you) might not remember to use this flag. A preferred method is to use a `LANGUAGE` pragma. The pragma looks like this:

```
{-# LANGUAGE <Extension Name> #-}
```

Here's a text.hs file that will allow you to use literal values for `Text` types.

Listing 23.4 Using `OverloadedStrings` to easily assign `Text` using a literal

```
{-# LANGUAGE OverloadedStrings #-}
import qualified Data.Text as T

aWord :: T.Text
aWord = "Cheese"
```

```
main :: IO ()
main = do
  print aWord
```

With the LANGUAGE pragma, you can compile this program just like any other Haskell program.

Language extensions are powerful and range from practical to experimental. In real-world Haskell, a few extensions are common and useful.

Other useful language extensions

Language extensions are common in practical Haskell. They're powerful, as they allow you to use features of Haskell that may not be available as a default in the language for years, if ever. `OverloadedStrings` is the most common. Here are a few others you may come across or find useful:

- `ViewPatterns`—Allows for more-sophisticated pattern matching.
- `TemplateHaskell`—Provides tools for Haskell metaprogramming.
- `DuplicateRecordFields`—Solves the annoying problem from lesson 16, where using the same field name for different types using record syntax causes a conflict.
- `NoImplicitPrelude`—As mentioned, some Haskell programmers prefer to use a custom `Prelude`. This language extension allows you to not use the default `Prelude`.

Quick check 23.2 There's a language extension called `TemplateHaskell`. How would you compile templates.hs to use this extension? How would you add it using a `LANGUAGE` pragma?

23.2.2 Basic Text utilities

The trouble with using `Text` instead of `String` is that most useful functions for working with text are intended to be used with the `String` type. You definitely don't want to be converting `Text` back to `String` in order to use functions such as `lines`. Luckily, nearly every important `String` function has its own version for working on `Text` in `Data.Text`. Here's some `sampleInput` you'll work with to show how these functions work.

QC 23.2 answer

```
$ghc templates.hs -XTemplateHaskell
```

```
{-# LANGUAGE TemplateHaskell -#}
```

Listing 23.5 `sampleInput` of type `Text`

```
sampleInput :: T.Text
sampleInput = "this\nis\ninput"
```

To use lines on this example, all you have to do is make sure you preface lines with `T.`, because of your qualified import. Here's an example in GHCi:

```
GHCi>T.lines sampleInput
["this","is","input"]
```

The following are a few other useful functions that exist for both `Text` and `String`.

words

The `words` function is the same as `lines`, but it works for any whitespace characters, rather than just new lines.

Listing 23.6 `someText` as a sample input for words

```
someText :: T.Text
someText = "Some\ntext for\t you"
```

In GHCi, you can easily see how this works:

```
GHCi> T.words someText
["Some","text","for","you"]
```

splitOn

Lesson 22 briefly mentioned `splitOn`. For strings, `splitOn` is part of the `Data.List.Split` module. Thankfully, the text version is included in `Data.Text` so no additional import is needed. `splitOn` lets you split up text by any substring of text.

Listing 23.7 Code for `splitOn` example

```
breakText :: T.Text
breakText = "simple"

exampleText :: T.Text
exampleText = "This is simple to do"
```

And in GHCi:

```
GHCi> T.splitOn breakText exampleText
["This is "," to do"]
```

unwords and unlines

Breaking up Text by using whitespace is fairly common when working with I/O. The inverse is also common, so two functions can undo what you've just done, conveniently called unlines and unwords. Their usage is fairly obvious, but they're useful functions to have in your tool belt:

```
GHCi> T.unlines (T.lines sampleInput)
"this\nis\ninput\n"
GHCi> T.unwords (T.words someText)
"Some text for you"
```

Intercalate

You've used the string version of intercalate before in lesson 18. It's the opposite of splitOn:

```
GHCi> T.intercalate breakText (T.splitOn breakText exampleText)
"This is simple to do"
```

Almost any useful function for working with strings works on text and has its own Text version.

Monoid operations

The exception to the rule that most useful functions on strings work on text is the ++ operator. So far, you've used ++ to combine strings:

```
combined :: String
combined = "some" ++ " " ++ "strings"
```

Unfortunately, ++ is defined only on the List type, so it won't work for Text. In lesson 17, we discussed the Monoid and Semigroup type classes, which allow you to combine like types and concatenate lists of the same type. This provides a general solution to combining both strings and text. You can either import Semigroup and use <> to combine text, or use mconcat:

```
{-# LANGUAGE OverloadedStrings #-}
import qualified Data.Text as T
import Data.Semigroup

combinedTextMonoid :: T.Text
combinedTextMonoid = mconcat ["some"," ","text"]

combinedTextSemigroup :: T.Text
combinedTextSemigroup = "some" <> " " <> "text"
```

Because `String` is also an instance of `Monoid` and `Semigroup`, strings can be combined in the same way.

> **Quick check 23.3** Create your own version of `T.lines` and `T.unlines` by using `splitOn` and `T.intercalate`.

23.3 Text and Unicode

The `Text` type has excellent support for working seamlessly with Unicode text. At one point, programmers could largely ignore the complications of working with non-ASCII text. If input had accents or umlauts, it could be squashed out of existence; it was acceptable to change *Charlotte Brontë to Charlotte Bronte*. But ignoring Unicode today and in the future is a recipe for disaster. There's no reason to be unable to record a user's name that includes diacritical marks, or to fail to handle Japanese Kanji.

23.3.1 Searching Sanskrit

To demonstrate how seamlessly you can use `Text` for working with Unicode characters, you'll build a simple program that highlights words in text. The trick is that you're going to be highlighting Sanskrit words written in Devanagari script! The Unicode text can be easily copied from this link if you want to paste this into your editor to follow along: https://gist.github.com/willkurt/4bced09adc2ff9e7ee366b7ad681cac6.

All of your code will go in a file named bg_highlight.hs. Your program will take a text query and a body of text, and use curly braces, {}, to highlight all cases of the word you're looking for. For example, if *dog* is your query text, and your main text is *a dog walking dogs*, you'd expect this output:

```
a {dog} walking {dog}s
```

QC 23.3 answer

```
myLines :: T.Text -> [T.Text]
myLines text = T.splitOn "\n" text

myUnlines :: [T.Text] -> T.Text
myUnlines textLines = T.intercalate "\n" textLines
```

In this task, you want to highlight the Sanskrit word *dharma* in a sample text from the *Bhavagad Gita*. The word *dharma* has many meanings in Sanskrit, ranging from *duty* to references of cosmic order and divine justice. Sanskrit is a language that has no singular writing system. The most popular today is Devanagari, an alphabet used by more than 120 languages, including Hindi. Here's the Sanskrit word *dharma* written in Devanagari script.

Listing 23.8 A Unicode text variable for dharma written in Devanagari script

```
dharma :: T.Text
dharma = "धर्म"
```

Next you'll take an excerpt from the *Bhavagad Gita*, itself a part of the Indian epic, *The Mahabharata*. Here's our section.

Listing 23.9 Your search text from the Bhavagad Gita

```
bgText :: T.Text
bgText = "श्रेयान्स्वधर्मो विगुणः परधर्मात्स्वनुष्ठितात् ।स्वधर्मे निधनं श्रेयः परधर्मो"
```

Your goal here is to highlight everywhere in your `bgText` where the word *dharma* appears. In English, your first thought might be to split a sentence by using `T.words`, and then look for the word you're looking for. But Sanskrit is more complicated. Because Sanskrit was a spoken language long before it was written, whenever words are naturally combined when speaking a sentence, they end up combined in text. To solve this, you can split your text on the target text query, wrap the query in brackets, and then put it all back together. You can use `T.splitOn` to split up the text, `mconcat` to add brackets to your query string, and `T.intercalate` to piece your words back together.

Here's your `highlight` function.

Listing 23.10 The `highlight` function for highlighting text segments

```
highlight :: T.Text -> T.Text -> T.Text
highlight query fullText = T.intercalate highlighted pieces
  where pieces = T.splitOn query fullText
        highlighted = mconcat ["{",query,"}"]
```

Using splitOn, you can find all locations of your query text and split the text based on these locations.

You can use mconcat to take the query and surround it in brackets.

After you have the query text format with brackets, you can use intercalate to stitch everything back together.

Finally, you can put this all together in your `main`. But first you have to learn how to use `IO` with your `Text` type.

23.4 Text I/O

Now that you have a `highlight` function, you want to print the results of your highlighting back to the users. The trouble is that so far you've always used an `IO String` type to send output to the user. One solution would be to unpack your end text back into a string. What you want is to have a `putStrLn` for `Text`; this way, you never have to convert your text to a string (and can hopefully forget about strings altogether). The `Data.Text` module includes only functions for manipulating text. To perform text I/O, you need to import the `Data.Text.IO` package. You'll do another qualified import:

```
import qualified Data.Text.IO as TIO
```

With `TIO.putStrLn`, you can print your `Text` type just as you would `String`. Any IO action you've used related to the `String` type has an equivalent in `Data.Text.IO`. Now you can put together your `main`, which calls your `highlight` function on your data. Here's your full file, including the necessary imports and `LANGUAGE` pragma.

Listing 23.11 Full file for your program

```
{-# LANGUAGE OverloadedStrings #-}
import qualified Data.Text as T
import qualified Data.Text.IO as TIO

dharma :: T.Text
dharma :: "धर्म"

bgText :: T.Text
bgText = " श्रेयान्स्वधर्मो विगुणः परधर्मात्स्वनुष्ठितात् ।स्वधर्मे निधनं श्रेयः परधर्मो भयावहः "

highlight :: T.Text -> T.Text -> T.Text
highlight query fullText = T.intercalate highlighted pieces
  where pieces = T.splitOn query fullText
        highlighted = mconcat ["{",query,"}"]

main = do
  TIO.putStrLn (highlight dharma bgText)
```

You can compile your program and see the highlighted text:

```
$./bg_highlight
ान्स्व{धर्म}ो वगिुणः पर{धर्म}ात्स्वनुष्ठतिात् ।स्व{धर्म} नधिनं श्रेयः पर{धर्म}ो भया
```

Now you have a program that easily handles Unicode and also works with text data much more efficiently than `String`.

Summary

In this lesson, our objective was to teach you how to efficiently process text (including Unicode) in Haskell by using `Data.Text`. Although strings as lists of characters are a useful tool for teaching Haskell, in practice they can lead to poor performance. The preferred alternative whenever you're working with text data is to use the `Data.Text` module. One issue you came across was that Haskell, by default, doesn't know how to understand string literals as `Data.Text`. This can be remedied by using the `OverloadedStrings` language extension. Let's see if you got this.

Q23.1 Rewrite the hello_world.hs program (reproduced here) from lesson 21 to use `Text` instead of `String` types.

```
helloPerson :: String -> String

helloPerson name = "Hello" ++ " " ++ name ++ "!"

main :: IO ()
main = do
   putStrLn "Hello! What's your name?"
   name <- getLine
   let statement = helloPerson name
   putStrLn statement
```

Q23.2 Use `Data.Text.Lazy` and `Data.Text.Lazy.IO` to rewrite the lazy I/O section from lesson 22 by using the `Text` type.

```
toInts :: String -> [Int]
toInts = map read . lines

main :: IO ()
main = do
  userInput <- getContents
  let numbers = toInts userInput
  print (sum numbers)
```

24 WORKING WITH FILES

After reading lesson 24, you'll be able to

- Work with file handles in Haskell
- Read from and write to files
- Understand limitations of lazy evaluation for I/O

One of the most important uses of I/O is to read and write from files. So far in this unit, you've learned a bit of the syntax behind `IO` types in Haskell, saw how to build command-line programs using lazy evaluation, and learned about efficient text processing by using the `Text` type. Now you'll look at working with files, including how they can make using lazy I/O a bit tricky. You'll start with the basics of opening, closing, reading from, and writing to simple files. Then you'll write a program that takes various statistics from an input file (including word count and character count) and writes them to a file. You'll discover that even in this rather straightforward task, lazy evaluation can be a major headache. The solution is to use strict data types to force the program to perform as you'd expect.

> **Consider this** In lesson 22, you saw a way to add up numbers entered in as user input. How can you write the same program that works with a file rather than user input (other than manually piping the file into your program)?

24.1 Opening and closing files

Before learning how files work in Haskell, you need to have a file to work with. You'll look at the basics of opening and closings files. Your first task is to open and close a text file. Here's the hello.txt file you'll start with.

Listing 24.1 hello.txt sample file

```
Hello world!
Good bye world!
```

Next you need a file that you'll put all of your code in. You'll call your file hello_file.hs. To start, you need to include the `System.IO` module, which will allow you to read and write files:

```
import System.IO
```

The first thing you need to do to work with your file is open it. To do this, you can use the `openFile` function, which has the following type signature (reminder: you can use `:t` to look up the type signature of a function in GHCi):

```
openFile :: FilePath -> IOMode -> IO Handle
```

As is usually the case, the more you understand the type of a function, the better you can understand how it works. If you open GHCi and use the `:info` command, you'll find that `FilePath` is just a type synonym for `String`:

```
type FilePath = String
```

Using `:info` on `IOMode`, you find it's a simple type like `Bool`, consisting of only single constructors:

```
data IOMode = ReadMode | WriteMode | AppendMode | ReadWriteMode
```

It should be clear from these constructor names that `IOMode` specifies whether you're reading, writing, appending, and so forth, your file. This is similar to nearly every other programming language, which typically requires programmers to specify what they're going to be doing with the file they're accessing.

Quick check 24.1 If you want to open a file named stuff.txt to read it, what will the function call look like?

You're then left with the `IO Handle`. The `Handle` type is a file handle that lets you pass around a reference to a file. As we've discussed throughout the unit, the `IO` type means that you have a handle in the context of `IO`. In order to get this file handle, you'll ultimately be doing the work in your main `IO` action.

Now you can put this all together and open hello.txt. The one missing piece is that just as in most other languages, whenever you open a file, you want to close it when you're finished. This can be achieved by using `hClose` (for *handle close*).

Listing 24.2 `main`, which opens and closes a file

```
main :: IO ()
main = do
   myFile <- openFile "hello.txt" ReadMode
   hClose myFile
   putStrLn "done!"
```

Opening and closing a file is boring if you don't do anything with what's inside! You clearly want to read and write to files. To do this, you can use two familiar functions, `hPutStrLn` and `hGetLine`. The only difference between these two functions and `putStrLn` and `getLine` is that you need to pass in a handle. It turns out that `putStrLn` is a specific instance of `hPutStrLn`. In `hPutStrLn` the handle is assumed to be `stdout`. Likewise, `getLine`is `hGetLine` where the handle is `stidn`. Here's a modified version of your code that reads the first line from hello.txt and writes it to the console, and then reads the second line and writes it to a new file, goodbye.txt.

Listing 24.3 Reading from a file and writing to `stdout` and another file

```
main :: IO ()
main = do
   helloFile <- openFile "hello.txt" ReadMode
```

QC 24.1 answer

```
openFile "stuff.txt" ReadMode
```

```
    firstLine <- hGetLine helloFile
    putStrLn firstLine
    secondLine <- hGetLine helloFile
    goodbyeFile <- openFile "goodbye.txt" WriteMode
    hPutStrLn goodbyeFile secondLine
    hClose helloFile
    hClose goodbyeFile
    putStrLn "done!"
```

This program works because you happen to know that `hello.txt` has two lines. What if you want to revise this program to read each line and print it out as it goes? You'd need to be able to check for the end of the file. To do this, you use `hIsEOF`. Here's a version of your program that checks the Hello file first before printing out the first line.

Listing 24.4 Checking whether helloFile is empty before printing the first line

```
main :: IO ()
main = do
   helloFile <- openFile "hello.txt" ReadMode
   hasLine <- hIsEOF helloFile
   firstLine <- if not hasLine
                then hGetLine helloFile
                else return "empty"
   putStrLn "done!"
```

Quick check 24.2 Write the code to check whether the second line is empty before writing it to a file.

QC 24.2 answer For this example, you'll return an empty `String` if there's no second line.

```
hasSecondLine <- hIsEOF helloFile
secondLine <- if not hasSecondLine
              then hGetLine helloFile
              else return ""
```

24.2 Simple I/O tools

Although it's important to understand how file handles work, in many cases you can get away without dealing with them directly. A few useful functions named `readFile`, `writeFile`, and `appendFile` hide away many of the details of reading, writing, and appending files. Here are the type signatures of these functions:

```
readFile :: FilePath -> IO String
writeFile :: FilePath -> String -> IO ()
appendFile :: FilePath -> String -> IO ()
```

To see how these functions are used, you'll create a program called fileCounts.hs. Your program will take a file as an argument, and then count the characters, words, and lines in the file. The program will display this data to the user as well as append the info to a stats.dat file. Here's an example of what stats.dat will look like, given that it has to be used on two files, hello.txt and what.txt.

Listing 24.5 Sample contents of stats.dat file for your fileCounts.hs program

```
hello.txt chars:  29  words:  5  lines:  2
what.txt chars:  30000  words:  2404  lines:  1
```

Now you can move on to write your code to perform this analysis.

The first step is to write a function that gets all of your counts. You can write this by assuming that your input data is a `String`. You'll represent your counts as a 3-tuple.

Listing 24.6 `getCounts` collects character, word, and line count info into a tuple

```
getCounts :: String -> (Int,Int,Int)
getCounts input = (charCount, wordCount, lineCount)
 where charCount = length input
       wordCount = (length . words) input
       lineCount = (length . lines) input
```

Next you'll create the `countsText` function to convert a 3-tuple of counts into a human-readable summary. You'll use `unwords` to join your text.

Listing 24.7 countsText renders count data in a human-readable form

```
countsText :: (Int,Int,Int) -> String
countsText (cc,wc,lc) =  unwords ["chars: "
                                 , show cc
                                 , " words: "
                                 , show wc
                                 , " lines: "
                                 ,  show lc]
```

In GHCi, you can see that this works great:

```
GHCi> (countsText . getCounts) "this is\n some text"
"chars: 18 words: 4 lines: 2"
```

Quick check 24.3 Why is it preferable to use unwords instead of combining your strings with ++?

You can now easily put these functions together with readFile and appendFile to build your program.

Listing 24.8 Putting your code together into main

```
main :: IO ()
main = do
  args <- getArgs
  let fileName = head args
  input <- readFile fileName
  let summary = (countsText . getCounts) input
  appendFile "stats.dat" (mconcat [fileName, " ",summary, "\n"])
  putStrLn summary
```

QC 24.3 answer The ++ operator is specific to lists. In lesson 23, we talked at length about the other text types beyond String. The unwords function has a version for Text as well as String, whereas ++ works only on type String. Using unwords makes it much, much easier to refactor your code if you decide to swap out String for Text.

If you compile this program, you can see that it works as expected:

```
$ ./fileCounts hello.txt
chars: 29 words: 5 lines: 2

$ cat stats.dat
hello.txt chars: 29 words: 5 lines: 2
```

Using `readFile` and `appendFile` made solving this problem much easier than if you were using handles and `openFile`.

24.3 The trouble with lazy I/O

Your fileCounts.hs program is clearly missing a lot of important checks: you don't bother to make sure there are arguments or that the file exists. These have been intentionally left out to make the code easier to read for learning. There's one interesting thing you can try that will create a bug that you might not expect. What happens if you try to use `fileCounts` on its own stats.dat file?

```
$ ./fileCounts stats.dat
fileCounts: stats.dat: openFile: resource busy (file is locked)
```

You get an error! The trouble here is that `readFile` doesn't close the file handle. Under the hood, `readFile` uses `hGetContents`, which works exactly like `getContents` except you're required to pass in a file handle. Here's how `readFile` is implemented in Haskell:

```
readFile :: FilePath -> IO String
readFile name = do
  inputFile <- openFile name ReadMode
  hGetContents inputFile
```

You can see that this code never closes the file handle, and just returns the results of `hGetContent`. If you ever need to view the source of a function in Haskell, you can look it up on Hackage, and the definition will contain a link to the source.

You can see why `readFile` doesn't close the handle if you attempt to fix your `main` by writing out the full operations you need. Here's your revised code.

Listing 24.9 Revised `main` with the `readFile` function expanded out

```
main :: IO ()
main = do
  args <- getArgs
  let fileName = head args
  file <- openFile fileName ReadMode
  input <- hGetContents file
  hClose file
  let summary = (countsText . getCounts) input
  appendFile "stats.dat" (mconcat [fileName, " ",summary, "\n"])
  putStrLn summary
```

That's a bit more verbose, but should prevent the error involving `appendFile` from trying to write a file that you still have open. Let's recompile and try this again:

```
$ ./fileCounts stats.dat
fileCounts: stats.dat: hGetContents: illegal operation (delayed read on
➥closed handle)
```

This time you have an even stranger error! Your program is completely broken now, as it will no longer work with hello.txt either:

```
$ ./fileCounts hello.txt
fileCounts: stats.dat: hGetContents: illegal operation (delayed read on
➥closed handle)
```

The problem here is lazy evaluation. The key to lazy evaluation is that no code is evaluated until it's absolutely needed. Your input isn't used until you define `summary`. But the problem doesn't end there: `summary` isn't used until you call `appendFile`. Because `appendFile` performs an `IO` action, it does force `summary` to be evaluated, which forces `input` to be evaluated. The real problem is that `hClose` closes the file immediately because it's an `IO` action and must happen as soon as you evaluate it. Figure 24.1 provides a visual of the process.

So you can put `hClose` after `appendFile` because that's when `summary` is finally evaluated, right?

```
  appendFile (mconcat [fileName, " ",summary, "\n"])
  hClose file
```

Because hGetContents is lazy, the value stored in input isn't used until it's needed. At this point, you can think of input as a substitute for "hGetContents file".

In terms of lazy evaluation, hClose has nothing to wait for and executes immediately. At this point in the program, the file is closed but input hasn't been evaluated yet.

```
main :: IO ()
main = do
  args <- getArgs
  let fileName = head args
  file <- openFile fileName ReadMode
  input <- hGetContents file
  hClose file
  let summary = (countsText . getCounts) input
  appendFile "stats.dat" (mconcat
  [fileName, " ", summary, "\n"])
  putStrLn summary
```

When you define summary, you're using input, but you still don't need to evaluate it. The input will be evaluated only when summary is evaluated.

Finally, you call appendFile which, like hClose, has something to do. At this point, summary is evaluated and because of this input is as well. But now the file is closed, and the OS won't let you read from it anymore!

Figure 24.1 The problem with closing a file before we use it when using lazy evaluation

But now you're back where you started; you're closing the file after you need a new handle! You need a solution that forces you to evaluate `summary` before you write to the file. One way to achieve this is to move `putStrLn summary` before you write to the file. This will force `summary` to be evaluated first. Then you can close the handle, finally appending the file.

Listing 24.10 `main` with the evaluation bugs fixed

```
main :: IO ()
main = do
  args <- getArgs
  let fileName = head args
  file <- openFile fileName ReadMode
  input <- hGetContents file
  let summary = (countsText . getCounts) input
  putStrLn summary
```

input still hasn't been evaluated yet.

Even though summary is defined, it hasn't been used. Neither summary nor input have been evaluated.

putStrLn needs to print summary; this forces summary to be evaluated, and thus the input to be read in so it can be used by summary.

```
hClose file
appendFile "stats.dat" (mconcat [fileName, " ",summary, "\n"])
```

Now closing the file causes no problem because the value inside summary has been evaluated.

Appending the file works as expected; your file will be updated correctly.

This should serve as an object lesson that although lazy I/O can be powerful, it can also lead to nasty bugs.

Quick check 24.4 Why doesn't `readFile` close the handle?

24.4 Strict I/O

The best solution to this problem is to use a strict (nonlazy) type. We mentioned in lesson 23 that `Data.Text` is preferred over `String` when working with text data. We also mentioned that `Data.Text` is a strict data type (it doesn't use lazy evaluation). You can rewrite your original program by using the `Text` type, and your problem will be solved!

```
{-# LANGUAGE OverloadedStrings #-}

import System.IO
import System.Environment
import qualified Data.Text as T
import qualified Data.Text.IO as TI

getCounts :: T.Text -> (Int,Int,Int)
getCounts input = (charCount, wordCount, lineCount)
 where charCount = T.length input
       wordCount = (length . T.words) input
       lineCount = (length . T.lines) input
```

QC 24.4 answer Because of lazy evaluation, if `readFile` closes the handle, you'd never be able to use the contents of the file. This is because a function acting on the contents of the file wouldn't be called until after the file handle was closed

```
countsText :: (Int,Int,Int) -> T.Text
countsText (cc,wc,lc) = T.pack (unwords ["chars: "
                                        , show cc
                                        , " words: "
                                        , show wc
                                        , " lines: "
                                        ,  show lc])

main :: IO ()
main = do
  args <- getArgs
  let fileName = head args
  input <- TI.readFile fileName
  let summary = (countsText . getCounts) input
  TI.appendFile "stats.dat"
              (mconcat [(T.pack fileName), " ",summary, "\n"])
  TI.putStrLn summary
```

Strict evaluation means that your I/O code works just as you'd expect it to in any other programming language. Although lazy evaluation has many great benefits, for any non-trivial I/O, reasoning about its behavior can be tricky. Your fileCounts.hs was a trivial demo program, but you still had a nasty bug to fix created by lazy evaluation.

24.4.1 When to use lazy vs. strict

In this unit, you've seen cases in which lazy evaluation in I/O can make life much easier and much more difficult. The key factor in deciding between the two is the complexity of your program's I/O. If your program is reading a single file and doing relatively little I/O work, sticking with lazy evaluation will likely provide many benefits and few problems. As soon as your I/O becomes even moderately complex, involving reading and writing files, or operations for which order is important, stick with strict evaluation.

Summary

In this lesson, our objective was to teach you the basics of reading and writing from files in Haskell. Most file I/O is similar to other forms of I/O in Haskell that you've seen. Issues can arise when you use lazy I/O without understanding how this will impact your program's behavior. Although lazy I/O can greatly simplify code, it becomes incredibly difficult to reason about as program complexity increases. Let's see if you got this.

Q24.1 Write a version of the Unix `cp` program that will copy a file and allow you to rename it (just mimic the basic functionality and don't worry about specific flags).

Q24.2 Write a program called capitalize.hs that will take a file as an argument, read that file, and then rewrite it capitalized.

LESSON 25

WORKING WITH BINARY DATA

After reading lesson 25, you'll be able to

- Use the `ByteString` type to efficiently work with binary data
- Treat `ByteString`s as regular ASCII strings by using `ByteString.Char8`
- Glitch JPEG images by using Haskell
- Work with binary Unicode data

In this lesson, you'll learn about working with binary file data by using Haskell's `ByteString` type. `ByteString` allows you to treat raw binary data as though it were a regular string. To demonstrate the use of `ByteString`, you'll focus on a fun project requiring you to manipulate binary file data. You'll create a simple command-line tool that will allow you to create *glitch art*, like that in figure 25.1.

Glitch art is the practice of deliberately corrupting binary data in order to create visual artifacts in an image or video. You'll work on the relatively simple task of "glitching" JPEG images. You'll also take a look at some of the issues around working with binary Unicode data.

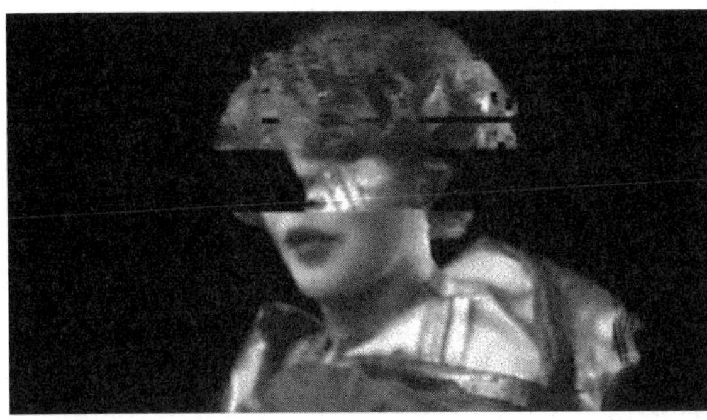

Figure 25.1 A scene from Michael Betancourt's glitch art video "Kodak Moment" (2013)

Consider this You have the name of the Japanese author Tatsuhiko Takimoto represented in Japanese Kanji using `T.Text`:

```
tatsuhikoTakimoto :: T.Text
tatsuhikoTakimoto = "滝本 竜彦"
```

You need to know the number of bytes in this text. For ASCII text, this would be the length of the text, but in this case, using `T.length` gives you only the number of characters (5). How can you find the number of bytes?

25.1 Working with binary data by using ByteString

So far in the unit, you've only looked at working with text in files. You started working with the basic `String` type and then learned that `Text` is a better type for working with textual data. Another important type that's similar to `String` and `Text` is called `ByteString`. The interesting thing about `ByteString` is that it's not specifically for text, as the name `String` might imply. `ByteString` is an efficient way to deal with any streams of binary data. Like `Data.Text`, you almost always import `Data.ByteString` with a qualified import by using a single letter:

```
import qualified Data.ByteString as B
```

Even though `ByteString` is an array of bytes and not a type of text, you can always use ASCII to represent strings of bytes. There are 256, or 2^8 (8 bits) ASCII characters, so every possible byte can be represented as an ASCII character. As long as you're using the `OverloadedStrings` extension, you can use literal ASCII strings to represent vectors of bytes.

Listing 25.1 `ByteString` defined by using the `OverloadedStrings` extension

```
sampleBytes :: B.ByteString
sampleBytes = "Hello!"
```

But you quickly run into a problem if you try to convert your `ByteString` into an ordinary `String` by using `B.unpack`. The following code will throw an error.

Listing 25.2 Trying to unpack a `ByteString` into a `String` causes an error

```
sampleString :: String
sampleString = B.unpack sampleBytes
```

As you can see by the type signature, `B.unpack` attempts to convert the `ByteString` into a list of bytes (of type `Word8`):

```
B.unpack :: B.ByteString -> [GHC.Word.Word8]
```

By default, `Data.ByteString` doesn't allow you to treat bytes just like `Char`, so instead you use `Data.ByteString.Char8`. The `Char8` stands for 8-bit `Chars` (ASCII characters). You need to import `Char8` separately, and usually use the qualifier `BC`:

```
import qualified Data.ByteString.Char8 as BC
```

You can see the difference between plain `ByteString` and `ByteString.Char8` by looking at the types of their `unpack` functions:

```
B.unpack :: BC.ByteString -> [GHC.Word.Word8]
BC.unpack :: BC.ByteString -> [Char]
```

You can see that `ByteString.Char8`'s `unpack` works just like `Data.Text`'s `unpack`. `ByteString.Char8` allows you to use the same core functions for working with text as `Data.Text` does. The careful reader will also notice that the type signature of `B.unpack` has changed! `B.unpack` now uses the `ByteString` representation from `ByteString.Char8`. This means you're free to treat your `ByteString`s as plain ASCII text from here on out.

Like `Text`, `ByteString` shares a common API with `String`. As you'll see in the next section, you can use all of the same functions you would when working with `Text` and `String` with binary data. This makes it easy to reason about efficiently stored binary data just as you would a normal list.

Quick check 25.1 Write a function that takes numbers in ASCII character form and converts them to Ints. For example, make the following an Int:

```
bcInt :: BC.ByteString
bcInt = "6"
```

25.2 Glitching JPEGs

Now that you've covered the basic use of `ByteString`, let's dive into creating glitch art. All the code for your program will be put in a file called glitcher.hs. You'll be working with an image that can be downloaded from Wikipedia (https://en.wikipedia.org/wiki/H._P._Lovecraft#/media/File:H._P._Lovecraft,_June_1934.jpg). For this exercise, you'll name this file lovecraft.jpg, shown in figure 25.2.

Figure 25.2 The target of your glitching is the lovecraft.jpg image.

QC 25.1 answer

```
bcInt :: BC.ByteString
bcInt = "6"

bcToInt :: BC.ByteString -> Int
bcToInt = read . BC.unpack
```

To get started with your program, let's see how to create the basic functionality you want for reading and writing your image. Here's the basic structure of the program:

1. Take a filename argument from the user.
2. Read in the binary data for the image file.
3. Randomly alter bytes in the image data.
4. Write a new file containing the glitched image.

You'll use both `Data.ByteString` and `Data.ByteString.Char8` in the program to work with the image's binary data. Because you're working with binary data, you want to read in your file by using `BC.readFile`. Here's the basic outline of your program without any of the glitching code.

Listing 25.3 Basic layout for your glitcher.hs file

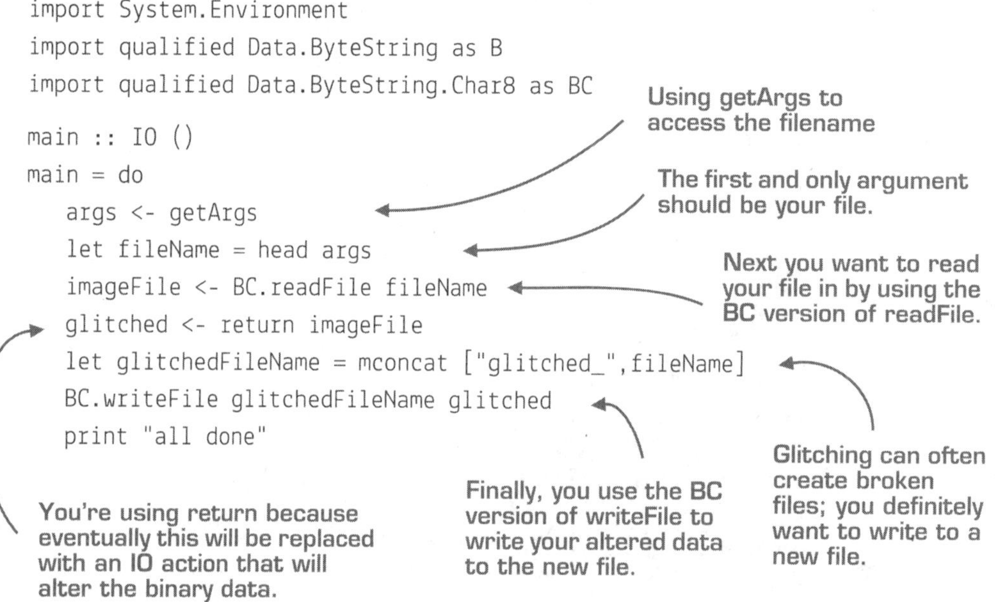

```
import System.Environment
import qualified Data.ByteString as B
import qualified Data.ByteString.Char8 as BC

main :: IO ()
main = do
   args <- getArgs
   let fileName = head args
   imageFile <- BC.readFile fileName
   glitched <- return imageFile
   let glitchedFileName = mconcat ["glitched_",fileName]
   BC.writeFile glitchedFileName glitched
   print "all done"
```

Using getArgs to access the filename
The first and only argument should be your file.
Next you want to read your file in by using the BC version of readFile.
Glitching can often create broken files; you definitely want to write to a new file.
Finally, you use the BC version of writeFile to write your altered data to the new file.
You're using return because eventually this will be replaced with an IO action that will alter the binary data.

With this bit of code, you can run your program, pass in a file, and get a new file that should be your glitched JPEG. The only thing missing is the code to glitch your image!

Quick check 25.2 At this point, the glitched variable in your `main` doesn't need to be an `IO` type. Change that line so that `glitched` is a regular variable.

25.2.1 Inserting random bytes

Part of the aesthetic of glitch art is to try different approaches to corrupting the data and see what works. You'll start with replacing a random byte in the file with another byte you pick at random. Creating a random number requires an `IO` action. But it's always best to separate as much code from `IO` actions as you possibly can, because your non-I/O code is pure and predictable. You can also easily test your code by loading it into GHCi and trying it out on a range of data samples.

Before you make your `IO` action, you'll start with a function that will convert an `Int` to a `Char`. Because `Char` is a member of `Enum`, you can use `toEnum`. You could use `toEnum` by itself, but if you do, you have no way to enforce the constraint that your `Char` is between 0 and 255. To enforce this, you'll take modulo 255 of the `Int` you pass to `toEnum`. You'll put all this together in an `intToChar` function.

Listing 25.4 `intToChar` creates a valid byte from an `Int`

```
intToChar :: Int -> Char
intToChar int =  toEnum safeInt
 where safeInt = int `mod` 255
```

Next you need a function that will convert this `Char` into a `ByteString`. You can do this by using `BC.pack` to take your `Char` and make it a `BC.ByteString`. Because `BC.pack` requires a string, you need to put your `Char` inside a list.

Listing 25.5 `intToBC` takes an `Int` and gives you a single-character `ByteString`

```
intToBC :: Int -> BC.ByteString
intToBC int = BC.pack [intToChar int]
```

QC 25.2 answer

```
let glitched = imageFile
```

Now that you have a way to make an Int into a single byte represented as a BC.ByteString, you can write the code to replace a byte with this value. You still don't need to use IO actions yet.

Your replaceByte function is the deterministic version of your random goal. This function will take the location of the byte to be replaced, the Int value of the new Char/Byte to go there, and the bytes of the image file. You'll use BC.splitAt to split your byte around the target byte. BC.splitAt will give you a pair of values representing the first part of the data and then the rest (just like calling take and drop at the same time). Then you'll drop one from the rest of the bytes to make room for your new byte. Finally, you'll concatenate the new byte in the middle of these two sections.

Listing 25.6 replaceByte removes a byte and replaces it with a new one

Your new ByteString is just the parts before and after the byte you're replacing concatenated with your newChar.

BC.splitAt will give you a pair of values, like drop and take at the same time. You can use pattern matching to assign these to two variables at once.

```
replaceByte :: Int -> Int -> BC.ByteString -> BC.ByteString
replaceByte loc charVal bytes = mconcat [before,newChar,after]
  where (before,rest) = BC.splitAt loc bytes
        after = BC.drop 1 rest
        newChar = intToBC charVal
```

You use BC.drop 1 here to remove the byte you're going to replace.

You're representing your byte as an ASCII Char.

Now you're ready for your IO action. You'll be using randomRIO from System.Random. randomRIO will take a pair of values in a tuple and randomly give you a number in that range. Your IO action will be named randomReplaceByte. All randomReplaceByte needs to do is pick two random numbers: one for the Char, and one for the location.

Listing 25.7 randomReplaceByte applies random numbers to replaceByte

```
randomReplaceByte :: BC.ByteString -> IO BC.ByteString
randomReplaceByte bytes = do
  let bytesLength = BC.length bytes
  location <- randomRIO (1,bytesLength)
```

```
  charVal <- randomRIO (0,255)
  return (replaceByte location charVal bytes)
```

Now you can use this `IO` action in your `main` to modify your image file:

```
main :: IO ()
main = do
  args <- getArgs
  let fileName = head args
  imageFile <- BC.readFile fileName
  glitched <- randomReplaceByte imageFile
  let glitchedFileName = mconcat ["glitched_",fileName]
  BC.writeFile glitchedFileName glitched
  print "all done"
```

You can compile your program and run it at the command line:

```
$ ghc glitcher.hs
$ ./glitcher lovecraft.jpg
```

These results are okay but not as dramatic as you'd hoped, as shown in figure 25.3.

Let's try something a bit more sophisticated to see if you can get better results.

Figure 25.3 The underwhelming effect of changing a single byte

Quick check 25.3 Write an IO action that returns a random Char.

25.2.2 Sorting random bytes

Another common technique for image glitching is to take a subsection of bytes and sort them. You can achieve this by splitting your `ByteString` at a point by using `BC.splitAt`, and then splitting the second half of this into a chunk of a fixed size; you sort the chunk and then put it all back together with `mconcat`. Here's your `sortSection` function, which takes a starting point of the section, a size of the section, and the byte stream.

Listing 25.8 `sortSection` **sorts a section of bytes in your file**

```
sortSection :: Int -> Int -> BC.ByteString -> BC.ByteString
sortSection start size bytes = mconcat [before,changed,after]
  where (before,rest) = BC.splitAt start bytes
        (target,after) = BC.splitAt size rest
        changed =  BC.reverse (BC.sort target)
```

All you need to use this in your `main` to create an `IO` action that picks a random starting point.

Listing 25.9 Randomizing your `sortSection` **by using an** `IO` **action**

```
randomSortSection :: BC.ByteString -> IO BC.ByteString
randomSortSection bytes = do
  let sectionSize = 25
  let bytesLength = BC.length bytes
  start <- randomRIO (0,bytesLength - sectionSize)
  return (sortSection start sectionSize bytes)
```

Here you're somewhat arbitrarily picking the size of the section you're going to sort. (annotates `let sectionSize = 25`)

Using randomRIO to figure out where you should sort your data from (annotates `start <- randomRIO ...`)

QC 25.3 answer

```
randomChar :: IO Char
randomChar = do
   randomInt <- randomRIO (0,255) -- could also use max and min bound
   return (toEnum randomInt)
```

You can replace randomReplaceByte with randomSortSection and try a revised approach.

Listing 25.10 Your main revised to use randomSortSection to glitch your file

```
main :: IO ()
main = do
  args <- getArgs
  let fileName = head args
  imageFile <- BC.readFile fileName
  glitched <- randomSortSection imageFile
  let glitchedFileName = mconcat ["glitched_",fileName]
  BC.writeFile glitchedFileName glitched
  print "all done"
```

With this trick, you get much more interesting results, as you can see in figure 25.4. But you could probably do better if you could combine these approaches!

Figure 25.4 A much more interesting result, achieved with randomSortSection

25.2.3 Chaining together IO actions with foldM

Suppose you want to use randomSortSection twice on your data and randomReplaceByte three times. You could rewrite your main like this.

Listing 25.11 A cumbersome approach to applying multiple actions

```
main :: IO ()
main = do
  args <- getArgs
  let fileName = head args
  imageFile <- BC.readFile fileName
  glitched1 <- randomReplaceByte imageFile
  glitched2 <- randomSortSection glitched1
  glitched3 <- randomReplaceByte glitched2
  glitched4 <- randomSortSection glitched3
  glitched5 <- randomReplaceByte glitched4
  let glitchedFileName = mconcat ["glitched_",fileName]
  BC.writeFile glitchedFileName glitched5
  print "all done"
```

This works, but it's clearly cumbersome to write code this way, and it's easy to make a simple typo with all the names you have to keep track of. Instead, you can use `foldM` from `Control.Monad`. Just as `mapM` generalizes `map` to monads (at this point, just code using do-notation), `foldM` does the same for folding. With `foldM`, you can take your original `imageFile` as the initial values, and then a list of `IO` actions that will transform your file. The only thing missing is a function that will apply these functions. In this case, you can use a simple lambda. Here's your `main` rewritten by using `foldM`.

Listing 25.12 An improved way to use multiple actions with `foldM`

```
main :: IO ()
main = do
  args <- getArgs
  let fileName = head args
  imageFile <- BC.readFile fileName
  glitched <- foldM (\bytes func -> func bytes) imageFile
                                                [randomReplaceByte
                                                ,randomSortSection
                                                ,randomReplaceByte
                                                ,randomSortSection
                                                ,randomReplaceByte]
```

```
let glitchedFileName = mconcat ["glitched_",fileName]
BC.writeFile glitchedFileName glitched
print "all done"
```

Now you can compile your program one last time and see what kind of glitches you can make! Figure 25.5 shows an example.

Figure 25.5 Now your beloved author looks more like a resident of Innsmouth!

There's still probably more you could do to make this image even more interesting, but now you have a setup that allows you to easily chain together whatever strange mutations you can come up with.

Quick check 25.4 Create a variable `glitchActions` outside your `main` that includes all your actions in a list. Don't forget to give it the correct type.

QC 25.4 answer

```
glitchActions :: [BC.ByteString -> IO BC.ByteString]
glitchActions = [randomReplaceByte
                ,randomSortSection
                ,randomReplaceByte
                ,randomSortSection
                ,randomReplaceByte]
```

25.3 ByteStrings, Char8, and Unicode

As you've seen in our glitch art example, `ByteString.Char8` is a helpful tool for treating binary data as though it were text. But it's important to be careful when using `ByteString`, `ByteString.Char8`, and Unicode data. Here's an example of setting a `BC.ByteString` to a Unicode string (for this Unicode, you're using the Devanagari script for the famous philosopher Nagarjuna).

Listing 25.13 Creating a Unicode `BC.ByteString`

```
nagarjunaBC :: BC.ByteString
nagarjunaBC = "नागर्जुनँ"
```

If you load this into GHCi, you see that the Unicode isn't preserved:

```
GHCi> nagarjunaBC
"(>\ETBOM\FSA("
```

This isn't too surprising, as `Char8` `ByteStrings` are only for ASCII. But you may want to transform text to just bytes for a variety of reasons, the primary one being writing Unicode to a file as `ByteStrings`. Suppose you have your Unicode safely represented as the `Text` type.

Listing 25.14 Same Unicode example, properly represented as `Text`

```
nagarjunaText :: T.Text
nagarjunaText = "नागर्जुनँ"
```

To convert `nagarjunaText` to a vector of bytes, you can't simply use `BC.pack` because `BC.pack` is of type `String -> ByteString`, so first you'd need to use `T.unpack` and then `BC.pack`.

Listing 25.15 Attempting to transform `Text` into a `ByteString`

```
nagarjunaB :: B.ByteString
nagarjunaB = (BC.pack . T.unpack) nagarjunaText
```

If you look at the type signature, you should have your Unicode safely represented as bytes. But if you convert back, you see this isn't the case. Note that you need to do a qualified import of `Data.Text.IO` to ensure that you're printing the text properly:

```
GHCi> TIO.putStrLn ((T.pack . BC.unpack) nagarjunaB)
"(>\ETBOM\FSA("
```

You're stuck with the same problem! If you had written `nagarjunaB` to a file, you'd have ultimately lost your Unicode. What you need is a way to convert `Text` directly to a `B.ByteString` and not a `BC.ByteString` along the way. For this, you use `Data.Text.Encoding`, and you'll do another qualified import:

```
import qualified Data.Text.Encoding as E
```

This module contains two essential functions that allow you to perform this direct transformation:

```
E.encodeUtf8 :: T.Text -> BC.ByteString
E.decodeUtf8 :: BC.ByteString -> T.Text
```

Now you can safely convert Unicode text to raw bytes and back again.

Listing 25.16 Converting between `Text` and `ByteString` with `de/encodeUtf8`

```
nagarjunaSafe :: B.ByteString
nagarjunaSafe = E.encodeUtf8 nagarjunaText

GHCi> TIO.putStrLn (E.decodeUtf8 nagarjunaSafe)
नागर्जुन
```

To be safe, never use the convenience of `Data.ByteString.Char8` if you're working with data that may contain Unicode. If you're working with purely binary data, as in the case of this lesson's example, the combination of regular `ByteString`s and `Char8` works great. For anything else, stick to `ByteString`, `Text`, and `Text.Encoding`. In this unit's capstone, you'll see an extended example of this latter case.

Summary

In this lesson, our objective was to teach you about writing binary data in Haskell. The `ByteString` type allows you to treat raw binary data similarly to the way you would ordinary strings. This can greatly simplify how you write programs editing binary data. But it's essential to remember not to mix single-byte representations of binary data (`Char8`) with Unicode text. Let's see if you got this.

Q25.1 Write a program that reads in a text file and outputs the difference between the number of characters in the file and the number of bytes in the file.

Q25.2 Add another glitching technique, `randomReverseBytes`, that randomly reverses a section of bytes in your data.

CAPSTONE: PROCESSING BINARY FILES AND BOOK DATA

This capstone covers

- Learning about a unique binary format used by libraries
- Writing tools to bulk-process binary data by using `ByteString`
- Working with Unicode data by using the `Text` type
- Structuring a large program performing a complicated I/O task

In this capstone, you're going to use the data on books created by libraries to make a simple HTML document. Libraries collectively spend a huge amount of time cataloging every possible book in existence. Thankfully, much of this data is freely available to anyone who wants to explore it. Harvard Library alone has released 12 million book records to be used for free by the public (http://library.harvard.edu/open-metadata). The Open Library project contains millions of additional records for use (https://archive.org/details/ol_data).

In a time when data science is a hot trend, it would be great to make some fun projects with all this data. But there's a big challenge to using this data. Libraries store their book-related metadata in a rather obscure format called a *MARC record* (for Machine-Readable Cataloging record). This makes using library data much more challenging than if it were in a more common format such as JSON or XML. MARC records are in a binary format that also makes heavy use of Unicode to properly store character encodings. To use

MARC records, you have to be careful about separating when you're working with bytes from when you're working with text. This is a perfect problem to explore all you've learned in this unit!

Our goal for this capstone is to take a collection of MARC records and convert it into an HTML document that lists the titles and authors of every book in the collection. This will leave you with a solid foundation to further explore extracting data from MARC records:

- You'll start your journey by creating a type for the book data you want to store and converting that to HTML.
- Next you have to learn how MARC records are formatted.
- Then you'll break apart a bulk of records serialized into a single file into a list of individual records.
- Once you've split the records up, you'll be able to parse individual files to find the information you need.
- Finally, you'll put all of this together into a single program that will process your MARC records into HTML files.

You'll be writing all of your code in a single file, marc_to_html.hs. To get started, you'll need the following imports (plus your `OverloadedStrings` extension).

Listing 26.1 The necessary imports for marc_to_html.hs

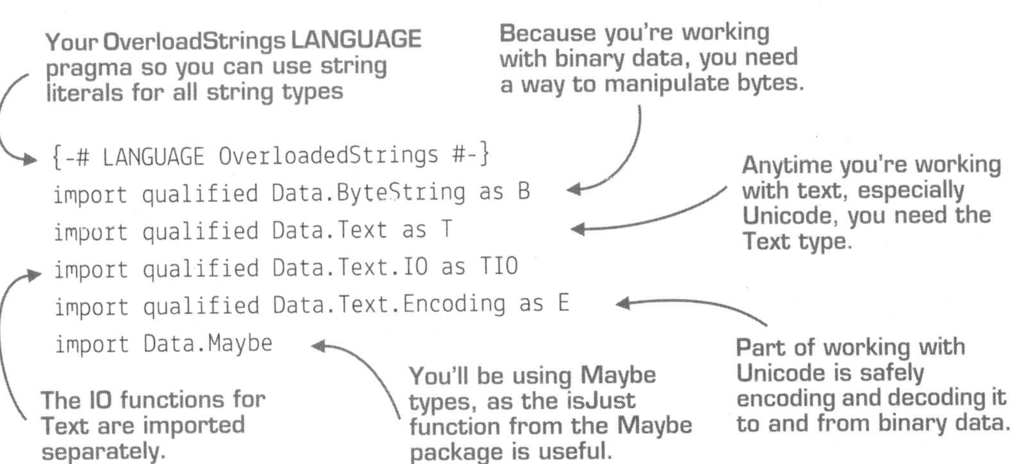
Your OverloadStrings LANGUAGE pragma so you can use string literals for all string types
Because you're working with binary data, you need a way to manipulate bytes.
Anytime you're working with text, especially Unicode, you need the Text type.
Part of working with Unicode is safely encoding and decoding it to and from binary data.
You'll be using Maybe types, as the isJust function from the Maybe package is useful.
The IO functions for Text are imported separately.

```
{-# LANGUAGE OverloadedStrings #-}
import qualified Data.ByteString as B
import qualified Data.Text as T
import qualified Data.Text.IO as TIO
import qualified Data.Text.Encoding as E
import Data.Maybe
```

You may have noticed that you're not importing `Data.ByteString.Char8`. This is because *when working with Unicode data, you never want to confuse Unicode text with ASCII text.* The best way to ensure this is to use plain old `ByteString`s for manipulating bytes and `Text` for everything else.

26.1 Working with book data

Unpacking MARC records is going to be a bit of work, so it's good to figure out where you want to end up before you get lost. Your primary goal is to convert a list of books into an HTML document. The books being in an obscure format is one obstacle to our goal. In this capstone, you're concerned with recording only the author and title of the books. You can use a type synonym for these properties. You could use `String`, but as mentioned in lesson 23, as a general rule it's much better to use `Text` when dealing with any large task consisting mostly of text data.

Now you can create your type synonyms for `Author` and `Title`.

Listing 26.2 Type synonyms for `Author` and `Title`

```
type Author = T.Text
type Title = T.Text
```

Your `Book` type will be the product type of `Author` and `Title`.

Listing 26.3 Create a `Book` type

```
data Book = Book {
    author :: Author
   ,title :: Title } deriving Show
```

Your final function for this will be called `booksToHtml` and will have the type `[Books] -> Html`. Before implementing this function, you first need to determine what type `Html` will be, and ideally how to make an individual book into a snippet of HTML. You can use the `Text` type once again to model your HTML.

Listing 26.4 `Html` type synonym

```
type Html = T.Text
```

To make transforming a list of books easier to turn into HTML, you'll start with creating a snippet of HTML for a single book. Your HTML will create a paragraph element, and then denote the title with a `<strong>` tag and the author with an `<em>` tag.

Listing 26.5 `bookToHtml` creates an individual snippet of HTML from a book

```
bookToHtml :: Book -> Html
bookToHtml book = mconcat ["<p>\n"
                          ,titleInTags
                          ,authorInTags
                          ,"</p>\n"]
   where titleInTags = mconcat["<strong>",(title book),"</strong>\n"]
         authorInTags = mconcat["<em>",(author book),"</em>\n"]
```

Next you need some sample books you can work with.

Listing 26.6 A collection of sample books

```
book1 :: Book
book1 = Book {
    title = "The Conspiracy Against the Human Race"
   ,author = "Ligotti, Thomas"
   }

book2 :: Book
book2 = Book {
    title = "A Short History of Decay"
   ,author = "Cioran, Emil"
   }

book3 :: Book
book3 = Book {
    title = "The Tears of Eros"
   ,author = "Bataille, Georges"
   }
```

In GHCi, you can test this bit of code:

```
GHCi> bookToHtml book1
"<p>\n<strong>The Conspiracy Against the Human Race</strong>\n<em>Ligotti,
➥Thomas</em>\n</p>\n"
```

To transform a list of books, you can map your bookToHtml function over the list. You also need to make sure you add html, head, and body tags as well.

Listing 26.7 Turning a list of books into an HTML document with booksToHtml

```
booksToHtml :: [Book] -> Html
booksToHtml books = mconcat ["<html>\n"
                            , "<head><title>books</title>"
                            ,"<meta charset='utf-8'/>"
                            ,"</head>\n"]
                            , "<body>\n"
                            , booksHtml
                            , "\n</body>\n"
                            , "</html>"]
  where booksHtml = (mconcat . (map bookToHtml)) books
```

Because you're dealing with Unicode data, it's important to declare your charset.

To test this out, you can put your books in a list:

```
myBooks :: [Book]
myBooks = [book1,book2,book3]
```

Finally, you can build a main and test out your code so far. You'll assume you're writing to a file called books.html. Remember that your Html type is Text. To write text to a file, you'll also need to include Text.IO.

Listing 26.8 Temporary main to write your books list to HTML

```
main :: IO ()
main = TIO.writeFile "books.html" (booksToHtml  myBooks)
```

Running this program will output your books.html file. Opening it up, you can see that it looks like you'd expect (see figure 26.1).

The Conspiracy Against the Human Race *Ligotti, Thomas*

A Short History of Decay *Cioran, Emil*

The Tears of Eros *Bataille, Georges*

Figure 26.1 Your book data rendered as HTML

With the ability to write books to a file, you can tackle the more complicated issue of working with MARC records.

26.2 Working with MARC records

The MARC record is the standard used in libraries for recording and transmitting information about books (called *bibliographic data*). If you're interested in data about books, MARC records are an important format to understand. There are many large, freely available collections of MARC records online. You'll be using the Oregon Health & Science University library records in this capstone. As noted earlier, *MARC* stands for *Machine-Readable Cataloging record*. As indicated by the name, MARC records are designed to be read by machines. Unlike formats such as JSON and XML, they *aren't* designed to be human-readable. If you open a MARC record file, you'll see something that looks like figure 26.2.


```
01292cam  2200337
4500001000300000003000600003005001700009008004100026010001600067019001
2000830290021000950350029001160400030001450430012001750490009001870500
0170019608200100021310000460022324502590026926000590052830000320058744
0007500619504003200694650005100726650003600777650003300813700003800846
7000042008849940012009269450016009382 OCoLC20060313170419.0690410s1963
laua     b    000 0 eng     a   63022268  a97725971 aNLGGCb861755170
a(OCoLC)2z(OCoLC)9772597  aDLCcDLCdOCLCQdTSEdOCL  an-us-la
aOCLC00aGB475.L6bM6 4a589.31 aMorgan, James P.q(James
Plummer),d1919-10aMudlumps at the mouth of South Pass, Mississippi
River;bsedimentology, paleontology, structure, origin, and relation to
deltaic processes,cby James P. Morgan, James M. Coleman [and] Sherwood
M. Gagliano. Including appendices by R.D. Adams ... [et al.].  aBaton
Rouge,bLouisiana State University Press,c1963.  axvi, 190 p.billus.c28
cm. 0aLouisiana State University studies.pCoastal studies series ;vno.
10.  aBibliography: p. [183]-190. 0aMud lumpszLouisianazMississippi
River Delta. 0aSediments (Geology)zLouisiana. 7aSciencesxPhilosophie.
2ram.1 aColeman, James M.,ejoint author.1 aGagliano, Sherwood
M.,ejoint author.  a02bOCL  aGB475.L6 M6
```


Figure 26.2 The content of a raw MARC record

If you've ever worked with the ID3 tag format for storing MP3 metadata, you'll find MARC records are similar.

26.2.1 Understanding the structure of a MARC record

The MARC record standard was developed in the 1960s with the primary aim of making it efficient to store and transmit information. Because of this, MARC records are much less flexible and extensible than formats such as XML or JSON. The MARC record consists of three main parts:

- The leader
- The directory
- The base record

Figure 26.3 shows an annotated version of your raw MARC record to help visualize how the record is laid out.

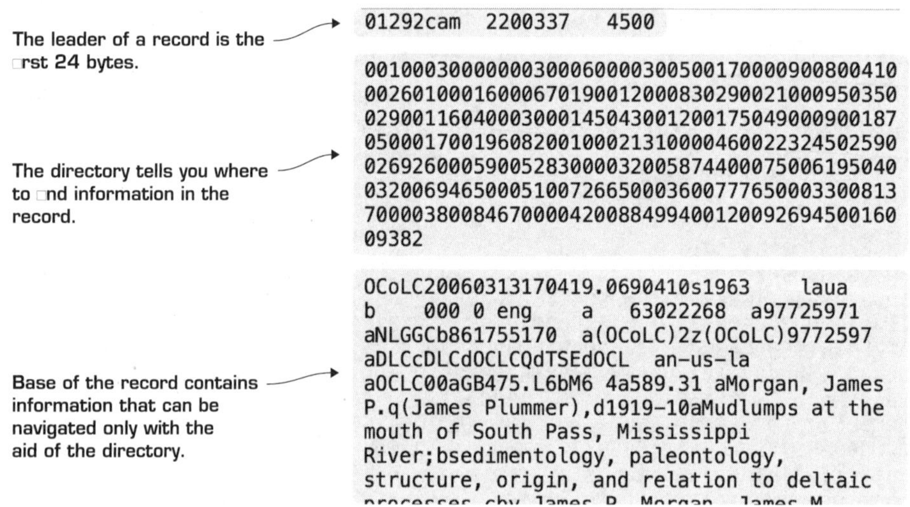
The leader of a record is the first 24 bytes.
01292cam 2200337   4500
The directory tells you where to find information in the record.
0010003000000030006000030050017000090080041000260100016000670190012000830290021000950350029001160400030001450430012001750490009001870500017001960820010002131000046002232450259002692600059005283000032005874400075006195040032006946500051007266500036007776500033008137000038008467000042008849940012009269450016009382
Base of the record contains information that can be navigated only with the aid of the directory.
OCoLC20060313170419.0690410s1963   laua
b   000 0 eng   a   63022268 a97725971
aNLGGCb861755170 a(OCoLC)2z(OCoLC)9772597
aDLCcDLCdOCLCQdTSEdOCL an-us-la
aOCLC00aGB475.L6bM6 4a589.31 aMorgan, James
P.q(James Plummer),d1919-10aMudlumps at the
mouth of South Pass, Mississippi
River;bsedimentology, paleontology,
structure, origin, and relation to deltaic

Figure 26.3 Annotated version of the MARC record

The *leader* contains information about the record itself, such as the length of the record and where to find the base record. The *directory* of the record tells you about the information contained in the record and how to access it. For example, you care only about the author and title of the book. The directory will tell you that the record contains this information and where to look in the file to find it. Finally, the *base record* is where all the information you need is located. But without the leader and directory, you don't have the information needed to make sense of this part of the file.

26.2.2 Getting the data

The first thing you need to do is get some MARC record data you can work with. Thankfully, archive.org has a great collection of freely available MARC records. For this project, you're going to use a collection of records from the Oregon Health & Science University library. Go to the project page on archive.org:

https://archive.org/download/marc_oregon_summit_records/catalog_files/

Download the ohsu_ncnm_wscc_bibs.mrc file. For this lesson, you'll rename the file sample.mrc. At 156 MB, this file is the smallest of the bunch, but if you'd like to play around with the others, they should all work equally as well.

26.2.3 Checking the leader and iterating through your records

Your .mrc file isn't a single MARC record but rather a collection of records. Before worrying about the details of a single record, you need to figure out how to separate all the records in this collection. Unlike many other formats for holding serialized data, there's no delimiter to separate files. You can't simply split your `ByteString` stream on a character in order to split your list of records. Instead, you need to look into the leader of each record to see how long it is. By looking at the length, you can then iterate through the list and collect records as you go. To begin, let's create synonyms for your `MarcRecord` and `MarcLeader`.

Listing 26.9 Type synonyms for `MarcRecordRaw` and `MarcLeaderRaw`

```
type MarcRecordRaw = B.ByteString
type MarcLeaderRaw = B.ByteString
```

Because you're primarily manipulating bytes, nearly all of your types when working with the raw MARC record are going to be `ByteString`s. But using type synonyms will make it much easier to read your code and understand your type signatures. The first take you want to do is to get the leader from the record:

```
getLeader :: MarcRecordRaw -> MarcLeaderRaw
```

The leader is the first 24 bytes of the record, as shown in figure 26.4.

```
01292cam  2200337
45000010003000000030006000003005001700009008004100026010001600
67019001200083029002100095035002900116040003000145043001200017
04900090018705000170019608200100021310000460022324502590026 92
00059000528300000320058744000075006195040003200694650000510072665 0
```

Figure 26.4 The leader in your record highlighted

You can declare a variable to keep track of your leader length.

Listing 26.10 Declaring the length of the leader to be 24

```
leaderLength :: Int
leaderLength = 24
```

Getting the leader from a MARC record is as straightforward as taking the first 24 characters of the `MarcRecord`.

Listing 26.11 `getLeader` grabs the first 24 bytes of the record

```
getLeader :: MarcRecordRaw -> MarcLeaderRaw
getLeader record = B.take leaderLength record
```

Just as the first 24 bytes of the MARC record is the leader, the first 5 bytes of the leader contain a number telling you the length of the record. For example, in figure 26.4 you see that the record starts with 01292, which means this record is 1,292 bytes long. To get the length of your entire record, you need to take these first five characters and then convert them to an `Int` type. You'll create a useful helper function, `rawToInt`, which will safely convert your `ByteString` to `Text`, then convert that `Text` to a `String`, and finally use `read` to parse an `Int`.

Listing 26.12 `rawToInt` and `getRecordLength`

```
rawToInt :: B.ByteString -> Int
rawToInt = (read . T.unpack . E.decodeUtf8)

getRecordLength :: MarcLeaderRaw -> Int
getRecordLength leader = rawToInt (B.take 5 leader)
```

Now that you have a way to figure out the length of a single record, you can think about separating all the records that you find into a list of `MarcRecords`. You'll consider your file a `ByteString`. You want a function that will take that `ByteString` and separate it into a pair of values: the first record and the rest of the remaining `ByteString`. You'll call this function `nextAndRest`, which has the following type signature:

```
nextAndRest :: B.ByteString -> (MarcRecordRaw,B.ByteString)
```

You can think of this pair of values as being the same as getting the head and tail of a list. To get this pair, you need to get the length of the first record in the stream and then split the stream at this value.

Listing 26.13 `nextAndRest` **breaks a stream of records into a head and tail**

```
nextAndRest :: B.ByteString -> (MarcRecordRaw,B.ByteString)
nextAndRest marcStream =  B.splitAt recordLength marcStream
  where recordLength = getRecordLength marcStream
```

To iterate through the entire file, you recursively use this function to take a record and the rest of the file. You then put the record in a list and repeat on the rest of the file until you reach the end.

Listing 26.14 Converting a stream of raw data into a list of records

```
allRecords :: B.ByteString -> [MarcRecordRaw]
allRecords marcStream = if marcStream == B.empty
                        then []
                        else next : allRecords rest
  where (next, rest) = nextAndRest marcStream
```

You can test `allRecords` by rewriting your `main` to read in your sample.mrc file and print out the length of that file:

```
main :: IO ()
main = do
  marcData <- B.readFile "sample.mrc"
  let marcRecords = allRecords marcData
  print (length marcRecords)
```

You can run your `main` by either compiling your program or loading it into GHCi and calling `main`:

```
GHCi> main
140328
```

There are 140,328 records in this collection! Now that you've split up all of your records, you can move on to figuring out exactly how to get all of your `Title` and `Author` data.

26.2.4 Reading the directory

MARC records store all the information about a book in *fields*. Each field has a tag and subfields that tell you more about the information that's in a book (such as author, title, subject, and publication date). Before you can worry about processing the fields, you need to look up all the information about those fields in the directory. Like everything else in our MARC records, the directory is a `ByteString`, but you can create another synonym for readability.

Listing 26.15 Type synonym for `MarcDirectoryRaw`

```
type MarcDirectoryRaw = B.ByteString
```

Unlike the leader, which is always the first 24 characters, the directory can be of variable size. This is because each record may contain a different number of fields. You know that the directory starts after the leader, but you have to figure out where the directory ends. Unfortunately, the leader doesn't tell you this information directly. Instead it tells you the base address, which is where the base record begins. The directory, then, is what's missing from where the leader ends and the base record begins.

Information about the base address is located in the leader starting with the 12th character and including the 16th byte (for a total of 5 bytes), assuming a 0 index. To access this, you can take the leader, drop the first 12 characters from it, and then take the next 5 in the remaining 12 of the leader. After this, you have to convert this value from a `ByteString` to an `Int`, just as you did with the `recordLength`.

Listing 26.16 Getting the base address to determine the size of the directory

```
getBaseAddress :: MarcLeaderRaw -> Int
getBaseAddress leader = rawToInt (B.take 5 remainder)
  where remainder = B.drop 12 leader
```

Then, to calculate the length of the directory, you subtract the `(leaderLength + 1)` from the base address, giving you the value of space between these two values.

Listing 26.17 Calculating the length of the directory with `getDirectoryLength`

```
getDirectoryLength :: MarcLeaderRaw -> Int
getDirectoryLength leader = getBaseAddress leader - (leaderLength + 1)
```

You can now put all these pieces together to get the directory. You start by looking up the directory length from the record, and then dropping the leader length and taking the length directly from that.

Listing 26.18 Putting everything together to `getDirectory`

```
getDirectory :: MarcRecordRaw -> MarcDirectoryRaw
getDirectory record = B.take directoryLength afterLeader
    where directoryLength = getDirectoryLength record
          afterLeader = B.drop leaderLength record
```

At this point, you've come a long way in understanding this rather opaque format. Now you have to make sense of what's inside the directory.

26.2.5 Using the directory to look up fields

At this point, your directory is a big `ByteString`, which you still need make sense of. As mentioned earlier, the directory allows you to look up fields in the base record. It also tells you what fields there are. Thankfully, each instance of this field metadata is exactly the same size: 12 bytes.

Listing 26.19 `MarcDirectoryRaw` type synonym and `dirEntryLength`

```
type MarcDirectoryEntryRaw = B.ByteString

dirEntryLength :: Int
dirEntryLength = 12
```

Next you need to split up your directory into a list of `MarcDirectoryEntries`. Here's the type signature of this function:

```
splitDirectory :: MarcDirectoryRaw -> [MarcDirectoryEntryRaw]
```

This is a fairly straightforward function: you take a chunk of 12 bytes and add them to a list until there's no more list left.

Listing 26.20 `splitDirectory` breaks down the directory into its entries

```
splitDirectory directory = if directory == B.empty
                           then []
                           else nextEntry : splitDirectory restEntries
  where (nextEntry, restEntries) = B.splitAt dirEntryLength directory
```

Now that you have this list of raw `DirectoryEntries`, you're close to finally getting your author and title data.

26.2.6 Processing the directory entries and looking up MARC fields

Each entry in the directory is like a miniature version of the record leader. The metadata for each entry has the following information:

- Tag of the field (first three characters)
- Length of the field (next four characters)
- Where the field starts relative to the base address (rest of the chars)

Because you want to use all this information, you're going to create a data type for your `FieldMetadata`.

Listing 26.21 `FieldMetadata` type

```
data FieldMetadata = FieldMetadata { tag         :: T.Text
                                   , fieldLength :: Int
                                   , fieldStart  :: Int } deriving Show
```

Next you have to process your list of `MarcDirectoryEntryRaw` into a list of `FieldMetadata`. As is often the case whenever you're working with lists, it's easier to start with transforming a single `MarcDirectoryEntryRaw` into a `FieldMetadata` type.

Listing 26.22 Converting a raw directory entry into a `FieldMetadata` type

```
makeFieldMetadata :: MarcDirectoryEntryRaw -> FieldMetadata
makeFieldMetadata entry = FieldMetadata textTag theLength theStart
  where (theTag,rest) = B.splitAt 3 entry
        textTag = E.decodeUtf8 theTag
        (rawLength,rawStart) = B.splitAt 4 rest
        theLength = rawToInt rawLength
        theStart = rawToInt rawStart
```

Now converting a list of one type to a list of another is as simple as using `map`.

Listing 26.23 Mapping `makeFieldMetadata` to `[FieldMetadata]`

```
getFieldMetadata ::  [MarcDirectoryEntryRaw] -> [FieldMetadata]
getFieldMetadata rawEntries = map makeFieldMetadata rawEntries
```

With `getFieldMetadata`, you can write a function that lets you look up the field itself. Now that you're looking up fields, you need to stop thinking in bytes and start thinking in text. Your fields will have information about author and title, and other text data. You'll create another type synonym for your `FieldText`.

Listing 26.24 Type synonym for `FieldText`

```
type FieldText = T.Text
```

What you want now is to take a `MarcRecordRaw`, `FieldMetadata` and get back a `FieldText` so you can start looking up useful values!

To do this, you first have to drop both the leader and the directory from your `MarcRecord` so you end up with the base record. Then you can drop the `fieldStart` from the record and finally take the `fieldLength` from this remaining bit.

Listing 26.25 Getting the `FieldText`

```
getTextField :: MarcRecordRaw -> FieldMetadata -> FieldText
getTextField record fieldMetadata = E.decodeUtf8 byteStringValue
  where recordLength = getRecordLength record
        baseAddress = getBaseAddress record
        baseRecord = B.drop baseAddress record
        baseAtEntry = B.drop (fieldStart fieldMetadata) baseRecord
        byteStringValue =  B.take (fieldLength fieldMetadata) baseAtEntry
```

You've come a long way in understanding this mysterious format. You have just one step to go, which is processing the `FieldText` into something you can use.

26.2.7 Getting Author and Title information from a MARC field

In MARC records, each special value is associated with a tag. For example, the `Title` tag is `245`. Unfortunately, this isn't the end of the story. Each field is made up of subfields that are separated by a delimiter, the ASCII character number 31. You can use `toEnum` to get this character.

Listing 26.26 Getting the field delimiter

```
fieldDelimiter :: Char
fieldDelimiter = toEnum 31
```

You can use T.split to split the FieldText into subfields. Each subfield is represented by a single character. Each subfield contains a value—for example, a title or author. Preceding the value is the subfield code, which is a single letter, as shown in figure 26.5.

```
aMudlumps at the mouth of South Pass, Mississippi River;
```

Figure 26.5 An example title subfield a. Notice that a is the first character of the title text you receive.

To fetch your title, you want field 245 and subfield a, with subfield a being the main title. For your author, you want field 100 and subfield a.

Listing 26.27 Tags and subfield codes for title and author

```
titleTag :: T.Text
titleTag = "245"

titleSubfield :: Char
titleSubfield = 'a'

authorTag :: T.Text
authorTag = "100"

authorSubfield :: Char
authorSubfield = 'a'
```

To get the value of a field, you need to look up its location in the record by using Field-Metadata. Then you split the raw field into its subfields. Finally, you look at the first character in each subfield to see whether the subfield you want is there.

Now you have another problem. You don't know for certain that the field you want will be in your record, and you also don't know that your subfield will be in your field. You need to use the Maybe type to check both of these. You'll start with lookupFieldMetadata, which will check the directory for the FieldMedata that you're looking for. If the field doesn't exist, it returns Nothing; otherwise, it returns just your field.

Listing 26.28 Safely looking up FieldMetadata from the directory

```
lookupFieldMetadata :: T.Text -> MarcRecordRaw -> Maybe FieldMetadata
lookupFieldMetadata aTag record = if length results < 1
                                  then Nothing
                                  else Just (head results)
```

```
  where metadata = (getFieldMetadata . splitDirectory . getDirectory)
                   record
        results = filter ((== aTag) . tag) metadata
```

Because you're going to be concerned with only looking up both a field and a subfield at the same time, you'll pass this `Maybe FieldMetadata` into the function that looks up a subfield. The `lookupSubfield` function will take a `Maybe FieldMetadata` argument, the subfield `Char`, and the `MarcRecordRaw`, returning a `Maybe BC.ByteString` of the data inside the subfield.

Listing 26.29 Safely looking up a potentially missing subfield

```
lookupSubfield :: (Maybe FieldMetadata) -> Char ->
                  MarcRecordRaw -> Maybe T.Text
lookupSubfield Nothing subfield record = Nothing
lookupSubfield (Just fieldMetadata) subfield record =
    if results == []
    then Nothing
    else Just ((T.drop 1 . head) results)
  where rawField = getTextField record fieldMetadata
        subfields = T.split (== fieldDelimiter) rawField
        results = filter ((== subfield) . T.head) subfields
```

If the metadata is missing, clearly you can't look up a subfield.

If the results of your search for the subfield are empty, the subfield isn't there.

Empty results mean you return nothing.

Otherwise, you turn your subfield value into Text and drop the first character, which is the subfield code.

All you care about is the value for a specific field/subfield combo. Next you'll create a specific `lookupValue` function that takes a tag, a subfield char, and a record.

Listing 26.30 General `lookupValue` function for looking up tag-subfield code pairs

```
lookupValue :: T.Text -> Char -> MarcRecordRaw -> Maybe T.Text
lookupValue aTag subfield record = lookupSubfield entryMetadata
                                                  subfield record
  where entryMetadata = lookupFieldMetadata aTag record
```

You can wrap up getting your values by making two helper functions for lookupAuthor and lookupTitle by using partial application.

Listing 26.31 Specific cases of looking up Title and Author

```
lookupTitle :: MarcRecordRaw -> Maybe Title
lookupTitle = lookupValue titleTag titleSubfield

lookupAuthor :: MarcRecordRaw -> Maybe Author
lookupAuthor = lookupValue authorTag authorSubfield
```

At this point, you've completely abstracted away the details of working with your MARC record format, and can build your final main, which will tie this all together.

26.3 Putting it all together

You've tackled the mess of writing a parser for your MARC records, but now you have access to a wide range of book information you can use. Remembering that you want as little in your main IO action as possible, and you also want to reduce all you have to do to converting a ByteString (representing the MARC file) to HTML (representing your output file). The first step is to convert your ByteString to a list of (Maybe Title, Maybe Author) pairs.

Listing 26.32 Raw MARC records to Maybe Title, Maybe Author pairs

```
marcToPairs :: B.ByteString -> [(Maybe Title, Maybe Author)]
marcToPairs marcStream = zip titles authors
 where records = allRecords marcStream
       titles = map lookupTitle records
       authors = map lookupAuthor records
```

Next you'd like to change these Maybe pairs into a list of books. You'll do this by only making a Book when both Author and Title are Just values. You'll use the fromJust function found in Data.Maybe to help with this.

Listing 26.33 Convert Maybe values into Books

```
pairsToBooks :: [(Maybe Title, Maybe Author)] -> [Book]
pairsToBooks pairs = map (\(title, author) -> Book {
                              title = fromJust title
```

```
                            ,author = fromJust author
                            }) justPairs
  where justPairs = filter (\(title,author) -> isJust title
                                           && isJust author) pairs
```

You already have your booksToHtml function from before, so now you can compose all these functions together to get your final processRecords function. Because there are so many records in your files, you'll also provide a parameter to specify the number of records you're looking up.

Listing 26.34 Putting it all together in processRecords

```
processRecords :: Int -> B.ByteString -> Html
processRecords n = booksToHtml . pairsToBooks . (take n) .  marcToPairs
```

Despite this being a lesson on I/O, and this being a fairly intensive I/O task, you might be surprised at how remarkably minimal your final main IO action is:

```
main :: IO ()
main = do
   marcData <- B.readFile  "sample.mrc"
   let processed = processRecords 500 marcData
   TIO.writeFile "books.html" processed
```

Now you've successfully converted your raw MARC records into a much more readable format. Notice that Unicode values also came out okay!

With lookupValue, you also have a nice, general tool you can use to look up any tag and subfield specified in the MARC standard.

Summary

In this capstone, you

- Modeled textual book data by using the Text type
- Wrote tools to perform binary fill processing by using ByteString to manipulate bits
- Safely managed Unicode text within a binary document by using decodeUtf8 and encodeUtf8
- Successfully transformed an opaque binary format into readable HTML

Extending the exercise

Now that you know the basics of processing MARC records, there's a world of interesting book data out there to explore. If you'd like to extend this exercise, look into fleshing out more of the details of processing the MARC record. For example, you may have noticed that trailing punctuation sometimes appears after our title. This is because a subfield `b` contains the rest of the extended title. Combining subfields `a` and `b` will give you the full title. The Library of Congress (LoC) provides extensive information on MARC records, and you can start exploring at www.loc.gov/marc/bibliographic/.

Another challenge you didn't tackle is dealing with an annoying non-Unicode character encoding that exists in a large number of MARC records called MARC-8. In MARC-8, a small subset of the Unicode characters is represented differently for historical reasons. The LoC has resources to add in this conversion: www.loc.gov/marc/specifications/speccharconversion.html. Whether a record is encoded in MARC-8 or standard Unicode can be determined from the leader. See the "Character Coding Scheme" section of the official LoC documentation: www.loc.gov/marc/bibliographic/bdleader.html.

Working with type in a context

In this unit, you'll take a look at three of Haskell's most powerful and often most confusing type classes: `Functor`, `Applicative`, and `Monad`. These type classes have funny names but a relatively straightforward purpose. Each one builds on the other to allow you to work in contexts such as `IO`. In unit 4, you made heavy use of the `Monad` type class to work in `IO`. In this unit, you'll get a much deeper understanding of how that works. To get a better feel for what these abstract type classes are doing, you'll explore types as though they were shapes.

One way to understand functions is as a means of transforming one type into another. Let's visualize two types as two shapes, a circle and a square, as shown in figure 1.

Figure 1 A circle and square visually representing two types

These shapes can represent any two types, `Int` and `Double`, `String` and `Text`, `Name` and `FirstName`, and so forth. When you want to transform a circle into a square, you use a function. You can visualize a function as a connector between two shapes, as shown in figure 2.

Figure 2 A function can transform a circle to a square.

This connector can represent any function from one type to another. This shape could represent (`Int -> Double`), (`String -> Text`), (`Name -> FirstName`), and so forth. When you want to apply a transformation, you can visualize placing your connector between the initial shape (in this case, a circle) and the desired shape (a square); see figure 3.

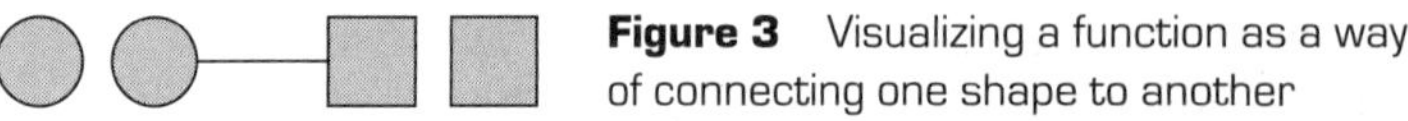

Figure 3 Visualizing a function as a way of connecting one shape to another

As long as each shape matches correctly, you can achieve your desired transformation.

In this unit, you'll look at working with types in context. The two best examples of types in context that you've seen are `Maybe` types and `IO` types. `Maybe` types represent a context in which a value might be missing, and `IO` types represent a context in which the value has interacted with I/O. Keeping with our visual language, you can imagine types in a context as shown in figure 4.

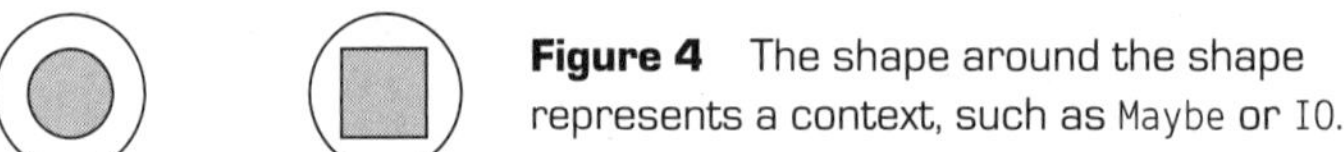

Figure 4 The shape around the shape represents a context, such as `Maybe` or `IO`.

These shapes can represent types such as `IO Int` and `IO Double`, `Maybe String` and `Maybe Text`, or `Maybe Name` and `Maybe FirstName`. Because these types are in a context, you can't simply use your old connector to make the transformation. So far in this book, you've relied on using functions that have both their input and output in a context as well. To perform the transformation of your types in a context, you need a connector that looks like figure 5.

Figure 5 A function that connects two types in a context

This connector represents functions with type signatures such as (`Maybe Int -> Maybe Double`), (`IO String -> IO Text`), and (`IO Name -> IO FirstName`). With this connector, you can easily transform types in a context, as shown in figure 6.

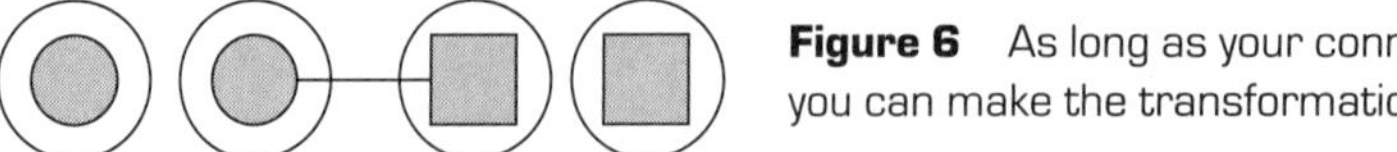

Figure 6 As long as your connector matches, you can make the transformation you want.

This may seem like a perfect solution, but there's a problem. Let's look at a function `halve`, which is of the type `Int -> Double`, and as expected halves the `Int` argument.

Listing 1 A `halve` function from `Int -> Double`

```
halve :: Int -> Double
halve n = fromIntegral n / 2.0
```

This is a straightforward function, but suppose you want to halve a `Maybe Int`. Given the tools you have, you have to write a wrapper for this that works with `Maybe` types.

Listing 2 `halveMaybe` wraps `halve` function to work with `Maybe` types

```
halveMaybe :: Maybe Int -> Maybe Double
halveMaybe (Just n) = Just (halve n)
halveMaybe Nothing = Nothing
```

For this one example, it's not a big deal to write a simple wrapper. But consider the wide range of existing functions from `a -> b`. To use any of these with `Maybe` types would require nearly identical wrappers. Even worse is that you have no way of writing these wrappers for `IO` types!

This is where `Functor`, `Applicative`, and `Monad` come in. You can think of these type classes as adapters that allow you to work with different connectors so long as the underlying types (circle and square) are the same. In the `halve` example, you worried about transforming your basic `Int`-to-`Double` adapter to work with types in context. This is the job of the `Functor` type class, illustrated in figure 7.

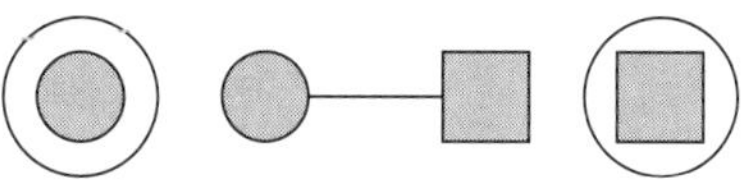

Figure 7 The `Functor` type class solves this mismatch between types in a context and a connector.

But you can have three other types of mismatches. The `Applicative` type class solves two of these. The first occurs when the first part of your connector is in a context, but not its result, as shown in figure 8.

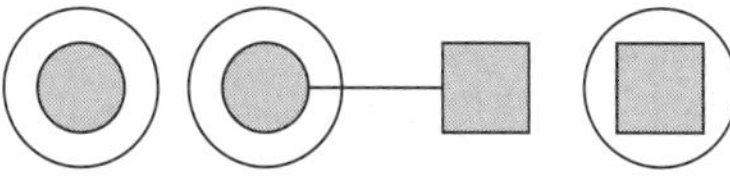

Figure 8 This is one of the mismatches that Applicative solves.

The other problem occurs when an entire function is in a context. For example, a function of the type `Maybe (Int -> Double)` means you have a function that might itself be missing. This may sound strange, but it can easily happen when using partial application with `Maybe` or `IO` types. Figure 9 illustrates this interesting case.

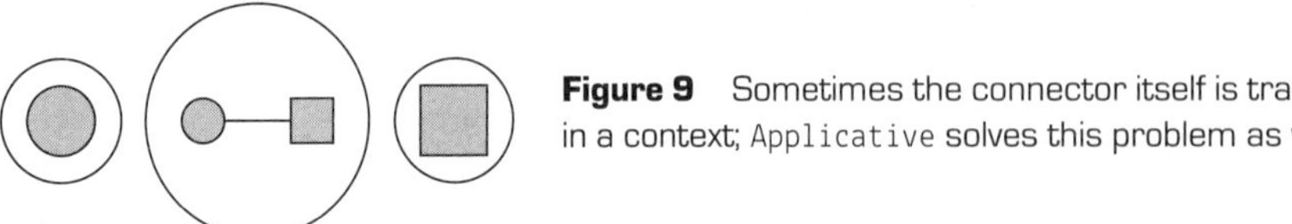

Figure 9 Sometimes the connector itself is trapped in a context; `Applicative` solves this problem as well.

There's only one possible mismatch between a function and types in a context left. This occurs when the argument to a function isn't in a context, but the result is. This is more common than you may think. Both `Map.lookup` and `putStrLn` have type signatures like this. This problem is solved by the `Monad` type class, illustrated in figure 10.

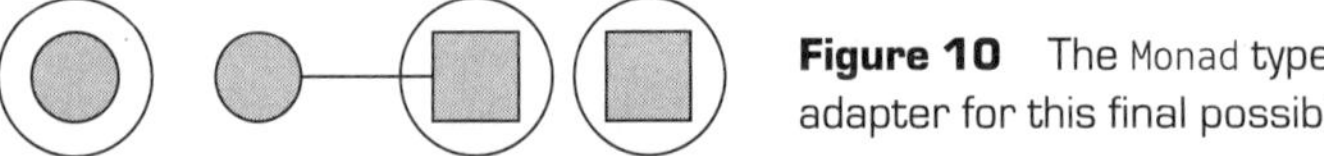

Figure 10 The `Monad` type class provides an adapter for this final possible mismatch.

When you combine all three of these type classes, there's no function that you can't use in a context such as `Maybe` or `IO`, so long as the underlying types match. This is a big deal because it means that you can perform any computation you'd like in a context and have the tools to reuse large amounts of existing code between different contexts.

LESSON

THE FUNCTOR TYPE CLASS

After reading lesson 27, you'll be able to

- Use the `Functor` type class
- Solve problems with `fmap` and `<$>`
- Understand kinds for `Functors`

So far in this book, you've seen quite a few parameterized types (types that take another type as an argument). You've looked at types that represent containers, such as `List` and `Map`. You've also seen parameterized types that represent a context, such as `Maybe` for missing values and `IO` for values that come from the complex world of I/O. In this lesson, you'll explore the powerful `Functor` type class. The `Functor` type class provides a generic interface for applying functions to values in a container or context. To get a sense of this, suppose you have the following types:

- `[Int]`
- `Map String Int`
- `Maybe Int`
- `IO Int`

These are four different types, but they're all parameterized by the same type: `Int` (`Map` is a special case, but the values are type `Int`). Now suppose you have a function with the following type signature:

```
Int -> String
```

This is a function that takes an `Int` and returns a `String`. In most programming languages, you'd need to write a custom version for your `Int -> String` function for each of these parameterized types. Because of the `Functor` type class, you have a uniform way to apply your single function to all these cases.

Consider this You have a potentially missing `Int` (a `Maybe Int`). You want to square this value, turn it into a string, and then add an `!` to the end. The function that you want to pass this value to, `printInt`, assumes that there might be missing values already:

```
printInt :: Maybe String -> IO ()
printInt Nothing = putStrLn "value missing"
printInt (Just val) = putStrLn val
```

How can you transform your `Maybe Int` into a `Maybe String` to be used by `printInt`?

27.1 An example: computing in a Maybe

`Maybe` has already proven a useful solution to your problem of potentially missing values. But when you were introduced to `Maybe` in lesson 19, you still had to deal with the problem of handling the possibility of a missing value as soon as you encountered it in your program. It turns out you can do computation on a potentially missing value without having to worry about whether it's actually missing.

Suppose you get a number from a database. There are plenty of reasons why a request to a database would result in a null value. Here are two sample values of type `Maybe Int`: `failedRequest` and `successfulRequest`.

Listing 27.1 Possibly null values: `successfulRequest` and `failedRequest`

```
successfulRequest :: Maybe Int
successfulRequest = Just 6

failedRequest :: Maybe Int
failedRequest = Nothing
```

Next imagine you need to increment the number you received from the database and then write it back to the database. From a design standpoint, assume that the logic that talks to the database handles the case of null values by not writing the value. Ideally, you'd like to keep your value in a Maybe. Given what you know so far, you could write a special incMaybe function to handle this.

Listing 27.2 Defining incMaybe to increment Maybe Int values

```
incMaybe :: Maybe Int -> Maybe Int
incMaybe (Just n) = Just (n + 1)
incMaybe Nothing = Nothing
```

In GHCi, this works just fine:

```
GHCi> incMaybe successfulRequest
Just 7
GHCi> incMaybe failedRequest
Nothing
```

The problem is that this solution scales horribly. The increment function is just (+ 1), but in our example, you need to rewrite it for Maybe. This solution means that you'd have to rewrite a special version of every existing function you want to use in a Maybe! This greatly limits the usefulness of tools such as Maybe. It turns out Haskell has a type class that solves this problem, called Functor.

Quick check 27.1 Write the function reverseMaybe :: Maybe String -> Maybe String that reverses a Maybe String and returns it as a Maybe String.

27.2 Using functions in context with the Functor type class

Haskell has a wonderful solution to this problem. Maybe is a member of the Functor type class. The Functor type class requires only one definition: fmap, as shown in figure 27.1.

QC 27.1 answer

```
reverseMaybe :: Maybe String -> Maybe String
reverseMaybe Nothing = Nothing
reverseMaybe (Just string) = Just (reverse string)
```

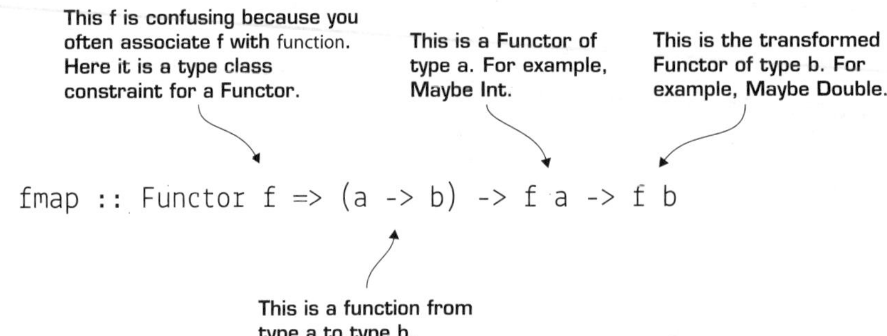
This f is confusing because you often associate f with function. Here it is a type class constraint for a Functor.
This is a Functor of type a. For example, Maybe Int.
This is the transformed Functor of type b. For example, Maybe Double.
fmap :: Functor f => (a -> b) -> f a -> f b
This is a function from type a to type b.

Figure 27.1 The type signature for the `fmap` function

Going back to your visual language from the introduction, `fmap` provides an adapter, as shown in figure 27.2. Notice that we're using `<$>`, which is a synonym for `fmap` (except it's a binary operator rather than a function).

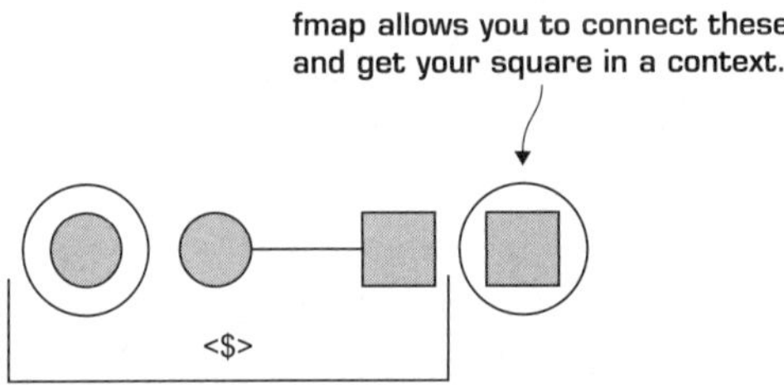
fmap allows you to connect these and get your square in a context.
<$>

Figure 27.2 Visualizing how `fmap`, also `<$>`, works as an adapter, allowing you to work with types in a context.

You can define `fmap` as a generalization of your custom `incMaybe` function.

Listing 27.3 Making `Maybe` an instance of `Functor`

```
instance Functor Maybe where
  fmap func (Just n) = Just (func n)
  fmap func Nothing = Nothing
```

With fmap, you no longer need a special function for keeping your value in a Maybe:

```
GHCi> fmap (+ 1) successfulRequest
Just 7
GHCi> fmap (+ 1) failedRequest
Nothing
```

Though fmap is the official function name, in practice the binary operator <$> is used much more frequently:

```
GHCi> (+ 1) <$> successfulRequest
Just 7
GHCi> (+ 1) <$> failedRequest
Nothing
```

In this example, (+ 1) adds 1 into the Maybe Int and returns a Maybe Int as well. But it's important to realize that the type signature of the function in fmap is (a -> b), meaning that the Maybe returned doesn't need to be parameterized by the same type. Here are two examples of going from a Maybe Int to a Maybe String.

Listing 27.4 Examples of using fmaps from one type to another

```
successStr :: Maybe String
successStr = show <$> successfulRequest

failStr :: Maybe String
failStr = show <$> failedRequest
```

This ability to transform the types of values inside a Maybe is the true power of the Functor type class.

Quick check 27.2 Use fmap or <$> to reverse a Maybe String.

QC 27.2 answer

```
GHCi> reverse <$> Just "cat"
Just "tac"
```

Strange type class names?

Semigroup, Monoid, and now Functor! What's up with these weird type class names? All these names come from fields of mathematics called abstract algebra and category theory. You absolutely don't need to know any advanced mathematics to use them. All of these type classes represent the design patterns of functional programming. If you've used Java, C#, or any enterprise programming language, you're likely familiar with object-oriented design patterns such as the Singleton, Observer, and Factory patterns. These names are more reasonable-sounding only because they've become part of the everyday vocabulary of OOP. Both OOP design patterns and category theoretic type classes abstract out common programming patterns. The only difference is that Haskell's are based on mathematical foundations, rather than ad hoc patterns discovered in code. Just as Haskell's functions derive power from their mathematical basis, so do Haskell's design patterns.

27.3 Functors are everywhere!

To understand instances of Functor, you'll run through some examples. Recall from lesson 18 that kinds are the types of types. Types of a kind * -> * are parameterized types that take just one type parameter. All Functors must be of kind * ->*. It also turns out that many parameterized types of kind * -> * are instances of Functor.

Members of Functor that you've seen so far in this book include List, Map, Maybe, and IO. To demonstrate how Functor allows you to generalize by solving a single problem the same way in multiple parameterized types, you'll explore how working with the same data type in multiple contexts can represent different problems. Then you'll see how Functor's <$> makes it easy to solve each of these problems in the same way. Rather than work with simple types such as Int or String, you'll work with something more complicated: a RobotPart data type.

27.3.1 One interface for four problems

In this example, you're going to assume that you're in the business of manufacturing robot parts. Here's the basic data type for your robot part.

Listing 27.5 RobotPart defined using record syntax

```
data RobotPart = RobotPart
   { name :: String
   , description :: String
```

```
  , cost :: Double
  , count :: Int
  } deriving Show
```

Here are some example robot parts you'll use in this section.

Listing 27.6 Example robot parts: `leftArm`, `rightArm`, and `robotHead`

```
leftArm :: RobotPart
leftArm  = RobotPart
   { name = "left arm"
   , description = "left arm for face punching!"
   , cost = 1000.00
   , count = 3
   }

rightArm :: RobotPart
rightArm  = RobotPart
   { name = "right arm"
   , description = "right arm for kind hand gestures"
   , cost = 1025.00
   , count = 5
   }

robotHead :: RobotPart
robotHead  = RobotPart
   { name = "robot head"
   , description = "this head looks mad"
   , cost = 5092.25
   , count = 2
   }
```

One of the most common things you'll need to do is to render the information contained in a `RobotPart` as HTML. Here's code for rendering an individual `RobotPart` as an HTML snippet.

Listing 27.7 Rendering a RobotPart as HTML

```
type Html = String

renderHtml :: RobotPart -> Html
renderHtml part = mconcat ["<h2>",partName, "</h2>"
                          ,"<p><h3>desc</h3>",partDesc
                          ,"</p><p><h3>cost</h3>"
                          ,partCost
                          ,"</p><p><h3>count</h3>"
                          ,partCount,"</p>"]
 where partName = name part
       partDesc = description part
       partCost = show (cost part)
       partCount = show (count part)
```

In many cases, you'll want to convert a RobotPart into an HTML snippet. Next you'll see four scenarios of this, using different parametrized types.

You'll start by using the Map type to create partsDB, which is your internal database of RobotParts.

Listing 27.8 Your RobotPart "database"

```
import qualified Data.Map as Map

partsDB :: Map.Map Int RobotPart
partsDB = Map.fromList keyVals
 where keys = [1,2,3]
       vals = [leftArm,rightArm,robotHead]
       keyVals = zip keys vals
```

Remember to include this in the top of your file if you're using Map.

Map is a useful type for this example because it naturally involves three instances of Functor: it's made from a List, returns Maybe values, and is itself a Functor.

27.3.2 Converting a Maybe RobotPart to Maybe Html

Now suppose you have a website driven by partsDB. It's reasonable that you'd have a request containing an ID for a part that you wish to insert into a web page. You'll assume that an insertSnippet IO action will take HTML and insert it into a page's template. It's also reasonable to assume that many data models might be generating snippets. Because any one of these models may have an error, you'll assume that `insertSnippet` accepts `Maybe Html` as its input, allowing the template engine to handle missing snippets as it sees fit. Here's the type signature of your imaginary function:

```
insertSnippet :: Maybe Html -> IO ()
```

The problem you need to solve is looking up a part and passing that part as `Maybe Html` to `insertSnippet`. Here's an example of fetching a `RobotPart` from your `partsDB`.

Listing 27.9 `partVal`: a `Maybe RobotPart` value

```
partVal :: Maybe RobotPart
partVal = Map.lookup 1 partsDB
```

Because `Maybe` is a `Functor`, you can use `<$>` to transform your `RobotPart` into HTML while remaining in a `Maybe`.

Listing 27.10 Using `<$>` to transform `RobotPart` to HTML, remaining in `Maybe`

```
partHtml :: Maybe Html
partHtml = renderHtml <$> partVal
```

You can now pass `partHtml` to `insertSnippet` easily because of `Functor`.

27.3.3 Converting a list of RobotParts to a list of HTML

Next suppose you want to create an index page of all your parts. You can get a list of parts from your `partsDB` like this.

Listing 27.11 A list of `RobotParts`

```
allParts :: [RobotPart]
allParts = map snd (Map.toList partsDB)
```

`List` is also an instance of `Functor`. In fact, `fmap` for a `List` is the regular map function you've been using since unit 1. Here's how you can apply `renderHtml` to a list of values by using `<$>`.

Listing 27.12 Transforming a list of `RobotParts` to HTML with `<$>` instead of `map`

```
allPartsHtml :: [Html]
allPartsHtml = renderHtml <$> allParts
```

Because <$> is just `fmap`, and for lists `fmap` is just `map`, this code is identical to the following.

Listing 27.13 The traditional way of transforming a list by using `map`

```
allPartsHtml :: [Html]
allPartsHtml = map renderHtml allParts
```

For lists, it's more common to use `map` over <$>, but it's important to realize these are identical. One way to think of the `Functor` type class is as "things that can be mapped over."

> **Quick check 27.3** Rewrite the definition of all parts to use <$> instead of `map`.

27.3.4 Converting a Map of RobotParts to HTML

The `partsDB` `Map` has been useful, but it turns out all you need it for is converting `RobotParts` to HTML. If that's the case, wouldn't it make more sense to have an `htmlPartsDB` so you don't have to continually convert? Because `Map` is an instance of `Functor`, you can do this easily.

Listing 27.14 Turning your `partsDB` into a `Map` of HTML rather than `RobotParts`

```
htmlPartsDB :: Map.Map Int Html
htmlPartsDB = renderHtml <$> partsDB
```

Now you can see that you've transformed your `Map` of `RobotParts` into a `Map` of `Html` snippets!

```
GHCi>Map.lookup 1 htmlPartsDB
Just "<h2>left arm</h2><p><h3>desc</h3>left ...
```

This example highlights just how powerful the simple interface that `Functor` provides can be. You can now trivially perform any transformation that you can on a `RobotPart` to an entire `Map` of robot parts.

QC 27.3 answer

```
allParts :: [RobotPart]
allParts = snd <$> Map.toList partsDB
```

The careful reader may have noticed something strange about `Map` being a `Functor`. `Map`'s kind is `* -> * -> *` because `Map` takes two type arguments, one for its keys and another for its values. Earlier we said that `Functor`s must be of kind `* -> *`, so how can this be? If you look at the behavior of `<$>` on your `partsDB`, it becomes clear. `Functor` for `Map` is concerned only about the `Map`'s values and not its keys. When `Map` is made an instance of `Functor`, you're concerned only about a single type variable, the one used for its values. So for the purposes of `Map` being a member of `Functor`, you treat it as being of kind `* -> *`. When we introduced kinds in lesson 18, they may have seemed overly abstract. But they can be useful for catching issues that arise with more advanced type classes.

27.3.5 Transforming an IO RobotPart into IO Html

Finally, you might have a `RobotPart` that comes from `IO`. You'll simulate this by using `return` to create an `IO` type of a `RobotPart`.

Listing 27.15 Simulating a `RobotPart` coming from an `IO` context

```
leftArmIO :: IO RobotPart
leftArmIO = return leftArm
```

Suppose you want to turn this into HTML so that you can write the HTML snippet to a file. By now, the pattern should start to be familiar.

Listing 27.16 Transforming

```
htmlSnippet :: IO Html
htmlSnippet = renderHtml <$> leftArmIO
```

Let's take a look at all of these transformations at once:

```
partHtml :: Maybe Html
partHtml = renderHtml <$> partVal

allPartsHtml :: [Html]
allPartsHtml = renderHtml <$> allParts

htmlPartsDB :: Map.Map Int Html
htmlPartsDB = renderHtml <$> partsDB

htmlSnippet :: IO Html
htmlSnippet = renderHtml <$> leftArmIO
```

As you can see, Functor's <$> provides a common interface to apply any function to a value in a context. For types such as List and Map, this is a convenient way to update values in these containers. For IO, it's essential to be able to change values in an IO context, because you can't take IO values out of their context.

Summary

In this lesson, our objective was to introduce you to the Functor type class. The Functor type class allows you to apply an ordinary function to values inside a container (for example, List) or a context (for example, IO or Maybe). If you have a function Int -> Double and a value Maybe Int, you can use Functor's fmap (or the <$> operator) to apply the Int -> Double function to the Maybe Int value, resulting in a Maybe Double value. Functors are incredibly useful because they allow you to reuse a single function with any type belonging to the Functor type class. [Int], Maybe Int, and IO Int can all use the same core functions. Let's see if you got this.

Q27.1 When we introduced parameterized types in lesson 15, you used a minimal type Box as the example:

```
data Box a = Box a deriving Show
```

Implement the Functor type class for Box. Then implement morePresents, which changes a box from type Box a to one of type Box [a], which has *n* copies of the original value in the box in a list. Make sure to use fmap to implement this.

QC27.2 Now suppose you have a simple box like this:

```
myBox :: Box Int
myBox = Box 1
```

Use fmap to put the value in your Box in another Box. Then define a function unwrap that takes a value out of a box, and use fmap on that function to get your original box. Here's how your code should work in GHCi:

```
GHCi> wrapped = fmap ? myBox
GHCi> wrapped
Box (Box 1)
GHCi> fmap unwrap wrapped
Box 1
```

Q27.3 Write a command-line interface for partsDB that lets the user look up the cost of an item, given an ID. Use the Maybe type to handle the case of the user entering missing input.

A PEEK AT THE APPLICATIVE TYPE CLASS: USING FUNCTIONS IN A CONTEXT

After reading lesson 28, you'll be able to

- Build an application that handles missing data
- Extend the power of the `Functor` type class with the `Applicative` type
- Use `Applicative` to use one data model in many contexts

In the preceding lesson, you learned how the `Functor` type class allows you to perform computation inside a container such as `List` or a context such as `Maybe` and `IO`. The key method behind `Functor` is `fmap` (more commonly, the `<$>` operator), which works just like `map` on a list. In this lesson, you'll work with a more powerful type class called `Applicative`. The `Applicative` type class extends the power of `Functor` by allowing you to use functions that are themselves in a context.

Although this may not seem useful, it allows you to chain together long sequences of computation in a context such as `IO` or `Maybe`.

In your first example, you'll see the limitations of `Functor` by building a command-line tool that allows the user to calculate the distance between two cities. The issue is that you need to pass two `Maybe` values to a function, which surprisingly `Functor` can't do. You'll then see how `Applicative` resolves this issue. After you learn about `Applicative`, you'll see how this can help you create data in the context of either `IO` or `Maybe`, while allowing you to reuse the majority of your code.

Consider this You want to combine a first- and last-name string to create a person's name: `"Alan" ++ " " ++ "Turing"`. The trouble is, both your first and last names are `Maybe Strings` because they come from an unreliable source and might be missing. How can you combine these `Strings` and return a `Maybe String` for the name?

28.1 A command-line application for calculating the distance between cities

In this section, you're going to build a simple command-line application that allows the user to enter cities by name and then returns the distance between them. The big challenge you'll face is ensuring that your application fails gracefully when the user enters a city not in your database. You'll use the `Maybe` type and the `Functor` type class to achieve this, but you'll find you need something a bit more powerful to deal with having two values in a `Maybe` context.

> **NOTE** Everything in this section should go in a file named dist.hs.

Let's assume you have a `Map` type (remember to add `import qualified Data.Map as Map`) for locations on the globe and their latitude and longitude as a tuple.

Listing 28.1 Using a Map as your database of city coordinates

```
type LatLong = (Double,Double)

locationDB :: Map.Map String LatLong
locationDB = Map.fromList [("Arkham",(42.6054,-70.7829))
                          ,("Innsmouth",(42.8250,-70.8150))
                          ,("Carcosa",(29.9714,-90.7694))
                          ,("New York",(40.7776,-73.9691))]
```

What you'd like to do is calculate the distance between two points on the globe from your `locationDB`. To do this, you need to use the formula for calculating distance on a globe. Because a globe curves, you can't calculate the straight-line distance between two points. Instead, you need to use the *Haversine formula*. Note that you need to convert your latitude and longitude to radians first. Here's an implementation of `haversine` (you don't need to understand the details of this function).

Listing 28.2 Computing the distance between two points with `haversine`

```
toRadians :: Double -> Double
toRadians degrees = degrees * pi / 180

latLongToRads :: LatLong -> (Double,Double)
latLongToRads (lat,long) = (rlat,rlong)
 where rlat = toRadians lat
       rlong = toRadians long

haversine :: LatLong -> LatLong -> Double
haversine coords1 coords2 = earthRadius * c
 where (rlat1,rlong1) = latLongToRads coords1
       (rlat2,rlong2) = latLongToRads coords2
       dlat = rlat2 - rlat1
       dlong = rlong2 - rlong1
       a = (sin (dlat/2))^2 + cos rlat1 * cos rlat2 * (sin (dlong/2))^2
       c = 2 * atan2 (sqrt a) (sqrt (1-a))
       earthRadius = 3961.0
```

Here's an example of using `haversine` to compute the distance between two points on the globe:

```
GHCi> haversine (40.7776,-73.9691) (42.6054,-70.7829)
207.3909006336738
```

Next you want to make a simple command-line tool that will let the user get the distance between two cities. You want the user to enter in two city names, and you'll return the distance. Given that you're dealing with user input, you definitely need to handle the case in which the user enters a city that doesn't exist in your database. If one of the names is missing, you'll let the user know that an error occurred in their input.

As is often helpful, you'll start reasoning backward from where you want to end up. What you want to end up with is an `IO` action that takes a `Maybe` value for your distance and either prints the distance or tells the user that an error occurred.

Listing 28.3 An `IO` action to handle printing your potentially missing distance

```
printDistance :: Maybe Double -> IO ()
printDistance Nothing = putStrLn "Error, invalid city entered"
printDistance (Just distance) = putStrLn (show distance ++ " miles")
```

Now you just have to tie everything together. You need to get two locations from your locationDB, calculate their distance, and then pass that distance to printDistance. The trouble is that your locationDB will give you Maybe values. Thinking in types, here's the problem. You have haversine, which is of this type:

```
haversine :: LatLong -> LatLong -> Double
```

What you need is a function that looks like figure 28.1.

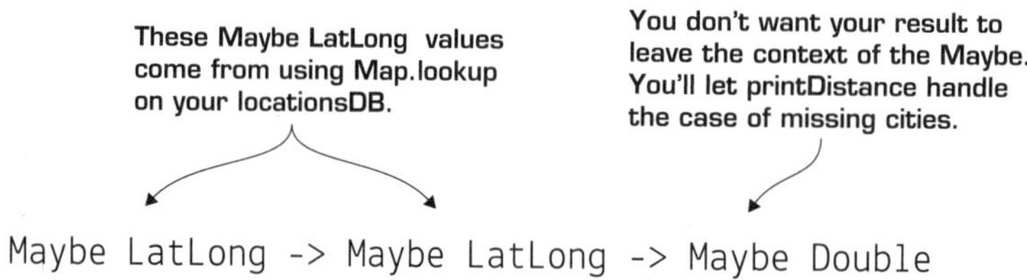

Figure 28.1 The signature of the function you need to connect your locationsDB with printDistance

This is almost exactly the type signature of haversine, but everything is in the context of a Maybe. This problem should be reminiscent of the problem you solved with Functor. You want to be able to use normal functions in a context. The naive solution is to put a wrapper function around haversine, which will work the specific case of Maybe.

Listing 28.4 One solution to working in a Maybe is to create wrapper functions

```
haversineMaybe :: Maybe LatLong -> Maybe LatLong -> Maybe Double
haversineMaybe Nothing _ = Nothing
haversineMaybe _ Nothing = Nothing
haversineMaybe (Just val1) (Just val2) = Just (haversine val1 val2)
```

The haversineMaybe solution is a poor one for two reasons. First, you have to write wrappers for any similar function, which is needlessly repetitive. Second, you have to write a different version of haversineMaybe for other similar context types such as IO. Because the promise of the Functor type is to provide a general way of working in different contexts, let's see if you can solve this problem with Functor.

Quick check 28.1 Write addMaybe for adding two Maybe Ints.

28.1.1 The limitations of Functor

Before you dive in, let's refresh your memory on `Functor`'s only method, `fmap`, and look at its type signature, shown in figure 28.2.

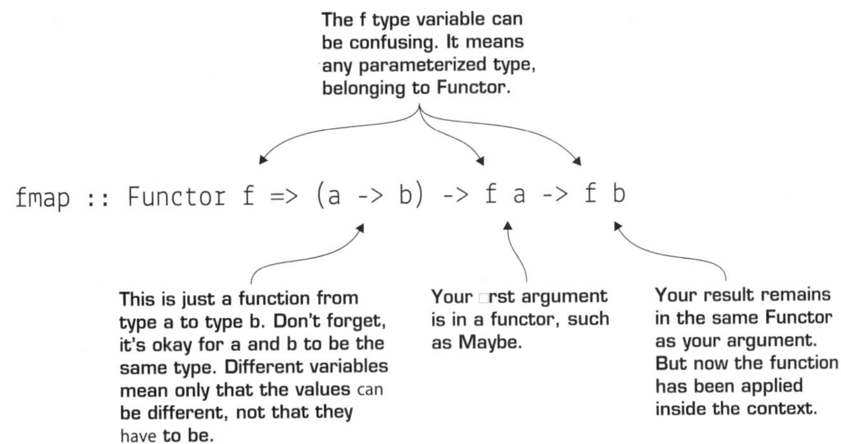

Figure 28.2 Annotated type signature for `Functor`'s only method, `fmap`

The `fmap` function takes any function from type `a` to type `b`, and the value of type `a` in the context of a `Functor` (like `Maybe`), and returns a value of type `b` in the same context. If you think of the problem in terms of types, this is pretty close. The major difference is you have one extra argument. What you want to do is this:

1. Take `haversine`, which is `(LatLong -> LatLong -> Double)`.
2. Take two arguments of type `Maybe`: `Maybe LatLong -> Maybe LatLong`.
3. And finally, you want your answer in a `Maybe`: `Maybe Double`.

QC 28.1 answer

```
addMaybe :: Maybe Int -> Maybe Int -> Maybe Int
addMaybe (Just x) (Just y) = Just (x + y)
addMaybe _ _ = Nothing
```

This leads to the following series of type transformations:

```
(LatLong -> LatLong -> Double) ->
      (Maybe LatLong ->  Maybe LatLong -> Maybe Double)
```

If you translate this to a more generic type signature, you get the following:

```
Functor f => (a -> b -> c) -> f a -> f b -> f c
```

This is nearly identical to `fmap`, except you're adding one argument. This is one of the limitations of `Functor`'s `fmap`: it only works on single-argument functions. Because your main problem is having an extra argument, using partial application should move you close to a solution.

> **Quick check 28.2** Suppose you don't have to worry about `Maybe`s and have raw coordinate pairs. If you have the pair `newYork`, how would you make a function `distanceFromNY` that's waiting for an additional location?

28.2 Using <*> for partial application in a context

The problem you need to solve now is generalizing `Functor`'s `fmap` to work with multiple arguments. In lesson 5, you learned that partial application means that calling an argument with fewer arguments than it requires results in a function waiting for the remaining arguments. Then in section 10.2.2, you saw that all functions are functions of one argument. Multi-argument functions are just a chain of single-argument functions. The key to solving your problem lies in being able to perform partial application in a context such as `Maybe` or `IO`.

The real limitation of `Functor`'s `<$>` is that if you end up with a function in a context, through partial application, you have no way of using that function. For example, you can use `<$>`, `(+)`, and the number 1 in a context to create a `maybeInc` function.

Listing 28.5 Using `Functor`'s `<$>` operator for partial application in a context

```
maybeInc = (+) <$> Just 1
```

QC 28.2 answer

```
distanceFromNY = haversine newYork
```

If you look up the type of this function, you find that it's as follows:

```
maybeInc :: Maybe (Integer -> Integer)
```

The (+) operator is a function that takes two values; by using <$> on a Maybe value, you created a function waiting for a missing value, but it's inside a Maybe. You now have a Maybe function, but there's no way to apply this function! Recalling the visual language of circles and squares in context, you've arrived at a problem of finding an adapter for the situation illustrated in figure 28.3.

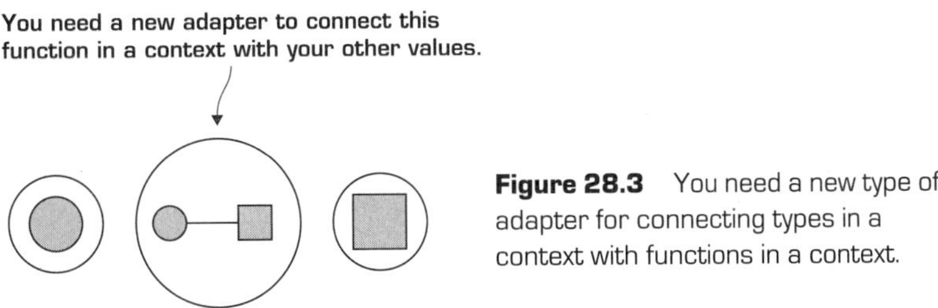

Figure 28.3 You need a new type of adapter for connecting types in a context with functions in a context.

Thankfully, there's another type class that solves precisely this problem!

28.2.1 Introducing the <*> operator

A powerful type class called Applicative contains a method that's the <*> operator (pronounced *app*). If you look at the type signature of <*>, you can see what this does, as shown in figure 28.4.

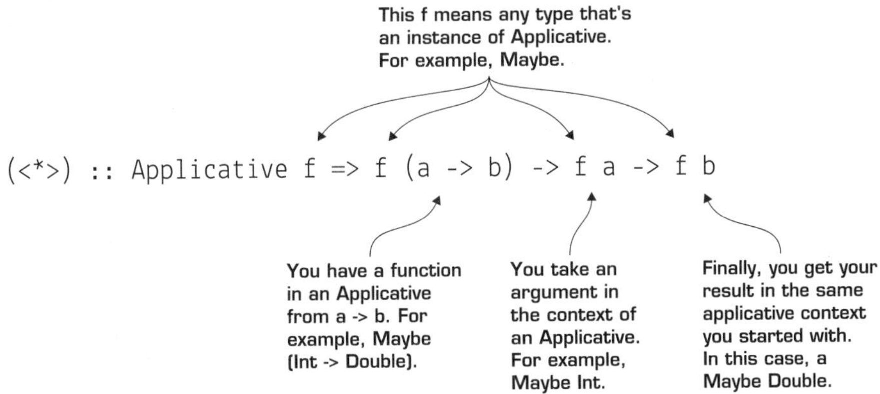

Figure 28.4 Annotated type signature for the <*> operator

Applicative's <*> allows you to apply a function in a context. Now you can use maybeInc to increment Maybe values. Here are a couple of examples in GHCi:

```
GHCi> maybeInc <*> Just 5
Just 6
GHCi> maybeInc <*> Nothing
Nothing
GHCi> maybeInc <*> Just 100
Just 101
```

You've not only solved the case of combining two values inside a Maybe, but also found a general way to use existing binary functions in a Maybe context.

You can use this to combine Strings in a Maybe context as well:

```
GHCi> (++) <$> Just "cats" <*> Just " and dogs"
Just "cats and dogs"
GHCi> (++) <$> Nothing <*> Just " and dogs"
Nothing
GHCi> (++) <$> Just "cats" <*> Nothing
Nothing
```

Because of the way partial application works, you can use <$> and <*> to chain together any number of arguments.

Quick check 28.3 Use the pattern for using binary values in a context for the functions (*), div, and mod on these two values:

```
val1 = Just 10
val2 = Just 5
```

QC 28.3 answer

```
val1 = (Just 10)
val2 = (Just 5)
result1 = (+) <$> val1 <*> val2
result2 = div <$> val1 <*> val2
result3 = mod <$> val1 <*> val2
```

28.2.2 Using <*> to finish your city distance program

With `Applicative` and `<*>`, you can finally solve your problem of wanting to use your `haversine` function with two `Maybe` values:

```
GHCi> startingCity = Map.lookup "Carcosa" locationDB
GHCi> destCity = Map.lookup "Innsmouth" locationDB
GHCi> haversine <$> startingCity <*> destCity
Just 1415.7942372467567
```

Because of heavy use of operators here, this can be difficult to parse. Figure 28.5 illustrates the key part of this to help clarify.

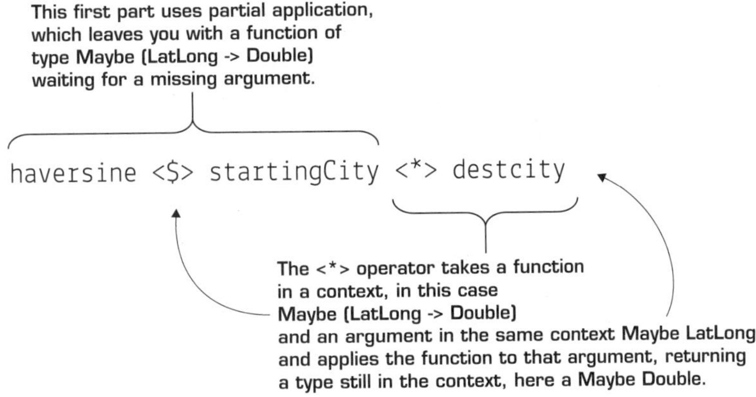

Figure 28.5 Combining `<$>` with `<*>` to compute `haversine` in a `Maybe` context

Now that you can extend the power of `fmap` with `<*>`, you can put everything together to build a program that will take two city names from user input, and output the distance. Here's the `main` for your program.

Listing 28.6 The `main` for dist.hs

```
main :: IO ()
main = do
   putStrLn "Enter the starting city name:"
   startingInput <- getLine
   let startingCity = Map.lookup startingInput locationDB
   putStrLn "Enter the destination city name:"
   destInput <- getLine
```

```
    let destCity = Map.lookup destInput locationDB
    let distance = haversine <$> startingCity <*> destCity
    printDistance distance
```

If you compile this program, you can see that you can now handle user input errors quite well:

```
$ ./dist
Enter the starting city name:
Carcosa
Enter the destination city name:
Innsmouth
1415.7942372467567 miles
```

And now an example with a city not in your database:

```
$ ./dist
Enter the starting city name:
Carcosa
Enter the destination city name:
Chicago
Error, invalid city entered
```

This example demonstrates the value of `Functors` and `Applicatives`. You just wrote a program that handles missing values well, but not once did you have to check whether a value was null using conditionals, or worry about exception handling. Even better, you could write the core functionality of your program, `haversine`, as though nothing in the world might go wrong.

Haskell's type system makes it impossible for you to accidentally pass a `Maybe LatLong` to `haversine`. In nearly every other programming language, even those with static types such as Java and C#, there's no way to ensure that a null value doesn't sneak into a function. `Functor` and `Applicative` complement this safety by making it easy to mix regular functions such as `haversine` with `Maybe` types or `IO` types, without compromising that safety.

28.2.3 Using a multi-argument function in IO using <$> and <*>

`IO` is also a member of `Applicative`. To show this off, let's see how to use `<$>` and `<*>` to make a simple command-line tool that returns the minimum of three numbers entered by the user, called min3.hs. You'll start with a three-argument function called `minOfThree`, which gives you the minimum of three values.

Listing 28.7 `minOfThree` function takes three arguments and returns the smallest

```
minOfThree :: (Ord a) => a -> a -> a -> a
minOfThree val1 val2 val3 = min val1 (min val2 val3)
```

Next you'll create a simple `IO` action, `readInt`, which will read an `Int` from the command line.

Listing 28.8 A simple `readInt` `IO` action made using <$>

```
readInt :: IO Int
readInt = read <$> getLine
```

Now you can use <$> with <*> to make an `IO` action that reads in three `Int`s and returns the minimum.

Listing 28.9 `minOfInts` shows using multiple arguments with <*>

```
minOfInts :: IO Int
minOfInts = minOfThree <$> readInt <*> readInt <*> readInt
```

Finally, you can put this in a `main`.

Listing 28.10 Your `main` for min3.hs

```
main :: IO ()
main = do
   putStrLn "Enter three numbers"
   minInt <- minOfInts
   putStrLn (show minInt ++ " is the smallest")
```

Now you can compile and run your min3.hs:

```
$ ghc min3.hs
$ ./min3.hs
Enter three numbers
1
2
3

1 is the smallest
```

Because of the power of partial application and <*>, you can chain together as many arguments as you'd like!

Quick check 28.4 Use `minOfThree` to get the `Maybe Int` value of these three `Maybe` values:

```
Just 10
Just 3
Just 6
```

28.3 Using <*> to create data in a context

One of the most common uses of `Applicatives` in practice occurs when you want to create data, but all the information you need for the data is in a context such as a `Maybe` or `IO`. For example, suppose you have user data for a video game.

Listing 28.11 User data for a game

```
data User = User
   { name :: String
   , gamerId :: Int
   , score :: Int
   } deriving Show
```

It's important to note that just because you're using record syntax doesn't mean that you can't create the type as you would without it. For example:

```
GHCi> User {name = "Sue", gamerId = 1337, score = 9001}
User {name = "Sue", gamerId = 1337, score = 9001}
GHCi> User "Sue" 1337 9001
User {name = "Sue", gamerId = 1337, score = 9001}
GHCi>
```

Let's look at two cases where you want to create a user from data that's in a context.

QC 28.4 answer

```
GHCi> minOfThree <$> Just 10 <*> Just 3 <*> Just 6
Just 3
```

28.3.1 Creating a user in the context of a Maybe

The first context is a `Maybe`. It's reasonable to assume that you've gathered the necessary information from sources in which the data might be missing. Here are some sample `Maybe` types that you'll pretend come from a server that might have accidently sent you missing data.

Listing 28.12 `Maybe` types for the necessary information to create a user

```
serverUsername :: Maybe String
serverUsername = Just "Sue"

serverGamerId :: Maybe Int
serverGamerId =  Just 1337

serverScore :: Maybe Int
serverScore = Just 9001
```

To create a user from this data, you can use `<$>` and `<*>`, because your data constructor `User` works as a function that takes three arguments. Here's your code to do this in GHCi:

```
GHCi> User <$> serverUsername <*> serverGamerId <*> serverScore
Just (User {name = "Sue", gamerId = 1337, score = 9001})
```

Another context in which you might want to create a user is from `IO`. You can make a command-line tool that reads three lines of input for the user values and outputs your user data. You'll reuse the `readInt` function from the preceding lesson to transform user input directly to an `Int`.

Listing 28.13 Using `Applicative` to create a user from `IO` types

```
readInt :: IO Int
readInt = read <$> getLine

main :: IO ()
main = do
   putStrLn "Enter a username, gamerId and score"
   user <- User <$> getLine <*> readInt <*> readInt
   print user
```

The powerful thing here is that you need to define only a single type, `User`, that works with regular `String`s and `Int`s. Because of the `Applicative` type class, you can trivially use the same code to create a user in different contexts.

Quick check 28.5 Show the result of creating a user with a missing (`Nothing`) `userName`.

Summary

In this lesson, our objective was to introduce you to the `Applicative` type class. The `Applicative`'s `<*>` operator allows you to use functions that are themselves in a context. For example, if you have a function that might not exist, `Maybe (Int -> Double)`, you can apply it to a value in the same context, `Maybe Int`, and get a result still in that context, `Maybe Double`. This may seem like a seldom-used operator, but it's essential to being able to extend `Functor` to multi-argument functions. Because of the prevalence of partial application in Haskell programs, it's fairly common to wind up with a function in a context. Without `Applicative`, it'd be impossible to use these functions in many cases. Let's see if you got this.

Q28.1 Writing `haversineMaybe` (listing 28.4) was straightforward. Write the function `haversineIO` without using `<*>`. Here's the type signature:

```
haversineIO :: IO LatLong -> IO LatLong -> IO Double
```

Q28.2 Rewrite `haversineIO`, this time using `<*>`.

Q28.3 Recall the `RobotPart` type from the preceding lesson:

```
data RobotPart = RobotPart
   { name :: String
   , description :: String
   , cost :: Double
   , count :: Int
   } deriving Show
```

Make a command-line application that has a database of various `RobotParts` (at least five), and then lets the user enter in two-part IDs and returns the one with the lowest cost. Handle the case of the user entering an ID that's not in the parts database.

QC 28.5 answer

```
GHCi> User <$> Nothing <*> serverGamerId <*> serverScore
Nothing
```

LISTS AS CONTEXT: A DEEPER LOOK AT THE APPLICATIVE TYPE CLASS

After reading lesson 29, you'll be able to

- Explain the formal definition of the `Applicative` type class
- Represent parameterized types as either containers or contexts
- Use `List` as a context to explore nondeterministic computing

In the preceding lesson, you learned how to use the <*> (pronounced *app*) operator to extend the power of `Functor`'s <$> (pronounced *fmap*) operator. In this lesson, you'll take a closer look at the `Applicative` type class. You'll explore the difference between types that represent a container and types that represent a context. You'll finish by looking at the powerful things you can achieve by using lists as a context.

Consider this

A breakfast place offers you the choice of the following:

- Coffee or tea
- Eggs, pancakes, or waffles
- Toast or a biscuit
- Sausage, ham, or bacon

What are all the possible meals you could choose, and how can you use `List` to help?

29.1 Introducing the Applicative type class

The `Applicative` type class allows you to use *functions* that are inside a context, such as `Maybe` or `IO`. As you saw in the preceding lesson, this extends the power of the `Functor` type class. Because of the way that `Applicative` works with `Functor`, `Functor` is a superclass of `Applicative`. See figure 29.1.

Functor

```
fmap :: Functor f :: (a -> b) -> f a -> f b
(<$>) :: Functor f :: (a -> b) -> f a -> f b
```

Applicative

```
fmap :: Functor f :: (a -> b) -> f a -> f b
(<$>) :: Functor f :: (a -> b) -> f a -> f b
(<*>) :: Applicative f :: f (a -> b) -> f a -> f b
pure :: Applicative f :: a -> f a
```

Figure 29.1 Functor is the superclass of applicative. Figure 29.2 provides the definition of `Applicative` with its two required methods.

One tricky thing in this definition is that there are two constraints on your type variable `f`. The first says that `f` is a `Functor`, which enforces that `Applicative` must be a `Functor`, and then you define `f` as your stand-in for `Applicative`. In your method signatures, `f` is a variable for any `Applicative` (see figure 29.2). Notice that the operator <*> has the same type signature as your `fmap`, except the function argument is also in a context. This small difference in <*> allows you to chain together larger sequences of functions inside members of the `Functor` type class. Here are a few examples of using <$> and <*> to perform mathematical operations on `Maybe` types:

```
GHCi> (*) <$> Just 6 <*> Just 7
Just 42
GHCi> div <$> Just 6 <*> Just 7
Just 0
GHCi> mod <$> Just 6 <*> Just 7
Just 6
```

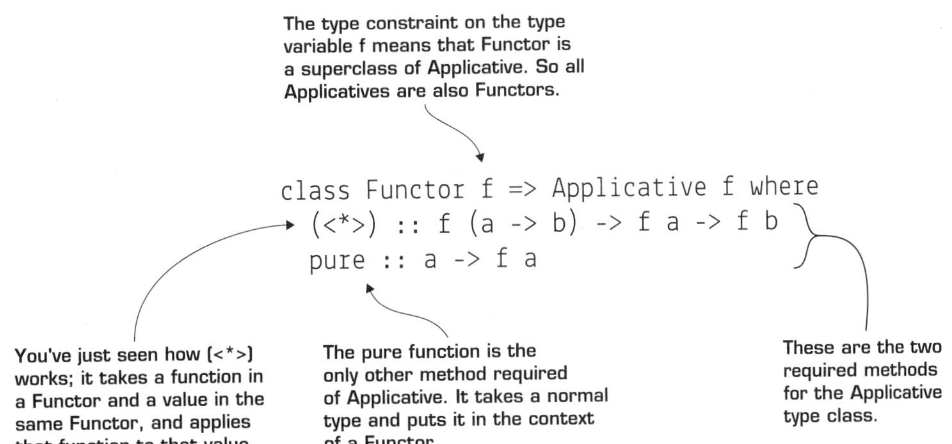
The type constraint on the type variable f means that Functor is a superclass of Applicative. So all Applicatives are also Functors.
class Functor f => Applicative f where
(<*>) :: f (a -> b) -> f a -> f b
pure :: a -> f a
You've just seen how (<*>) works; it takes a function in a Functor and a value in the same Functor, and applies that function to that value.
The pure function is the only other method required of Applicative. It takes a normal type and puts it in the context of a Functor.
These are the two required methods for the Applicative type class.

Figure 29.2 Type class definition for `Applicative`

This solution may seem either elegant or confusing, depending on how comfortable you are with Haskell's infix binary operators. Undoubtedly, using `<$>` and `<*>` can initially seem confusing. Further complicating the issue is that unlike `<$>` and `fmap`, `<*>` has no equivalent function. If you're struggling with these operators, the best solution is practice. Try going back to some of the examples in unit 1 and change values used as arguments to `Maybe` values. Remember, because of `fmap` and `<*>`, you don't need to rewrite any functions to work with `Maybe` values.

> **Quick check 29.1** Use `<$>` and `<*>` to combine two `Maybe String` types with `++`.

29.1.1 The pure method

The function `pure` is the second method required by the `Applicative` type class. The `pure` method is a useful helper function for taking an ordinary value or function and putting

QC 29.1 answer

```
GHCi>(++) <$> Just "Learn" <*> Just " Haskell"
Just "Learn Haskell"
```

it into a context. The best way to understand `pure` is to play around with it in GHCi. In the example of a `Maybe`, `pure` will return a `Just`:

```
GHCi> pure 6 :: Maybe Int
Just 6
```

You can also use `pure` to put a function into the context of `Applicative`. For example, if you want to add `6` to `(Just 5)`, you can use either `fmap` or `pure`:

```
GHCi> (6+) <$> Just 5
Just 11
GHCi> pure (6+) <*> Just 5
Just 11
```

Though these examples are fairly simple, in practice you'll frequently want a quick way to transform a value into the desired `Applicative` type. In our visual language, `pure` also performs an important role, as shown in figure 29.3.

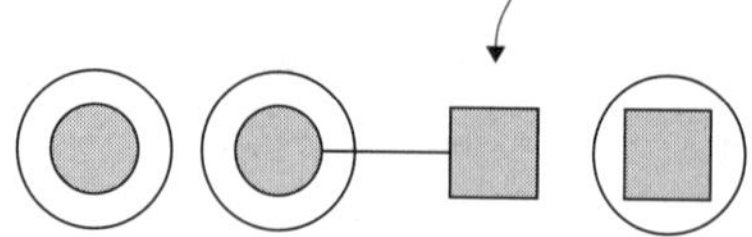

The pure method provides an adapter for when you simply need to put a regular type into a context.

Figure 29.3 The `pure` method means you always have a way to take an ordinary type and put it in a context.

Because of `pure`, you can take any value that's not in a context and trivially put it in one. This is vital to allowing all possible computations in a context.

Quick check 29.2 Make the `String` `"Hello World"` into an `IO String`.

QC 29.2 answer

```
hello :: IO String
hello = pure "Hello World"
```

29.2 Containers vs. contexts

So far, we've talked somewhat loosely about the difference between parameterized types that represent containers and contexts. At this point, you need to be a bit clearer about what you mean by these terms. The reason is that unlike `Functor`, `Applicative` and the next lesson's type class `Monad` make sense only when you're talking about types as a context. Here's the distinction in a nutshell:

- Parameterized types that represent a container are types that represent a data structure.
- When a type is a context, extra information is implied about the type, beyond its structure.

Let's explore this further. The best test of whether a type is a *container* is whether you can tell what it does, independent of its name. For example, consider the 2-tuple `(a,b)`. You could implement the same type named `Blah`.

Listing 29.1 A poorly named 2-tuple is still the same thing

```
data Blah a b = Blah a b
```

Even with a completely useless name like `Blah`, it's hard to argue that this type is any different than a regular tuple pair `(a,b)`.

The `Data.Map` type is another, similar structure. You could call this a `Dictionary`, a `BinarySearchTree`, a `MagicLookupBox`, and so forth. But what the type means is implied by the data structure itself. Even if the entire set of functions around `Map` were written in an alien language, you'd still quickly figure out what the type is used for. (Probably…eventually.)

It's worth pointing out that the 2-tuple `(,)` and `Data.Map` are both instances of `Functor` but *not* instances of `Applicative`. Remember that the key power of `Applicative` is that it lets you apply a function in a parameterized type. Another good way to differentiate containers from contexts is to ask, "Does it make sense to have a `<type>` function?" `Maybe (a -> b)` is a function from `a -> b` that itself might not exist because it was made via partial application with a `Nothing` value. An `IO (a -> b)` function is any function that's operating in the world of `IO`. What does a `Data.Map` function mean? Likewise, what does a 2-tuple function mean? If you can answer these questions, you have the starting ground for figuring out the `Applicative` instance for these types.

When a type is a context, on the other hand, extra information is implied about the type, beyond its structure. The most obvious case is the `IO` type. When you first introduce parameterized types, you introduce the idea of a `Box` type.

Listing 29.2 The trivial `Box` type doesn't seem much different from `IO`

```
data Box a = Box a
```

Clearly, `Box` is a uselessly trivial type. But there's no difference at the data constructor level between `Box` and `IO`. `IO`, from our perspective, is just a data constructor that wraps types that came from `IO` (there's much more to the `IO` type, but not that you can immediately see).

The `Maybe` type is another context type. Suppose you want to create a parameterized type for a resource-constrained computation. You could imagine this type as follows.

Listing 29.3 A type representing if there are enough resources to continue

```
data ResourceConstrained a = NoResources | Okay a
```

Behind the scenes, there would be a lot of magic determining resource usage, but this type is no different from `Maybe` at the type-constructor level. Most of the information about this type is in a context that you assume about the type itself.

The best way to understand this distinction between container and context is to look at an example. `List` turns out to be the perfect case. It's easy to understand `List` as a container because it's a common data structure. But `List` also describes a context. If you understand how `List` can be a container and a context, you're on the path to truly understanding `Applicatives`.

Quick check 29.3 Suppose you want to make it so that `(pure +) <*> (1,2) <*> (3,4) = (1+2,1+4,2+3,2+4) = (3,5,5,6)`. Why doesn't this work?

QC 29.3 answer This doesn't work because `(3,5,5,6)` is an entirely different type than `(1,2)` or `(3,4)`. The first is type `(a,b,c,d)`, and the other two are `(a,b)`.

29.3 List as a context

The List type, being a fundamental example of nearly everything in Haskell, is both a container *and* a context. List as a container is easy to understand. List is basically a chain of buckets of whatever type of data you want to hold. But List is a member of Applicative, so there must be a way to view List as a context.

The reason context matters for a list is that to use Applicative, you need to be able to answer the question, "What does it mean to apply a function to two or more values in the context of a list?" For example, what does [1000,2000,3000] + [500,20000] mean? The naive assumption might be as follows:

```
[1000,2000,3000] + [500,20000] = [1000,2000,3000,500,20000]
```

But this would be just adding two lists, which is concatenation (the ++ operator for lists). What you're curious about is what it means to combine two values in the context of List by using addition. In terms of Applicative, you'd read this statement as follows:

```
pure (+) <*> [1000,2000,3000] <*> [500,20000]
```

The List data structure alone doesn't give you enough information to say what this means. To understand how you add two values in a list, you need extra context to interpret the general idea of applying a binary function to values in lists.

The best way to understand List as a context is that it describes *nondeterministic* computation. Normally, you think of programming as purely deterministic. Each step in the computation is followed by another in a precise order that yields one, final result. In nondeterministic computing, you're computing multiple possibilities all at once. In terms of thinking nondeterministically, when you add values in the context of a list, you're adding together all possible values from the two contexts. You can see the somewhat surprising result of using <*> with Lists in GHCi:

```
GHCi> pure (+) <*> [1000,2000,3000] <*> [500,20000]
[1500,21000,2500,22000,3500,23000]
```

Adding together two Ints in the context of a List means adding all possible combinations of the values in those lists.

29.3.1 Exploring container vs. context with a list

It's important to take a moment and point out the major differences between a list as a container and a list as a context:

- A list as a *container* is a sequence of values that can hold any type. Each item in the list points to the next one or to the empty list.
- A list as a *context* represents a set of possibilities. Think of a list as a context as being a single variable that can contain many possible values.

Don't be fooled by your familiarity with `List` as a container. Both `Maybe` and `IO` are much simpler contexts to reason about. A `Maybe Int` is a single `Int` value in the context that it may be missing. An `IO Int` is an `Int` value in the context that it was produced by an `IO` action that may have produced side effects or other issues. An `[Int]` is an `Int` in the context that there are many possible values for that `Int`. Because there are many possible values for that `[Int]`, when you apply a function `(Int -> Int -> Int)` in the context of a list, you must think nondeterministically and compute all possible results of that operation.

29.3.2 A game show example

As an example, suppose you're on a game show and you get to choose one of three doors and then one of two boxes. Behind the doors are prizes worth $1,000, $2,000, and $3,000. You don't know which you'll get, so you can represent this as a list.

Listing 29.4 Nondeterministic possibilities for door values

```
doorPrize :: [Int]
doorPrize = [1000,2000,3000]
```

After the door, you choose one of two boxes; a box can contain either $500 or $20,000. You can represent these possibilities as a list as well.

Listing 29.5 Nondeterministic possibilities for box prizes

```
boxPrize :: [Int]
boxPrize = [500,20000]
```

In a deterministic context, you can open only one door, and pick only one box, getting only one prize. But if you nondeterministically think about this problem, you're computing all possible combinations of doors you can open and boxes you can pick. Deterministically, if you want to talk about prizes, you're talking about the one prize you can win. Figure 29.4 presents the deterministic and nondeterministic ways to understand your prize.

The equation for your `totalPrize` in a deterministic world would be the following (you use the prefix `(+)` so it's easy to compare with the `Applicative` version).

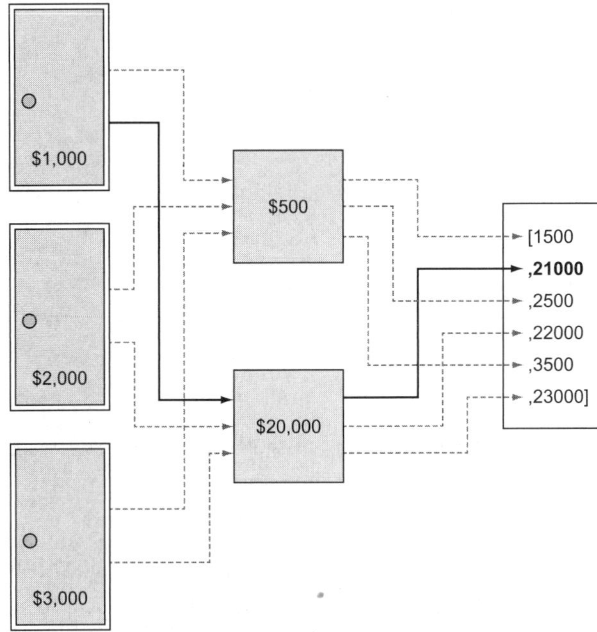
Deterministic computing means following a single path to a single answer. Follow the solid line to the bold answer.
$1,000
$2,000
$3,000
$500
$20,000
[1500
,21000
,2500
,22000
,3500
,23000]
Nondeterministic computing means following all possible paths at once to all possible answers. Lists as context represent nondeterministic computing.

Figure 29.4 Thinking of lists as nondeterministic computing is hard because you normally think deterministically.

Listing 29.6 Deterministic door prize can represent only a single path

```
totalPrize :: Int
totalPrize = (+) doorPrize boxPrize
```

In a nondeterministic context, you're talking about all possible prizes that can be won. You can describe the nondeterministic `totalPrize` with the function shown in figure 29.5.

In GHCi, you can see that `totalPrize` represents all possible prizes that can be won:

```
GHCi> totalPrize
[1500,21000,2500,22000,3500,23000]
```

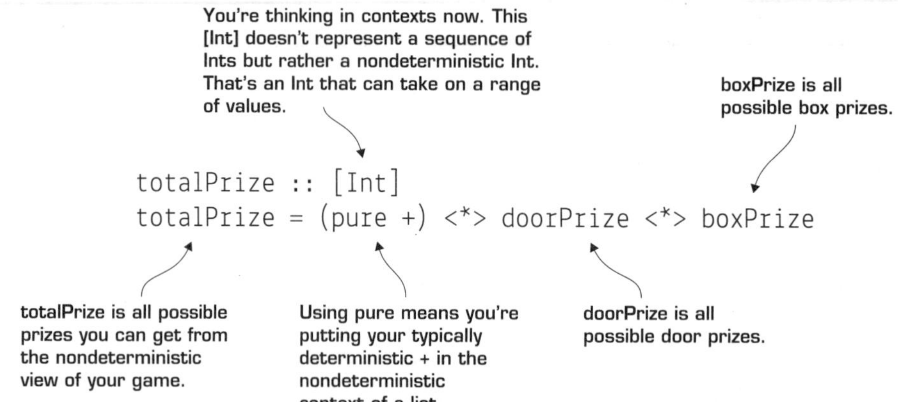

Figure 29.5 Nondeterministic computing computes on all possible paths, rather than just one.

When you add two lists in context, you get the combination of all possible worlds. For each door prize, you can pick one of the two possible box prizes. The results of adding two lists within the context of a list are all possible solutions in your nondeterministic world.

Next you'll look at two more examples of practical nondeterministic computing. You'll use nondeterministic computing to compute all nonprime numbers, allowing you to easily identify primes. Then you'll use nondeterministic computing to quickly generate a set of possible test data.

> **Quick check 29.4** Solve this problem if the boxes contain a prize multiplier instead of just an additional prize. The multipliers are 10× and 50×.

29.3.3 Generating the first N prime numbers

A *prime number* is any number divisible by only 1 and itself. Suppose you want to generate a list of prime numbers. There's an amazingly simple method for computing a list of primes using the `Applicative` properties of a list. Here's the basic process:

QC 29.4 answer

```
boxMultiplier = [10,50]
newOutcomes = pure (*) <*> doorPrize <*> boxMultiplier

GHCi> newOutcomes
[10000,50000,20000,100000,30000,150000]
```

1 Start with your list from 2 to *n*.
2 Determine all the nonprime numbers (composite numbers).
3 Filter out all items from the list that aren't composite.

The only question remaining then is, "How do you compute the composite numbers?" A *composite number* is any number that results from multiplying two or more other numbers together. You can easily build this list by multiplying each number in your `[2 .. n]` list by itself. How can you do this easily? With `Applicative`! For example, if you have `[2..4]`, you can use multiplication `*`, `pure`, and `<*>` to build your list of all possible numbers that are made from these numbers:

```
GHCi> pure (*) <*> [2 .. 4] <*> [2 .. 4]
[4,6,8,6,9,12,8,12,16]
```

This list is inefficient, as it includes numbers out of your range as well as duplicate numbers. But it'll include every composite number in your range. Given this bit of code, you can easily write your function for listing all prime numbers to *n*.

Listing 29.7 `primesToN`, a simple but inefficient primer algorithm

```
primesToN :: Integer -> [Integer]
primesToN n = filter isNotComposite twoThroughN
 where twoThroughN = [2 .. n]
       composite = pure (*) <*> twoThroughN <*> twoThroughN
       isNotComposite = not . (`elem` composite)
```

Although not the most efficient prime-number-generating algorithm, this is incredibly easy to implement and works well enough for reasonably small ranges:

```
GHCi> primesToN 32
[2,3,5,7,11,13,17,19,23,29,31]
```

If you ever need to whip up a quick prime-number generator, this little trick can be a useful tool to have.

29.3.4 Quickly generating large amounts of test data

In the preceding lesson, we showed how a `User` could be created in different contexts by using `Applicative`. You used this `User` type for a user in a video game:

```
data User = User {
     name :: String
   , gamerId :: Int
```

```
  , score :: Int
  } deriving Show
```

You used `Applicative` to create instances of `User` in the context of both `IO` and `Maybe`. To demonstrate how powerful the list context is, you'll do the same thing, only to create a large amount of test data.

Suppose you have a list of usernames, some typical and others problematic in certain cases. Thinking of lists as context, `testNames` represents possible names.

Listing 29.8 Some `testNames` for your data

```
testNames :: [String]
testNames = ["John Smith"
            ,"Robert'); DROP TABLE Students;--"
            ,"Christina NULL"
            ,"Randall Munroe"]
```

You want to test possible gamer IDs with `gamerIds`.

Listing 29.9 `testIds` with different values

```
testIds :: [Int]
testIds = [1337
          ,0123
          ,999999]
```

And you also want to make sure you have possible troublesome scores as well.

Listing 29.10 Sample `testScores` for testing

```
testScores :: [Int]
testScores = [0
             ,100000
             ,-99999]
```

What you want to do is generate test data that includes all possible combinations of these values. This means nondeterministically computing a list of possible users. You could do that by hand, but that would mean writing out 4 × 3 × 3 = 36 entries! Plus, if you later decide to add another value to any of those lists, it means a lot of work for you.

Instead, you can use the Applicative properties of List to nondeterministically generate your test data for you. You'll do this exactly the same way you created User types for IO and Maybe in the preceding lesson.

Listing 29.11 Same pattern used for IO and Maybe to generate many test users

```
testData :: [User]
testData = pure User <*> testNames
                     <*> testIds
                     <*> testScores
```

In GHCi, you can see that you've successfully created a list of all 36 possible combinations of these values. Even better, to update your list, you have to add whatever values you like to testNames, testIds, or testScores:

```
GHCi> length testData
36
GHCi> take 3 testData
[User {name = "John Smith", gamerId = 1337, score = 0}
,User {name = "John Smith", gamerId = 1337, score = 100000}
,User {name = "John Smith", gamerId = 1337, score = -99999}]
```

Using the List type to perform nondeterministic computing shows how powerful the Applicative type class can be when working with contexts!

> **Quick check 29.5** Add your own name to testNames and regenerate the data. How many examples are there now?

QC 29.5 answer

```
testNames = ["Will Kurt"
            , "John Smith"
            ,"Robert'); DROP TABLE Students;--"
            ,"Christina NULL"
            ,"Randall Munroe"]

testData :: [User]
testData = pure User <*> testNames
                     <*> testIds
                     <*> testScores
```

There are now 45 examples.

Summary

In this lesson, our objective was to give you a deeper insight into the `Applicative` type class. You were formally introduced to the full `Applicative` type class, which includes the `<*>` operator you learned in the preceding lesson, as well as the `pure` method. The role of `pure` is to take normal values and put them into the context you need; for example, turning an `Int` into a `Maybe Int`. You also focused on the differences between containers and contexts by exploring a list as a context. Contexts differ from containers in that they require you to understand something about the computation happening beyond what the data structure alone tells you. For lists, this means representing nondeterministic computation, rather than just a container for sequential data. Let's see if you got this.

Q29.1 To prove that `Applicative` is strictly more powerful than `Functor`, write a universal version of `fmap`, called `allFmap`, that defines `fmap` for all members of the `Applicative` type class. Because it works for all instances of `Applicative`, the only functions you can use are the methods required by the `Applicative` type class. To get you started, here's your type signature:

```
allFmap :: Applicative f => (a -> b) -> f a -> f b
```

When you're finished, test this out on `List` and `Maybe`, which are both members of `Applicative`:

```
GHCi> allFmap (+ 1) [1,2,3]
[2,3,4]
GHCi> allFmap (+ 1) (Just 5)
Just 6
GHCi> allFmap (+ 1) Nothing
Nothing
```

Q29.2 Translate the following expression into one where the result is a `Maybe Int`. The catch is that you may not add (or remove) anything to the code except `pure` and `<*>`. You can't use the `Just` constructor or any extra parentheses.

```
example :: Int
example = (*) ((+) 2 4) 6
```

Here's the type signature for your answer:

```
exampleMaybe :: Maybe Int
```

Q29.3 Take the following example and use nondeterministic computing with `Lists` to determine how much beer you need to purchase to assure there will be enough:

- You bought beer last night but don't remember whether it was a 6-pack or a 12-pack.
- You and your roommate each had two beers last night.
- You're having either two or three friends coming over tonight, depending on who can come.
- For a long night of gaming, you expect the average person to drink three to four beers.

30

INTRODUCING THE MONAD TYPE CLASS

After reading lesson 30, you'll be able to

- Understand the limitations of both `Functor` and `Applicative`
- Use `Monad`'s `(>>=)` operator to chain together functions in a context
- Write `IO` code without do-notation

You've just finished learning about two important type classes, `Functor` and `Applicative`. Each has allowed you to perform increasingly powerful computations within a context such as `Maybe` or `IO`. `Functor` allows you to change individual values in a context:

```
GHCi> (+ 2) <$> Just 3
Just 5
```

`Applicative` increases your power by enabling you to use partial application in a context. This, in turn, allows you to use multiple arguments in a context:

```
GHCi> pure (+) <*> Just 3 <*> Just 2
Just 5
```

In this lesson, you'll look at the final evolution of this process, the `Monad` type class. Through one more operator, the `Monad` type class will allow you to perform any arbitrary computation in a context you'd like. You already saw this power in unit 4 with do-notation, which is syntactic sugar for the methods of the `Monad` type class.

Listing 30.1 A quick reminder of do-notation

```
main :: IO ()
main = do
  putStrLn "Remember do-notation!"
  putStrLn "It makes things easy!"
```

To understand why you need the `Monad` type class, you'll ignore do-notation for this lesson and see why you need `Monad`s at all, given how powerful `Functor` and `Applicative` are. Because do-notation does make life much easier, you'll revisit it in the next lesson.

You'll start this lesson by looking at two relatively straightforward problems that are frustratingly challenging to solve with `Functor` or `Applicative`. You'll then learn about `Monad`'s powerful *bind* operator, and how it can make these problems easy to solve. You'll conclude this lesson by using `Monad`'s methods to write `IO` actions similar to what you used do-notation for in unit 4.

> **Consider this** How would you write a single `IO` action that reads in a number from the user, doubles it, and prints that value back to the user, without using do-notation?

30.1 The limitations of Applicative and Functor

Remembering back to our visual representation of `Functor`, `Applicative`, and `Monad`, you've solved three of the four possible mismatches. The `Functor`'s `fmap` provides an adapter when you have a value in a context and a regular function, and want your result in a context, as shown in figure 30.1.

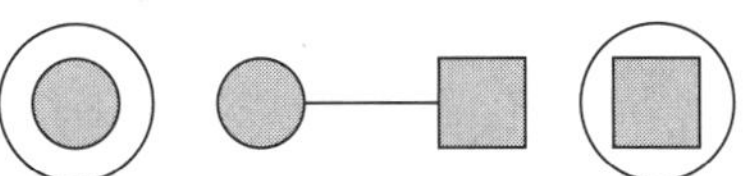

Figure 30.1 A visualization of the mismatch between function and context that `Functor` solves

`Applicative`'s `<*>` allows you to connect a function in a context with values in a context, as shown in figure 30.2.

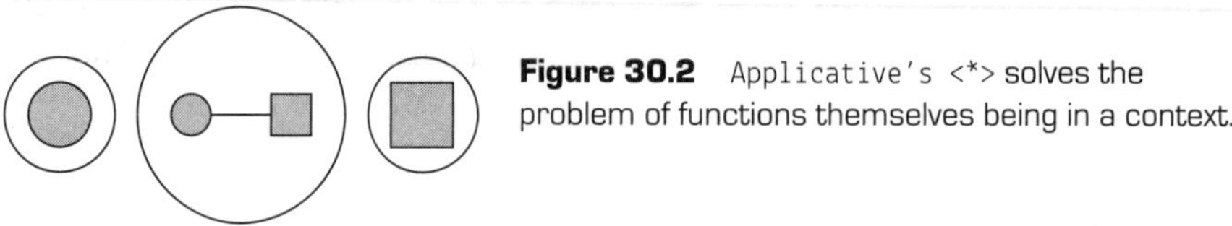

Figure 30.2 Applicative's <*> solves the problem of functions themselves being in a context.

And finally, `Applicative`'s `pure` method allows you to handle the case of your final result not being in a context, as shown in figure 30.3.

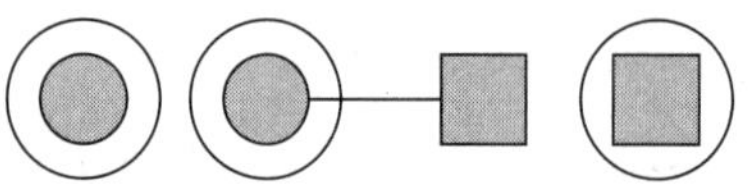

Figure 30.3 Applicative's pure method means you can always put a result into a context.

This leaves one problem left to solve, when the initial argument isn't in a context but its result is, as shown in figure 30.4.

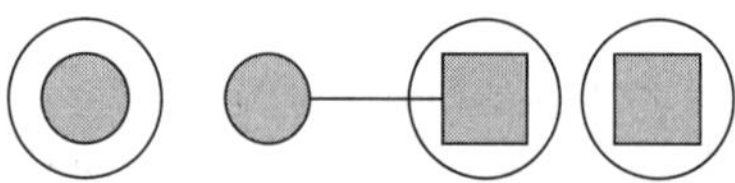

Figure 30.4 This is the only pattern you need a solution for; the `Monad` type class provides an answer.

After you have a solution for this last pattern, you have a solution for using any possible function in a context. This last case may initially seem like an odd one, but it appears often. Next you'll investigate two examples of when this comes up and how `Functor` and `Applicative` can't help.

30.1.1 Combining two Map lookups

In this section, you'll explore a common issue of needing to look up a value in one `Map` in order to access another value in a second `Map`. This can happen anytime you need one value to look up another, such as the following:

- Looking up a zip code to find a city, and then looking up the city to find the state
- Using an employee name to look up an employee ID, and then using the ID to look up a record
- Taking a stock ticker and looking up the company name, and then looking up the company location

You're writing code for managing user credits for a mobile gaming platform. Currently, each user is identified as a unique `GamerId` that's just an `Int`. Suppose that earlier instances of your program used a unique `Username`, a `String`, to associate a user with the credits in their account. Because of this legacy dependence of `Username` as an identity, to look up user credits on newer users, you still have to look up a `Username` given a `GamerId` and then use the `Username` to look up the credits in their account. Here's the basic code to get you started.

Listing 30.2 Basic setup for the problem of combining two `Map` lookups

```
import qualified Data.Map as Map

type UserName = String
type GamerId = Int
type PlayerCredits = Int

userNameDB :: Map.Map GamerId UserName
userNameDB = Map.fromList [(1,"nYarlathoTep")
                          ,(2,"KINGinYELLOW")
                          ,(3,"dagon1997")
                          ,(4,"rcarter1919")
                          ,(5,"xCTHULHUx")
                          ,(6,"yogSOThoth")]

creditsDB :: Map.Map UserName PlayerCredits
creditsDB = Map.fromList [("nYarlathoTep",2000)
                         ,("KINGinYELLOW",15000)
                         ,("dagon1997",300)
                         ,("rcarter1919",12)
                         ,("xCTHULHUx",50000)
                         ,("yogSOThoth",150000)]
```

This Map represents the database you're getting your UserName from, given a GamerId.

This Map represents the database; you'll use the UserName to look up PlayerCredits.

With your sample data in place, you can start working on your main problem: writing a function to look up a user's credits given that user's `GamerId`. You want a function that will look up `PlayerCredits` given a `GamerId`. You still want your `PlayerCredits` value to be a `Maybe PlayerCredits` because it's entirely possible that either you have a missing `GamerId` or there's a missing entry for your `GamerID` in `creditsDB`. The function you want is as follows.

Listing 30.3 Type signature of your goal function, `creditsFromId`

```
creditsFromId :: GamerId -> Maybe PlayerCredits
```

To create this function, you have to combine two `Map.lookup` functions. You'll create helper functions that abstract out your databases. The `lookupUserName` function will take a `GamerID` and give you a `Maybe UserName` result, and the `lookupCredits` function will take a `UserName` and give the user a `Maybe Credits` result.

Listing 30.4 The functions to combine: `lookupUserName` and `lookupCredits`

```
lookupUserName :: GamerId -> Maybe UserName
lookupUserName id = Map.lookup id userNameDB

lookupCredits :: UserName -> Maybe PlayerCredits
lookupCredits username = Map.lookup username creditsDB
```

Before you dive deeper, you should think about the type signature of the missing function that you need. You need to connect the result of `lookupUserName, Maybe Username`, with the function `lookupCredits, UserName -> Maybe PlayerCredits`. For this concrete case, the type signature of your function is as follows:

```
Maybe UserName -> (UserName -> Maybe PlayerCredits) -> Maybe PlayerCredits
```

`Applicative` and `Functor` have taught you to think more abstractly about solving problems in types such as `Maybe`. The general form of the combining function you want is as follows:

```
Applicative f => f a -> (a -> f b) -> f b
```

You'll assume the `Applicative` constraint rather than `Functor` only because `Applicative` is more powerful. If you can't solve your problem with `Applicative`, you can't solve it with `Functor` either. Now let's take a look at the tools you get from `Applicative` and `Functor`:

```
(<$>) :: Functor f => (a -> b) -> f a -> f b
(<*>) :: Applicative f => f (a -> b) -> f a -> f b
pure :: Applicative f => a -> f a
```

Unfortunately, for all the power you've gained with `Applicative`, it doesn't look like any combination of these tools will solve this rather straightforward problem of wanting to chain together two functions. You can solve this problem by writing a wrapper for `lookupCredits` to be a function of `Maybe UserName -> Maybe PlayerCredits`.

Listing 30.5 `altLookupCredits`, a solution without using `Functor` or `Applicative`

```
altLookupCredits :: Maybe UserName -> Maybe PlayerCredits
altLookupCredits Nothing = Nothing
altLookupCredits (Just username) = lookupCredits username
```

Now you can put together your final `creditsFromId` function.

Listing 30.6 Going straight from `GamerId -> Maybe PlayerCredits`

```
creditsFromId :: GamerId -> Maybe PlayerCredits
creditsFromId id = altLookupCredits (lookupUserName id)
```

And you can see in GHCi that this works well:

```
GHCi> creditsFromId 1
Just 2000
GHCi> creditsFromId 100
Nothing
```

This solution works, but having to write a wrapper function to make it work for `Maybe` should be a warning at this point. In lesson 28, you saw a similar pattern of being forced to write a wrapper function to work in a context as motivating more powerful type classes. But at this point, you might not be convinced of the need for yet another, even more powerful type class.

Quick check 30.1 Interestingly enough, the following function seems to do what you want and compiles just fine. What's the issue? (Hint: Look at its type signature in GHCi.)

```
creditsFromIdStrange id = pure lookupCredits <*> lookupUserName id
```

30.1.2 Writing a not-so-trivial echo IO action

The reason your problem with `Maybe` doesn't seem so bad is that `Maybe` is an easy context to work in. You can always manually create a solution to any `Maybe` problem by a clever use of pattern matching on `Just` and `Nothing`. The `IO` type, on the other hand, isn't nearly as friendly. To demonstrate this, let's attempt to solve an easy-looking problem. You want to write a simple `IO` action, `echo`. The `echo` action is a single action that reads in user input and immediately prints it back. To do this, you need to combine two `IO` actions that you already know well:

```
getLine :: IO String
putStrLn :: String -> IO ()
```

QC 30.1 answer The trouble with this function is that it returns a `Maybe (Maybe PlayerCredits)`. That's a nested `Maybe`!

And of course the type of `echo` is as follows:

```
echo :: IO ()
```

You need to combine `getLine` with `putStrLn`. If you once again think of this problem in types, you'll see a familiar pattern. You need a function that combines `getLine` and `putStrln` and returns an `IO String`:

```
IO String -> (String -> IO ()) -> IO ()
```

If you abstract this out, you have this:

```
Applicative f => f a -> (a -> f b) -> f b
```

This is exactly the same type signature you ended up with before. To solve this problem, you need something strictly more powerful than either `Functor` or `Applicative`. This finally brings you to the `Monad` type class!

Quick check 30.2 Why can't you write a function like `creditsFromId` to solve this problem?

```
altLookupCredits :: Maybe UserName -> Maybe PlayerCredits
altLookupCredits Nothing = Nothing
altLookupCredits (Just username) = lookupCredits username

creditsFromId :: GamerId -> Maybe PlayerCredits
creditsFromId id = altLookupCredits (lookupUserName id)
```

30.2 The bind operator: >>=

The missing operator you need is `>>=` (pronounced *bind*) and has the following type signature:

```
(>>=) :: Monad m => m a -> (a -> m b) -> m b
```

As you can see, `(>>=)` has exactly the signature you were looking for! From the type class constraint, you can see that `>>=` is a member of the `Monad` type class. `Maybe` and `IO` are both instances of `Monad`, which means you can use `>>=` to solve your problems. With bind, you can find a more elegant solution to your `creditFromId` function.

QC 30.2 answer You have no way of getting a value out of an `IO` context as you do a `Maybe` context. You need more powerful tools such as `Applicative` and `Functor` to work with `IO` types.

Listing 30.7 `creditsFromId` rewritten to use bind instead of pattern matching

```
creditsFromId :: GamerId -> Maybe PlayerCredits
creditsFromId id = lookupUserName id >>= lookupCredits
```

As you can see, `>>=` allows you to chain together a function of a type `(a -> m b)`. In the case of `Maybe`, this means you can endlessly chain together lookups. For example, suppose you have yet another level of indirection. Imagine your mobile gaming company was purchased by WillCo Industries, and now each `GamerId` is itself associated with a `WillCoId`.

Listing 30.8 Adding yet another `Map` to `lookup` in order to get a user's credit

```
type WillCoId = Int

gamerIdDB :: Map.Map WillCoId GamerId
gamerIdDB = Map.fromList [(1001,1)
                         ,(1002,2)
                         ,(1003,3)
                         ,(1004,4)
                         ,(1005,5)
                         ,(1006,6)]

lookupGamerId :: WillCoId -> Maybe GamerId
lookupGamerId id = Map.lookup id gamerIdDB
```

Now you need a new function, `creditsFromWCId`, of type `WillCoId -> Maybe PlayerCredits`. You can easily create this by chaining all three of your lookup functions with `>>=`.

Listing 30.9 You can chain together arbitrarily many lookups with >>=

```
creditsFromWCId :: WillCoId -> Maybe PlayerCredits
creditsFromWCId id = lookupGamerId id >>= lookupUserName >>= lookupCredits
```

In GHCi, you can see that this works as expected:

```
GHCi> creditsFromWCId 1001
Just 2000
GHCi> creditsFromWCId 100
Nothing
```

Although using `>>=` made chaining together `Maybe` functions much easier, it's essential to solving your `IO` action problem. When you left off, you wanted to chain together `getLine` and putStrLn. But you were absolutely stuck because there was no way to combine these actions and there was no way to crack open the IO type to write a wrapper as you did for Maybe. With >>=, creating an echo function is trivially easy. Let's put what you know into an echo.hs file and see how it behaves.

Listing 30.10 Using >>= to create your echo function

```
echo :: IO ()
echo = getLine >>= putStrLn

main :: IO ()
main = echo
```

If you compile this program, you can see that it behaves as expected:

```
$ ghc echo.hs
$ ./echo
Hello World!
Hello World!
```

The >>= operator is the heart of the Monad type class. Though relatively simple, the >>= operator is the final piece in your puzzle. Now that you have <$>, <*>, pure, and >>=, you can chain together any computation you need in a context.

Quick check 30.3 Combine readInt and printDouble (defined next) into a single IO action:

```
readInt :: IO Int
readInt = read <$> getLine

printDouble :: Int -> IO ()
printDouble n = print (n*2)
```

QC 30.3 answer

```
readInt :: IO Int
readInt = read <$> getLine

printDouble :: Int -> IO ()
printDouble n = print (n*2)

readInt >>= printDouble
```

30.3 The Monad type class

In the same way the `Applicative` type class extends the power of `Functor`, the `Monad` type class extends the power of `Applicative`. See figure 30.5.

Functor
fmap :: Functor f :: (a -> b) -> f a -> f b
(<$>) :: Functor f :: (a -> b) -> f a -> f b
Applicative
fmap :: Functor f :: (a -> b) -> f a -> f b
(<$>) :: Functor f :: (a -> b) -> f a -> f b
(<*>) :: Applicative f :: f (a -> b) -> f a -> f b
pure :: Applicative f :: a -> f a
Monad
fmap :: Functor f :: (a -> b) -> f a -> f b
(<$>) :: Functor f :: (a -> b) -> f a -> f b
(<*>) :: Applicative f :: f (a -> b) -> f a -> f b
pure :: Applicative f :: a -> f a
(>>=) :: Monad m :: m a -> (a -> m b) -> m b
(>>) :: Monad m :: m a -> m b -> m b
return :: Monad m :: a -> m a
fail :: Monad m :: String -> m a

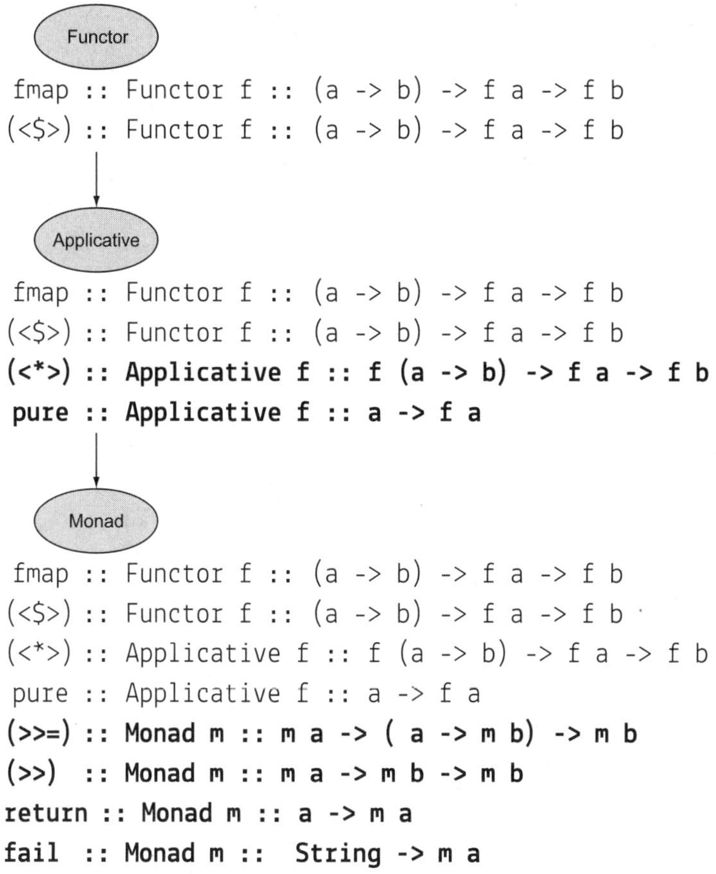

Figure 30.5 `Functor` is a superclass of `Applicative`, which is a superclass of `Monad`.

Here's the definition of `Monad`:

```
class Applicative m => Monad (m :: * -> *) where
  (>>=) :: m a -> (a -> m b) -> m b
```

```
(>>) :: m a -> m b -> m b
return :: a -> m a
fail :: String -> m a
```

Here you have four important methods in your type class definition. The only method required for the minimum definition of Monad is >>=. You've already seen how >>= lets you chain together a sequence of functions that put a normal value into a context. The fail method handles the case of errors happening in your Monad. For Maybe, fail returns Nothing; and for IO, fail raises an I/O error. You'll discuss fail in more depth in unit 7 when we discuss handling errors in Haskell. That leaves only >> and return to explain.

The return method should look awfully familiar. If you compare this to pure, you'll find they're nearly identical:

```
pure :: Applicative f => a -> f a
return :: Monad m => a -> m a
```

The only difference is that pure has a type class restraint on Applicative, whereas return has a constraint on the Monad type class. It turns out that pure and return *are* identical and have different names only for historical reasons. The Monad type class predates the Applicative type class, so the return method exists for legacy reasons. Because every Monad must be an Applicative, it would be reasonable to use pure over return because pure will work everywhere return does. But this isn't typically the case. When using pure in the context of Monad, it's preferable to stick with return.

Finally, you can look at the >> operator. If you look carefully, >> has a rather strange type signature, as shown in figure 30.6.

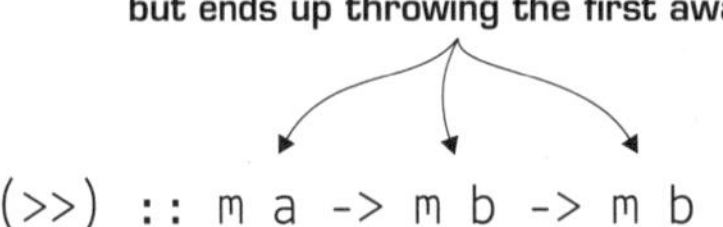
The >> operator takes two arguments but ends up throwing the first away.
(>>) :: m a -> m b -> m b

Figure 30.6 The >> operator has a strange type signature but is useful for Monads with side effects.

It looks like this operator throws away the first m a type. It turns out this is exactly what >> does. Why would you want this? It's particularly useful in contexts that produce side effects such as IO (there are others, which we'll discuss in unit 7). So far, the only context you've seen like this is IO. Whenever you use putStrLn, you don't get anything back. It's common that you'll want to print something to the user and just throw away the IO ()

result. For example, you might want to modify your echo.hs program so that it lets your user know what it's doing.

Listing 30.11 Showing the benefit of >> with a verbose version of echo

```
echoVerbose :: IO ()
echoVerbose = putStrLn "Enter a String an we'll echo it!" >>
              getLine >>= putStrLn

main :: IO ()
main = echoVerbose
```

When working with `IO`, `>>` is useful anytime you need to perform an `IO` action that doesn't meaningfully return a value.

30.3.1 Using Monad to build a Hello <Name> program

To demonstrate how you tie all these together, let's write a simple `IO` action that will ask a user's name, and then print out `"Hello, <NAME>!"`. You need to chain together a few basic functions to do this. The first is an `IO` action that will ask for the name; this is simply `putStrLn` with your question.

Listing 30.12 askForName IO action

```
askForName :: IO ()
askForName = putStrLn "What is your name?"
```

The next `IO` action you need to use is `getLine`. After that, you need to take the result of `getLine` and make your `"Hello, <NAME>!"` string. This function is a regular function of the form `String -> String`.

Listing 30.13 nameStatement works on normal String rather than IO String

```
nameStatement :: String -> String
nameStatement name = "Hello, " ++ name ++ "!"
```

Then you have to send the results of this to `putStrLn`, and your action is finished. You start with chaining together `askForName` and `getLine` with `>>`, because you don't need the results:

```
(askForName >> getLine)
```

The next part is tricky; you now have an `IO String`, but you need to connect it with `nameStatement`, which is a regular `String -> String` function. You can use `>>=` to do this if you can make `nameStatement` return an `IO String`. You could rewrite `nameStatement`, but a more common solution is to wrap `nameStatement` in a lambda and use `return` at the end. Because of type inference, Haskell knows which context to put the type into, as shown in figure 30.7.

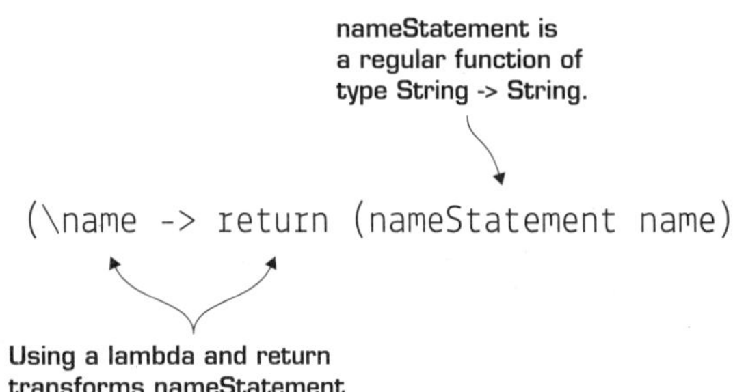
nameStatement is
a regular function of
type String -> String.
(\name -> return (nameStatement name))
Using a lambda and return
transforms nameStatement
into the type String -> IO String.

Figure 30.7 Using a lambda expression with `return` to transform a type `a -> a` into `a -> m a`

> **Quick check 30.4** Turn `(+ 2)` from type `Num a => a -> a` to type `Num a => a -> IO a` using a lambda and `return`. Use `:t` in GHCi to double-check that you're getting the correct type.

This is your program so far:

```
(askForName >> getLine) >>= (\name -> return (nameStatement name))
```

To finish, you use `>>=` to return the results to `putStrLn`. Here's your final `helloName IO` action.

Listing 30.14 Your Hello Name program using `Monad` methods

```
helloName :: IO ()
helloName = askForName >>
            getLine >>=
            (\name ->
              return (nameStatement name)) >>=
            putStrLn
```

QC 30.4 answer

```
(\n -> return ((+ 2) n))
```

You can either make this its own program or use GHCi to test it out. Here's the result in GHCi:

```
GHCi> helloName
What is your name?
Will
Hello, Will!
```

The great thing about using `Monad` to solve this problem is that you were able to chain all your functions and actions together relatively easily. The bad part is that if you had to add more `IO` functions such as `nameStatement`, all these lambdas would get a bit annoying. Additionally, going back and forth with all these operators can be confusing. In the next lesson, you'll see how the do-notation from unit 4 is just syntactic sugar over `Monad`'s methods.

Summary

In this lesson, our objective was to introduce you to the `Monad` type class. The `Monad` type class is the final refinement of computing in a context that you started with `Functor`. The most important method of the `Monad` type class is the `>>=` (pronounced *bind*) operator. You use `>>=` to chain together functions of the type `(a -> m b)`. This is particularly important for working with the `IO` type. Unlike `Maybe`, you can't trivially use pattern matching to access values inside the `IO` context. The `Monad` type class is what makes I/O programming possible. Let's see if you got this.

Q30.1 To prove that `Monad` is strictly more powerful than `Functor`, write a universal version of `<$>`, as in the preceding lesson's exercise, called `allFmapM`, that defines `<$>` for all members of the `Monad` type class. Because it works for all instances of `Monad`, the only functions you can use are the methods required by the `Monad` type class (and lambda functions). To get you started, here's your type signature:

```
allFmapM :: Monad m => (a -> b) -> m a -> m b
```

Q30.2 To prove that `Monad` is strictly more powerful than `Applicative`, write a universal version of `<*>`, called `allApp`, that defines `<*>` for all members of the `Monad` type class. Because it works for all instances of `Monad`, the only functions you can use are the methods required by the `Monad` type class (and lambda functions). To get you started, here's your type signature:

```
allApp :: Monad m => m (a -> b) -> m a -> m b
```

This question is much trickier than the last one. Two hints:

- Try to think exclusively in terms of the type signatures.
- Use <$> if you want and replace it with your answer to Q29.1

Q30.3 Implement a bind function which is the same as (>>=) for Maybe:

```
bind :: Maybe a -> (a -> Maybe b) -> Maybe b
```

LESSON 31

MAKING MONADS EASIER WITH DO-NOTATION

After reading lesson 31, you'll be able to

- Use do-notation to simplify working with Monads
- Translate from Monad methods and lambdas to do-notation
- Generate code from one instance of Monad to all Monads

The Monad type class allows for powerful abstraction when using types in context. But the use of the Monad methods >>=, >>, and return quickly becomes cumbersome. In this lesson, you'll look at two useful tools that make working with Monads significantly easier. The first is do-notation, which you already made heavy use of in unit 4. Now you'll get a sense of how do-notation works behind the scenes. After this, you'll learn about how List works as a Monad. This leads to another abstraction over Monads that makes them even easier to work with: list comprehensions. Although it's important to understand the methods of the Monad type class, in practice most of the work you'll do with Monads involves using these methods of simplifying your code.

In the preceding lesson, you left off with a helloName IO action that asks the user for their name and then says hello to them.

Listing 31.1 helloName

```
askForName :: IO ()
askForName = putStrLn "What is your name?"

nameStatement :: String -> String
nameStatement name = "Hello, " ++ name ++ "!"

helloName :: IO ()
helloName = askForName >>
            getLine >>=
            (\name ->
              return (nameStatement name)) >>=
            putStrLn
```

You were able to achieve this by using the methods of the `Monad` type class. As a refresher, here are those methods:

- `>>` allows you to perform an `IO` action and chain it with another action, ignoring its value.
- `>>=` allows you to perform an `IO` action and then hand off the return value of that function to another waiting for a value.
- `(\x -> return (func x))` allows you to take an ordinary function and have it work in the context of `IO`.

The good thing about all this is that now you have the tool to do basically anything that you'd like inside a context such as `IO` or `Maybe`. Unfortunately, this code is messy, and is difficult to read and write. Thankfully, Haskell has a great solution to this problem!

Consider this Write a program by using the tools of the `Monad` type class that takes a pair of values in a context, and then returns the maximum of each pair. Here's your type signature to get you started:

```
maxPairM :: (Monad m, Ord a) => m (a,a) -> m a
```

The resulting function should work on `IO (a,a)`, `Maybe (a,a)`, and `[(a,a)]`.

31.1 Do-notation revisited

It turns out that you've already seen the solution to making your monadic code look cleaner: do-notation. Do-notation is syntactic sugar for using `>>`, `>>=`, and `(\x -> return (func x))`. Here's the previous example rewritten in do-notation.

Listing 31.2 Rewriting `helloName` using do-notation

```
helloNameDo :: IO ()
helloNameDo = do
   askForName
   name <- getLine
   putStrLn (nameStatement name)
```

Figure 31.1 provides an annotated version of this transformation.

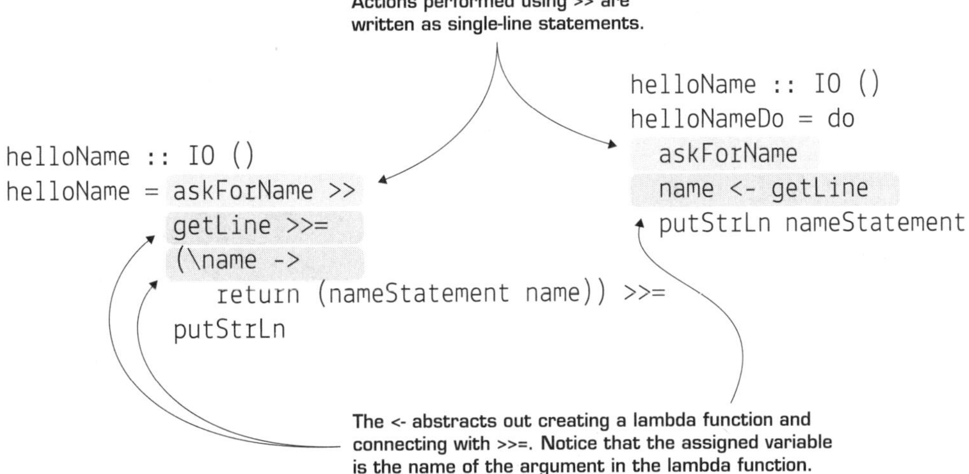

Figure 31.1 Mapping `Monad` methods to do-notation

It's a useful exercise to learn how to translate back and forth between using `Monad`'s operators and do-notation. In unit 4, you saw this simple Hello World program.

Listing 31.3 A program illustrating do-notation

```
helloPerson :: String -> String
helloPerson name = "Hello" ++ " " ++ name ++ "!"

main :: IO ()
main = do
   name <- getLine
   let statement = helloPerson name
   putStrLn statement
```

You can desugar `main`, as shown in figure 31.2.

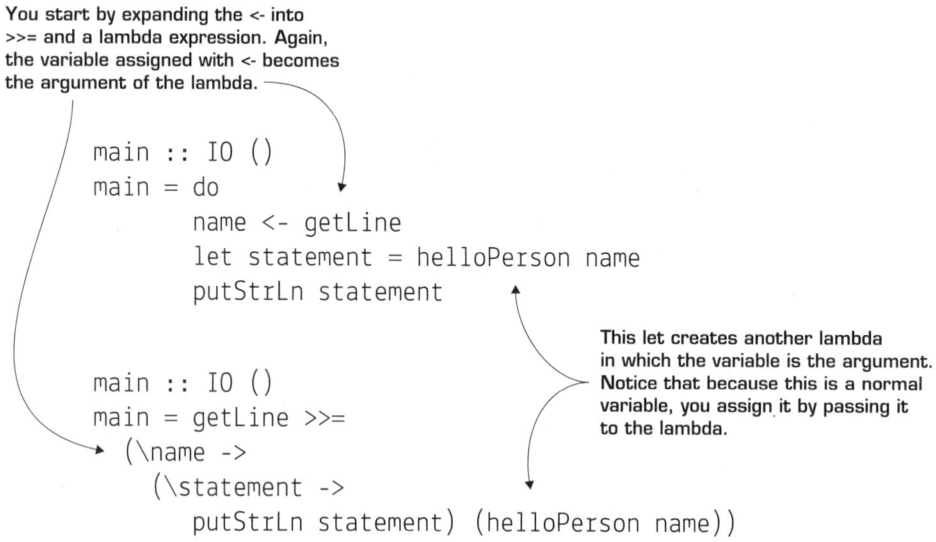

You start by expanding the <- into >>= and a lambda expression. Again, the variable assigned with <- becomes the argument of the lambda.

```
main :: IO ()
main = do
       name <- getLine
       let statement = helloPerson name
       putStrLn statement
```

This let creates another lambda in which the variable is the argument. Notice that because this is a normal variable, you assign it by passing it to the lambda.

```
main :: IO ()
main = getLine >>=
  (\name ->
    (\statement ->
       putStrLn statement) (helloPerson name))
```

Figure 31.2 Desugaring do-notation

If you're having trouble understanding the translation of `let` and `<-` into lambda expressions, it'd be a good idea to review lesson 3 from unit 1. For reasons that should be clear, do-notation is strongly preferred for nontrivial use of monadic operators. But for simple cases such as an `echo` function, using `>>=` is often easier than doing things with do-notation.

Listing 31.4 A trivial `IO` action in which >>= makes more sense than do

```
echo :: IO ()
echo = getLine >>= putStrLn
```

When learning Haskell, it's okay if translating back and forth between do-notation and lambda with `Monad` methods takes some work. The important thing is to realize that there's nothing magic about do-notation.

Quick check 31.1 Rewrite `echo` by using do-notation.

31.2 Using do-notation to reuse the same code in different contexts

In unit 4, when you first saw do-notation, you briefly touched on the idea that the power of the `Monad` type class is that it allows you to create different programs by using the same code in different contexts. The example you used in lesson 21 was creating an I/O program that asked a user for information about comparing the costs of two pizzas. Because do-notation works on all members of `Monad`, you were able to trivially translate this program to work with `Maybe` types when your values came from `Data.Maps` rather than `IO`.

To further demonstrate the idea that `Monad` allows you to easily reuse code across different contexts, you're going to look at a series of examples of using the same code in different contexts. The fundamental issue is processing data on job candidates for your company. You want to determine whether they've passed or failed your interview process. You'll see how the same code can handle candidates in the context of `IO`, `Maybe`, and even `List`. In the end, you'll be able to refactor the code you've reused in each section to a single function that works on all instances of `Monad`.

31.2.1 The problem setup

To get started, you need to model your candidate data. Each `Candidate` is tracked by a unique ID. During the interview, candidates are given a code review and a culture fit interview. Each of these is scored by using a grade.

QC 31.1 answer

```
echo :: IO ()
echo = do
 val <- getLine
 putStrLn val
```

Listing 31.5 The `Grade` data type code review and culture fit

```
data Grade = F | D | C | B | A deriving (Eq, Ord, Enum, Show, Read)
```

Because you have a variety of research positions, you also keep track of the candidates' education level, and some positions require a minimum degree.

Listing 31.6 The `Degree` data type for highest level of education

```
data Degree = HS | BA | MS | PhD deriving (Eq, Ord, Enum, Show, Read)
```

Here's your final model for your `Candidate`.

Listing 31.7 The `Candidate` data type representing performance on an interview

```
data Candidate = Candidate
   { candidateId :: Int
   , codeReview :: Grade
   , cultureFit :: Grade
   , education :: Degree } deriving Show
```

The big thing you want to do is determine whether a candidate is viable. If a candidate is viable, you'll pass that person on to a committee for review. Here's your code for `viable`, which makes sure a candidate passes your minimum requirements.

Listing 31.8 The `viable` function checks how well your `Candidate` did

```
viable :: Candidate -> Bool
viable candidate = all (== True) tests
   where passedCoding = codeReview candidate > B
         passedCultureFit = cultureFit candidate > C
         educationMin = education candidate >= MS
         tests = [passedCoding
                 ,passedCultureFit
                 ,educationMin]
```

Next you'll look at three contexts in which you might want to check whether a candidate is viable.

Quick check 31.2 Create a `Candidate` type and see whether that candidate is viable.

31.2.2 The IO context—building a command-line tool

Your first case is building a command-line tool so that someone can manually enter in the data about a candidate. This task should be similar to the types of problems you solved in unit 4. The only difference is that in unit 4 you treated do-notation a bit like magic. The first thing you need is a bunch of simple `IO` actions to read in `Int`, `Grade`, and `Degree` types. You could use do-notation to implement these actions, but this is a great example of when using `>>=` comes in handy. Each of these actions needs a way to connect `getLine` with reading the result, and finally returning that result back as an `IO` type.

Listing 31.9 Useful `IO` actions for building your `Candidate`

```
readInt :: IO Int
readInt = getLine >>= (return . read)

readGrade :: IO Grade
readGrade = getLine >>= (return . read)

readDegree :: IO Degree
readDegree = getLine >>= (return . read)
```

With these helper actions, you can create a single `IO` action that reads in a candidate. For this action, all you're doing is adding output to help the user understand what to enter.

QC 31.2 answer

```
testCandidate :: Candidate
testCandidate = Candidate
   { candidateId = 1
   , codeReview = A
   , cultureFit = A
   , education = PhD }

GHCi> viable testCandidate
True
```

This use of do-notation is exactly the same type of problem you solved in unit 4, so it should feel fairly familiar.

Listing 31.10 A single function to read your candidate in from the command line

```
readCandidate :: IO Candidate
readCandidate = do
   putStrLn "enter id:"
   cId <- readInt
   putStrLn "enter code grade:"
   codeGrade <- readGrade
   putStrLn "enter culture fit grade:"
   cultureGrade <- readGrade
   putStrLn "enter education:"
   degree <- readDegree
   return (Candidate { candidateId = cId
                     , codeReview = codeGrade
                     , cultureFit = cultureGrade
                     , education = degree })
```

The core logic of your program is an `assessCandidateIO` action. This will take in a candidate, check whether the candidate is viable, and then return a `String` as `passed` if the candidate passed; otherwise it will return `failed`. You can write this action easily by using do-notation.

Listing 31.11 An `IO` action that lets you know if candidate passed/failed

```
assessCandidateIO :: IO String
assessCandidateIO = do
   candidate <- readCandidate
   let passed = viable candidate
   let statement = if passed
                   then "passed"
                   else "failed"
   return statement
```

You could put this in a `main`, compile your program, and run it, but in this case it's easier to use GHCi:

```
GHCi> assessCandidateIO
enter id:
1
enter code grade:
A
enter culture fit grade:
B
enter education:
PhD
"passed"
```

Because you have the `Monad` type class, you have an easy way to take a `Candidate` that wasn't designed with I/O in mind and use that `Candidate` in the `IO` context.

> **Quick check 31.3** Rewrite `readGrade` with do-notation.

31.2.3 The Maybe context—working with a map of candidates

Entering users one by one in the command line is a tedious way to check candidate data. In our next example, you'll use `Data.Map` to store a bunch of candidates and then look them up. First you need a few candidates to work with.

Listing 31.12 Example candidates

```
candidate1 :: Candidate
candidate1 = Candidate { candidateId = 1
                       , codeReview = A
                       , cultureFit = A
                       , education = BA }

candidate2 :: Candidate
candidate2 = Candidate { candidateId = 2
```

QC 31.3 answer

```
readGradeDo :: IO Grade
readGradeDo = do
   input <- getLine
   return (read input)
```

```
                        , codeReview = C
                        , cultureFit = A
                        , education = PhD }

candidate3 :: Candidate
candidate3 = Candidate { candidateId = 3
                        , codeReview = A
                        , cultureFit = B
                        , education = MS }
```

Then you can put all these candidates into `candidateDB`.

Listing 31.13 Putting your example candidates in a `Data.Map`

```
candidateDB :: Map.Map Int Candidate
candidateDB = Map.fromList [(1,candidate1)
                           ,(2,candidate2)
                           ,(3,candidate3)]
```

Once again you want to assess your candidates and return a string if you've found them. Now you can use your `candidateDB`. Because each lookup will return a `Maybe` type, you have a problem in a different context than the `IO` case before. In the last example, you were worried about interacting with a user; now you're concerned with passing around potentially missing values. To handle this, you need a function that looks a lot like `assessCandidateIO` but works for `Maybe` types.

Listing 31.14 Similarity between `assessCandidateMaybe` and `assessCandidateIO`

```
assessCandidateMaybe :: Int -> Maybe String
assessCandidateMaybe cId = do
   candidate <- Map.lookup cId candidateDB
   let passed = viable candidate
   let statement = if passed
                   then "passed"
                   else "failed"
   return statement
```

Now all you have to do is pass in a potential candidate's ID and you'll get your result in a `Maybe` context:

```
GHCi> assessCandidateMaybe 1
Just "failed"
GHCi> assessCandidateMaybe 3
Just "passed"
GHCi> assessCandidateMaybe 4
Nothing
```

Notice that your code is essentially identical. This is because after you assign a variable with `<-` in do-notation, you get to pretend it's an ordinary type that's not in a particular context. The `Monad` type class and do-notation have abstracted away the context you're working in. The immediate benefit in this case is you get to solve your problem without having to think about missing values at all. The larger benefit in terms of abstraction is that you can start thinking about all problems in a context in the same way. Not only is it easier to reason about potentially missing values, but along the way you can start designing programs that work in *any* context.

Quick check 31.4 Write a simple function `Maybe String -> String` that will print `failed/passed` if there's a result and `error id not found` for the `Nothing` constructor.

31.2.4 The List context—processing a list of candidates

It should come as no surprise that `List` is also a `Monad`, as `List` is an example of virtually every feature of Haskell. In the next lesson, you'll look more into what this means, but for now let's see what happens when you want to look at a list of candidates.

Listing 31.15 A list of possible candidates

```
candidates :: [Candidate]
candidates = [candidate1
             ,candidate2
             ,candidate3]
```

QC 31.4 answer

```
failPassOrElse :: Maybe String -> String
failPassOrElse Nothing = "error id not found"
failPassOrElse (Just val) = val
```

Because `List` is an instance of `Monad`, you should be able to convert your other `assessCandidate` function into an `assessCandidateList` function. If you do and pass in a list, you get a useful result.

Listing 31.16 Assessing a list of candidates using `List` as a `Monad`

```
assessCandidateList :: [Candidate] -> [String]
assessCandidateList candidates = do
   candidate <- candidates
   let passed = viable candidate
   let statement = if passed
                   then "passed"
                   else "failed"
   return statement
```

As you can see in GHCi, this checks each of your candidates in the list to see whether they pass and returns a list indicating whether candidates have passed or failed:

```
GHCi> assessCandidateList candidates
["failed","failed","passed"]
```

Once again, you haven't done much to change the core logic of your `assessCandidateX` functions. Working with lists by using the tools of the `Monad` type class, you can treat entire lists as single values. If you didn't know Haskell, you could easily read the body of your `assessCandidateList` function, but you'd likely assume it was for a single value. You could've written this code by using a list function such as `map`.

Listing 31.17 A list-specific way to assess candidates

```
assessCandidates :: [Candidate] -> [String]
assessCandidates candidates = map (\x -> if x
                                         then "passed"
                                         else "failed") passed
   where passed  = map viable candidates
```

But this code has two issues in terms of abstraction. The first is that you're forced to think of the problem in terms of a list. Showing this same code to someone unfamiliar with Haskell, they'd likely be much more confused by the use of `map`. The second, and more important, is that there's no way to generalize this code to other types in a context. The `assessCandidates` code is completely distinct from the `assessCandidateIO` and `assessCandidateMaybe` code you've written, even though it does the exact same thing.

In the next section, you'll start thinking about problems in terms of `Monad`s and realize that you have a general solution that you can easily put together to solve all three of the contexts you've explored so far.

Quick check 31.5 Does `assessCandidateList` handle the empty list?

31.2.5 Putting it all together and writing a monadic function

So far, you've focused primarily on the way that do-notation and the `Monad` type class allow you to solve problems while abstracting away the context:

- You can write code for `IO` types and not worry about the mismatch between `IO String`s and regular `String`s.
- You can write code for `Maybe` and forget about dealing with missing values.
- You can even write code for lists and pretend you have only a single value.

But there's another benefit to `Monad` that can emerge as a consequence of letting you forget context when you write programs. The action and two functions you wrote—`assessCandidateIO`, `assessCandiateMaybe`, and `assessCandidateList`—all share nearly identical code. Not only is it easier to solve a problem in a specific context with the `Monad` type class, but you end up with a single solution that works in any context.

The only limitation to using the same code in all three contexts is that the type signatures are too restrictive. Because `IO`, `Maybe`, and `List` are all instances of `Monad`, you can use a type class constraint in your definition of a universal `assessCandidate` function. The amazing thing here is you need to change only the type signature of your `assessCandidateList` function to do this.

Listing 31.18 The monadic `assessCandidate` works on `IO`, `Maybe`, and `List`

```
assessCandidate :: Monad m =>  m Candidate -> m String
assessCandidate candidates = do
   candidate <- candidates
   let passed = viable candidate
   let statement = if passed
```

QC 31.5 answer It does! Passing any empty list to `assessCandidateList` returns the empty list.

```
                    then "passed"
                    else "failed"
   return statement
```

In GHCi, you can now demonstrate by using this single function in three contexts:

```
GHCi> assessCandidate readCandidate
enter id:
1
enter code grade:
A
enter culture fit grade:
B
enter education:
PhD
"passed"
```

```
GHCi> assessCandidate (Map.lookup 1 candidateDB)
Just "failed"
GHCi> assessCandidate (Map.lookup 2 candidateDB)
Just "failed"
GHCi> assessCandidate (Map.lookup 3 candidateDB)
Just "passed"
```

```
GHCi> assessCandidate candidates
["failed","failed","passed"]
```

Many of the examples you've seen so far show how the `Monad` type class allows you to write code for regular types and use them in increasingly powerful ways in a context such as `Maybe`, `IO`, or `List`. Here you see how to take code that does work in one of these contexts and generalize it to work in all contexts because of `Monad`.

Summary

In this lesson, our objective was to teach you do-notation for working with `Monads`. The good news is that you already have plenty of experience using do-notation, as it was used heavily in unit 4. It's still important to understand desugared monadic code as it can help tremendously in debugging and understanding issues when working with `Monads`. You also saw how code written for `IO` using do-notation can be trivially rewritten for `Maybe` types. Although this is useful in itself, it also means you can write more generalized code that will work on all `Monad`s. Let's see if you got this.

Q31.1 At the end of lesson 21, you saw the following program used to calculate the cost of pizza:

```
main :: IO ()
main = do
   putStrLn "What is the size of pizza 1"
   size1 <- getLine
   putStrLn "What is the cost of pizza 1"
   cost1 <- getLine
   putStrLn "What is the size of pizza 2"
   size2 <-  getLine
   putStrLn "What is the cost of pizza 2"
   cost2 <- getLine
   let pizza1 = (read size1, read cost1)
   let pizza2 = (read size2, read cost2)
   let betterPizza = comparePizzas pizza1 pizza2
   putStrLn (describePizza betterPizza)
```

Desugar this code to use `>>=`, `>>`, `return` and lambda functions rather than do-notation.

Q31.2 At the end of lesson 21 in unit 4, we first introduced the idea that do-notation isn't specific to `IO`. You ended up with this function for a `Maybe` type:

```
maybeMain :: Maybe String
maybeMain = do
   size1 <- Map.lookup 1 sizeData
   cost1 <- Map.lookup 1 costData
   size2 <- Map.lookup 2 sizeData
   cost2 <- Map.lookup 2 costData
   let pizza1 = (size1,cost1)
   let pizza2 = (size2,cost2)
   let betterPizza = comparePizzas pizza1 pizza2
   return  (describePizza betterPizza)
```

Rewrite this function so it works with the `List` type (don't worry if the results seem strange).

Q31.3 Refactor the `maybeMain` function from the preceding exercise so that it works with any `Monad`. You'll need to change the type signature as well as remove the type-specific parts from the body of the function.

32

THE LIST MONAD AND LIST COMPREHENSIONS

After reading lesson 32, you'll be able to

- Use do-notation to generate lists
- Filter results in do-notation by using `guard`
- Further simplify do-notation with list comprehensions

At the end of the preceding lesson, you saw that `List` is an instance of `Monad`. You saw only a simple example of using `List` as a `Monad` to process a list of candidates.

Listing 32.1 The `assessCandidateList` function from the previous lesson

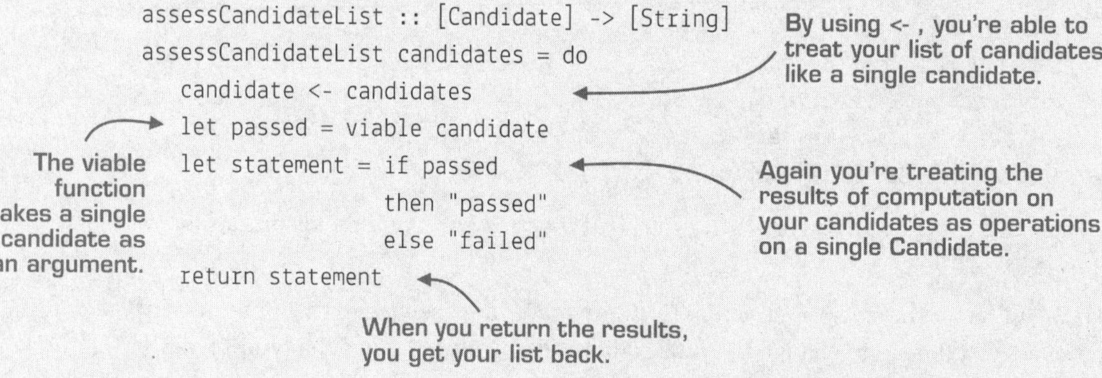

```
assessCandidateList :: [Candidate] -> [String]
assessCandidateList candidates = do
   candidate <- candidates
   let passed = viable candidate
   let statement = if passed
                   then "passed"
                   else "failed"
   return statement
```

By using <- , you're able to treat your list of candidates like a single candidate.
The viable function takes a single candidate as an argument.
Again you're treating the results of computation on your candidates as operations on a single Candidate.
When you return the results, you get your list back.

What makes using `List` as a `Monad` so interesting is that when you assign your list to a variable using <-, you get to treat it as though it were a single value. The rest of this code looks like it's operating on one candidate, and yet the final result is the same as applying your logic to every candidate in a list.

When you looked at `List` as `Applicative`, you saw some initially confusing examples of nondeterministic computing. For example, if you have two lists and use `pure (*)` to multiply them with <*>, you get every possible combination of the values from the two lists combined:

```
GHCi> pure (*) <*> [1 .. 4] <*> [5,6,7]
[5,6,7,10,12,14,15,18,21,20,24,28]
```

You may expect `List` as `Monad` to be even more confusing, but it turns out to be surprisingly familiar. The list monad allows you to trivially build complicated lists in an easy-to-program fashion. This is similar to LINQ in C# or list comprehensions in Python and other languages. It turns out there's even a way to further simplify do-notation for lists that makes generating lists even easier.

> **Consider this** What's the simplest way to create a list of the square of every odd number less than 20?

32.1 Building lists with the list monad

The main use of the list monad is to quickly generate lists. Figure 32.1 shows an example of using the list monad to create a list of powers of 2.

```
powersOfTwo :: Int -> [Int]
powersOfTwo n = do
  value <- [1 :: n]
  return (2^value)
```

When you assign values by using <-, you can pretend that values aren't in its context. In this case, the context is an [Int], so you can treat this as an Int.

Even though you're working with a list of values, you can raise 2 to the power of value as if it were a single value. The magic of the Monad class is that you can pretend that types in context are just plain types.

Figure 32.1 Generating lists by thinking of `List` as a `Monad`

In GHCi, you can use this to create the first 10 powers of 2:

```
GHCi> powersOfTwo 10
[2,4,8,16,32,64,128,256,512,1024]
```

Notice that in this definition you can treat the entire list as a single value and the results are as you'd expect. You could easily solve this with `map`, as you would have in unit 1:

```
powersOfTwoMap :: Int -> [Int]
powersOfTwoMap n = map (\x -> 2^x) [1 .. n]
```

But in this case, you're thinking of a list as a list data structure, not abstracting out the context of the list. For this case, the version using `map` is probably much easier to write and read. But as you generate more complicated lists, being able to focus on how you'd transform a single value can be helpful. Here are some more examples of generating lists with do-notation.

You can combine two lists easily. Suppose you want powers of 2 and 3 as *n* pairs.

Listing 32.2 Making a list of pairs by using do-notation

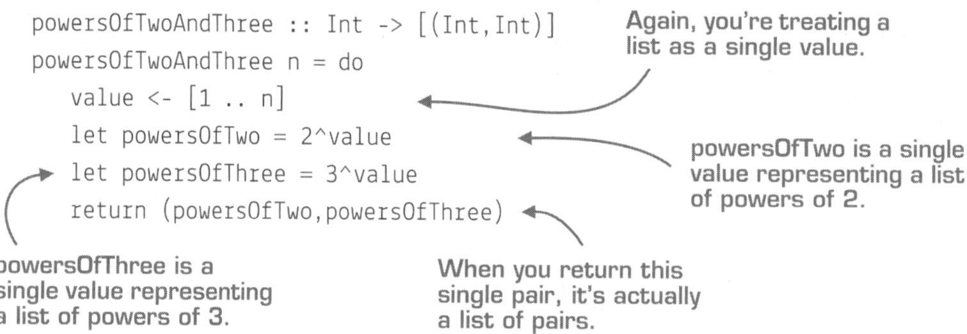
Again, you're treating a list as a single value.
powersOfTwo is a single value representing a list of powers of 2.
powersOfThree is a single value representing a list of powers of 3.
When you return this single pair, it's actually a list of pairs.

```
powersOfTwoAndThree :: Int -> [(Int,Int)]
powersOfTwoAndThree n = do
   value <- [1 .. n]
   let powersOfTwo = 2^value
   let powersOfThree = 3^value
   return (powersOfTwo,powersOfThree)
```

Now you have a list for pairs of powers of 2 and powers of 3:

```
GHCi> powersOfTwoAndThree 5
[(2,3),(4,9),(8,27),(16,81),(32,243)]
```

In the preceding example, you used one list, `value`, to generate your powers of 2. If you make two lists and combine them into pairs the same way, you get different results. Here's a function that will generate all possible combinations of odd and even numbers up to *n*:

```
allEvenOdds :: Int -> [(Int,Int)]
allEvenOdds n = do
   evenValue <- [2,4 .. n]
   oddValue <- [1,3 .. n]
   return (evenValue,oddValue)
```

evenValue is a single value representing a list.

oddValue is another single value representing a list.

Because evenValue and oddValue were created with <-, this pair represents all possible pairs from the two values.

As you can see in GHCi, you don't get a list of size *n*, but rather all possible combinations of even and odd values:

```
GHCi> allEvenOdds 5
[(2,1),(2,3),(2,5),(4,1),(4,3),(4,5)]
GHCi> allEvenOdds 6
[(2,1),(2,3),(2,5),(4,1),(4,3),(4,5),(6,1),(6,3),(6,5)]
```

Quick check 32.1 Use do-notation to generate pairs of numbers up to 10 and their squares.

32.1.1 The guard function

Another useful trick is to filter lists. Again you could use `filter`, but when working with monads, you'd like to be able to reason about a value outside its context. In `Control.Monad`, a function called `guard` allows you to filter your values in a list. You have to import `Control.Monad` to use `guard`. Here's a method of generating even numbers by using `guard`:

```
evensGuard :: Int -> [Int]
evensGuard n = do
```

QC 32.1 answer

```
valAndSquare :: [(Int,Int)]
valAndSquare = do
   val <- [1 .. 10]
   return (val,val^2)
```

```
value <- [1 .. n]
guard(even value)
return value
```

guard filters out all the values that don't satisfy your test.

Although do-notation makes it easy to generate arbitrarily complex lists by using the methods of `Monad`, there's a more familiar interface for this.

Quick check 32.2 Write `filter` by using `guard` and do-notation.

The guard function and the Alternative type class

If you look at `guard`'s type signature, you find that it's a strange function. Most notably, it has a type class constraint you haven't seen before:

```
guard :: Alternative f => Bool -> f()
```

The `Alternative` type class is a subclass of `Applicative` (meaning all instances of `Alternative` must be instances of `Applicative`). But, unlike `Applicative`, `Alternative` isn't a superclass of `Monad`; not all `Monad`s are instances of `Alternative`. For the `guard` function, the key method of `Alternative` is `empty`, which works exactly like `mempty` from `Monoid`. Both `List` and `Maybe` are instances of `Alternative`. `List`'s empty value is `[]`, and `Maybe`'s is `Nothing`. IO, however, isn't an instance of `Alternative`. You can't use `guard` with `IO` types.

When you first encounter `guard`, it might seem like magic. Surely, there must be some stateful mischief going on behind the scenes! Surprisingly, `guard` is a completely pure function. It's far beyond the scope of this book, but if you feel comfortable with `Monad`s, revisit `guard` and see whether you can implement it yourself. To understand `guard`, it helps tremendously to translate from do-notation back to >>=, >>, and lambdas. Learning about `guard` will also teach you a lot about the subtleties of >>. Again, this isn't a particularly useful exercise for beginners, but highly recommended after you're comfortable working with `Monad`s.

QC 32.2 answer

```
guardFilter :: (a -> Bool) -> [a] -> [a]
guardFilter test vals = do
   val <- vals
   guard(test val)
   return val
```

32.2 List comprehensions

If you're a Python developer, you likely find this method of generating lists a bit verbose. Python uses a special syntax to generate lists, called *list comprehensions*. Here's a Python list comprehension to generate powers of 2:

```
Python> [n**2 for n in range(10)]
[1, 2, 4, 8, 16, 32, 64, 128, 256, 512]
```

Python's list comprehensions also allow you to filter a list on a condition. Here's a list of squares that are even:

```
Python> [n**2 for n in range(10) if n**2 % 2 == 0]
[0, 4, 16, 36, 64]
```

Because you've been playing with do-notation and lists, this should look close, though more compact, to what you've been doing. Here's the do-notation version of the last Python list comprehension in Haskell, `evenSquares`.

Listing 32.3 `evenPowersOfTwo` emulates Python's list comprehensions

```
evenSquares :: [Int]
evenSquares = do
   n <- [0 .. 9]
   let nSquared = n^2
   guard(even nSquared)
   return nSquared
```

It may come as a bit of a surprise to any Python programmer, but list comprehensions are just specialized applications of monads! Of course, our Haskell example is significantly more verbose than Python's. By this point in your journey to learning Haskell, the phrase "Haskell is more verbose than ..." should be surprising. Not to be outdone in terseness, Haskell has a further refinement of do-notation specifically for lists: Haskell's list comprehensions.

List comprehensions provide an even simpler way of generating lists than do-notation. Figure 32.2 shows how to translate a function, `powersOfTwo`, from do-notation to a list comprehension.

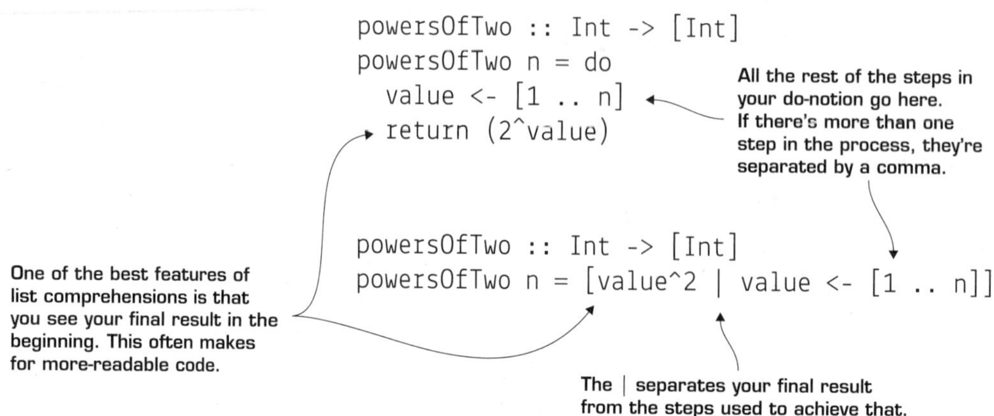

powersOfTwo :: Int -> [Int]
powersOfTwo n = do
value <- [1 .. n]
return (2^value)
All the rest of the steps in your do-notation go here. If there's more than one step in the process, they're separated by a comma.
powersOfTwo :: Int -> [Int]
powersOfTwo n = [value^2 | value <- [1 .. n]]
One of the best features of list comprehensions is that you see your final result in the beginning. This often makes for more-readable code.
The | separates your final result from the steps used to achieve that.

Figure 32.2 List comprehensions simplify do-notation even further for generating lists.

The conversion is reasonably straightforward; here's `powersOfTwoAndThree` converted:

```
powersOfTwoAndThree :: Int -> [(Int,Int)]
powersOfTwoAndThree n = [(powersOfTwo,powersOfThree)
                        | value <- [1 .. n]
                        , let powersOfTwo = 2^value
                        , let powersOfThree = 3^value]
```

As you can see, this is nearly identical to do-notation, except lines are separated by a commas and the new line is purely optional.

For clarity, the full variable names are used. Typically, shorter variables are used to keep the comprehension a one-liner if possible.

One thing that makes list comprehensions much easier to work with is that you start with the result and then show how it's generated. It's often easier to understand what a list comprehension is doing just by looking at the beginning of it:

```
allEvenOdds :: Int -> [(Int,Int)]
allEvenOdds n = [(evenValue,oddValue) | evenValue <- [2,4 .. n]
                                      , oddValue <- [1,3 .. n]]
```

The `guard` function is completely abstracted out of list comprehensions:

```
evensGuard :: Int -> [Int]
evensGuard n = [ value | value <- [1 .. n], even value]
```

List comprehensions are a nice way to make working with the list monad even easier. The other great insight here is that if you've used them in another language, you already have experience writing monadic code! Despite their prominence in Haskell, nothing prevents monads from existing in other languages that support the basics of functional programming covered in unit 1: first-class functions, lambda expressions, and closures. You could build a primate list comprehension system in any language that supports this. You'd simply have to implement `>>=`, `>>`, and `return`.

Quick check 32.3 Write a list comprehension that takes the following words

```
["brown","blue","pink","orange"]
```

and capitalizes the first letter, and prepends Mr. in front. (Hint: use `Data.Char`'s `toUpper`.)

32.3 Monads: much more than just lists

In this unit's capstone, you're going to take abstracting operations on lists one step further by creating a SQL-like interface for working with lists. All of this time thinking about the list monad may leave you thinking that monads are all about lists. Don't forget about unit 4! Even though we didn't discuss it much, nearly every line of code you wrote in that lesson used the `Monad` type class.

By the end of this unit, you'll have taken a deep dive into two ways of thinking in `Monads`: `IO` and `List`. The goal here is to show you how powerful an abstraction the idea of working in a context can be. For `IO`, you used working in a context to separate stateful, nonpure code necessary for I/O from the rest of your safe, predictable program logic. For lists, you've seen how to make generating complex data much easier by using the `Monad` type class. You've also seen many examples of using monads to write programs with

QC 32.3 answer

```
import Data.Char

answer :: [String]
answer = ["Mr. " ++ capVal | val <-
                              ["brown","blue","pink","organge","white"]
                            , let capVal = (\(x:xs) ->
                                               toUpper x:xs) val]
```

Maybe types. This has allowed you to write complex programs dealing with missing values while never having to think about how you'll handle those missing values. All three of these contexts are extremely different, and yet the Monad type class allows you to think about them the exact same way.

Summary

In this lesson, our objective was to further explain the Monad type class by exploring how List behaves as a member of Monad. It may be surprising for many people learning Haskell to discover that list comprehensions, popular in the Python programming language, are equivalent to Monads. Any list comprehension can be trivially converted to do-notation, and any code using do-notation can be trivially desugared to >>= and lambdas. The amazing thing about the Monad type class is that it allows you to abstract out the logic you might use in a list comprehension and seamlessly apply it to both Maybe types and IO types! Let's see if you got this.

Q32.1 Use a list comprehension that generates a list of correct calendar dates, given that you know the number of days in each month. For example, it should start with `1 .. 31` for January and be followed by `1 .. 28` for February.

Q32.2 Translate the preceding question into do-notation, and then into Monad methods and lambdas.

CAPSTONE: SQL-LIKE QUERIES IN HASKELL

This capstone covers

- Using the Monad type class to create SQL-like queries on lists
- Generalizing functions written for one Monad (for example, List) to many
- Organizing functions with types

In the preceding lesson, you saw how List as a Monad can also be understood as a list comprehension, which is used heavily in Python. In this capstone, you're going to take your use of lists and monads one step further to create a SQL-like interface to lists (and other monads). SQL is used as the primary means to query relational databases. It has a clean syntax for representing the relationships between data. For example, if you had data about teachers teaching classes, you could query the teachers teaching English like this:

```
select teacherName from
teacher inner join course
on teacher.id = course.teacherId
where course.title = "English";
```

This allows you to easily combine two data sets, the teacher table and course table, to extract relevant information. You'll build a set of tools you'll call HINQ (borrowing its name from the similar .NET tool LINQ). HINQ will allow you to query your data relationally. You'll make extensive use of the `Monad` type class to make this possible. In the end, you'll have a query tool that

- Provides a familiar interface for querying relational data in Haskell
- Is strongly typed
- Uses lazy evaluation to allow you to pass around queries without executing them
- Can be used seamlessly with other Haskell functions

You'll start by making some select queries on a list, learn to filter your queries with a where function, and finally build a join function that allows you to easily combine complex data inside a monad.

33.1 Getting started

Let's start with some basic data. You can put everything you need in a file named hinq.hs. Because you want to see how well you can treat lists such as tables in a relational database, you'll use an example involving students, teachers, courses, and enrollments. Figure 33.1 illustrates this setup.

You'll start with modeling your student. Each student has a name, which you'll keep to `firstName` and `lastName`.

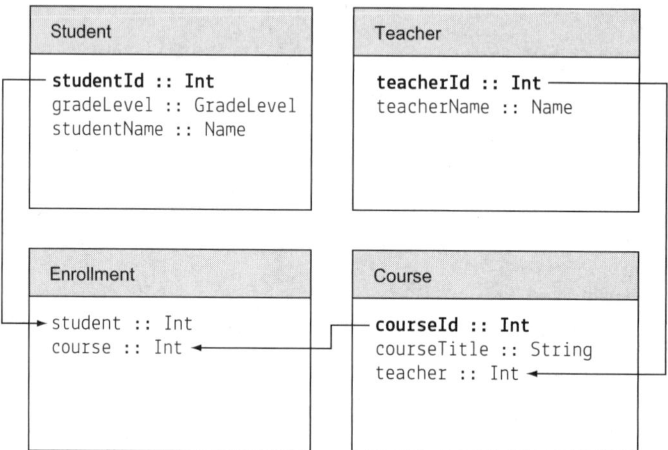

Figure 33.1 The relationships among the basic data you'll be working with

Listing 33.1 A simple `Name` data type with its `Show` instance

```
data Name = Name
            { firstName ::String
            , lastName :: String }

instance Show Name where
   show (Name first last) = mconcat [first," ",last]
```

Then each student has a grade level.

Listing 33.2 `GradeLevel` represents the student's grade

```
data GradeLevel = Freshman
   | Sophmore
   | Junior
   | Senior deriving (Eq,Ord,Enum,Show)
```

In addition to these two things, you'll include a unique student ID. Here's your `Student` data type.

Listing 33.3 The `Student` data type

```
data Student = Student
   { studentId :: Int
   , gradeLevel :: GradeLevel
   , studentName :: Name } deriving Show
```

And you want a list of students you can play with.

Listing 33.4 A list of example students that you can query

```
students :: [Student]
students = [(Student 1 Senior (Name "Audre" "Lorde"))
           ,(Student 2 Junior (Name "Leslie" "Silko"))
           ,(Student 3 Freshman (Name "Judith" "Butler"))
           ,(Student 4 Senior (Name "Guy" "Debord"))
           ,(Student 5 Sophmore (Name "Jean" "Baudrillard"))
           ,(Student 6 Junior (Name "Julia" "Kristeva"))]
```

With just this list, you can move on to building out your basic operations, select and where. In addition to select and where, you'll also want a join function that will allow you to combine two lists based on a common property.

Thinking in types, you can reason about these three functions as follows: Your select function needs to take a function representing the property being selected and a list of items to select from. Then the result will be a list of the selected property. Figure 33.2 shows the type signature of select.

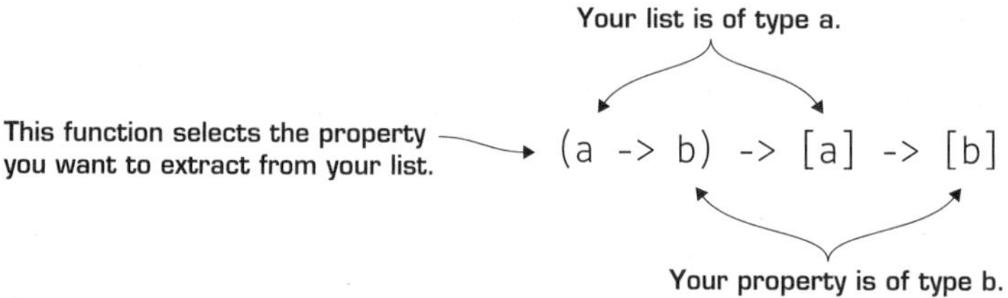

Figure 33.2 The type signature of your select function

Your where function will take a test function (which is just a function from `a -> Bool`) and a list and will return only the remaining values in the list. The type signature of where is shown in figure 33.3.

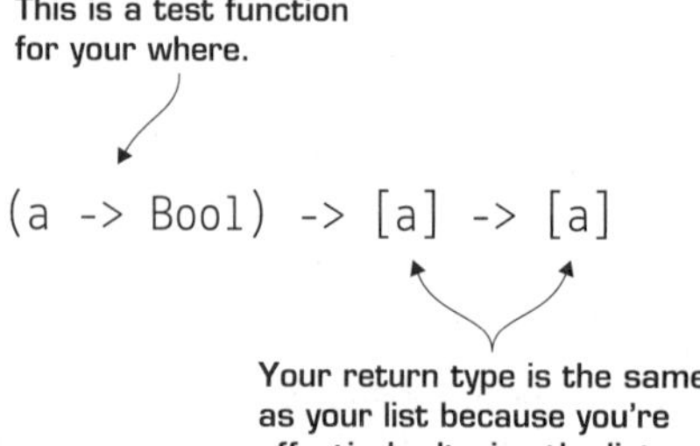

Figure 33.3 The type signature for your where function

Finally, your join function will take two lists of potentially different types, and then two functions that extract a property from each list. It's important that both properties are of the same type and instances of `Eq` so they can be compared. The result of join will be a list of tuples of the matching values from the original lists. Here's the type signature for the join function (we'll explain this in more detail when you implement it):

```
Eq c => [a] -> [b] -> (a -> c) -> (b -> c) -> [(a,b)]
```

Next you'll get started with implementing your select and where functions, which will make it easy to perform simple queries on lists.

33.2 Basic queries for your list: select and where

The functions you'll start with are select and where. The `select` clause in SQL allows you to select properties from a table:

```
select studentName from students;
```

This query gives you all the student names from the students table. In the case of your HINQ queries, you'd expect `select` to give you all the names from a list of students. The `where` clause in SQL allows you to condition your `select` on a given value:

```
select * from students where gradeLevel = 'Senior';
```

In this SQL statement, you'd select all the entries in the student table that have a grade level of `Senior`. Notice that in most databases, you'd have to represent the grade level as a `String`, but in Haskell you get the benefit of using a specific type.

Now you can move on to implementing these as functions. You'll preface all the functions for HINQ with an underscore (_), not only because you haven't covered modules and want to avoid collision, but also because `where` is a reserved keyword.

33.2.1 Implementing _select

The easiest operation to implement is `_select`. The `_select` function works just like `fmap`, only you'll use the `Monad` syntax in this case.

Listing 33.5 The `_select` function is just `fmap`

```
_select :: (a -> b) -> [a] -> [b]
_select prop vals = do
   val <- vals
   return (prop val)
```

Here are a few examples of selecting properties from your students in GHCi:

```
GHCi> _select (firstName . studentName) students
["Audre","Leslie","Judith","Guy","Jean","Julia"]
GHCi> _select gradeLevel students
[Senior,Junior,Freshman,Senior,Sophmore,Junior]
```

This example may make it seem like `_select` can choose only a single property, but you can easily use a lambda to make a single function that selects two properties:

```
GHCi> _select (\x -> (studentName x, gradeLevel x)) students
[(Audre Lorde,Senior),(Leslie Silko,Junior),(Judith Butler,Freshman),
➥(Guy Debord,Senior),(Jean Baudrillard,Sophmore),(Julia Kristeva,Junior)]
```

Even after all the tricks of functional programming you've learned so far, it's easy to forget how much power combining first-class functions with lambda functions can provide.

One more thing to notice is that your `_select` function is strictly less powerful than `fmap` solely because of its type signature. If you had literally defined `_select` as `_select = fmap`, your `_select` function would work on all members of the `Functor` type class. Later in this capstone, you'll refactor your code (though for monads), but it's worth realizing just how powerful a type signature can be.

33.2.2 Implementing _where

Your `_where` function will also be surprisingly simple. You'll create a simple wrapper around `guard`, which will take a test function and your list. Remember, to use `guard`, you'll have to import `Control.Monad`. The `_where` function is more complicated than `_select` because it's not just the `guard` function (whereas `_select` could be defined as `fmap`). You'll use the `<-` assignment to treat your list like a single value and then use your `test` function with `guard` to filter out the results that don't pass your test.

Listing 33.6 `_where` allows you to filter your queries

```
_where :: (a -> Bool) -> [a] -> [a]
_where test vals = do
         val <- vals
         guard (test val)
         return val
```

To show off `_where`, you'll start with a helper function that tests whether a `String` starts with a specific letter.

Listing 33.7 Check whether a `String` starts with a particular character using `startsWith`

```
startsWith :: Char -> String -> Bool
startsWith char string = char == (head string)
```

Now you can use `where` and `select` together to select only the students with names starting with *J*:

```
GHCi> _where (startsWith 'J' . firstName) (_select studentName students)
[Judith Butler,Jean Baudrillard,Julia Kristeva]
```

With the basics of `_select` and `_where` down, you can start to look at the heart of relational queries: `_join`.

33.3 Joining Course and Teacher data types

Before you join two data sets, you need to create more data. You'll look at teachers and courses next. Your `Teachers` have a `teacherId` and a `teacherName`.

Listing 33.8 A `Teacher` data type

```
data Teacher = Teacher
 { teacherId :: Int
 , teacherName :: Name } deriving Show
```

Here are some example teachers.

Listing 33.9 A list of example teachers

```
teachers :: [Teacher]
teachers = [Teacher 100 (Name "Simone" "De Beauvior")
           ,Teacher 200 (Name "Susan" "Sontag")]
```

Your courses have a `courseId`, a `courseTitle`, and a `teacher`. The `teacher` is an `Int` that represents the `teacherId` of the `Teacher` leading the `Course`.

Listing 33.10 `Course` data type references a `Teacher` by ID

```
data Course = Course
 { courseId :: Int
 , courseTitle :: String
 , teacher :: Int } deriving Show
```

And you need some examples.

Listing 33.11 A list of example courses

```
courses :: [Course]
courses = [Course 101 "French" 100
          ,Course 201 "English" 200]
```

Now what you want is to join these two data sets. In SQL terms, the join you're describing is an *inner join*, meaning that you care only about matching pairs. In SQL, the following query returns pairs of teachers and the class they teach:

```
select * from
teachers inner join courses
on (teachers.teacherId = courses.teacher);
```

You're going to assume that for your `_join`, you'll be checking to see whether a given property of data in one list is equal to another property in another list. This will have a rather large type signature. What you want to pass into your `_join` function is two lists, and then a function to select the property to join those lists on, and finally it will return those lists combined. Figure 33.4 shows the type signature to help you understand the process.

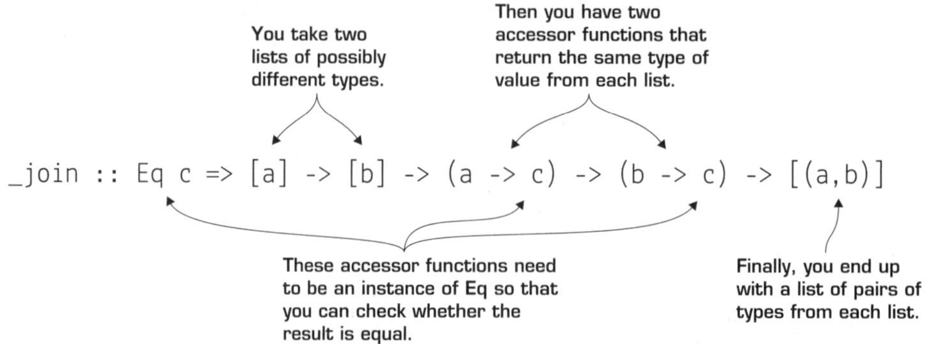

Figure 33.4 Reading the type signature for `_join`

You'll create your `_join` the same way a join works in the relational algebra used to create databases. You'll start by computing the Cartesian product of your two lists (by itself, this is a *cross join* in SQL). The *Cartesian product* is the combination of all possible pairs. Before you return the result, you'll filter these pairs out by matching property values (based on the properties you passed in, as shown in figure 33.5).

By using <-, you treat each of the lists of data as though it were as single value.

```
_join data1 data2 prop1 prop2 = do
  d1 <- data1
  d2 <- data2
  let dpairs = (d1,d2)
  guard ((prop1 (fst dparis)) == (prop2 (snd dpairs)))
  return dpairs
```

You then create pairs of these two lists. Remember, in do-notation this represents the combination of all possible pairs of d1 and d2.

The guard means you accept only pairs in which the two properties you passed in match.

You finally return the filtered set of pairs, containing only matches.

Figure 33.5 The `_join` function joins two data sets on matching properties.

You can use `_join` to combine your teachers and courses:

```
GHCi> _join teachers courses teacherId teacher
[(Teacher {teacherId = 100, teacherName = Simone De Beauvior},
➥Course {courseId = 101, courseTitle = "French", teacher = 100}),
➥(Teacher {teacherId = 200, teacherName = Susan Sontag},Course
➥{courseId = 201, courseTitle = "English", teacher = 200})]
```

With the three major parts of your query language together, you can start packaging `_select`, `_where`, and `_join` into an easier-to-use format.

33.4 Building your HINQ interface and example queries

You want to make it a bit easier to stick together the pieces of your query. Here's an example of using all three functions to find a list of English teachers (there's only one).

Listing 33.12 You need a way to pleasantly combine `_join`, `_select` , and `_where`

```
joinData = (_join teachers courses teacherId teacher)
whereResult = _where ((== "English") . courseTitle . snd) joinData
selectResult = _select (teacherName . fst) whereResult
```

This solution is okay, but what you want is your query to feel like a SQL query. Typically, SQL queries are structured like this:

```
select <elements> from <data> where <tests>
```

Your data can be either a list or data created from joining two lists together. You want to be able to restructure your query so it looks like this:

```
(_select (teacherName . fst))
(_join teachers courses teacherId teacher)
(_where ((== "English") .courseTitle . snd))
```

You can achieve this by using lambda functions to restructure your code so it looks the way you want it to. You'll create a function called `_hinq` that will take the `_select`, `_join`, and `_where` queries in the order you expect and then use lambdas behind the scenes to restructure everything.

Listing 33.13 `_hinq` function allows you to restructure your query

```
_hinq selectQuery joinQuery whereQuery = (\joinData ->
                                            (\whereResult ->
                                              selectQuery whereResult)
                                            (whereQuery joinData)
                                           ) joinQuery
```

The `_hinq` function can be used to run your query. Obviously, this code isn't a perfect replication of SQL or LINQ, but it's pretty close and allows you to think about combining two lists in the same way you would a relational query. Here's the previous query restructured using your `_hinq` function.

Listing 33.14 Using `_hinq` allows you to approximate SQL syntax in Haskell

```
finalResult :: [Name]
finalResult = _hinq (_select (teacherName . fst))
                    (_join teachers courses teacherId teacher)
                    (_where ((== "English") .courseTitle . snd))
```

There's one small annoyance left. Suppose you want to get the first names from your `finalResult` for all teachers, not just those teaching English. To do this, you wouldn't need a `_where` clause. You can solve this by using `(\_ -> True)`, which will automatically make everything `True`.

Listing 33.15 One possible solution to a missing _where

```
teacherFirstName :: [String]
teacherFirstName = _hinq (_select firstName)
                         finalResult
                         (_where (\_ -> True))
```

This works, but it's no fun to have to remember to pass in this universally true statement. And Haskell doesn't support default arguments. How can you make an easier way to deal with cases with missing `where` clauses? You'll use a `HINQ` type that will have two constructors.

33.5 Making a HINQ type for your queries

In this section, you'll create a `HINQ` type that represents a query. You know that a query can be a select clause, join/data clause, and a where clause, or just the first two. This will allow you to run queries with and without `_where` statements. Before moving on, though, you need to make one more improvement in your `_select`, `_where`, and `_join` functions. Currently, these all operate on lists, but you can generalize this so they work on other monads. To fix this, you don't need to change your code at all, only make your type signatures less restrictive. But you'll have to add a type class constraint. The `guard` function works on types of the `Alternative` type class. `Alternative` is a subtype of `Applicative`, and includes defining an empty element for the type (a lot like `Monoid`). Both `List` and `Maybe` are members of `Alternative`, but `IO` isn't. To use the `Alternative` type class, you need to import `Control.Applicative`. Here are your refactored type signatures that will extend the power of your HINQ queries.

Listing 33.16 `_select`, `_where`, and `_join` functions can work for all monads

```
_select :: Monad m => (a -> b) -> m a -> m b
_where :: (Monad m, Alternative m) => (a -> Bool) -> m a -> m a
_join :: (Monad m, Alternative m, Eq c) => m a -> m b ->
                                        (a -> c) -> (b -> c) -> m (a,b)
```

This is a great example of why writing monadic code is so useful. You start by solving your problem for just the `List` type. But you can make your code dramatically more generalized by changing the type signatures! If you had used list-specific functions, such as map and filter, this would require much more work to refactor. Now that your types are refactored, you can make a generic HINQ type to represent the queries you're interested in running, as shown in figure 33.6.

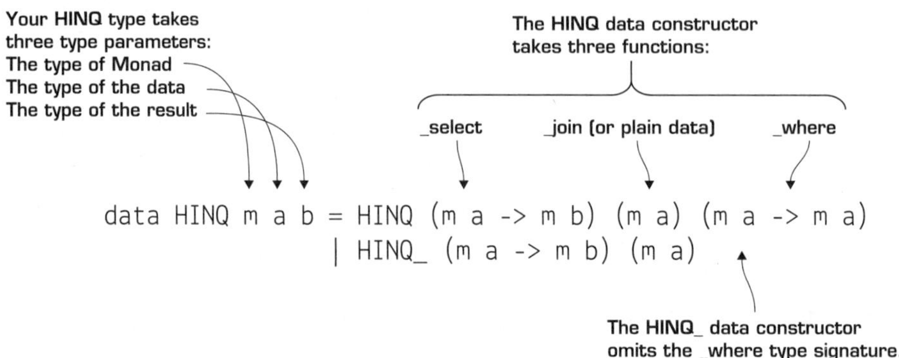

Figure 33.6 Understanding the HINQ data type

This constructor uses the types of your _selector, _join, and possibly _where functions. With this data type, you can write a runHINQ function that takes a HINQ type and runs the query.

Listing 33.17 runHINQ function allows you to execute HINQ queries

```
runHINQ :: (Monad m, Alternative m) => HINQ m a b -> m b
runHINQ (HINQ sClause jClause wClause) = _hinq sClause jClause wClause
runHINQ (HINQ_ sClause jClause) = _hinq sClause jClause
                                        (_where (\_ -> True))
```

The other benefit of having the HINQ type is that it clarifies the originally long type you were working with. Let's run a few queries to see how it does!

 33.6 Running your HINQ queries

With your HINQ type, you can start exploring different queries you might want to run. You'll start by revisiting your English teacher query. Here's the full HINQ query with a type signature:

```
query1 :: HINQ [] (Teacher, Course) Name
query1  = HINQ (_select (teacherName . fst))
               (_join teachers courses teacherId teacher)
               (_where ((== "English") .courseTitle . snd))
```

Because Haskell uses lazy evaluation, simply defining this query doesn't run it. This is great because it emulates the behavior of .NET LINQ (which also uses lazy evaluation) and it means you can pass around expensive computation without worrying about running the queries until you need the result. Another great thing about HINQ is that it's strongly typed. You'll easily be able to find bugs in your query because Haskell's type checker will yell at you. Because of type inference, you can always choose to leave the type out for quick queries. Run `query1` and look at the result:

```
GHCi> runHINQ query1
[Susan Sontag]
```

If you want to select teacher names from a similar data set, you can omit the `where` clause and use `HINQ_`:

```
query2 :: HINQ [] Teacher Name
query2 = HINQ_  (_select teacherName)
                teachers
```

This is the same as using `_select` on teachers by itself, but it shows that your query type works even for extremely simple cases. You can see that you get the results you expect in GHCi:

```
GHCi> runHINQ query2
[Simone De Beauvior,Susan Sontag]
```

Lists are the most common use of something like HINQ, but remember that you refactored it to work with all members of `Monad` and `Alternative`. Next you'll look at an example of querying a `Maybe`.

33.6.1 Using HINQ with Maybe types

It's not hard to imagine that you could end up with a `Maybe Teacher` and a `Maybe Course`. Just because you don't have a list of values doesn't mean you don't want to join your teacher with the course. Here's an example of a possible `Teacher` and a possible `Course`.

Listing 33.18 Because it's written for monads you can query `Maybe` types

```
possibleTeacher :: Maybe Teacher
possibleTeacher = Just (head teachers)

possibleCourse :: Maybe Course
possibleCourse = Just (head courses)
```

Running a query with a Maybe type means that you'll get results only if the query doesn't fail. It can fail from missing data *or* because it doesn't find a match. Here's your English teacher query again for Maybe types.

Listing 33.19 An example of a Maybe query

```
maybeQuery1 :: HINQ Maybe (Teacher,Course) Name
maybeQuery1  = HINQ (_select (teacherName . fst))
                    (_join possibleTeacher possibleCourse
                                           teacherId teacher)
                    (_where ((== "French") .courseTitle . snd))
```

Even in a Maybe context, you can still think relationally, run queries, and get your results:

```
GHCi> runHINQ maybeQuery1
Just Simone De Beauvior
```

If you had a missing course, you can still safely run the query.

Listing 33.20 You can join Maybe data and easily handle the case of missing data

```
missingCourse :: Maybe Course
missingCourse = Nothing

maybeQuery2 :: HINQ Maybe (Teacher,Course) Name
maybeQuery2  = HINQ (_select (teacherName . fst))
               (_join possibleTeacher missingCourse teacherId teacher)
               (_where ((== "French") .courseTitle . snd))
```

In GHCi, you can see that the missing data is still handled safely:

```
GHCi> runHINQ maybeQuery2
Nothing
```

You'll end this capstone by using HINQ to solve a more complicated problem involving multiple joins.

33.6.2 Joining multiple lists to get all enrollments

Next you'll look at querying your data to determine course enrollment. To do this, you need another data type to represent an enrollment. Enrollment is a student ID and a course ID. Here's the type you'll use to represent this.

Listing 33.21 `Enrollment` relates a `Student` to a `Course`

```
data Enrollment = Enrollment
   { student :: Int
   , course :: Int } deriving Show
```

You can represent all of your student enrollments by creating a list of them, each pairing a student's ID with a course ID.

Listing 33.22 A list of example enrollments

```
enrollments :: [Enrollment]
enrollments = [(Enrollment 1 101)
              ,(Enrollment 2 101)
              ,(Enrollment 2 201)
              ,(Enrollment 3 101)
              ,(Enrollment 4 201)
              ,(Enrollment 4 101)
              ,(Enrollment 5 101)
              ,(Enrollment 6 201) ]
```

Suppose you want to get a list of all the students' names paired with the name of the course they're enrolled in. To do this, you need to join students with enrollments, and then join the result of that with courses. You can get all of the student enrollments in one go by using a `HINQ_` query. This is a great example of the occasional times you may want to take advantage of type inference. How your queries combine types can get complicated, so writing out the full type signature can be tough. Thankfully, type inference takes care of all the work for you! This query will join students and enrollments to get a list of courses the students are enrolled in.

Listing 33.23 Queries students and the course they're enrolled in

```
studentEnrollmentsQ = HINQ_ (_select (\(st,en) ->
                                  (studentName st, course en))
                           (_join students enrollments studentId student)
```

Even though you didn't want to have to worry about the type signature of the query, you know the result should be a Name and an Id. When you run this query, you can make sure that this is the type of your result.

Listing 33.24 Running a query for studentEnrollments

```
studentEnrollments :: [(Name, Int)]
studentEnrollments = runHINQ studentEnrollmentsQ
```

In GHCi, you can double-check that your query ran as expected.

```
GHCi> studentEnrollments
[(Audre Lorde,101),(Leslie Silko,101),(Leslie Silko,201),
➥(Judith Butler,101),(Guy Debord,201),(Guy Debord,101),
➥(Jean Baudrillard,101),(Julia Kristeva,201)]
```

Now suppose you want to get a list of all English students. To do this, you need to join studentEnrollments with courses. Here's your query for selecting the name of students enrolled in an English course.

Listing 33.25 Joining studentEnrollments with courses

```
englishStudentsQ = HINQ  (_select (fst . fst))
                         (_join studentEnrollments
                                courses
                                snd
                                courseId)
                         (_where ((== "English") . courseTitle . snd))
```

Notice that your _where clause used data in courses, but your select is concerned only about which students are in the course. Now you can run your query and get a list of englishStudents.

Listing 33.26 Running the englishStudentsQ query to list English students

```
englishStudents :: [Name]
englishStudents = runHINQ englishStudentsQ
```

With HINQ, you were able to join three lists together just as though they were tables in a relational database.

You can also use HINQ inside a function to make generic tools for querying your data. Suppose you want a function getEnrollments that would list all the students enrolled in a class. You can pass in the course's name to the query you used last.

Listing 33.27 getEnrollments queries your data for enrollments

```
getEnrollments :: String -> [Name]
getEnrollments courseName =  runHINQ courseQuery
 where courseQuery = HINQ  (_select (fst . fst))
                           (_join studentEnrollments
                                courses
                                snd
                                courseId)
                           (_where ((== courseName) . courseTitle . snd))
```

In GHCi, you can see that this function works as expected:

```
GHCi> getEnrollments "English"
[Leslie Silko,Guy Debord,Julia Kristeva]
GHCi> getEnrollments "French"
[Audre Lorde,Leslie Silko,Judith Butler,Guy Debord,Jean Baudrillard]
```

And there you have it! With the power of monads, you've been able to successfully approximate a relational query engine that's reasonably similar to both SQL and LINQ. Not only are your queries easier to read, but you also get lazy evaluation and a powerful type system to make your system more efficient and robust. Furthermore, for any new types you have, if you implement Monad and Alternative, you can use HINQ on those data types for free! Nearly all the code you wrote to implement used the Monad type class. By combining monads, sum types (your HINQ type), lazy evaluation, and first-class functions, you were able to build a powerful query engine from scratch!

Summary

In this capstone you

- Learned how to easily implement _select and _where for lists
- Used the Cartesian product of two lists to replicate a database join
- Easily changed functions on lists to functions on monads in general

- Saw how lambda functions can allow you to restructure the way functions are called
- Made working with HINQ queries easier by using a `HINQ` data type

Extending the exercise

Now that you have the basics of your HINQ queries down, try to extend them the Haskell way! See if you can implement `Semigroup` and `Monoid` for HINQ. For `Monoid`, you might have to refactor your `HINQ` type to include the empty query. If you can define `Monoid` for `HINQ`, you can concatenate a list of HINQ queries into a single query!

Organizing code and building projects

Congratulations! You've made it through the most challenging topics in the book. Starting with this unit, the rest of this book focuses on practical uses of the topics we've covered so far. After you're finished, you should be comfortable building a wide range of common programming projects in Haskell.

In this unit, you'll look at a topic that will be familiar if you're an experienced programmer: organizing code and building projects. Haskell still has some fun tricks up its sleeve, but nothing that's as strange as you've experienced on your journey to get here.

You'll start this unit learning about Haskell's module system. Surprisingly, there's nothing strange or unique about the purpose of Haskell's modules. Just as in any other programming language, they serve to group functions into a single namespace and help organize reusable code. After that, you'll learn about Haskell's build system: stack. Again, stack is a typical, though solid, build system used to help automate the building of projects. The one interesting, but not particularly challenging, topic we'll cover is Haskell's QuickCheck testing library. QuickCheck automatically generates test cases for your code based on a set of properties that you define.

After you've completed this unit, coding in Haskell should feel more like everyday software development. You'll conclude this unit by building a library for working with prime numbers, and in many ways, this should feel like building a library in just about any programming language.

34

LESSON

ORGANIZING HASKELL CODE WITH MODULES

After reading lesson 34, you'll be able to

- Understand the `main` module implicitly used when you create a program
- Create namespaces for your functions by using modules
- Separate programs into multiple files
- Selectively import functions from modules

Up to this point in the book, we've covered a wide range of interesting topics related to Haskell. But we haven't discussed one of the most basic topics: creating namespaces for your functions. Haskell uses a system of modules to create separate namespaces for functions and allow you to organize your code much better. This works similarly to modules in languages such as Ruby and Python, and to packages and namespaces in languages such as Java and C#.

You've already used Haskell's module system. Every time you use `import`, you're including a new module in your program. Additionally, all the built-in functions and types you have—such as `[]`, `length`, and `(:)`—are all included in the standard module named `Prelude` that's automatically imported. The full documentation for `Prelude` can be found on Hackage (https://hackage.haskell.org/package/base/docs/Prelude.html).

So far in this book, we've avoided modules by keeping all of your code in the same file and giving your functions unique names when there's a conflict. In this lesson, you'll start organizing your code correctly into modules. You'll focus on a simple example: writing a command-line tool that prompts the user for a word and indicates whether the word is a palindrome. Ideally, you'd like to keep the `main` `IO` action in a separate file from the functions that work to determine whether text is a palindrome. This keeps your code better organized and makes it easier to extend your program with more code in the future. You'll start by writing your program as a single file, and then correctly separating the code into two files.

Consider this You have a type for books and a type for magazines. Each has the same field names, but they represent different things:

```
data Book = Book
    { title :: String
    , price :: Double }

data Magazine = Magazine
    { title :: String
    , price :: Double }
```

Both types are written using record syntax, which creates a problem. Record syntax automatically creates accessor functions `title` and `price`. Unfortunately, this causes an error because you're attempting to define two functions of the same name. You want to avoid giving these fields such as `bookTitle` and `bookPrice`. How can you resolve this conflict?

34.1 What happens when you write a function with the same name as one in Prelude?

To get started, let's create a better version of the default `head` function that you've been using throughout the book. In `Prelude`, `head` is defined as follows.

Listing 34.1 The definition in `Prelude` of `head`

```
head                :: [a] -> a
head (x:_)          = x
head []             = errorEmptyList "head"
```

errorEmptyList is a List-specific way to throw an error.

The head function has a problem in that it throws an error when it's applied to an empty list. This isn't ideal for Haskell, and lesson 38 covers this in more detail when we talk about handling errors. The reason head throws an error is that there often isn't a sensible value you can return. Languages such as Lisp and Scheme will return the empty list as the result of calling head on an empty list, but Haskell's type system doesn't allow this (because the empty list is usually a different type than values in the list itself). But you can come up with a solution to this problem if you constrain head to work on members of the Monoid type class. You'll recall from lesson 17 that the Monoid type class is defined as follows.

Listing 34.2 The definition of the Monoid type class

```
class Monoid m where
    mempty :: m
    mappend :: m -> m -> m
    mconcat :: [m] -> m
```

All Monoids are required to define a mempty element. The mempty element represents the empty value for instances of Monoid. List is an instance of Monoid, and mempty is just the empty list, []. For members of Monoid, you can return the mempty element when you have an empty list. Here's your new, safer version of head.

Listing 34.3 Oops, you accidentally created a function that already has a name!

```
head :: Monoid a => [a] -> a
head (x:xs) = x
head [] = mempty
```

If you write this code in a file, it'll compile just fine, even though you've "accidentally" used the name of an existing function. That's because the head you use all the time is part of the Prelude module. To test your new head function, you need an example of a list with values that are members of Monoid. In this case, you'll use an empty list of lists (remember, the elements of your list must be an instance of Monoid).

Listing 34.4 An example list that's a list of values that are an instance of Monoid

```
example :: [[Int]]
example = []
```

You can compile this code just fine, but something happens if you try to use `head` in GHCi. Because there's already a function called `head` when you run this code in GHCi, you get an error that looks something like this:

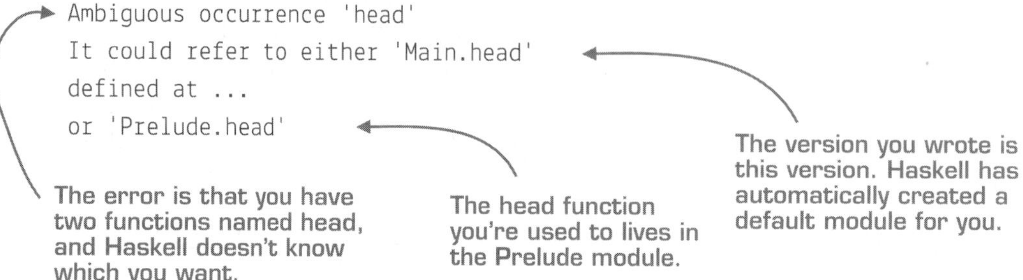

Ambiguous occurrence 'head'
It could refer to either 'Main.head'
defined at ...
or 'Prelude.head'
The error is that you have two functions named head, and Haskell doesn't know which you want.
The head function you're used to lives in the Prelude module.
The version you wrote is this version. Haskell has automatically created a default module for you.

The problem is that Haskell doesn't know which `head` you mean—the one defined in `Prelude` or the one you just wrote. What's interesting is that the complaint is that there's a `Main.head` function. When you don't explicitly tell Haskell that you're in a module, Haskell assumes that you're the `Main` module. You can make this explicit by using the following line at the top of your file.

Listing 34.5 Explicitly defining a module for your code

```
module Main where

head :: Monoid a => [a] -> a
head (x:xs) = x
head [] = mempty

example :: [[Int]]
example = []
```

This line is the only code that's different from your original code.

To specify precisely which `head` you mean, you can fully qualify your function's name with the name of the module. You use `Main.head` to specify your head, and `Prelude.head` to use the default `Prelude` definition of head. Here's an example in GHCi:

```
GHCi> Main.head example
[]
GHCi> Prelude.head example
*** Exception: Prelude.head: empty list
```

Next, you'll expand on your use of modules to build a simple program that's spread over two files.

Quick check 34.1 Suppose you need to store the length of an object as a variable. For example:

```
length :: Int
length = 8
```

How would you use that value without conflicting with the existing `length` function in `Prelude`?

34.2 Building a multifile program with modules

In this section, you'll build a simple program that reads a line of user input and then indicates whether the word is a palindrome. You'll start with a quick, single-file version of the program that can detect palindromes such as *racecar* but fails on *Racecar!* You'll then refactor your code into two files, one dealing with the main program logic and the other a library to put all your code for properly detecting palindromes.

It's generally good practice to separate groups of related functions into separate modules. The main module should primarily be concerned with the execution of your program. All of the logic for reasoning about palindromes should be kept in a separate file, because this makes it easier to keep track of the locations of library functions. Additionally, you can hide functions in a module the same way classes in Java or C# can have private methods. This allows you to have encapsulation so that only the functions you wish to export are available for use.

34.2.1 Creating the Main module

So far, you've been pretty casual with your filenames. Now that you're starting to think about properly organizing code, you should be more careful. As you saw in unit 4, each Haskell program has a `main` function the same way that Java programs have a `main` method. Normally, you expect the `main` function to live in the `Main` module. Convention in Haskell is that modules should live in files of the same name as the module. When creating your palindrome project, you should start with a file named Main.hs. Here's your program.

QC 34.1 answer You need to qualify the value as `Main.length`:

```
length :: Int
length = 8

doubleLength :: Int
doubleLength = Main.length * 2
```

Listing 34.6 A first draft of your `Main` module

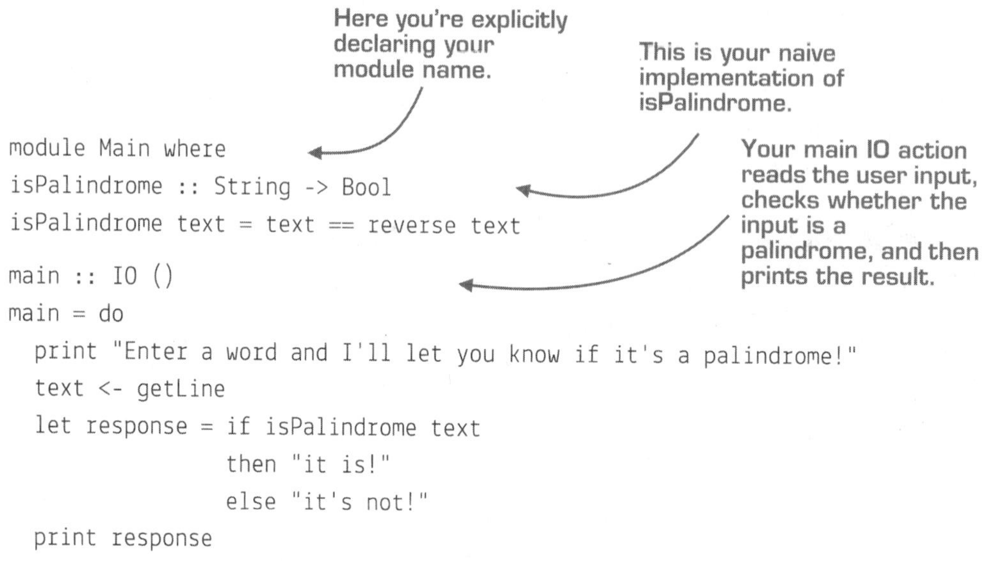
Here you're explicitly declaring your module name.
This is your naive implementation of isPalindrome.
Your main IO action reads the user input, checks whether the input is a palindrome, and then prints the result.

```
module Main where
isPalindrome :: String -> Bool
isPalindrome text = text == reverse text

main :: IO ()
main = do
  print "Enter a word and I'll let you know if it's a palindrome!"
  text <- getLine
  let response = if isPalindrome text
                 then "it is!"
                 else "it's not!"
  print response
```

You can compile this program and test out your code or just load it into GHCi. You can see that your palindrome program isn't as robust as you'd like:

```
GHCi> main
"Enter a word and I'll let you know if it's a palindrome!"
racecar
"it is!"
GHCi> main
"Enter a word and I'll let you know if it's a palindrome!"
A man, a plan, a canal: Panama!
"it's not!"
```

Your program correctly identifies *racecar* as a palindrome, but fails to identify *A man, a plan, a canal: Panama!* What you need is a bit of preprocessing for your strings to strip out whitespace, remove punctuation, and ignore case. In the past, you would just add this code to your file. But it makes sense to pull out your palindrome code into a separate file for two reasons. First, it makes your `Main` cleaner, and second, you can then more easily reuse your palindrome code in other programs.

34.2.2 Putting your improved isPalindrome code in its own module

You'll put your palindrome code in a separate module. The module's name will be `Palindrome`, so your code should be in a file named Palindrome.hs. Your `Palindrome` module will have a function, also named `isPalindrome`, which will be the function used by the `Main` module. You want to write a more robust version of `isPalindrome` so your module will also contain a series of helper functions: `stripWhiteSpace`, `stripPunctuation`, `toLowerCase`, and `preprocess`, which performs all of these. Here's your full Palindrome.hs file.

Listing 34.7 The Palindrome.hs file

You declare that your module is named Palindrome and that it exports a single function isPalindrome.

You could import the entire Data.Char module, but you need only the three functions listed.

The rest of the code is just like any other code written in this book.

```
module Palindrome(isPalindrome) where

import Data.Char (toLower,isSpace,isPunctuation)

stripWhiteSpace :: String -> String
stripWhiteSpace text = filter (not . isSpace) text

stripPunctuation :: String -> String
stripPunctuation text = filter (not . isPunctuation) text

toLowerCase :: String -> String
toLowerCase text = map toLower text

preprocess :: String -> String
preprocess = stripWhiteSpace . stripPunctuation . toLowerCase

isPalindrome :: String -> Bool
isPalindrome text = cleanText == reverse cleanText
  where cleanText = preProcess text
```

Let's walk through this file step-by-step to get a better sense of what's happening. You could've started your `Palindrome` function this way:

```
module Palindrome where
```

By default, this will export all the functions that you're defining in Palindrome.hs. But you don't want to export your helper functions; all you care about is `isPalindrome`. You can achieve this by listing all the functions you want to export in parentheses after the module name:

```
module Palindrome(isPalindrome) where
```

Here's another way to format your export functions so that you can easily accommodate exporting additional functions:

```
module Palindrome
    ( isPalindrome
    ) where
```

Now the only function available from your `Palindrome` module is `isPalindrome`.

To create your helper functions, you need a few functions from the `Data.Char` module. In the past, you've crudely imported the entire module whenever you need to use one. But just as you can selectively export functions, you can also selectively import them. This `import` statement imports only the three functions you'll need.

Listing 34.8 Importing only a specific subset of functions from `Data.Char`

```
import Data.Char (toLower,isSpace,isPunctuation)
```

The primary benefits of importing functions this way are that it improves readability and reduces the possibility that you'll have an unexpected namespace collision when performing a nonqualified import.

Now the rest of your file is just like any other Haskell file you've used so far. All your helper functions are relatively self-explanatory.

Listing 34.9 The code in your module for properly detecting palindromes

```
stripWhiteSpace :: String -> String
stripWhiteSpace text = filter (not . isSpace) text

stripPunctuation :: String -> String
stripPunctuation text = filter (not . isPunctuation) text

toLowerCase :: String -> String
toLowerCase text = map toLower text
```

This function strips out the whitespace from your text.

Next you can remove all the punctuation.

The last step is to make sure your String is all lowercase.

```
preprocess :: String -> String
preprocess = stripWhiteSpace . stripPunctuation . toLowerCase

isPalindrome :: String -> Bool
isPalindrome text = cleanText == reverse cleanText
  where cleanText = preprocess text
```

You use function composition to put these all together.

Finally, you end up with a much-improved version of isPalindrome.

Your Palindrome module doesn't have a `main` because it's just a library of functions. Even without a `main`, you can still load your file into GHCi and test it out:

```
GHCi> isPalindrome "racecar"
True
GHCi> isPalindrome "A man, a plan, a canal: Panama!"
True
```

Now that you understand your `Palindrome` module, let's go back and refactor your `Main` module.

Quick check 34.2 Modify the module declaration so that you also export `preprocess`.

34.2.3 Using your Palindrome module in your Main module

To use `Palindrome`, you add the import to your `Main` as you would any other module. As you'll soon see, when your module is in the same directory as your `Main`, compiling your `Main` will automatically compile your other module.

Let's suppose you'd like to keep your existing definition of `isPalindrome` in your `Main`. In the past, you've used `import qualified Module as X` to provide a named import for the modules you'd like to use (such as `import qualified Data.Text as T`). If you leave off the `as X` part

QC 34.2 answer

```
module Palindrome(
                  isPalindrome
                 ,preprocess
                 ) where
```

of your qualified import, you use the name of the module itself to reference functions in that module. Here's the start of your `main` refactored.

Listing 34.10 Performing a qualified import of your `Palindrome` module

```
module Main where
import qualified Palindrome
```

Now all you have left to do is change your call to `isPalindrome` to `Palindrome.isPalindrome` and you're all set.

Listing 34.11 Using the qualified `Palindrome.isPalindrome` function

```
  let response = if Palindrome.isPalindrome text
```

Here's your fully refactored Main.hs.

Listing 34.12 Your Main.hs file that uses your Palindrome.hs file

```
module Main where
import qualified Palindrome

isPalindrome :: String -> Bool
isPalindrome text = text == (reverse text)

main :: IO ()
main = do
  print "Enter a word and I'll let you know if it's a palindrome!"
  text <- getLine
  let response = if Palindrome.isPalindrome text
                 then "it is!"
                 else "it's not!"
  print response
```

Compiling this program is surprisingly simple. You can compile your Main.hs file with GHC and it'll automatically find your module:

```
$ ghc Main.hs
[1 of 2] Compiling Palindrome       ( Palindrome.hs, Palindrome.o )
[2 of 2] Compiling Main             ( Main.hs, Main.o )
Linking Main ...
```

Finally, you can run your `Main` executable:

```
$ ./Main
"Enter a word and I'll let you know if it's a palindrome!"
A man, a plan, a canal, Panama!
"it is!"
```

This is a trivial case of having a simple module in the same directory. In the next lesson, you'll explore stack, which is a powerful and popular build tool for Haskell. If you're going to be building anything nontrivial, make sure you do it with stack. Nonetheless, it's still helpful to understand how to compile multiple-file programs by hand.

Quick check 34.3 You shouldn't leave `Main.isPalindrome` there, as it's no longer necessary. If you remove the code for `Main.isPalindrome`, how can you refactor your code so you no longer need to qualify `Palindrome.isPalindrome`?

Summary

In this lesson, our goal was to teach you how to use modules to organize your Haskell programs. You learned how most of your programs automatically belong to a `Main` module. Next, you saw how to organize programs into separate files and compile them into a single program. You also learned how to export specific functions from your modules while hiding the rest. Let's see if you got this.

Q34.1 Recall that in unit 4 we mentioned that `Data.Text` is strongly preferred over `String` for working with text data. Refactor this project to use `Data.Text` instead of `String` (in both the `Main` and `Palindrome` modules).

Q34.2 In unit 4, lesson 25, you wrote a program to "glitch" binary images. Revisit that program and pull out all the code specific to glitching images into its own `Glitch` module.

QC 34.3 answer Change `import qualified Palindrome` to `import Palindrome`. Then remove `Palindrome.` from `Palindrome.isPalindrome`.

LESSON 35

BUILDING PROJECTS WITH STACK

After reading lesson 35, you'll be able to

- Work with Haskell's stack build tool
- Build stack projects
- Configure key files generated by stack

When moving beyond learning a programming language to using it for more serious projects, one of the most important things to have is proper build automation. One universal option is to use a tool such as GNU Make. But many languages have their own build tools. Java has several industrial-strength options such as Ant and Maven, Scala has sbt, and Ruby has rake. Given Haskell's academic history, it might come as a surprise that Haskell too has a powerful build tool: stack. The stack build tool is a relatively recent addition to the Haskell ecosystem, but it has had a tremendous impact. stack automates and manages several parts of Haskell projects:

- Provides an isolated installation of GHC per project to ensure that you're always using the correct version
- Handles the installation of packages and their dependencies
- Automates the building of the project
- Aids you in organizing and running tests on your project

This lesson introduces the basics of creating and building a project by using stack. In the preceding lesson, you saw how modules in Haskell let you separate your code into multiple files. In this lesson, you're going to build the same project but change two things. First, you'll use `Data.Text` rather than `String` for your program. As mentioned in unit 4, `Data.Text` is strongly preferred over `String` for real-world text. Second, this time, rather than compile modules, you'll use stack. stack comes with the Haskell platform (recommended in lesson 1), or if you prefer you can download stack by itself from https://docs.haskellstack.org/. Because stack handles installing copies of GHC and GHCi, after you're familiar with stack, it's the only tool you need to install to get started with Haskell.

> **Consider this** Like all languages, Haskell is always changing over time. How can you make sure that code you've written today still builds in five years?

35.1 Starting a new stack project

The first thing you need to do is make sure that stack is up-to-date. You can do this with the stack `update` command:

```
$ stack update
```

It's common for this operation to take a long time the first time you run stack (or when it has been a long time). Because stack is making sure you have a clean environment to build projects in, many first-time tasks might take a few minutes for everything to run. Rest assured that after you're using stack, many of these tasks will run much faster, as stack is good at managing the resources it needs.

Now that you're up-to-date, you can build your project. For this, you can use the `new` command. You'll name your project palindrome-checker:

```
$ stack new palindrome-checker
```

Running this command causes stack to create a new project. After this command has run, you should have a new directory named palindrome-checker. If you look inside palindrome-checker, you'll find the following files and directories:

```
LICENSE                    src
Setup.hs                   stack.yaml
app                        test
palindrone-checker.cabal
```

Next you'll make sense of everything that stack has created for you.

35.2 Understanding the project structure

When you run `stack new`, stack builds a new project from a template. You didn't supply an argument for your template, so stack uses the default one. For now, you're going to stick with the default template, but many templates exist that you can choose from (https://github.com/commercialhaskell/stack-templates is a source for many).

35.2.1 The project .cabal file and autogenerated files

In the top-level directory for your project, you have the following files, and all of these were created by stack for you:

- LICENSE
- Setup.hs
- palindrome-checker.cabal
- stack.yaml

The only file that you're primarily interested in at this point is palindrome-checker.cabal, which is your project configuration file. It contains all the metadata related to your project. In the beginning of the file, you have the basic information you'd expect about the project name, version, description, and so forth:

```
name:                palindrome-checker
version:             0.1.0.0
synopsis:            Initial project template from stack
description:         Please see README.md
homepage:            https://github.com/githubuser/palindrone-checker#readme
license:             BSD3
license-file:        LICENSE
author:              Author name here
maintainer:          example@example.com
copyright:           2016 Author name here
```

A section of palindrome-checker.cabal includes information about where your library files are stored in the project, which libraries you use, and which version of the Haskell language you're using:

```
library
  hs-source-dirs:      src
  exposed-modules:     Lib
```

```
  build-depends:        base >= 4.7 && < 5
  default-language:     Haskell2010
```

The most important lines in this part of the configuration are `hs-source-dirs` and `exposed-modules`. The `hs-source-dirs` value tells you which subdirectory of your project your library files live in. You can see that the default value for this is `src`. You'll notice that stack already generated a source directory for you. The `exposed-modules` value tells you which libraries you're using. By default, stack creates a `Lib` module that's located in src/Lib.hs. You can add more values to `exposed-modules` by placing them on separate lines with commas, like this:

```
exposed-modules:     Lib,
                     Palindrome,
                     Utils
```

When first getting started with stack, especially for smaller projects, you can put all the library functions you write in src/Lib.hs. You'll cover the `build-depends` argument in a later section, and for the most part you shouldn't need to worry about the `default-language` value.

You also have information on where the files you'll be using to build your executable will be stored, the name of your `Main` module, and default command-line arguments you're going to use when running your program:

```
executable palindrome-checker-exe
  hs-source-dirs:      app
  main-is:             Main.hs
  ghc-options:         -threaded -rtsopts -with-rtsopts=-N
  build-depends:       base
                     , palindrone-checker
  default-language:    Haskell2010
```

stack separates the code for your libraries from the code for running your program into separate directories. The hs-source-dirs value specifies the name of the directory where the program's `Main` module lives. Just like the library section of the .cabal file, the executable section tells you in which file your `main` is located with the `main-is` value. Once again, stack has automatically created the app directory (specified by hs-source-dirs) for you and placed a Main.hs file inside.

There's a lot more in the .cabal file, but what we've discussed so far should cover the basics you'll need for creating new projects. Next you'll look at some of the directories and code generated for you by stack. We'll point out other interesting parts of the .cabal file as you work through projects that use them in the rest of this book.

Quick check 35.1 Set your name as the project's author.

35.2.2 The app, src, and test directories

stack also automatically creates three directories for you:

- app
- src
- test

In the preceding section, you saw that app and src are created for your executable and library modules. You'll ignore test for now, as you'll explore testing in much more depth in lesson 36. We also mentioned that stack automatically includes two files in these: app/Main.hs and src/Lib.hs. These files and directories serve as a template for a minimal Haskell project.

The Main.hs file generated looks like this.

Listing 35.1 The default `Main` module generated by stack

```
module Main where

import Lib

main :: IO ()
main = someFunc
```

This is a simple file, but it provides guidance on how to think about stack projects. The only thing this `Main` module does is import the `Lib` module and then define a `main IO` action that's just the `someFunc` function. Where does `someFunc` come from? It's defined in the `Lib` module. The `Lib` module is located in src/Lib.hs and looks like this.

QC 35.1 answer Change the author line in the project's .cabal file to your name, like this:

```
author:     Will Kurt
```

Listing 35.2 The default `Lib` module generated by stack

```
module Lib
    ( someFunc
    ) where

someFunc :: IO ()
someFunc = putStrLn "someFunc"
```

`someFunc` is a trivial function that prints `someFunc`. Though simple, these two files give you a solid foundation for getting started building a project using stack. Your `Main` module logic should be minimal, relying primarily on library functions defined in the `Lib` module. Now let's start translating your project from the last lesson to work with stack!

> **Quick check 35.2** We haven't covered building a project in stack yet, but when you run this project, what should it do based on the default code you have?

35.3 Writing your code

Let's start with your `Palindrome` module. Remember, unlike last time, this time you're going to write a library that works with the `Data.Text` type, rather than just `Strings`. Because you're using stack, you want to put this file into the src directory. Rather than create a Palindrome.hs file, you'll go ahead and overwrite the Lib.hs stack created for you. For simple programs like this, you can put all of your utilities into a single module.

Listing 35.3 Rewriting `Palindrome` from the preceding lesson to work with `Text`

```
{-# LANGUAGE OverloadedStrings #-}
module Lib
    ( isPalindrome
    ) where

import qualified Data.Text as T
import Data.Char (toLower,isSpace,isPunctuation)
```

QC 35.2 answer The program should print out `someFunc`.

```
stripWhiteSpace :: T.Text -> T.Text
stripWhiteSpace text = T.filter (not . isSpace) text

stripPunctuation :: T.Text -> T.Text
stripPunctuation text = T.filter (not . isPunctuation) text

preProcess :: T.Text -> T.Text
preProcess = stripWhiteSpace . stripPunctuation . T.toLower


isPalindrome :: T.Text -> Bool
isPalindrome text = cleanText == T.reverse cleanText
  where cleanText = preProcess text
```

Next you need to write your `Main`. This time you won't use a qualified import (but you'll need to make a small change so that your code works with `Data.Text`). Because your `Main` is essential to building your executable, it goes in the app directory (this is declared in your project's .cabal file!). You overwrite the generated Main.hs with your own. Here's your revised Main.hs.

Listing 35.4 Writing the Main.hs file for your palindrome checker

```
{-# LANGUAGE OverloadedStrings #-}
module Main where

import Lib
import Data.Text as T
import Data.Text.IO as TIO

main :: IO ()
main = do
  TIO.putStrLn "Enter a word and I'll let you know if it's a palindrome!"
  text <- TIO.getLine
  let response = if isPalindrome text
                 then "it is!"
                 else "it's not!"
  TIO.putStrLn response
```

Now you're almost ready, except you have to add edit your .cabal file. You have to tell stack about any modules you're depending on. For both your Main.hs file and your

Lib.hs file, you're using `Data.Text`. For both your library and executable sections of palindrome-checker.cabal, you need to add the text package to the list of dependencies:

```
library
  hs-source-dirs:      src
  exposed-modules:     Lib
  build-depends:       base >= 4.7 && < 5
                     , text
  default-language:    Haskell2010

executable palindrome-checker-exe
  hs-source-dirs:      app
  main-is:             Main.hs
  ghc-options:         -threaded -rtsopts -with-rtsopts=-N
  build-depends:       base
                     , palindrome-checker
                     , text
  default-language:    Haskell2010
```

Now you're all set to build your project!

> **Quick check 35.3** If you wanted to keep your Palindrome module named `Palindrome` and in the original Palindrome.hs file, what would you have to change about your .cabal file?

35.4 Building and running your project!

Finally, you're ready to put everything together and build your project. The first command you need to run is `setup`. In your project directory, run this command:

```
$ stack setup
```

This command ensures that stack is using the correct version of GHC. For simple projects like ours, this isn't a big deal, but with the ever-changing nature of Haskell, ensur-

QC 35.3 answer Change the `exposed-modules` value to `Palindrome`:

```
library
  hs-source-dirs:      src
  exposed-modules:     Palindrome
```

ing that your project is built with the version of GHC you used to write it is important. Specifying the version of GHC you want to use is done indirectly by choosing your stack resolver version. The stack resolver is set in the stack.yaml file:

```
resolver: lts-7.9
```

This book was written using the lts-7.9 version of the stack resolver, which uses GHC version 8.0.1. By default, stack uses the most recent stable resolver. Most of the time, this is what you want, but if you have any trouble building a project in this book, setting the resolver to lts-7.9 will likely fix this. You can find a listing of the current resolver versions at www.stackage.org, and info about a specific resolver can be found by appending the resolver version to that URL (for example, www.stackage.org/lts-7.9 for the lts-7.9 resolver).

Next you have to build your project. This can be done with the following:

```
$ stack build
```

Don't be concerned if this command takes a bit of time to run the first time you use stack or build your project. Future builds will go much faster.

After you run this command, you're ready to run your project. In the past, you manually used GHC to compile an executable, and then you could run it like any other program. In the case of stack, you'll use the `exec` command. You need to pass in the name of your executable, which is defined in your palindrome-checker.cabal file:

```
executable palindrone-checker-exe
```

The name of the executable comes right after the `executable` in the executable section. By default, it's <project-name>-exe:

```
$ stack exec palindrone-checker-exe
Enter a word and I'll let you know if it's a palindrome!
A man, a plan, a canal: Panama!
it is!
```

Great, your program works!

35.4.1 A quick improvement: getting rid of language pragmas

One annoying thing about your program, and any large program involving `Data.Text`, is that you have to remember to add your `OverloadedStrings` pragma to every file. Thankfully, stack has a great fix for this. You can add the following line to your palindrome-checker.cabal file and universally apply the `OverloadString` language extension.

You add the following line after `default-language: Haskell2010` to both your library and executable sections of palindrome-checker.cabal:

```
extensions: OverloadedStrings
```

With this in place, you no longer have to add your pragma or remember compiler flags. You can build your project again, and everything should run fine.

Summary

In this lesson, our objective was to teach you how to use the stack tool to build and manage Haskell projects. You learned by creating a new stack project and exploring the files and directories it created for you. Next you organized the code from the preceding lesson into separate files in the stack project directory. Finally, you built your palindrome project in a reliable and repeatable way. Let's see if you got this.

Q35.1 Make the following changes to this project:

- Set the author, description, and maintainer email to the correct info.
- Return the definition of Lib.hs to the original one created by stack.
- Add the code for `isPalindrome` into a `Palindrome` module in src/Palindrome.hs.
- Make sure that `OverloadedStrings` is set at the project level.

Q35.2 Refactor the code in unit 4, lesson 21, for comparing the cost of two pizzas into a stack project. All of the supporting code in the original program file should be in either Lib.hs or an additional library module.

LESSON 36

PROPERTY TESTING WITH QUICKCHECK

After reading lesson 36, you'll be able to

- Use `stack ghci` to interact with a stack project
- Run tests with `stack test`
- Use QuickCheck for property testing
- Install packages with `stack install`

The preceding lesson introduced Haskell's powerful build tool, stack. You saw how to build a project, but we cheated a bit. You copied the code you wrote when learning about modules and pasted it in. In this lesson, you're going to rebuild your palindrome project, but this time you'll develop it as though you were building a project from the beginning. Your focus this time will be on testing your code. So far in this book, you've done only manual testing of your functions. With stack, you can make automated tests from the beginning. You'll start this lesson by learning about using GHCi with stack for manual testing of your modules. Then you'll learn to use `stack test` to run simple unit tests you'll write. Finally, you'll learn about property testing and the amazing tool QuickCheck, which allows you to quickly generate many tests.

One thing you may have noticed in this unit is that everything should seem more familiar to you than nearly every other topic we've covered in Haskell. Even QuickCheck, which is a more powerful approach to testing then you may have seen before, is not so much mind-bending as interesting and useful. The reason for this familiarity is that stack has been largely developed by real-world software engineers interested in shipping and maintaining production code. It's likely that any standard approach to software engineering you prefer (such as test-driven development or behavior-driven development) can be supported easily with stack. Because of tools such as stack, Haskell is more able to be used for real software than at any time in its history. This unit is meant to give you only a quick introduction to software development with Haskell and stack. For more detailed information, visit haskellstack.org and stackage.org.

Consider this When developing projects with stack, how can you interact with your code and make sure it behaves as you'd like?

36.1 Starting a new project

Let's start a new palindrome project, pretending for a moment that this is a brand new problem you're solving. You'll stick with the same problem you've been working on so you don't have to worry too much about what your code does and can focus on how you think about writing programs when using stack. Because the focus of this unit is on testing, you'll call this project palindrome-testing. Here's your command for creating this new project:

```
$ stack new palindrome-testing
```

Rather than jump straight to your `Main` module, let's see how to start building out the functionality you'll be using in src/Lib.hs. Stack created a default `Main` for you, so you'll want to clean that out because you'll be overwriting Lib. You'll replace the default `someFunc` function with a simple `"Hello World!"`.

Listing 36.1 Small refactor to Main.hs file so you can focus on your Lib.hs file

```
module Main where

import Lib

main :: IO ()
main = putStrLn "Hello World!"
```

For most of this project, you'll be working in your src/Lib.hs, creating the library functions that you'll eventually use in your `Main`. You'll start with implementing the simplest version of `isPalindrome`, just as you would if you were starting this project completely from scratch.

Listing 36.2 A minimal definition of `isPalindrome`

```
module Lib
    ( isPalindrome
    ) where

isPalindrome :: String -> Bool
isPalindrome text = text == reverse text
```

Now that you have some code, you can start interacting with it and testing it the stack way!

Quick check 36.1 You're going to be adding only a few functions to the Lib module, and you'll end up exporting all of them. Given that's the case, what's a more efficient way to define this module?

36.2 Different types of testing

When we typically think of testing code, we often think about unit testing individual cases of potential bugs. But testing doesn't need to mean specifically unit testing. Whenever you load your code into GHCi to play with a function you wrote, you're testing your code; you're just doing it manually. You'll start this section by looking at how to use GHCi with stack to manually test your code. Then you'll use the `stack test` command to automatically run crude unit tests you'll write. Finally, you'll see that Haskell offers a powerful alternative to unit testing called *property testing*. If unit testing is essentially automating manual tests, then property testing is automating unit tests.

This lesson takes a rather traditional approach to testing. You'll start with writing code, manually testing it, and only then move on to writing more formal tests for your code.

QC 36.1 answer

```
module Lib where

isPalindrome :: String -> Bool
isPalindrome text = text == reverse text
```

But there's nothing inherent to Haskell that requires this approach. If you prefer to take a test-driven development (TDD) approach, you can certainly revisit this lesson in reverse, writing all of your tests first. Even if you prefer behavior-driven development, popularized by Ruby's RSpec, Haskell has an equivalent testing library, Hspec. (Hspec isn't covered here but should be straightforward to implement after you finish this unit.)

36.2.1 Manual testing and calling GHCi from stack

Because you're using stack, you have to approach using GHCi a bit differently. First set up and build your project to make sure everything works okay:

```
$ cd palindrome-testing
$ stack setup
...
$ stack build
...
```

Because stack is creating a safe, reproducible, isolated environment for your project, you don't want to run `ghci` from the command line to interact with your project. This is because each project has its own libraries and even possibly its own version of GHC installed just for it. To safely interact with your project, you need to run `stack ghci`. For this section, rather than use the `GHCi>` prompt as you have throughout the book, you'll use the actual prompt you get from `stack ghci`:

```
$ stack ghci
*Main Lib>
```

Because you've built your project and are running stack GHCi, you'll notice that you have the `Main` and `Lib` modules loaded as indicated by the prompt. You can test out your code from here:

```
*Main Lib> isPalindrome "racecar"
True
*Main Lib> isPalindrome "cat"
False
*Main Lib> isPalindrome "racecar!"
False
```

And here you find the first error! The string `"racecar!"` should be a palindrome, but it's not. Now you can go back and add a quick fix for this.

Listing 36.3 Iteratively testing and fixing `isPalindrome`

```
isPalindrome :: String -> Bool
isPalindrome text = cleanText == reverse cleanText
  where cleanText = filter (not . (== '!')) text
```

You don't even have to run `stack build` again to test this; you can `quit ghci` and restart with `stack ghci`. If your changes have been made only to code files and no configuration changes have been made, you can also type `:r` into GHCi to reload your code without exiting:

```
*Main Lib> :r
*Main Lib> isPalindrome "racecar!"
True
```

And you see that your code works!

Quick check 36.2 Test whether `sam I mas` is a palindrome

36.2.2 Writing your own unit tests and using stack test

Manually testing as you just did is fine for hashing out new ideas. As your program grows in complexity, you'll want to automate this. Thankfully, stack has a built-in command for running tests. In the test directory, you'll find another file autogenerated for you called Spec.hs. Like Main.hs and Lib.hs, stack has autogenerated some code there for you.

Listing 36.4 The contents of Spec.hs generated by stack

```
main :: IO ()
main = putStrLn "Test suite not yet implemented"
```

Haskell has packages for unit testing (such as Hspec, similar to Ruby's RSpec, and HUnit, similar to Java's JUnit), but for now you'll start with a simple unit-testing framework of

QC 36.2 answer

```
*Main Lib> isPalindrome "sam I mas"
True
```

your own. All you'll do is define an `assert IO` action that takes a `Bool` (in this case, a test of a function) and prints either a passing message or a fail message.

Listing 36.5 A minimal function for unit testing

```
assert :: Bool -> String -> String -> IO ()
assert test passStatement failStatement = if test
                                          then putStrLn passStatement
                                          else putStrLn failStatement
```

Next you can fill out your `main` with a few tests. You'll also need to import the `Lib` module. Here's your first round of a test suite.

Listing 36.6 Your Spec.hs file with a few simple unit tests

```
import Lib

assert :: Bool -> String -> String -> IO ()
assert test passStatement failStatement = if test
                                          then putStrLn passStatement
                                          else putStrLn failStatement


main :: IO ()
main = do
  putStrLn "Running tests..."
  assert (isPalindrome "racecar") "passed 'racecar'" "FAIL: 'racecar'"
  assert (isPalindrome "racecar!") "passed 'racecar!'" "FAIL: 'racecar!'"
  assert ((not . isPalindrome) "cat") "passed 'cat'" "FAIL: 'cat'"
  putStrLn "done!"
```

To run these tests, you use the `stack test` command:

```
$ stack test

Running tests...
passed 'racecar'
passed 'racecar!'
passed 'cat'
done!
```

Great! Next let's add another test, the word `racecar.` (with a period at the end).

Listing 36.7 Adding another test to your main IO action

```
assert (isPalindrome "racecar.") "passed 'racecar.'" "FAIL: 'racecar.'"
```

If you run your tests again, you see that your `isPalindrome` function is lacking:

```
Running tests...
passed 'racecar'
passed 'racecar!'
passed 'cat'
FAIL: 'racecar.'
done!
```

You can come up with a lame fix for this problem by redefining `isPalindrome` once again.

Listing 36.8 Another minimal fix for the issues in your `isPalindrome` function

```
isPalindrome :: String -> Bool
isPalindrome text = cleanText == reverse cleanText
  where cleanText = filter (not . (`elem` ['!','.'])) text
```

You already know that the correct solution to this problem is to use the `isPunctuation` function in `Data.Char`. But this iterative approach to fixing bugs is common, if often less trivial. If you run your tests again, you find you've fixed this bug:

```
Running tests...
passed 'racecar'
passed 'racecar!'
passed 'cat'
passed 'racecar.'
done!
```

But this fix feels unsatisfactory because you know there's more punctuation you're missing. Even though you know that `isPunctuation` is the better solution, in order to test this solution, you still have to think of a huge range of possible tests: `race-car`, `:racecar:`, `racecar?`, and so forth. In the next section, you'll learn about a powerful type of testing available in Haskell called *property testing*. This automates much of the hassle of creating individual unit tests.

Quick check 36.3 Add a test for `:racecar:` to your list of tests and rerun the test suite.

36.3 Property testing QuickCheck

Before diving into property testing, let's clean up your library a bit. It's pretty clear that the part of `isPalindrome` that gives you `cleanText` is going to get large fast, so you'll refactor this out into a `preprocess` function.

Listing 36.9 Your code is starting to get a bit cleaner

```
module Lib
    ( isPalindrome
    , preprocess
    ) where

preprocess :: String -> String
preprocess text = filter (not . (`elem` ['!','.'])) text

isPalindrome :: String -> Bool
isPalindrome text = cleanText == reverse cleanText
  where cleanText = preprocess text
```

QC 36.3 answer

```
main :: IO ()
main = do
  putStrLn "Running tests..."
  assert (isPalindrome "racecar") "passed 'racecar'" "FAIL: 'racecar'"
  assert (isPalindrome "racecar!") "passed 'racecar!'" "FAIL: 'racecar!'"
  assert ((not . isPalindrome) "cat") "passed 'cat'" "FAIL: 'cat'"
  assert (isPalindrome "racecar.") "passed 'racecar.'" "FAIL: 'racecar.'"
  assert (isPalindrome ":racecar:")
         "passed ':racecar:'" "FAIL: ':racecar:'"
  putStrLn "done!"
```

This passes because `:racecar:` is a palindrome even with punctuation.

Now the function you really care about testing is `preprocess`. You want to test `preprocess`, but you've already seen that unit testing is going to quickly get tedious, and you're still likely to miss something.

36.3.1 Testing properties

In the abstract, what you want to test about the `preprocess` function is that it has a certain property. Mainly, you want to test that the output, given the input, is `punctuation invariant`, which is a fancy way of saying you don't care about whether the input string has punctuation.

You can write a function to express this property. You'll need to import `Data.Char (isPunctuation)` and put this function in your Spec.hs file.

Listing 36.10 Expressing the property you want to test in a function

```
prop_punctuationInvariant text = preprocess text ==
                                 preprocess noPuncText
  where noPuncText = filter (not . isPunctuation) text
```

If you read what this code says, it expresses the core of what you're trying to achieve:

```
"Calling preprocess on text should give the same answer as calling
           preprocess on the same text with no punctuation"
```

Having this property written in code is great, but you still don't have a way to test it. You need a way get a range of possible values for your text automatically. This is where the QuickCheck library comes in.

> **Quick check 36.4** Write a property `prop_reverseInvariant` that demonstrates the obvious fact that the results of `isPalindrome` should be the same whether or not you reverse the input.

QC 36.4 answer

```
prop_reverseInvariant text = isPalindrome text ==
➥(isPalindrome (reverse text))
```

36.3.2 Introducing QuickCheck

Haskell's QuickCheck library is built around the idea of property testing. The `prop_punctuationInvariant` function was your first example of a property. The way QuickCheck works is that you supply properties that your code is supposed to uphold, and then QuickCheck automatically generates values and tests them on the functions, making sure the properties are upheld. Now let's replace your simple unit tests with some property tests.

The first thing you have to do is add QuickCheck to your `build-depends` in the .cabal file.

Listing 36.11 Modified palindrome-testing.cabal file

```
test-suite palindrome-testing-test
  type:                exitcode-stdio-1.0
  hs-source-dirs:      test
  main-is:             Spec.hs
  build-depends:       base
                     , palindrome-testing
                     , QuickCheck
  ghc-options:         -threaded -rtsopts -with-rtsopts=-N
  default-language:    Haskell2010
```

Now you can include import `Test.QuickCheck` at the top of Spec.hs file. To use QuickCheck, you call the `quickCheck` function on your property inside the `main`.

Listing 36.12 Using the `quickCheck` function in your Spec.hs file

```
main :: IO ()
main = do
  quickCheck prop_punctuationInvariant
  putStrLn "done!"
```

When you run your test, see that you get a failure (as expected):

```
Progress: 1/2*** Failed! Falsifiable (after 4 tests and 2 shrinks):
"\187"
```

In passing in values to your `prop_punctuationInvariant`, QuickCheck tried `\187`, which is a Unicode punctuation mark. In a sense, QuickCheck has automatically created a bunch of unit tests for you. To show how well QuickCheck catches bugs, let's take the lazy approach to removing punctuation and modify your `preprocess` function to handle `\187` as well.

Listing 36.13 Refactoring `preprocess` based on feedback from QuickCheck

```
preprocess :: String -> String
preprocess text = filter (not . (`elem` ['!','.','\187'])) text
```

If you run your tests again, you find that QuickCheck still isn't happy:

```
Failed! Falsifiable (after 11 tests and 2 shrinks):
";"
```

This time, the semicolon is the problem.

> **NOTE** QuickCheck uses carefully chosen but random values, so you might get different errors when you run this locally.

This time let's refactor your code the correct way, using `isPunctuation`.

Listing 36.14 Fixing the issue with punctuation the correct way

```
import Data.Char(isPunctuation)

preprocess :: String -> String
preprocess text = filter (not . isPunctuation) text
```

This time you get a much happier response when you run `stack test`:

```
OK, passed 100 tests.
```

As you might guess from this message, QuickCheck strategically tried 100 strings on your property, and they all passed! Is 100 tests not enough to make you feel secure? Let's try 1,000 using `quickCheckWith`. To do this, you'll use record syntax to update a standard argument value passed in to the function (see lesson 12).

Listing 36.15 You can tell QuickCheck to run as many tests as you'd like

```
main :: IO ()
main = do
  quickCheckWith stdArgs { maxSuccess = 1000}  prop_punctuationInvariant
  putStrLn "done!"
```

If you run your tests, you'll see that QuickCheck is still happy, and you might feel more secure that you've tried enough inputs:

```
OK, passed 1000 tests.
```

Even though you've just written a single property test for `isPalindrome`, you've replaced the need to write countless unit tests!

Quick check 36.5 Add a `quickCheck` test for the `prop_reverseInvariant` defined in the preceding exercise

36.3.3 Using QuickCheck with more types and installing packages

The tricky part of QuickCheck is generating the input values to test on. All types that QuickCheck can automatically test must be an instance of the type class `Arbitrary`. A detailed explanation of implementing `Arbitrary` is beyond the scope of this book. The bad news is that only a few base types are instances of `Arbitrary`. The good news is that you can install a package that greatly extends the types covered by QuickCheck.

For example, `Data.Text` by default isn't an instance of `Arbitrary` and won't work with QuickCheck. You can remedy this by installing the quickcheck-instances package. You can do this with the `stack install` command:

```
$ stack install quickcheck-instances
```

This installs a new package in your palindrome-testing project.

Let's first see how to refactor your Lib.hs file to work with text.

Listing 36.16 Refactoring your `Lib` module to use `Data.Text` instead of `String`

```
module Lib
    ( isPalindrome
    , preprocess
    ) where
```

QC 36.5 answer

```
prop_reverseInvariant text = isPalindrome text == isPalindrome
➥(reverse text)

main :: IO ()
main = do
  quickCheckWith stdArgs { maxSuccess = 1000}  prop_punctuationInvariant
  quickCheck prop_reverseInvariant
  putStrLn "done!"
```

```
import Data.Text as T
import Data.Char(isPunctuation)

preprocess :: T.Text -> T.Text
preprocess text = T.filter (not . isPunctuation) text

isPalindrome :: T.Text -> Bool
isPalindrome text = cleanText == T.reverse cleanText
  where cleanText = preprocess text
```

Don't forget to add `text` to `build-depends` in the library section of your project's .cabal file. You can make a similar refactor to your Spec.hs file.

Listing 36.17 Refactoring Spec.hs to work with `Data.Text`

```
import Lib
import Test.QuickCheck
import Test.QuickCheck.Instances
import Data.Char(isPunctuation)
import Data.Text as T

prop_punctuationInvariant text = preprocess text == preprocess noPuncText
  where noPuncText = T.filter (not . isPunctuation) text

main :: IO ()
main = do
  quickCheckWith stdArgs { maxSuccess = 1000}  prop_punctuationInvariant
  putStrLn "done!"
```

For this to run, you need to add both `text` and `quickcheck-instances` to your test suite `build-depends` in the .cabal file.

Finally, you can test your newly refactored code:

```
$ stack test
...
 OK, passed 1000 tests.
```

Here you can also see another benefit of property testing. This refactor was relatively straightforward. Imagine how much work this would have taken if you had handwritten a suite of unit tests and needed to change the type on all of them!

Summary

In this lesson, our objective was to teach you how to test your Haskell code. You started by manually testing your code by using `stack ghci`. Using GHCi inside stack ensures that your code will build as expected. After manual testing, you used the `stack test` command to build and run a series of simple unit tests. Finally, you generalized your unit testing by creating property tests with QuickCheck. Let's see if you got this.

Q36.1 Complete this palindrome-testing project so it's the same as the code in the preceding lesson. Then implement property tests to fully test `preprocess`, ensuring that whitespace doesn't matter and that capitalization doesn't matter.

37

LESSON

CAPSTONE: BUILDING A PRIME-NUMBER LIBRARY

This capstone covers

- Building a new project by using stack
- Writing basic library functions for working with prime numbers
- Using stack test and QuickCheck to check for bugs as you go
- Refactoring code to fix errors
- Adding new functions and tests to your project as you go

So far in this unit, you've focused on one problem: creating a program for working with palindromes. For this capstone, you'll be reiterating over all the work you've done creating modules and learning about stack with a new problem. This time you'll be working on creating a library to work with prime numbers. You'll focus on three essential problems:

- Listing out primes less than a specified number
- Determining whether a given number is prime
- Breaking a number into its prime factors

The first thing that you'll need is a way to create a list of prime numbers. Here's the type signature for that list:

```
primes :: [Int]
```

You'll achieve this by using a prime sieve, which works by filtering out the prime numbers. In terms of types, this will require you to take an `[Int]` of possible primes and then return an `[Int]` of just primes. The function that will perform this work is `sieve`:

```
sieve :: [Int] -> [Int]
```

With a list of primes in hand, you can easily check whether a number is prime by seeing if it's a member of the list. Normally, you'd think of this as simply a function `Int -> Bool`, but because there are some numbers that you don't want to consider valid for your primality check (such as negative numbers), you'll return a `Maybe Bool`:

```
isPrime :: Int -> Maybe Bool
```

Finally, you'll look at factoring numbers into primes. Because of the same issue of having `isPrime` return a `Maybe Bool`, your `primeFactors` function will return a `Maybe [Int]` representing a possible list of factors:

```
primeFactors :: Int -> Maybe [Int]
```

You'll build this entire project by using stack, making sure to build out useful tests along the way to help you design your program. Your code for this capstone will remain relatively straightforward, as our main goal is to reinforce the basics of using stack to build a project.

37.1 Starting your new project

As always, your first step in creating a new project is to use the `stack new` command to create your project. You'll call this project `primes`:

```
$ stack new primes
```

When stack has finished, you should have a nice, new project directory waiting for you. Let's go ahead and change to that directory:

```
$ cd primes
```

As a refresher, you can look at the files and directories that stack has created. The directories are as follows:

- *app*—Where your `Main` module will live; by default contains Main.hs
- *src*—All your library files will be here; by default contains Lib.hs
- *test*—You'll keep all your testing code in this directory; by default contains Spec.hs

The files created for you are as follows, and shown in figure 37.1:

- *primes.cabal*—The file where you'll do most of your configuration
- *LICENSE*—Describes the license you're using for your software
- *stack.yaml*—Contains some extra configuration data used by stack
- *Setup.hs*—A file used by the underlying cabal system that you can ignore

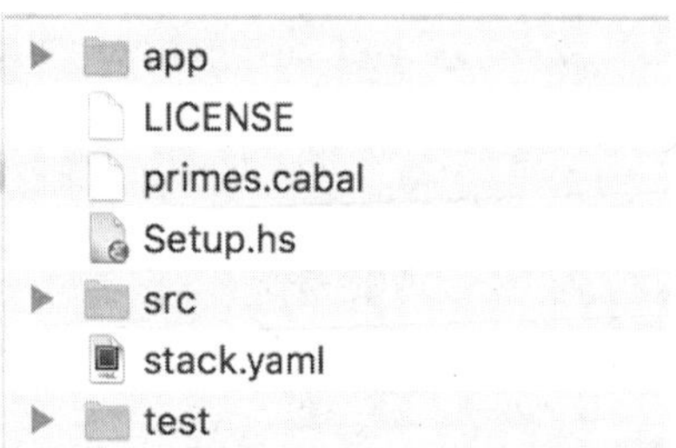
app
LICENSE
primes.cabal
Setup.hs
src
stack.yaml
test

Figure 37.1 The files created by stack

With these files in place, you have everything you need to get started writing your code!

37.2 Modifying the default files

Stack generated a bunch of useful starter files for you in app/Main.hs and src/Lib.hs, including example code that you don't need for this project. Because you're mostly concerned about your library functions, you'll start by changing your app/Main.hs into something that does essentially nothing other than import the `Primes` module you'll be making.

Listing 37.1 Your modified `Main` module in app/Main.hs

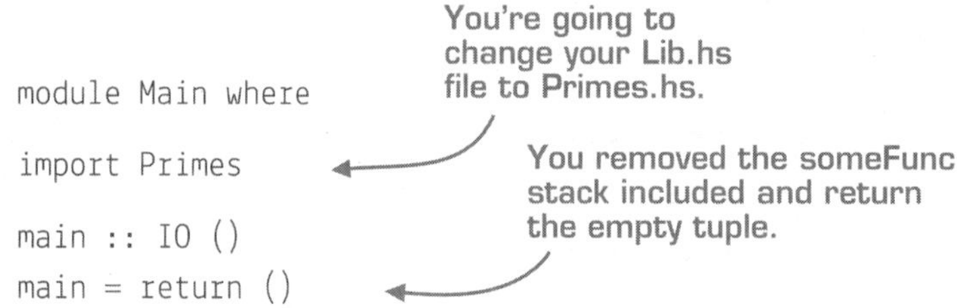

```
module Main where

import Primes

main :: IO ()
main = return ()
```

You're going to change your Lib.hs file to Primes.hs.
You removed the someFunc stack included and return the empty tuple.

Next, you want to change your src/Lib.hs. Because you're creating a library of functions for working with prime numbers, you want to change the name of this file to Primes.hs and likewise change the module name to `Primes`. You'll also start by creating a dummy list of primes that your other functions will use. You'll start with a list of all numbers and refactor this later.

Listing 37.2 Changing src/Lib.hs to src/Primes.hs

```
module Primes where

primes :: [Int]
primes = [1 .. ]
```

Remember that you must also tell stack that you changed the name of your library file. To do this, open the primes.cabal file. Find the library section and change the `exposed-modules` value.

Listing 37.3 Modifying primes.cabal to reflect the change of your library module

```
library
  hs-source-dirs:       src
  exposed-modules:      Primes
  build-depends:        base >= 4.7 && < 5
  default-language:     Haskell2010
```

This value was previously Lib.

As a sanity check, set up and build your project:

```
$ stack setup
...
$ stack build
...
```

At this point, you haven't done anything too complex, so if you do get an error, it's likely due to a spelling mistake or forgetting to save a modified default file.

37.3 Writing your core library functions

With the basics all set, you're ready to start writing code. The first thing you need to do is to generate a list of prime numbers that your other functions will use. In unit 5, you saw how to use the `Applicative` type's <*> operator to generate a list of primes. But this technique is inefficient. This time you'll use a better option called the *sieve of Eratosthenes*. This algorithm works by iterating through a list of numbers and filtering out all the nonprimes. You start with 2, which is the first prime, and then remove all the other numbers that are evenly divisible by 2. Then you take the next number in your list, which is 3. You remove all the remaining numbers that are evenly divisible by 3. Here's the step-by-step process for finding the primes less than 10:

1 Start with 2–10: `[2,3,4,5,6,7,8,9,10]`
2 2 is the next number, so you put it in a primes list and remove all the rest:
  `[2]` and `[3,5,7,9]`
3 Then you get 3, which you add to your list and remove all numbers divisible by 3:
  `[2,3]` and `[5,7]`
4 You repeat with 5:
  `[2,3,5]` and `[7]`
5 And finally, with `[7]`:
  `[2,3,5,7]` and `[]`

You can implement this function recursively. As with many recursive functions, you know that you're finished when you reach the end of the list. Otherwise, you repeat the process described previously. Here's the code in Haskell for your sieve (this function belongs in src/Primes.hs).

Listing 37.4 Recursive implementation of the sieve of Eratosthenes

```
sieve :: [Int] -> [Int]
sieve [] = []
sieve (nextPrime:rest) = nextPrime : sieve noFactors
  where noFactors = filter (not . (== 0) . (`mod` nextPrime)) rest
```

You can use the `stack ghci` command to interact with your new function:

```
GHCi> sieve [2 .. 20]
[2,3,5,7,11,13,17,19]
GHCi> sieve [2 .. 200]
[2,3,5,7,11,13,17,19,23,29,31,37,41,43,47,53,59,61,67,71,73,79,83,89,97,101,
➥103,107,109,113,127,131,137,139,149,151,157,163,167,173,179,181,191,193,
➥197,199]
```

The sieve isn't an end to itself. You're going to use this sieve to generate a list of prime numbers that you'll use for other functions, such as `isPrime`.

37.3.1 Defining primes

You can easily replace your dummy primes variable with a list of primes generated by your sieve function. You could write this value as follows.

Listing 37.5 Creating a list of all possible primes

```
primes :: [Int]
primes = sieve [2 .. ]
```

This generates a list of all primes smaller than the maximum `Int` value. Although this is philosophically great, you can see just how large the `maxBound` for `Int` is in GHCi:

```
GHCi> maxBound :: Int
9223372036854775807
```

Even with your much more efficient method of computing primes, you don't want to allow users of your library to use this algorithm to test for large prime numbers, because this would still take a long time. Furthermore, the approximate number of primes less than your `maxBound` is around 2×10^{17}! If you naively assume that each `Int` is stored as 4 bytes (which isn't the case), you'd need over 800 petabytes to store this list! Lazy evaluation can be great in these cases, but you don't want to allow the user of this library to accidentally request that much memory.

Instead you'll start with a reasonable upper bound on the primes you'll be searching for. For this simple example, you'll leave it at primes less than 10,000.

Listing 37.6 Using sieve to generate a reasonable list of primes

```
primes :: [Int]
primes = sieve [2 .. 10000]
```

You can play with your new list of primes in GHCi:

```
GHCi> length primes
1229
GHCi> take 10 primes
[2,3,5,7,11,13,17,19,23,29]
```

If you do decide to make your limit of primes higher (say, primes less than 100,000), something annoying happens. The first time you use the primes list, returning your answer will take an extremely long time. This is partially due to tricky issues that can come up with lazy evaluation, and because you're using a list. In most other programming languages, you'd want to implement your sieve as an array and update the values in place. In unit 7, you'll look at how to achieve this in Haskell.

37.3.2 Defining an isPrime function

Now that you have a list of primes, defining an `isPrime` function seems trivial: you just check whether the value is in your list. You'd start with a type signature like this:

```
isPrime :: Int -> Bool
```

But things aren't quite that simple. Here are a couple of edge cases:

- What about negative numbers?
- What about values greater than the size of your sieve?

What should you do for these? One solution would be to simply return `False`. But this doesn't seem correct. The biggest issue is that the user of your function could put in a legitimate, albeit large, prime number and get the wrong answer. Additionally, although it's true that –13 isn't prime, it's not *not prime* the same way that 4 isn't prime. The number 4 isn't prime because it's a composite number. A composite number is one that has two or more prime factors—in this case, 2 and 2. The number –13 isn't prime because we typically don't consider negative numbers to be prime.

This is a great case for using `Maybe`. You'll return `Just True` for primes within your range, `Just False` for composite numbers within your range, and `Nothing` for all the exceptions we mentioned. Here's your slightly more complicated `isPrimes` function.

Listing 37.7 A more robust version of `isPrime`

```
isPrime :: Int -> Maybe Bool
isPrime n | n < 0 = Nothing
          | n >= length primes = Nothing
          | otherwise = Just (n `elem` primes)
```

In the past, you've thought of `Maybe` types as being just for null values, but you can see here how this can be used for other cases of missing values. In this case, your result is missing because the answer doesn't make sense for several reasons.

After you add your `isPrime` function to Primes.hs, you can test it out in GHCi:

```
GHCi> isPrime 8
Just False
GHCi> isPrime 17
Just True
GHCi> map isPrime [2 .. 20]
```

```
[Just True,Just True,Just False,Just True,Just False,Just True,Just
➥False,Just False,Just False,Just True,Just False,Just True,Just False,
➥Just False,Just False,Just True,Just False,Just True,Just False]
GHCi> isPrime (-13)
Nothing
```

Because you're working with a more complicated definition of `isPrime` than you expected, now would also be a good time to start with more rigorous testing.

37.4 Writing tests for your code

The next step is to start testing your code by using more than just GHCi, and that means using the test suite you saw in the previous lesson, QuickCheck. Let's start with the basic setup. First, you need to edit your primes.cabal file so that the `test-suite` section includes QuickCheck. You won't need the quickcheck-instances package this time because you'll use `Ints`, which work with QuickCheck by default.

Listing 37.8 Changing `test-suite` in primes.cabal to include QuickCheck

```
test-suite primes-test
  type:                exitcode-stdio-1.0
  hs-source-dirs:      test
  main-is:             Spec.hs
  build-depends:       base
                     , primes
                     , QuickCheck
  ghc-options:         -threaded -rtsopts -with-rtsopts=-N
  default-language:    Haskell2010
```

This is the only addition you need to make to use QuickCheck.

The next file you need to modify is test/Spec.hs. You'll start by adding some imports that you need.

Listing 37.9 Adding necessary imports to test/Spec.hs

```
import Test.QuickCheck
import Primes

main :: IO ()
main = putStrLn "Test suite not yet implemented"
```

Even though you haven't written any tests yet, you should still run `stack test` to make sure that everything is in good working order:

```
$ stack test
Test suite not yet implemented
```

If you get this message, everything should be working. Time to start with some basic properties that your `isPrime` function needs to have.

37.4.1 Defining properties for isPrime

The first property to define is a basic one that makes sure that you're getting your `Maybe` types correct. Remember that numbers larger than your list of primes, and numbers less than 0, should return a `Nothing` value; anything else should be a `Just` value. You'll import `Data.Maybe` so that you can use the `isJust` function to quickly check whether a `Maybe` value is a `Just` value. Here's the definition of `prop_validPrimesOnly`.

Listing 37.10 `prop_validPrimesOnly` tests that you get `Nothing` and `Just` values

```
import Data.Maybe

prop_validPrimesOnly val = if val < 0 || val >= length primes
                           then result == Nothing
                           else isJust result
  where result = isPrime val
```

All you need to do for this test is refactor your `main IO` action to run the new test.

Listing 37.11 Adding `prop_validPrimesOnly` to your `main`

```
main :: IO ()
main = do
  quickCheck prop_validPrimesOnly
```

Before running your test suite, you'll add a few more tests.

Testing that primes are, in fact, prime

The most obvious property that needs to be upheld is that primes are prime. You can do this by generating a list of all the numbers less than your prime, starting at 2. Then you'll filter this list to see if any of the values evenly divide your input number. In this test, you're concerned only with the case in which the function returns `Just True`, indicating a prime. Here's the definition of `prop_primesArePrime`.

Listing 37.12 Testing that numbers your function thinks are prime, are prime

```
prop_primesArePrime val = if result == Just True
                          then length divisors == 0
                          else True
  where result = isPrime val
        divisors = filter ((== 0) . (val `mod`)) [2 .. (val - 1)]
```

This way to verify primes isn't as efficient as the way you generate them, but that's okay because you'll run this test only occasionally. This is a great demonstration of how powerful property tests can be. You can use a method that's less efficient but easier to reason about to test a wide range of possible inputs.

Testing that nonprimes are composite

The final test to add for your `isPrime` function is the opposite of the preceding one. You'll check that if your function returns `Just False`, the input number has at least one number that's less than it and evenly divides it.

Listing 37.13 Testing that the nonprimes are composite numbers

```
prop_nonPrimesAreComposite val = if result == Just False
                                 then length divisors > 0
                                 else True
  where result = isPrime val
        divisors = filter ((== 0) . (val `mod`)) [2 .. (val - 1)]
```

This is another nice example of a property you want your function to uphold. Rather than just testing a handful of composite number examples, you're defining what it means to be *not prime*.

Running your tests

All you have to do now is to add a few more calls to `quickCheck` to your `main`. This time you'll do `quickCheckWith` and run 1,000 tests rather than just 100. After all, a lot of numbers are possible inputs for an `Int` type, so you want to make sure you check a good number of them.

Listing 37.14 Modifying your `main` to test your additional properties

```
main :: IO ()
main = do
  quickCheck prop_validPrimesOnly
  quickCheckWith stdArgs { maxSuccess = 1000} prop_primesArePrime
  quickCheckWith stdArgs { maxSuccess = 1000} prop_nonPrimesAreComposite
```

Now if you run this test, you see you missed something!

```
+++ OK, passed 100 tests.
+++ OK, passed 1000 tests.
*** Failed! Falsifiable (after 1 test):
0
```

You fail because 0 isn't composite! When you decided which numbers should be `Nothing`, you decided on numbers less than zero. But your property test has led you to an interesting problem: 0 (and 1 for that matter) isn't composite and isn't prime. So what should you do? Perhaps the best part of your property test is that you have an answer already written down. You've decided that `isPrime` should return `Just True` for primes and `Just False` for *composite* numbers. This decision means that any user of `isPrime` can safely assume that `Just False` means that the number used as an input is composite. Your property test caught an error in your thinking and helped you to understand what the right solution should be.

37.4.2 Fixing the bug

Fixing this bug is straightforward. You have to refactor your `isPrime` function so it returns `Nothing` for all values less than 2, rather than 0.

Listing 37.15 Fixing the bug in `isPrime`

```
isPrime :: Int -> Maybe Bool
isPrime n | n < 2 = Nothing
          | n >= length primes = Nothing
          | otherwise = Just (n `elem` primes)
```

You need to change your `prop_validPrimesOnly` test to reflect this change as well.

Listing 37.16 Updating your `prop_validPrimesOnly` after updated `isPrime`

```
prop_validPrimesOnly val = if val < 2 || val >= length primes
                           then result == Nothing
                           else isJust result
  where result = isPrime val
```

Now if you rerun your tests, you get an `OK` for everything:

```
+++ OK, passed 100 tests.
+++ OK, passed 1000 tests.
+++ OK, passed 1000 tests.
```

With the ability to list primes and detect primes, you can move on to a slightly more interesting problem, which is dividing a number into its prime factors.

37.5 Adding code to factor numbers

The final function you'll add is a function to generate all the prime factors of a number. The prime factors are the prime numbers that when multiplied together give you the original number. For example:

```
4 = [2,2]
6 = [2,3]
18 = [2,3,3]
```

For the same reason you needed to with `isPrime`, you want to return a `Maybe` list of prime factors. This is in case your number is negative, or larger than your largest prime number.

You'll start by making an unsafe version of this function that returns a regular list, rather than a `Maybe` list. The algorithm is simple. You'll start with a number and a list of primes. Then you check whether the number is easily divisible by each prime in the list. You'll remove the primes from the list if they aren't evenly divisible. You can define this function recursively as follows.

Listing 37.17 An unsafe version of your prime factorization algorithm

```
unsafePrimeFactors :: Int -> [Int] -> [Int]
unsafePrimeFactors 0 [] = []
unsafePrimeFactors n [] = []
```

```
unsafePrimeFactors n (next:primes) = if n `mod` next == 0
                                     then next:unsafePrimeFactors
                                     ➥(n `div` next) (next:primes)
                                     else unsafePrimeFactors n primes
```

Now all you have to do is wrap this unsafe function in code that handles the cases in which you want to return missing values.

Listing 37.18 Wrapping `unsafePrimeFactors` to make it safe

```
primeFactors :: Int -> Maybe [Int]
primeFactors n | n < 2 = Nothing
               | n >= length primes = Nothing
               | otherwise = Just (unsafePrimeFactors n primesLessThanN)
  where primesLessThanN = filter (<= n) primes
```

The final step is to add tests for your new function.

The most obvious property of your factors is that the product of these factors should return the original values. You'll test this with the `prop_factorsMakeOriginal` property.

Listing 37.19 Making sure the product of your factors is the original value

```
prop_factorsMakeOriginal val = if result == Nothing
                               then True
                               else product (fromJust result) == val
  where result = primeFactors val
```

One more error you could have is somehow having a nonprime value in your results. The `prop_allFactorsPrime` property tests that all your prime factors are truly prime. Because you already tested `isPrime`, you can feel free to use that in this test.

Listing 37.20 Ensuring that all your factors are prime

```
prop_allFactorsPrime val = if result == Nothing
                           then True
                           else all (== Just True) resultsPrime
  where result = primeFactors val
        resultsPrime = map isPrime (fromJust result)
```

Your last step is to update your `main`.

Listing 37.21 Your final `main` in src/Spec.hs to run all your property tests

```
main :: IO ()
main = do
  quickCheck prop_validPrimesOnly
  quickCheckWith stdArgs { maxSuccess = 1000} prop_primesArePrime
  quickCheckWith stdArgs { maxSuccess = 1000} prop_nonPrimesAreComposite
  quickCheck prop_factorsSumToOriginal
  quickCheck prop_allFactorsPrime
```

Running these five property tests, which in this case are the equivalent of 2,300 unit tests, you can see that your code works as you'd expect:

```
+++ OK, passed 100 tests.
+++ OK, passed 1000 tests.
+++ OK, passed 1000 tests.
+++ OK, passed 100 tests.
+++ OK, passed 100 tests.
```

You've just completed your second project using stack, and this time you've walked through everything in one go. As you can see, stack is a useful tool that makes writing code in Haskell much more manageable. In the next unit, you'll use stack for all the practical code examples.

Summary

In this capstone, you

- Created a new stack project
- Modified the default source files and configuration
- Wrote your basic library code and manually tested it in GHCi
- Implemented property tests to check for bugs
- Used QuickCheck and `stack test` to find errors in your functions
- Refactored your code to fix the bugs
- Extended your library functions with new code and tests

Extending the exercise

The easiest way to extend this exercise is to go ahead and put some code in your app/Main.hs file to allow a user to test numbers for primality, factor primes, or both. An interesting challenge would be to handle the case of `Nothing` results from either function. Here's an example of how this might look:

```
$ stack exe primes-exe
Enter a number to check if it's prime:
4
It is prime!

$ stack exe primes-exe
Enter a number to Factor:
100000000000
Sorry, this number is not a valid candidate for primality testing
```

A trickier challenge would be to consider more sophisticated prime checking algorithms. For example, there's a probabilistic primality test called the Miller-Rabin primality test. By implementing this algorithm, you could allow your `isPrime` function to work with much larger inputs. Wikipedia provides a good overview of this algorithm: https://en.wikipedia.org/wiki/Miller%E2%80%93Rabin_primality_test.

Practical Haskell

Welcome to the last unit of *Get Programming with Haskell*! By this point, you've come a long way from learning the basics of referential transparency and the benefits of functional programming. This last unit is different from most of the others. The goal of unit 7 is to ease the transition from learning Haskell to writing real-world code. I've often found that many students of Haskell (myself included) find the transition from reading about Haskell to writing everyday code in Haskell to be more challenging than expected.

To ease this transition, this unit will ensure that you have some familiarity with a range of tasks that provide a solid foundation for building larger and more complex programs. You'll start by learning how Haskell handles errors and will then be introduced to a useful type called `Either`.

Next, you'll build three practical projects. In the first, you'll make a simple HTTP request in Haskell by using a RESTful API. Interacting with HTTP is an increasingly large part of what most programmers have to deal with every day. Even if you aren't interested in web development, it won't be long until you find yourself needing to fetch data from the web. You'll then use the results from this project to learn how to parse JSON data in Haskell by using the Aeson library. JSON is perhaps the most ubiquitous format for data today; parsing JSON comes up in many common programming projects. After that, you'll learn how to use Haskell with a SQL database by building a command-line tool for a community tool-sharing library. Your application will cover all of the basic CRUD database tasks.

In the final lesson of this unit, you'll say goodbye to *Get Programming with Haskell* by learning to do something you don't normally think of using Haskell for: classic array algorithms. In this lesson, you'll use the `STUArray` type to implement a sorting algorithm that's stateful, doesn't use lazy evaluation, and should perform as well as in most non-functional languages. If you can implement a proper bubble sort in a purely functional language, you can use Haskell for anything.

ERRORS IN HASKELL AND THE EITHER TYPE

After reading lesson 38, you'll be able to

- Throw errors by using the `error` function
- Understand the dangers of throwing errors
- Use `Maybe` as a method for handling errors
- Handle more sophisticated errors with the `Either` type

Most of what makes Haskell so powerful is based on the language being safe, predictable, and reliable. Although Haskell reduces or eliminates many problems, errors are an unavoidable part of real-world programming. In this lesson, you'll learn how to think about handling errors in Haskell. The traditional approach of throwing an exception is frowned upon in Haskell, as this makes it easy to have runtime errors the compiler can't catch. Although Haskell does allow you to throw errors, there are better ways to solve many problems that come up in your programs. You've already spent a lot of time with one of these methods: using the `Maybe` type. The trouble with `Maybe` is that you don't have a lot of options for communicating what went wrong. Haskell provides a more powerful type, `Either`, that lets you use any value you'd like to provide information about an error.

In this lesson, you'll use the `error` function, `Maybe` type, and `Either` type in Haskell to resolve exceptions in your programs. You'll start by exploring the `head` function. Though head is one of the first functions you learned, its implementation has a major issue: it's easy to use head and create runtime errors that can't be captured by Haskell's type system. You'll look at several alternative ways to handle the case where head fails. This problem can be better solved by using the familiar Maybe type, and you can give more informative errors by using a new type you'll learn about, called Either. You'll conclude by building a simple command-line tool that checks whether a number is prime. You'll use the Either type and your own error data type to represent errors and display them to the user.

Consider this You have a list representing employee ID numbers. Employee IDs can't be larger than 10000 or less than 0. You have an idInUse function that checks whether a specific ID is being used. How can you write a function that lets a programmer using idInUse distinguish between a user that isn't in the database and a value that's outside the range of valid employee IDs?

38.1 Head, partial functions, and errors

One of the first functions you were introduced to was head. The head function gives you the first element in the list, if there is one. The trouble with head is what to do when there's no first element in the list (an empty list). See figure 38.1.

Initially, head seems like an incredibly useful function. Many recursive functions you write in Haskell use lists, and accessing the first item in a list is a common requirement.

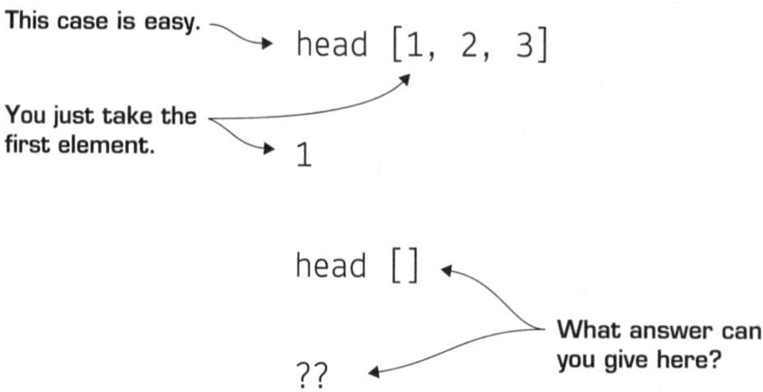

Figure 38.1 How can you solve the case of calling head on an empty list?

But head has one big issue. When you call head on an empty list, you get an error:

```
GHCi> head [1]
1
GHCi> head []
*** Exception: Prelude.head: empty list
```

In most programming languages, throwing an exception like this is common practice. In Haskell, this is a big problem, because throwing an exception makes your code unpredictable. One of the key benefits of using Haskell is that your programs are safer and more predictable. But nothing about the head function, or its type signature, gives you any indication that it could suddenly blow up:

```
head :: [a] -> a
```

By this point in the book, you've seen firsthand that if a Haskell program compiles, it likely runs as expected. But head violates this rule by making it easy to write code that compiles but then causes an error at runtime.

For example, suppose you naively implement a recursive myTake function using head and tail.

Listing 38.1 A function that easily causes an error when used but compiles fine

```
myTake :: Int -> [a] -> [a]
myTake 0 _ = []
myTake n xs = head xs : myTake (n-1) (tail xs)
```

Let's compile this code, only this time you'll set a compiler flag to warn of any potential problems with the code. You can do this by using the -Wall flag. This can be done in stack by adding -Wall to the ghc-options value in the executable section of the .cabal file. As a refresher from lesson 35, open the headaches.cabal file in the projects root directory, find the executable section of the .cabal file, and append -Wall to the list of ghc-options as shown here:

```
executable headaches-exe
  hs-source-dirs:      app
  main-is:             Main.hs
  ghc-options:         -threaded -rtsopts -with-rtsopts=-N -Wall
  build-depends:       base
                     , headaches
  default-language:    Haskell2010
```

The -Wall argument sets all warnings to be checked when the program is compiled.

After you change your file, you need to restart GHCi (which will automatically rebuild your project). Now if you build your project, you'll get no complaints from the compiler. But it's trivial to see that this code produces an error:

```
GHCi> myTake 2 [1,2,3] :: [Int]
[1,2]
GHCi> myTake 4 [1,2,3] :: [Int]
[1,2,3,*** Exception: Prelude.head: empty list
```

Imagine that this code is running and processing requests from a user. This kind of failure would be frustrating, especially given that you're using Haskell.

To understand why `head` is so dangerous, let's compare this to the exact same version using pattern matching.

Listing 38.2 An identical function to `myTake`, which throws a compiler warning

```
myTakePM :: Int -> [a] -> [a]
myTakePM 0 _ = []
myTakePM n (x:xs) = x : myTakePM (n-1) xs
```

This code is identical in behavior to `myTake`, but when you compile with `-Wall`, you get a helpful error:

```
Pattern match(es) are non-exhaustive
    In an equation for 'myTakePM':
        Patterns not matched: p [] where p is not one of {0}
```

This tells you that your function doesn't have a pattern for the empty list! Even though this is identical to the code using `head`, GHC can warn you about this.

NOTE If you don't want to miss warnings on large projects, you can compile with `-error`, which causes an error anytime a warning is found.

Quick check 38.1 Which of the following is the missing pattern that would fix myTakePM?

```
myTakePM _0 [] = []

myTakePM _ [] = []

myTakePM 0 (x:xs) = []
```

38.1.1 Head and partial functions

The head function is an example of a *partial function*. In lesson 2, you learned that every function must take an argument and return a result. Partial functions don't violate this rule, but they have one significant failing. They aren't defined on all inputs. The head function is undefined on the empty list.

Nearly all errors in software are the result of partial functions. Your program receives input you don't expect, and the program has no way of dealing with it. Throwing an error is an obvious solution to this problem. Throwing errors in Haskell is simple: you use the error function. Here's myHead with an error.

Listing 38.3 myHead, an example of throwing an error

```
myHead :: [a] -> a
myHead [] = error "empty list"
myHead (x:_) = x
```

Throws an error whenever myHead matches an empty list

In Haskell, throwing errors is considered bad practice. This is because, as you saw with myTake, it's easy to introduce bugs into code that the compiler can't check. In practice, you should *never* use head, and instead use pattern matching. If you replace any instance of using head and tail in your code with pattern matching, the compiler can warn you of errors.

The real question is, what do you do about partial functions in general? Ideally, you want a way to transform your partial function into one that works on all values. Another common partial function is (/), which is undefined for 0. But Haskell avoids throwing an error in this case by providing a different solution:

```
GHCi> 2 / 0
Infinity
```

QC 38.1 answer You need to add the following pattern:

```
myTakePM _ [] = []
```

This is a nice solution to the problem of dividing by zero, but solutions like this exist for only a few specific cases. What you want is a way to use types to capture when errors might happen. Your compiler can help in writing more error-resistant code.

Quick check 38.2 The following are all partial functions included in `Prelude`. For what inputs do they fail?

- `maximum`
- `succ`
- `sum`

38.2 Handling partial functions with Maybe

It turns out you've already seen one of the most useful ways to handle partial functions: `Maybe`. In many of the examples of `Maybe` that you've used, there would be a `Null` value in other languages. But `Maybe` is a reasonable way to transform any partial function into a complete function. Here's your code for `maybeHead`.

Listing 38.4 Using `Maybe` to make `head` a complete function

```
maybeHead :: [a] -> Maybe a
maybeHead [] = Nothing
maybeHead (x:_) = Just x
```

With `maybeHead`, you can safely take the `head` of a list:

```
GHCi> maybeHead [1]
Just 1
GHCi> maybeHead []
Nothing
```

In unit 5, you learned that `Maybe` is an instance of `Monad` (and therefore `Functor` and `Applicative`), which allows you to perform computation on values in a `Maybe` context. Recall that the

QC 38.2 answer

- `maximum`—Fails on the empty list
- `succ`—Fails on `maxBound` for the type
- `sum`—Fails on infinite lists

Functor type class allows you to use <$> to apply a function to a Maybe value. Here's an example of using the maybeHead function, as well as using <$> to operate on the values it produces:

```
GHCi> (+2) <$> maybeHead [1]
Just 3
GHCi> (+2) <$> maybeHead []
Nothing
```

The Applicative type class provides the <*> operator, so you can chain together functions in a context, most commonly used for multi-argument functions. Here's how to use <$> with <*> to cons a result from maybeHead with a Just []:

```
GHCi> (:) <$> maybeHead [1,2,3] <*> Just []
Just [1]
GHCi> (:) <$> maybeHead [] <*> Just []
Nothing
```

You can combine maybeHead with <$> and <*> to write a new, safer version of myTake.

Listing 38.5 A safer version of myTake using maybeHead instead of head

```
myTakeSafer :: Int -> Maybe [a] -> Maybe [a]
myTakeSafer 0 _ = Just []
myTakeSafer n (Just xs) = (:) <$> maybeHead xs
                              <*> myTakeSafer (n-1) (Just (tail xs))
```

In GHCi, you can see that the myTakeSafer function works just fine with error-causing inputs:

```
GHCi> myTakeSafer 3 (Just [1,2,3])
Just [1,2,3]
GHCi> myTakeSafer 6 (Just [1,2,3])
Nothing
```

As you can see, myTakeSafer works as you'd expect (though differently than take, which would return the full list). Note that the reason you named it safer, not safe, is that, unfortunately, *tail is also a partial function.*

38.3 Introducing the Either type

We've spent a lot of time in this book talking about the power of `Maybe`, but it does have one major limitation. As you write more sophisticated programs, the `Nothing` result becomes harder to interpret. Recall that in our unit 6 capstone you had an `isPrime` function. Here's a simplified version of `isPrime`:

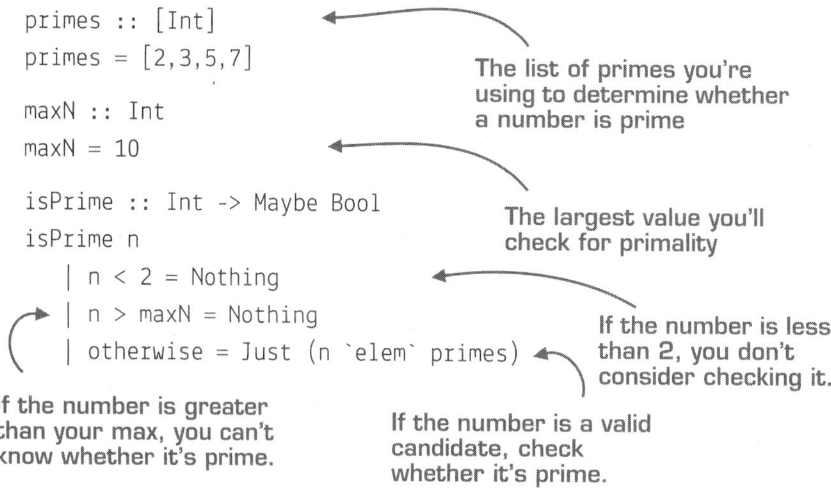

```
primes :: [Int]
primes = [2,3,5,7]

maxN :: Int
maxN = 10

isPrime :: Int -> Maybe Bool
isPrime n
   | n < 2 = Nothing
   | n > maxN = Nothing
   | otherwise = Just (n `elem` primes)
```

The list of primes you're using to determine whether a number is prime
The largest value you'll check for primality
If the number is less than 2, you don't consider checking it.
If the number is greater than your max, you can't know whether it's prime.
If the number is a valid candidate, check whether it's prime.

You made this function of type `Int -> Maybe Bool` because you wanted to handle your edge cases. The key issue is that you want a `False` value for `isPrime` to mean that a number is composite. But there are two problems. Numbers such as 0 and 1 are neither composite nor prime. Additionally, the `isPrime` function limits how large a number can be, and you don't want to return `False` just because a value is too expensive to compute.

Now imagine you're using `isPrime` in your own software. When you call `isPrime 9997`, you get `Nothing` as a result. What in the world does this mean? You'd have to look up the documentation (hoping there is any) to find out. The nice thing about errors is that you get an error message. Although `Maybe` does give you lots of safety, unless `Nothing` has an obvious interpretation, as in the case of `Null` values, it's not useful. Fortunately, Haskell has another type, similar to `Maybe`, that allows you to create much more expressive errors while remaining safe.

Quick check 38.3 Suppose you have this list:

```
oddList :: [Maybe Int]
oddList = [Nothing]
```

The type you'll be looking at is called `Either`. Though only a bit more complicated than `Maybe`, its definition can be confusing. Here's the definition of `Either`:

```
data Either a b = Left a | Right b
```

`Either` has two confusingly named data constructors: `Left` and `Right`. For handling errors, you can consider the `Left` constructor as the case of having an error, and the `Right` constructor for when things go as planned. A more user-friendly, but less general way to define `Either` is as follows:

```
data Either a b = Fail a | Correct b
```

In practice, the `Right` constructor works exactly like `Just` for `Maybe`. The key difference between the two is that `Left` allows you to have more information than `Nothing`. Also notice that `Either` takes two type parameters. This allows you to have a type for sending error messages and a type for your actual data. To demonstrate, here's an example of making a safer `head` function with `Either`.

Listing 38.6 A safer version of `head` written using `Either`

```
eitherHead :: [a] -> Either String a
eitherHead [] = Left "There is no head because the list is empty"
eitherHead (x:xs) = Right x
```

Notice that the `Left` constructor takes a `String`, whereas the `Right` constructor returns the value from the first item in your list. Here are some example lists you can test on:

```
intExample :: [Int]
intExample = [1,2,3]

intExampleEmpty :: [Int]
intExampleEmpty = []
```

QC 38.3 answer

```
Maybe Int
```

```
charExample :: [Char]
charExample = "cat"

charExampleEmpty :: [Char]
charExampleEmpty = ""
```

In GHCi, you can see how `Either` works, as well as the types you get back:

```
GHCi> eitherHead intExample
Right 1
GHCi> eitherHead intExampleEmpty
Left "There is no head because the list is empty"
GHCi> eitherHead charExample
Right 'c'
GHCi> eitherHead charExampleEmpty
Left "There is no head because the list is empty"
```

The `Either` type is also a member of `Monad` (and thus `Functor` and `Applicative` as well). Here's a simple example of using `<$>` to increment the `head` of your `intExample`:

```
GHCi> (+ 1) <$> (eitherHead intExample)
Right 2
GHCi> (+ 1) <$> (eitherHead intExampleEmpty)
Left "There is no head because the list is empty"
```

The `Either` type combines the safety of `Maybe` with the clarity that error messages provide.

Quick check 38.4 Use `<$>` and `<*>` to add the first and second numbers in `intExample` by using `eitherHead`.

38.3.1 Building a prime check with Either

To demonstrate working with `Either`, let's see how to build a basic command-line tool to check whether a number is prime. You'll keep your `isPrime` function minimal, focusing on using the `Either` type. You'll begin by using a `String` for your error message. Then

QC 38.4 answer

```
(+) <$> eitherHead intExample <*> eitherHead (tail intExample)
```

you'll take advantage of the fact that `Either` lets you use any type you want to, allowing you to create your own error types.

The nice thing about `Either` is you don't have to stick to a single error message. You can have as many as you'd like. Your improved `isPrime` function will let you know whether a value isn't a valid candidate for primality checking, or whether the number is too large.

Listing 38.7 `isPrime` refactors to use multiple messages when a number is invalid

```
isPrime :: Int -> Either String Bool
isPrime n
  | n < 2 = Left "Numbers less than 2 are not candidates for primes"
  | n > maxN = Left "Value exceeds limits of prime checker"
  | otherwise = Right (n `elem` primes)
```

Here are a few tests of this function in GHCi:

```
GHCi> isPrime 5
Right True
GHCi> isPrime 6
Right False
GHCi> isPrime 100
Left "Value exceeds limits of prime checker"
GHCi> isPrime (-29)
Left "Numbers less than 2 are not candidates for primes"
```

So far, you haven't taken advantage of `Either` being able to take two types; you've exclusively used `String` for the `Left` constructor. In most programming languages, you can represent errors by using a class. This makes it easier to model specific types of errors. `Either` allows you to do this as well. You'll start by making your errors into a type of their own.

Listing 38.8 The `PrimeError` types for representing your errors as types

```
data PrimeError = TooLarge | InvalidValue
```

Now you can make this an instance of `Show` so you can easily print out these errors.

Listing 38.9 Making `PrimeError` an instance of `Show`

```
instance Show PrimeError where
  show TooLarge = "Value exceed max bound"
  show InvalidValue = "Value is not a valid candidate for prime checking"
```

With your new PrimeError type, you can refactor your isPrime function to show off these errors.

Listing 38.10 Refactoring isPrime to use PrimeError

```
isPrime :: Int -> Either PrimeError Bool
isPrime n
   | n < 2 = Left InvalidValue
   | n > maxN = Left TooLarge
   | otherwise = Right (n `elem` primes)
```

This makes your code much more readable. Additionally, you now have an easily reusable data type that will work with your errors. Here are some examples of your new function in GHCi:

```
GHCi> isPrime 99
Left Value exceed max bound
GHCi> isPrime 0:
Left Value is not a valid candidate for prime checking
```

Next you'll create a displayResult function that will convert your Either response into a String.

Listing 38.11 Translating your isPrime result to be human-readable

```
displayResult :: Either PrimeError Bool -> String
displayResult (Right True) = "It's prime"
displayResult (Right False) = "It's composite"
displayResult (Left primeError) = show primeError
```

Finally, you can put together a simple main IO action that reads as follows.

Listing 38.12 The main to check for primes from user input

```
main :: IO ()
main = do
  print "Enter a number to test for primality:"
  n <- read <$> getLine
  let result = isPrime n
  print (displayResult result)
```

Now you can build and run your program:

```
$ stack build
$ stack exec primechecker-exe
"Enter a number to test for primality:"
6
"It's composite"

$ stack exec headaches-exe
"Enter a number to test for primality:"
5
"It's prime"

$ stack exec headaches-exe
"Enter a number to test for primality:"
213
"Value exceed max bound"

$ stack exec headaches-exe
"Enter a number to test for primality:"
0
"Value is not a valid candidate for prime checking"
```

With your `PrimeError` type, you were able to replicate more sophisticated ways of modeling errors in OOP languages. The great thing about `Either` is that because the `Left` constructor can be any type, there's no limit to how expressive you can be. If you wanted to, you could return a function!

Summary

In this lesson, our objective was to teach you how to safely handle errors in Haskell. You started by looking at the way `head` uses `error` to signal when you have an empty list with no head. Neither your type checker nor GHC's warnings let you know this is a problem. This is ultimately caused by `head` being a partial function, a function that doesn't return a result for all possible inputs. This can be solved by using a `Maybe` type. Although `Maybe` types do make your code safer, they can make errors hard to understand. Finally, you saw that the `Either` type provides the best of both worlds, allowing you to safely handle errors as well as providing detailed information about them.

Q38.1 Make a function `addStrInts` that takes two `Ints` represented as `Strings` and adds them. The function would return an `Either String Int`. The `Right` constructor should return the result, provided that the two arguments can be parsed into `Ints` (use `Data.Char isDigit` to check). Return a different `Left` result for the three possible cases:

- First value can't be parsed.
- Second value can't be parsed.
- Neither value can be parsed.

Q38.2 The following are all partial functions. Use the type specified to implement a safer version of the function:

- `succ`—`Maybe`
- `tail`—`[a]` (Keep the type the same.)
- `last`—`Either` (`last` fails on empty lists and infinite lists; use an upper bound for the infinite case.)

39

MAKING HTTP REQUESTS IN HASKELL

After reading lesson 39, you'll be able to

- Fetch web pages by using Haskell
- Generate more complex requests by setting headers and using HTTPS
- Understand how to approach learning new Haskell types and libraries

In this lesson, you'll learn how to make an HTTP request in Haskell and save the results to a file. The data you'll fetch is from the National Oceanic and Atmospheric Administration (NOAA) Climate Data API. This API requires you to send a custom HTTP request that uses SSL and has a custom header for authentication. You'll use the `Network.HTTP.Simple` library, which will allow you to make simple requests as well as create custom HTTP requests. You'll start by learning how to use `Network.HTTP.Simple` to fetch a web page from a URL. Then you'll create a specific request for the NOAA API. In the end, you'll have fetched JSON data from this API to be used in the next lesson.

Consider this How would you go about writing a Haskell program that when ran would fetch the homepage of reddit.com and write it to a local .html file?

39.1 Getting your project set up

In this lesson, you'll look at one of the most common tasks in contemporary programming: making an HTTP request. The aim of this project is to create a script that makes a request to the NOAA Climate Data API. The NOAA Climate Data API contains access to a wide range of climate-related data. On the API's website (https://www.ncdc.noaa.gov/cdo-web/webservices/v2#gettingStarted), you can find a list of endpoints that the API offers. Here are a few of them:

- /datasets—Tells you which data sets are available
- /locations—Gives the locations available to look up
- /stations—Provides information on available weather observation stations
- /data—Provides access to the raw data

Building a full wrapper for the NOAA API would be a project beyond the scope of a single lesson. You'll focus on the first step in this process: getting results from the /datasets endpoint. The /datasets endpoint provides essential metadata you need to pass to the /data endpoint to request your data. Here's an example entry:

```
"uid":"gov.noaa.ncdc:C00822",
"mindate":"2010-01-01",
"maxdate":"2010-12-01",
"name":"Normals Monthly",
"datacoverage":1,
"id":"NORMAL_MLY"
```

Even though fetching this data is a small part of the overall API, after you understand the basics of working with HTTP in Haskell, extending the project is straightforward. After you've made the request, you'll write the body of the request to a JSON file. Although this is a fairly straightforward task, you'll learn much about working with real-world Haskell along the way.

You'll create a new stack project called `http-lesson`. As a quick refresher, the following steps will create and build your project:

```
$ stack update
$ stack new http-lesson
$ cd http-lesson
$ stack setup
$ stack build
```

For this simple project, you'll keep everything in the `Main` module located in app/Main.hs.

NOTE This project uses the NOAA Climate Data API to fetch JSON and save it to a file. In the next lesson, you'll parse that JSON. This API is free to use but does require the user to request an API token. To get your token, go to www.ncdc.noaa.gov/cdo-web/token and fill in the form with your email address. Your token should be sent quickly. You'll be making a request to see which data sets the API allows access to.

After you have your API token, you can start coding up your project.

39.1.1 Your starter code

You'll start with adding imports to your `Main` module. Notice that you'll import both `Data.ByteString` and `Data.ByteString.Lazy`. Importing multiple text or `ByteString` types is common in real-world Haskell. In this case, you're doing so because different parts of the library you'll be using require using either strict or lazy `ByteString`s. You'll import the `Char8` module for both of these libraries, as it will make using them much easier, as we discussed in lesson 25. Finally, you'll add the `Network.HTTP.Simple` library, which you'll use for your HTTP requests.

Listing 39.1 The imports for your app/Main.hs file

```
module Main where

import qualified Data.ByteString as B
import qualified Data.ByteString.Char8 as BC
import qualified Data.ByteString.Lazy as L
import qualified Data.ByteString.Lazy.Char8 as LC
import Network.HTTP.Simple
```

Before you continue, you also need to update your http-lesson.cabal file to support these imports. You'll add `bytestring` and `http-conduit` to your `build-depends` section. Because you're working with `ByteString`s and `Char8`, it's also helpful to include the `OverloadedStrings` extension.

Listing 39.2 Modifying your project's .cabal file

```
executable http-lesson-exe
  hs-source-dirs:      app
  main-is:             Main.hs
  ghc-options:         -threaded -rtsopts -with-rtsopts=-N
```

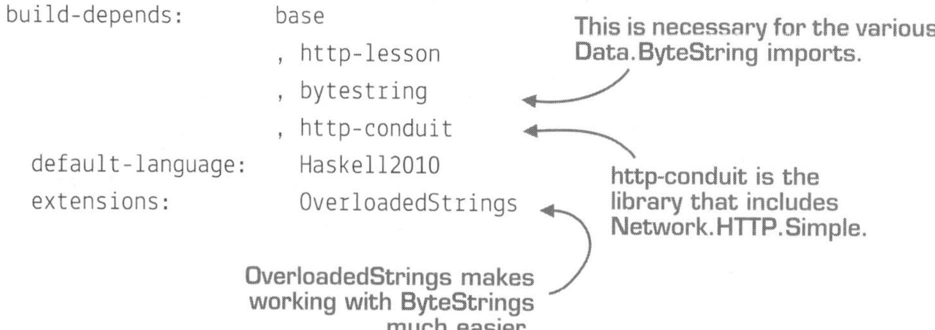
build-depends: base
, http-lesson
, bytestring
, http-conduit
default-language: Haskell2010
extensions: OverloadedStrings
This is necessary for the various Data.ByteString imports.
http-conduit is the library that includes Network.HTTP.Simple.
OverloadedStrings makes working with ByteStrings much easier.

Note that stack will handle downloading all of your dependencies for `http-conduit`, and you don't need to explicitly use the `stack install` command.

Next you can start fleshing out your `Main` with variables for the data you need. You're only going to be concerned about a single API request, which will allow you to list all the data sets in the NOAA Climate Data API.

Listing 39.3 Variables that will be helpful in making your HTTP requests

```
myToken :: BC.ByteString
myToken = "<API TOKEN HERE>"

noaaHost :: BC.ByteString
noaaHost = "www.ncdc.noaa.gov"

apiPath :: BC.ByteString
apiPath = "/cdo-web/api/v2/datasets"
```

You also need placeholder code in your `main IO` action to ensure that your code will compile.

Listing 39.4 Placeholder code for your `main` action

```
main :: IO ()
main = print "hi"
```

> **Quick check 39.1** If you didn't include your `OverloadedStrings` extension in the .cabal file, how could you modify Main.hs to support `OverloadedStrings`?

QC 39.1 answer You could use the `LANGUAGE` pragma:

```
{-# LANGUAGE OverloadedStrings -#}
```

39.2 Using the HTTP.Simple module

Now that you have the basics in place, you can start playing around with HTTP requests. You'll use the module `Network.HTTP.Simple`, which is part of the `http-conduit` package. As the name indicates, `HTTP.Simple` makes it easy for you to make simple HTTP requests. You'll use the `httpLBS` (the *LBS* stands for *lazy ByteString*) function to submit your request. Normally, you'd have to create an instance of the `Request` data type to pass into this function. But `httpLBS` is able to cleverly take advantage of `OverloadedStrings` to make sure the correct type is passed in. Here's a quick sample of fetching the data from the popular tech news site, Hacker News (https://news.ycombinator.com):

```
GHCi> import Network.HTTP.Simple
GHCi> response = httpLBS "http://news.ycombinator.com"
```

If you type this into GHCi, you'll notice that the `response` variable is set instantly, even though you're making an HTTP request. Typically, an HTTP request results in a noticeable delay in time due to the nature of making the request itself. Your variable is assigned instantly because of lazy evaluation. Even though you've defined a request, you still haven't used it. If you enter `response` again, you'll notice a slight delay:

```
GHCi> response
<large output>
```

You want to be able to access different pieces of your response. The first thing to check is the status code of the response. This is the HTTP code that tells whether your request was successful.

> **Common HTTP codes**
>
> In case you're unfamiliar, here are some common HTTP status codes:
>
> - 200 OK—The request was successful.
> - 301 Moved Permanently—The resource being requested has moved.
> - 404 Not Found—The resource is missing.

`Network.HTTP.Simple` contains the function `getResponseStatusCode` that gives you the status of your response. If you run this in GHCi, you immediately come across a problem:

```
GHCi> getResponseStatusCode response

<interactive>:6:23: error:
    No instance for (Control.Monad.IO.Class.MonadIO Response)
      arising from a use of 'response'
```

What happened here? The issue is that getResponseStatusCode is expecting a plain response type, as you can see from its type signature:

```
getResponseStatusCode :: Response a -> Int
```

But to make your HTTP request, you had to use IO, which means that your response variable is an IO (Response a) type.

A popular alternative to HTTP.Simple

Although Network.HTTP.Simple is fairly straightforward, it's relatively bare bones. Many other Haskell packages are available for making HTTP requests. One of the more popular is the wreq package (https://hackage.haskell.org/package/wreq). Although wreq is a nice library, it would require you to learn another abstract Haskell topic: Lens. It's worth pointing out that it's common for Haskell packages to use new and interesting abstractions. If you loved unit 5 on monads, you may find this one of the more exciting parts of writing Haskell. But the love of abstraction can also be a frustration for beginners who may not want to learn yet another new idea when they just want to fetch data from an API.

You can solve this problem in two ways. The first way is to use your Functor <$> operator:

```
GHCi> getResponseStatusCode <$> response
200
```

Remember that <$> allows you to take a pure function and put it in a context. If you look at the type of your result, you'll see it's also in a context:

```
GHCi> :t getResponseStatusCode <$> response
getResponseStatusCode <$> response
:: Control.Monad.IO.Class.MonadIO f => f Int
```

An alternative solution is to assign response by using <- rather than =. Just as when you're using do-notation, this allows you to treat a value in a context as though it were a pure value:

```
GHCi> response <- httpLBS "http://news.ycombinator.com"
GHCi> getResponseStatusCode response
200
```

Now that you understand the basics of an HTTP request, you'll move on to make a more sophisticated request.

Quick check 39.2 There's also a `getResponseHeader` function. Use both `<$>` and `<-` to get the header of the response.

39.3 Making an HTTP request

Although your simple use of `httpLBS` is convenient, you need to change a few things. Your request to the API requires you to use HTTPS rather than plain HTTP, as well as to pass your token in the header. You can't simply put a URL into your request; you also need to do the following:

- Add your token to the header.
- Specify the host and path for your request.
- Make sure you're using the `GET` method for your request.
- Make sure your request works for an SSL connection.

You can do this by using a series of functions that set these properties for your request. The code to build your request follows. Even though making this request is straightforward, you're using an operator that you haven't used in this book so far: the `$` operator. The `$` operator automatically wraps parentheses around your code (for more details, see the following sidebar).

Listing 39.5 The code for building an HTTPS request for the API

```
buildRequest :: BC.ByteString -> BC.ByteString -> BC.ByteString
             -> BC.ByteString -> Request
```

QC 39.2 answer

Method 1:

```
GHCi> import Network.HTTP.Simple
GHCi> response = httpLBS "http://news.ycombinator.com"
GHCi> getResponseHeader <$> response
```

Method 2:

```
GHCi> response <- httpLBS "http://news.ycombinator.com"
GHCi> getResponseHeader response
```

```
buildRequest token host method path  = setRequestMethod method
                                     $ setRequestHost host
                                     $ setRequestHeader "token" [token]
                                     $ setRequestPath path
                                     $ setRequestSecure True
                                     $ setRequestPort 443
                                     $ defaultRequest

request :: Request
request = buildRequest myToken noaaHost "GET" apiPath
```

The $ operator

The $ operator is most commonly used to automatically create parentheses. You can visualize the opening parentheses as starting with the $ and ending at the end of the function definition (covering multiple lines if necessary). For example, suppose you want to double 2 + 2. You need to add parentheses to make sure the operation works correctly:

```
GHCi> (*2) 2 + 2
6
GHCi> (*2) (2 + 2)
8
```

You could alternatively write this:

```
GHCi> (*2) $ 2 + 2
8
```

Here's another example:

```
GHCi> head (map (++"!") ["dog","cat"])
"dog!"
GHCi> head $ map (++"!") ["dog","cat"]
"dog!"
```

For beginners, the $ often makes Haskell code more difficult to parse. In practice, the $ operator is used frequently, and you'll likely find you prefer using it over many parentheses. There's nothing magical about $; if you look at its type signature, you can see how it works:

```
($) :: (a -> b) -> a -> b
```

The arguments are just a function and a value. The trick is that $ is a binary operator, so it has lower precedence than the other functions you're using. Therefore, the argument for the function will be evaluated as though it were in parentheses.

The interesting thing about this code is the way you're handling changing the state of your request. You have a bunch of `setValue` functions, but how are they setting a value? You'll get a better sense of what's going on if you explore the types of these `set` methods:

```
GHCi> :t setRequestMethod
setRequestMethod :: BC.ByteString -> Request -> Request

GHCi> :t setRequestHeader
setRequestHeader:: HeaderName -> [BC.ByteString] -> Request -> Request
```

Here you see one functional solution to having state. Each `setValue` function takes the argument for the parameter it's going to set and existing request data. You start with an initial request, `defaultRequest`, which is provided by the `Network.HTTP.Simple` module. You then create a new copy of the request data with the modified parameter, finally returning the modified request as a result. You saw this type of solution in unit 1, only much more verbose. You could rewrite your function, explicitly controlling your state with a `let` clause. Notice that these function calls are in reverse order.

Listing 39.6 `buildRequest` rewritten with the state saved as variables

```
buildRequest token host method path  =
   let state1 = setRequestPort 443 defaultRequest
   in let state2 = setRequestSecure True state1
      in let state3 = setRequestPath path state2
         in let state4 = setRequestHeader "token" [token] state3
            in setRequestHost host state4
```

Using the `$` operator to make each `setValue` function serve as the argument to the next function makes the code much more compact. Haskellers strongly prefer terse code whenever possible, though this can sometimes make reading the code more difficult when starting out.

39.4 Putting it all together

Now you have to put together your `main IO` action. You can pass your request into `httpLBS`. Then you'll get the status. After you have the status, you'll check whether it's 200. If it's 200, you'll write the data to a file by using the `getResponseBody` function. Otherwise, you'll alert the user that there was an error in your request. When you write your file, it's important to notice that you're using the raw lazy `ByteString`s with `L.writeFile` rather than the Char8 version LC.writeFile. In lesson 25, we mentioned that when you use binary data that may include Unicode, you should never write it using the Char8 interface, as it can corrupt your data.

Listing 39.7 Your final main for writing your request to a JSON file

```
main :: IO ()
main = do
  response <- httpLBS request
  let status = getResponseStatusCode response
  if status == 200
    then do
         print "saving request to file"
         let jsonBody = getResponseBody response
         L.writeFile "data.json" jsonBody
    else print "request failed with error"
```

Now you have a basic application that can fetch data from the REST API and write it to a file. This is just a taste of the type of HTTP request you can make using Haskell. The full documentation for this library can be found at https://haskell-lang.org/library/http-client.

Summary

In this lesson, our objective was to give you a quick overview of how to make an HTTP request in Haskell. In addition to learning how to make an HTTP request, you learned how to go about learning new libraries in Haskell. Let's see if you got this.

Q39.1 Build a function buildRequestNOSSL that works exactly like buildRequest, only it doesn't support SSL.

Q39.2 Improve the output of your code when something goes wrong. getResponseStatus will give you a data type including both the statusCode and the statusMessage. Fix main so that if you do get a non-200 statusCode, you print out the appropriate error.

WORKING WITH JSON DATA BY USING AESON

After reading lesson 40, you'll be able to

- Transform Haskell types into JSON
- Read JSON into a Haskell type
- Use the `DeriveGeneric` extension to implement needed classes
- Write you own instances of `ToJSON` and `FromJSON`

In this lesson, you'll work with JavaScript Object Notation (JSON) data, one of the most popular ways to store and transmit data. The JSON format originates in simple JavaScript objects and is heavily used in transmitting data through HTTP APIs. Because the format is so simple, it has seen widespread adoption outside the web, frequently being used as a method of storing data and for tasks such as creating configuration files. Figure 40.1 shows an example JSON object used with the Google Analytics API.

In the previous lesson, you ended up downloading a JSON file containing information on data sets available through the NOAA Climate Data API. In this lesson, you're going to build a simple command-line application that opens that JSON file and prints out the data sources in the file. Before you get there, you'll learn how to work with JSON. You'll create types that you can turn into JSON as well as create types representing JSON that you'll read in.

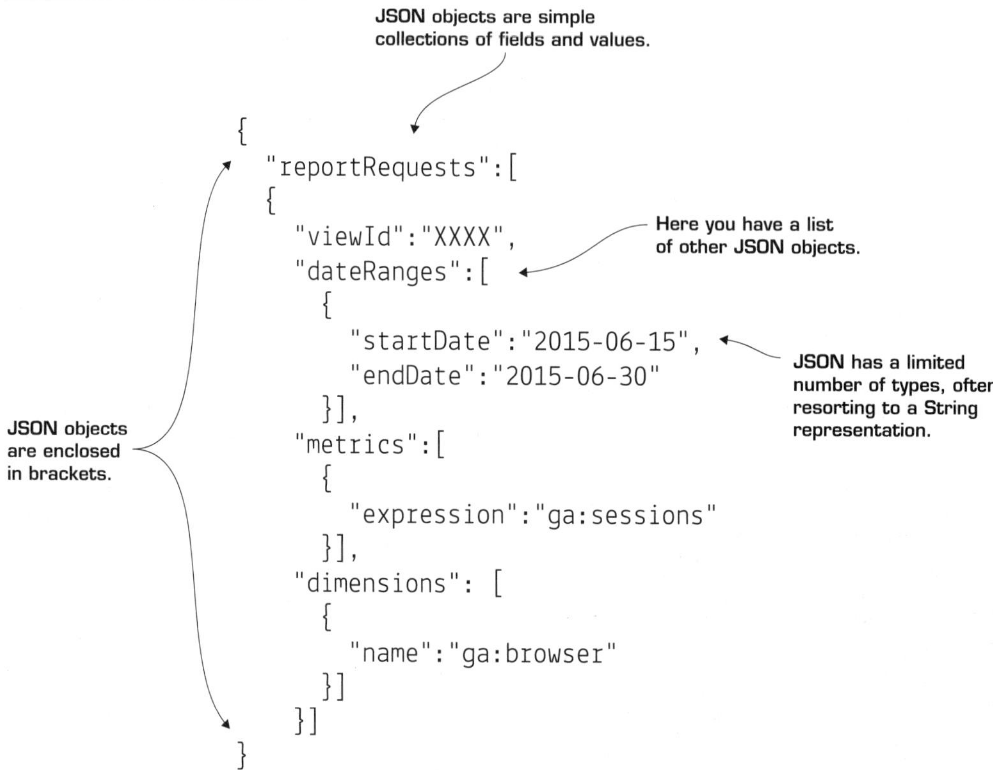
JSON objects are simple collections of fields and values.
Here you have a list of other JSON objects.
JSON has a limited number of types, often resorting to a String representation.
JSON objects are enclosed in brackets.
{
"reportRequests":[
{
"viewId":"XXXX",
"dateRanges":[
{
"startDate":"2015-06-15",
"endDate":"2015-06-30"
}],
"metrics":[
{
"expression":"ga:sessions"
}],
"dimensions": [
{
"name":"ga:browser"
}]
}]
}

Figure 40.1 An example of JSON data from the Google Analytics API

Consider this You have a data type representing a user:

```
data User = User
    { userId :: Int
    , userName :: T.Text
    , email :: T.Text
    }
```

The process of transforming objects into and out of JSON is known as serialization and deserialization, respectively. You may have come across this in other languages. If you have a data type representing a user, how did you serialize and deserialize to and from this type?

40.1 Getting set up

The key challenge of working with JSON in Haskell is that JSON supports only a few simple types: objects, strings, numbers (technically just floats), Booleans, and lists. In many programming languages, JSON is supported by using a dictionary-like data structure. You'll use the Aeson library, which provides a much more appropriate solution for Haskell. Aeson allows you to translate back and forth between Haskell's powerful data types and JSON.

Aeson relies on two key functions for translating back and forth between Haskell data types and JSON: `encode` and `decode`. To use these two functions, you need to make your data an instance of two type classes: `ToJSON` (encode) and `FromJSON` (decode). We'll demonstrate two ways to do this. The first is automatically deriving the type classes with the help of a language extension. The other is to implement these classes yourself.

After you've learned how to use Aeson, you can create a data type representing the JSON data you downloaded from NOAA. The JSON response from the NOAA Climate Data API involves nested objects, so you'll implement a nontrivial data type to interact with this data. Finally, you'll put everything together that will allow you to list the contents of your file.

40.1.1 Setting up stack

You'll use a stack project called `json-lesson` for this lesson. As you did last time, for convenience, you'll keep all of your code in the `Main` module. The first thing you need to do is set up your Main.hs file. You'll start by importing the basics. You'll use the popular Aeson library for working with JSON (Aeson was the father of the ancient Greek mythical hero Jason). In this lesson, all the textual data you're working with will be in the form of `Data.Text`, because this is the preferred method in Haskell for representing text. You also need to import lazy `ByteString`s and the `Char8` helper for these. Your JSON will be represented as `ByteString`s by default until you transform it into more meaningful types. Here's your starter Main.hs file, which includes all the imports you need for this lesson.

Listing 40.1 Your Main.hs file

```
module Main where
import Data.Aeson
import Data.Text as T
import Data.ByteString.Lazy as B
```

```
import Data.ByteString.Lazy.Char8 as BC
import GHC.Generics

main :: IO ()
main = print "hi"
```

You also have to add these libraries to your json-lesson.cabal file. You want to make sure you're using the `OverloadedStrings` extension. You'll also use a new extension for this lesson.

Listing 40.2 Adding your build depends on language extensions

```
build-depends:       base
                   , json-lesson
                   , aeson
                   , bytestring
                   , text
default-language:    Haskell2010
extensions:          OverloadedStrings
                   , DeriveGeneric
```

Now you can start exploring how you're going to model JSON in Haskell.

40.2 Using the Aeson library

To work with JSON, you'll use the most popular Haskell library for JSON: Aeson. The main challenge you face when working with JSON and Haskell is that JSON has little regard for types, representing most of its data as strings. The great thing about Aeson is that it lets you apply Haskell's strong type system to JSON data. You get the ease of working with a widely adopted and flexible data format without having to sacrifice any of Haskell's power and type-related safety.

Aeson relies on two straightforward functions to do the bulk of the work. The `decode` function takes JSON data and transforms it into a target type. Here's the type signature for `decode`:

```
decode :: FromJSON a => ByteString -> Maybe a
```

Two things are worth noticing here. First is that you return a `Maybe` type. As mentioned in lesson 38, `Maybe` is a good way to handle errors in Haskell. In this case, the type of errors you're concerned with are parsing the JSON data correctly. There are many ways your parse could go wrong; for example, the JSON could be malformed or not match the type you expect. If something goes wrong with parsing the JSON data, you'll get a `Nothing` value. You also learned that `Either` is often a better type because it can tell you what went wrong. Aeson also offers an `eitherDecode` function that will give you more informative error messages by using the `Left` constructor (remember that `Left` is the constructor used for errors):

```
eitherDecode :: FromJSON a => ByteString -> Either String a
```

The other important thing to notice is that the type parameter of your `Maybe` (or `Either`) type is constrained by the type class `FromJSON`. Making a type an instance of `FromJSON` enables you to convert raw JSON into a `Maybe` instance of your type. You'll explore ways of making data an instance of `FromJSON` in the next section.

The other important function in Aeson is `encode`, which performs the opposite function as `decode`. Here's the type signature of `encode`:

```
encode :: ToJSON a => a -> ByteString
```

The `encode` function takes a type that's an instance of `ToJSON` and returns a JSON object represented as a `ByteString`. `ToJSON` is the counterpart to `FromJSON`. If a type is an instance of both `FromJSON` and `ToJSON`, it can trivially be converted to and from JSON. Next you'll look at how to take your data and make it an instance of each of these type classes.

Quick check 40.1 Why does `encode` return a `ByteString` rather than a `Maybe ByteString`?

40.3 Making your data types instances of FromJSON and ToJSON

The aim of Aeson is to make it trivial to convert back and forth between Haskell data types and raw JSON. This is a particularly interesting challenge because JSON has a limited number of types to work with: numbers (technically just floats), strings, Booleans, and arrays of values. To do this, Aeson uses two type classes: `FromJSON` and `ToJSON`. The `FromJSON` type class allows you to parse JSON and turn it into a Haskell data type, and `ToJSON` allows you to turn Haskell data types into JSON. Aeson does a remarkably good job of making this easy in many cases.

QC 40.1 answer Because there's no way that your data type could fail to be turned into JSON. The issue arises only when you have JSON that may not be able to be parsed into your original type.

40.3.1 The easy way

For many data types in Haskell, implementing both `ToJSON` and `FromJSON` is remarkably easy. Let's start with a `Book` type, which you'll make an instance of both `ToJSON` and `FromJSON`. Your `Book` type will be incredibly simple, having only a text value for the title, another text value for the author, and an `Int` for the year of publication. Later in this lesson, you'll look at more complicated data. Here's the definition of your `Book` type.

Listing 40.3 A straightforward `Book` type

```
data Book = Book
            { title :: T.Text
            , author :: T.Text
            , year :: Int
            } deriving Show
```

There's an easy way to make the `Book` type both an instance of `FromJSON` and `ToJSON`. To do this, you need to use another language extension called `DeriveGeneric`. This extension adds support for better generic programming in Haskell. This makes it possible to write generic instances of a type class definition, allowing for new data to easily be an instance of a class with no extra code required. The `DeriveGeneric` extension makes it possible to easily derive instances of `FromJSON` and `ToJSON`. All you have to do is add `Generic` to your `deriving` statement.

Listing 40.4 Adding `deriving Generic` to your `Book` type

```
data Book = Book
            { title :: T.Text
            , author :: T.Text
            , year :: Int
            } deriving (Show,Generic)
```

Finally, you have to declare `Book` an instance of `FromJSON` and `ToJSON`. You need to do nothing more than add these two lines (no additional `where` clause or definition is necessary).

Listing 40.5 Making your `Book` type an instance of both `FromJSON` and `ToJSON`

```
instance FromJSON Book
instance ToJSON Book
```

To demonstrate the power of these type classes, let's take an example of your type and encode it.

Listing 40.6 Taking a Book type and converting it to JSON

```
myBook :: Book
myBook = Book {author="Will Kurt"
              ,title="Learn Haskell"
              ,year=2017}

myBookJSON :: BC.ByteString
myBookJSON = encode myBook
```

In GHCi, you can see how this looks:

```
GHCi> myBook
Book {title = "Learn Haskell", author = "Will Kurt", year = 2017}
GHCi> myBookJSON
"{\"author\":\"Will Kurt\",\"title\":\"Learn Haskell\",\"year\":2017}"
```

You can also do the reverse just as easily. Here's a raw JSON `ByteString` that you'll parse into your data type.

Listing 40.7 Taking a JSON representation of your book and converting it to a Book

```
rawJSON :: BC.ByteString
rawJSON = "{\"author\":\"Emil Ciroan\",\"title\":
➥\"A Short History of Decay\",\"year=1949}"

bookFromJSON :: Maybe Book
bookFromJSON = decode rawJSON
```

In GHCi, you can see that you've successfully created a `Book` from this JSON:

```
GHCi> bookFromJSON
Just (Book { title = "A Short History of Decay"
           , author = "Emil Ciroan"
           , year = 1949})
```

This is a powerful feature of Aeson. From a string of JSON, which usually has little type information, you were able to successfully create a Haskell type. In many languages, parsing JSON means getting a hash table or a dictionary of keys and values. Because of Aeson, you can get something much more powerful from your JSON.

Notice that your result is wrapped in the `Just` data constructor. That's because a parsing error could have easily made it impossible to make an instance of your type. If you have malformed JSON that doesn't work, you get nothing.

Listing 40.8 Parsing JSON that doesn't match your type

```
wrongJSON :: BC.ByteString
wrongJSON = "{\"writer\":\"Emil Cioran\",\"title\":
➥\"A Short History of Decay\",\"year\"=1949}"

bookFromWrongJSON :: Maybe Book
bookFromWrongJSON = decode wrongJSON
```

As expected, when you load this into GHCi, you see that your result is `Nothing`:

```
GHCi> bookFromWrongJSON
Nothing
```

This is also a great example of the limitations of `Maybe`. You know what went wrong when parsing this JSON because you purposefully wrote this code with an error. But in a real project, this would be an amazingly frustrating error, especially if you didn't have easy access to the raw JSON data to inspect. As an alternative, you can use `eitherDecode`, which gives you much more information:

```
GHCi> eitherDecode wrongJSON :: Either String Book
Left "Error in $: The key \"author\" was not found"
```

Now you know exactly why your parse failed.

Although using `DeriveGeneric` makes using Aeson incredibly easy, you won't always be able to take advantage of this. Occasionally, you'll have to help Aeson figure out how exactly to parse your data.

Quick check 40.2 Use `Generic` to implement `ToJSON` and `FromJSON` for this type:

```
data Name = Name
    { firstName :: T.Text
    , lastName :: T.Text
    } deriving (Show)
```

QC 40.2 answer

```
data Name = Name
    { firstName :: T.Text
    , lastName :: T.Text
    } deriving (Show,Generic)

instance FromJSON Name
instance ToJSON Name
```

40.3.2 Writing your own instances of FromJSON and ToJSON

In the preceding example, you started with a type you defined and made it work with JSON. In practice, you're just as often working with someone else's JSON data. Here's an example of an error message you might get as a response to a JSON request because of an error on the other person's server.

Listing 40.9 An example of JSON you don't have control over

```
sampleError :: BC.ByteString
sampleError = "{\"message\":\"oops!\",\"error\": 123}"
```

To use Aeson, you need to model this request with your own data type. When you do this, you'll immediately see there's a problem. Here's the first attempt to model this error message.

Listing 40.10 Unfortunately, you can't model this JSON by using Haskell

```
data ErrorMessage = ErrorMessage
                    { message :: T.Text
                    , error :: Int          -- The error is because of this property.
                    } deriving Show
```

The problem here is that you have a property named `error`, but you can't have this, because `error` is already defined in Haskell. You could rewrite your type to avoid this collision.

Listing 40.11 Haskell code that works but doesn't match the original JSON

```
data ErrorMessage = ErrorMessage
                    { message :: T.Text
                    , errorCode :: Int
                   } deriving Show
```

Unfortunately, if you try to automatically derive `ToJSON` and `FromJSON`, your programs will expect an `errorCode` field instead of `error`. If you were in control of this JSON, you could rename the field, but you're not. You need another solution to this problem.

To make your `ErrorMessage` type an instance of `FromJSON`, you need to define one function: `parseJSON`. You can do this in the following way.

Listing 40.12 Making `ErrorMessage` an instance of `FromJSON`

```
instance FromJSON ErrorMessage where
  parseJSON (Object v) =
    ErrorMessage <$> v .: "message"
                 <*> v .: "error"
```

This code is confusing, so breaking it down is worthwhile. The first part shows the method you need to define and the argument it takes:

```
parseJSON (Object v)
```

The `(Object v)` is the JSON object being parsed. When you take just the `v` inside, you're accessing that value of that JSON object. Next you have a bunch of infix operators you need to make sense of. You've seen this pattern before, in unit 5, when you learned about common uses of applicatives:

```
ErrorMessage <$> value <*> value
```

As a refresher, suppose the values for your `ErrorMessage` were in a `Maybe` context.

Listing 40.13 Values for constructing an `ErrorMessage` in a `Maybe` context

```
exampleMessage :: Maybe T.Text
exampleMessage = Just "Opps"

exampleError :: Maybe Int
exampleError = Just 123
```

If you want to make an `ErrorMessage`, you can combine `<$>` and `<*>` to safely make this `ErrorMessage` in the context of a `Maybe`:

```
GHCi> ErrorMessage <$> exampleMessage <*> exampleError
Just (ErrorMessage {message = "Opps", errorCode = 123})
```

This pattern works with any instance of `Monad`. In this case, you're not working with values in a `Maybe` context but in a `Parser` context. This brings you to the final mystery: what's the `(.:)` operator? You can figure this out by looking at its type:

```
(.:) :: FromJSON a => Object -> Text -> Parser a
```

This operator takes an `Object` (your JSON object) and some text and returns a value parsed into a context. For example, this line of code is trying to parse the `message` field from your JSON object:

```
v .: "message"
```

The result is a value in a `Parser` context. The reason you need a context for your parse is that it can fail if there's trouble parsing.

> **Quick check 40.3** Make the `Name` type into an instance of `FromJSON` without `Generic`:
>
> ```
> data Name = Name
>     { firstName :: T.Text
>     , lastName :: T.Text
>     } deriving (Show)
> ```

Now that your `ErrorMessage` type is an instance of `FromJSON`, you can finally parse the incoming JSON `ErrorMessages`.

Listing 40.14 With your custom `FromJSON`, you can now parse your JSON

```
sampleErrorMessage :: Maybe ErrorMessage
sampleErrorMessage = decode sampleError
```

In GHCi, you find this works as expected:

```
GHCi> sampleErrorMessage
Just (ErrorMessage {message = "oops!", errorCode = 123})
```

And of course you want to go back again. The syntax for creating your message is different:

```
instance ToJSON ErrorMessage where
  toJSON (ErrorMessage message errorCode) =
    object [ "message" .= message
           , "error" .= errorCode
           ]
```

QC 40.3 answer

```
instance FromJSON Name where
    parseJSON (Object v) =
        Name <$> v .: "firstName"
             <*> v .: "lastName"
```

Once again you have a confusing bit of code. This time you're defining the `toJSON` method. You can see that the method takes your data constructor and pattern matches on its two arguments, `message` and `errorCode`:

```
toJSON (ErrorMessage message errorCode)
```

You then use the `object` function to create your JSON object, passing the values of your data type into the correct fields for the JSON object:

```
    object [ "message" .= message
           , "error" .= errorCode
           ]
```

You have another new operator here, (`.=`). This operator is used to create a key/value pair matching the value of your data with the field name for the JSON object.

Quick check 40.4 Finally, make `Name` an instance of `ToJSON` without `Generic`:

```
data Name = Name
    { firstName :: T.Text
    , lastName :: T.Text
    } deriving (Show)
```

Now you can create your own raw JSON, just like the one you received.

Listing 40.15 Creating an error message to test your instance of `ToJSON`

```
anErrorMessage :: ErrorMessage
anErrorMessage = ErrorMessage "Everything is Okay" 0
```

Again, you can see that this works exactly as you expect:

```
GHCi> encode anErrorMessage
"{\"error\":0,\"message\":\"Everything is Okay\"}"
```

QC 40.4 answer

```
instance ToJSON Name where
    toJSON (Name firstName lastName) =
        object [ "firstName" .= firstName
               , "lastName" .= lastName
               ]
```

Now that you have down all the basics of working with JSON data in Haskell, let's take a look at a more complex problem.

40.4 Putting it all together: reading your NOAA data

In the preceding lesson, you learned how to use `HTTP.Simple` to save a JSON file to disk. You saved a list of NOAA data sets to a file named data.json. If you didn't run the code from lesson 39, you can get the data here: https://gist.github.com/willkurt/9dc14babbffea1a30c2a1e121a81bc0a. Now you're going to read in that file and print the names of the data sets. The interesting thing about this file is that the JSON isn't a simple type. Your JSON data has nested results and looks like this.

Listing 40.16 The JSON from the NOAA has a nested structure

```
{
   "metadata":{
      "resultset":{
         "offset":1,
         "count":11,
         "limit":25
      }
   },
   "results":[
      {
          "uid":"gov.noaa.ncdc:C00861",
         "mindate":"1763-01-01",
         "maxdate":"2017-02-01",
         "name":"Daily Summaries",
         "datacoverage":1,
         "id":"GHCND"
      },
   .....
```

You're going to model the entire response with a `NOAAResponse` data type. `NOAAResponse` is made up of two types: `Metadata` and `Results`. `Metadata` itself contains another type, `Resultset`. Then you have `NOAAResults`, which contains values.

You'll start with your basic result, because that's ultimately what you're interested in, and it doesn't contain any more sophisticated types. Because `Result` contains an `id` value, you need to define a custom implementation of your instances. Here's the data type for `Result`. You'll name this type `NOAAResult` to distinguish it from the `Result` type in Aeson.

Listing 40.17 Use `NOAAResult` type to print the names of the data sets

```
data NOAAResult = NOAAResult
                  { uid :: T.Text
                  , mindate :: T.Text
                  , maxdate :: T.Text
                  , name :: T.Text
                  , datacoverage :: Int
                  , resultId :: T.Text
                  } deriving Show
```

Because the data uses `id` instead of `resultId`, you need to make your own instance of `FromJSON`. You're not concerned about `ToJSON`, because you'll be reading only from the data.

Listing 40.18 Making `NOAAResult` an instance of `FromJSON`

```
instance FromJSON NOAAResult where
  parseJSON (Object v) =
    NOAAResult <$> v .: "uid"
               <*> v .: "mindate"
               <*> v .: "maxdate"
               <*> v .: "name"
               <*> v .: "datacoverage"
               <*> v .: "id"
```

Next you need to tackle the `Metadata` type. The first part of your `Metadata` is `Resultset`. Thankfully, you don't need a custom implementation of `FromJSON`. You just need to define your type, add `deriving (Generic)`, and make it an instance of your type class.

Listing 40.19 Using `Generic` to derive the `FromJSON` instance for `Resultset`

```
data Resultset = Resultset
                 { offset :: Int
                 , count :: Int
                 , limit :: Int
```

```
                } deriving (Show,Generic)

instance FromJSON Resultset
```

The `Metadata` data type itself has only the `Resultset` value, and it's simple to write.

Listing 40.20 Making the `Metadata` type

```
data Metadata = Metadata
               {
                 resultset :: Resultset
               } deriving (Show,Generic)

instance FromJSON Metadata
```

Finally, you put together these other types into your `NOAAResponse`. Like your other types, there's no issue with the naming of your values so you can derive the necessary class.

Listing 40.21 Putting all your types together into a `NOAAResponse` type

```
data NOAAResponse = NOAAResponse
                   { metadata :: Metadata
                   , results :: [NOAAResult]
                   } deriving (Show,Generic)

instance FromJSON NOAAResponse
```

Your goal is to print out all the types in the file. To do this, you'll create a `printResults IO` action. Because your data will be a `Maybe` type, you need to handle the case of the parse failing. For this, you'll print a message that an error occurred. Otherwise, you'll use `forM_` from the `Control.Monad` module (remember to import `Control.Monad`) to loop through your results and print them. The `forM_` function works just like the `mapM_` function, only it reverses the order of the data and the function used to map over the data.

Listing 40.22 Printing the results

```
printResults :: Maybe [NOAAResult] -> IO ()
printResults Nothing = print "error loading data"
printResults (Just results) =  do
   forM_ results (print . name)
     print dataName
```

Now you can write your `main`, which will read in the file, parse the JSON, and iterate through your results.

Listing 40.23 Putting everything together into your `main`

```
main :: IO ()
main = do
       jsonData <- B.readFile "data.json"
       let noaaResponse = decode jsonData :: Maybe NOAAResponse
       let noaaResults = results <$> noaaResponse
       printResults noaaResults
```

Now you can load your project into GHCi (or use `stack build` to run it if you'd prefer) and see how it works:

```
GHCi> main
"Daily Summaries"
"Global Summary of the Month"
"Global Summary of the Year"
"Weather Radar (Level II)"
"Weather Radar (Level III)"
"Normals Annual/Seasonal"
"Normals Daily"
"Normals Hourly"
"Normals Monthly"
"Precipitation 15 Minute"
"Precipitation Hourly"
```

And there you have it; you've successfully used Haskell to parse a nontrivial JSON file.

Summary

In this lesson, our objective was to teach you how to parse and create JSON files by using Haskell. You used the popular Aeson library, which makes it possible to convert back and forth between Haskell data types and JSON. The conversion between data types and JSON is achieved with two type classes: `FromJSON` and `ToJSON`. In the best case, you can use the `DeriveGeneric` language extension to derive these classes automatically. Even in the worst case, where you have to help Aeson translate your data types, doing this is still relatively easy. Let's see if you got this.

Q40.1 Make your `NOAAResponse` type an instance of `ToJSON`. This requires making all the types used by this type instances of `ToJSON` as well.

Q40.2 Make a `Sum` type called `IntList` and use `DerivingGeneric` to make it an instance of `ToJSON`. Don't use the existing `List` type, but rather write it from scratch. Here's an example of an `IntList`:

```
intListExample :: IntList
intListExample = Cons 1 $
                 Cons 2 EmptyList
```

41

LESSON

USING DATABASES IN HASKELL

After reading lesson 41, you'll be able to

- Connect to a SQLite database from Haskell
- Translate SQL rows into Haskell data types
- Create, read, update, and delete database data with Haskell

In this lesson, you'll learn how to work with databases when using Haskell. In particular, you'll use the SQLite3 relational database management system (RDBMS) and the `sqlite-simple` Haskell library. You'll explore this topic by building a command-line interface for a tool-lending library. This will require you to perform all of the essential CRUD tasks commonly associated with RDBMS use. The CRUD tasks are as follows:

- *Create*—Adding new data to the database
- *Read*—Querying the database for information
- *Update*—Modifying existing data in the database
- *Delete*—Removing data from the database

You'll use the `sqlite-simple` library to interact with your database. `sqlite-simple` is a *mid-level* abstraction over the database, meaning that while many of the low-level connection details are abstracted away, you'll still be writing a large amount of raw SQL queries. The most important abstraction that `sqlite-simple` helps with is transforming SQL queries into lists of Haskell data types.

Here's the rundown of the project you'll be building. Suppose you have a friend who's setting up a basic community tool-lending library. Your friend needs a system to help manage the basics of keeping track of the inventory and checking out tools from the library. From the RDBMS side of things, this project will involve three tables: tools, users, and checkedout. From the Haskell standpoint, you'll worry about modeling only users and tools. By the end of this lesson, you'll have a command-line application that supports the following operations:

- Listing all of the users and tools
- Listing all the checked-out and available tools
- Adding new users to the database
- Checking items back in
- Recording the number of times a tool has been checked out, and how recently

By the end of this lesson, we'll have covered performing the majority of database operations through Haskell.

41.1 Setting up your project

In this lesson, you'll keep all of your code in a stack project named `db-lesson`. As in all the lessons in this unit, you'll keep your code in the `Main` module for simplicity (though this project could easily be refactored into multiple files). You'll start with your app/Main.hs file. Here's the starter code, including the imports you'll use for this lesson.

Listing 41.1 The app/Main.hs file starter code

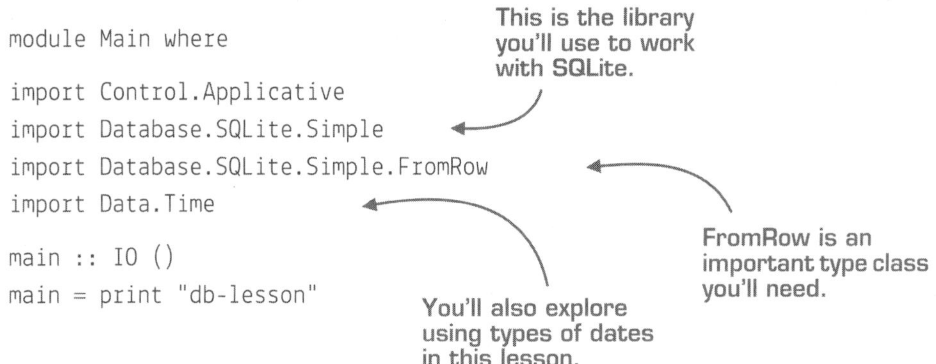

```
module Main where

import Control.Applicative
import Database.SQLite.Simple
import Database.SQLite.Simple.FromRow
import Data.Time

main :: IO ()
main = print "db-lesson"
```

This is the library you'll use to work with SQLite.
FromRow is an important type class you'll need.
You'll also explore using types of dates in this lesson.

The `build-depends` you need to add to the project's .cabal file is `sqlite-simple`, the module you'll be using to interact with SQLite, and `time`, which will help you manage dates.

Listing 41.2 The changes to `build-depends` in db-lesson.cabal

```
build-depends:       base
                   , db-notes
                   , time
                   , sqlite-simple
```

You'll also use the `OverloadedStrings` extension, because many of your strings will be interpreted as SQL queries by the SQLite Simple library.

Listing 41.3 Use the `OverloadedStrings` extension in db-lesson.cabal

```
extensions:          OverloadedStrings
```

After all of this code is in place, you can run the `setup` and `build` commands in stack to ensure that your project is set up correctly.

41.2 Using SQLite and setting up your database

For this lesson, you'll use the SQLite3 database management system, because it's easy to install and get started with. SQLite can be downloaded from www.sqlite.org. Because SQLite3 is designed to be easy to deploy, setup should be straightforward on your system (if you don't already have it installed).

Your tool library will use a database that consists of a users table, a tools table, and a checkedout table that represents which tools are checked out to which person. Figure 41.1 provides a basic entity-relationship diagram to show how your tables are set up.

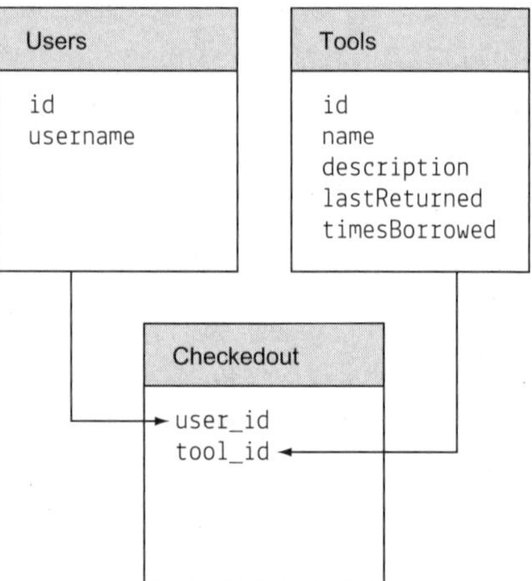

Figure 41.1 The setup of your database

You'll start your project off with sample data as well. Here's the code to build your database; this code will go in a file named build_db.sql, which should be kept in the root directory of your `db-lesson` project.

Listing 41.4 The code for building your database

```
DROP TABLE IF EXISTS checkedout;
DROP TABLE IF EXISTS tools;
DROP TABLE IF EXISTS users;

CREATE TABLE users (
       id INTEGER PRIMARY KEY,
       username TEXT
       );

CREATE TABLE tools (
       id INTEGER PRIMARY KEY,
       name TEXT,
       description TEXT,
       lastReturned TEXT,          <-- SQLite doesn't support date types.
       timesBorrowed INTEGER
       );

CREATE TABLE checkedout (
       user_id INTEGER,
       tool_id INTEGER
       );

INSERT INTO users (username) VALUES ('willkurt');

INSERT INTO tools (name,description,lastReturned,timesBorrowed)
VALUES ('hammer','hits stuff','2017-01-01',0);

INSERT INTO tools (name,description,lastReturned,timesBorrowed)
VALUES ('saw','cuts stuff','2017-01-01',0);
```

To run SQLite, you have to call `sqlite3` from the command line. You also need to pass in the database name, which is tools.db. Finally, you'll pipe in the build.sql file you just saved. Here's the command you need:

```
$ sqlite3 tools.db < build_db.sql
```

You can check out your database by using the `sqlite3` command along with the path to your database file. Once there, you can run SQL queries to ensure that everything has been installed correctly. The `sqlite>` prompt indicates that you're using your RDBMS interactively:

```
$ sqlite3 tools.db
sqlite> select * from tools;
1|hammer|hits stuff|2017-01-01|0
2|saw|cuts stuff|2017-01-01|0
```

Because your goal is to work with SQLite through Haskell, you won't be directly using the `sqlite` command again. If you like, you can always use `sqlite` directly to double-check the results of the code you've run.

41.2.1 Your Haskell data

One of the challenges when working with Haskell and an RBDMS such as SQLite is that your types in Haskell are typically much richer and more expressive than those in the RBDMS. SQLite, for example, doesn't support any types representing dates. This is a similar problem to what you have working with JSON data. Before diving into creating data in your database, let's look at your data from the Haskell perspective. Here's the definition of your `Tool` data type.

Listing 41.5 The definition of `Tool`, which should live in app/Main.hs

```
data Tool = Tool
 { toolId :: Int
 , name :: String
 , description :: String
 , lastReturned :: Day
 , timesBorrowed :: Int
 }
```

There's one type you haven't seen before in this definition of `Tool`, which is the `Day` type. The `Day` type is part of the `Data.Time` module. `Data.Time` contains a variety of useful time-related functions. Here's an example of getting the current time with `getCurrentTime` and transforming it into a `Day` type by using `utctDay`:

```
GHCi> getCurrentTime
2017-02-26 07:05:12.218684 UTC
GHCi> utctDay <$> getCurrentTime
2017-02-26
```

The other type you need to model is your `User`. The `User` type is much simpler than your `Tool` type, having values only for its `id` and `userName`.

Listing 41.6 The `User` data type

```
data User = User
 { userId :: Int
 , userName :: String
 }
```

The `User` and `Tool` types enable you to perform computation on any data that comes from your database. The most common computation will be displaying data about the users and tools you query. You can make sure the results look as you prefer by making these types instances of `Show`.

Listing 41.7 Making `User` and `Tool` instances of `Show`

```
instance Show User where
   show user = mconcat [ show $ userId user
                       , ".)  "
                       , userName user]

instance Show Tool where
   show tool = mconcat [ show $ toolId tool
                       , ".) "
                       , name tool
                       , "\n description: "
                       , description tool
                       , "\n last returned: "
                       , show $ lastReturned tool
                       , "\n times borrowed: "
                       , show $ timesBorrowed tool
                       , "\n"]
```

When you print your results, they should look like this:

```
1.) willkurt

1.) hammer
 description: hits stuff
 last returned: 2017-01-01
 times borrowed: 0
```

Now you're ready to start interacting with your database!

> **Quick check 41.1** Why is `mconcat` preferred for combining your strings over `++`?
>
> 1 Fewer characters to type
> 2 `++` works only on lists, not text
> 3 `mconcat` makes your code easier to refactor with text types

41.3 Creating data—inserting users and checking out tools

Of the four operations covered under CRUD, the first is Create. You've just used raw SQL to create your tables and data; now you're going to do this in Haskell. To insert data into your database, you need to connect to the database, create a SQL string, and then execute the SQL.

41.3.1 Adding new users to your database

At this point, you have only one user in your database. You need a command to add a user. You'll start with a function that takes a `userName` and inserts it into your database. To do this, you'll use the `execute` command, which allows you to insert users into your database. Your query string will contain a `(?)`, which allows you to safely pass values into your string. Before you can insert the user, you also need to establish a connection to your database. This connection is then passed along with your query and query parameters to the `execute` action. Here's your `addUser` action.

Listing 41.8 `addUser` action connects to database and inserts a user

```
addUser :: String -> IO ()
addUser userName = do
   conn <- open "tools.db"
   execute conn "INSERT INTO users (username) VALUES (?)"
```

First you have to open a connection to your database.

You execute a command by using the connection, a query, and query parameters.

QC 41.1 answer The answer is 3. Although you used `String` in this lesson, you often would prefer to use the `Text` type. `mconcat` works on all major string types: `String`, `Text`, and `ByteString`. This makes refactoring code to change types as easy as changing type signatures.

```
    (Only userName)
    print "user added"
  close conn
```

The Only constructor is used for your single-element tuple of parameters.

It's important to close the connection when you're finished.

The `Only` constructor is used to create single-element tuples. This is needed because `execute` expects you to pass in a tuple of a particular size for your values.

This is a good start, but most of your code will have to access the database, so the bulk of this `IO` action will need to be repeated verbatim. You can abstract this out by creating a `withConn` action to automatically handle opening and closing your database.

Listing 41.9 `withConn` lets you abstract out connecting to the database

```
withConn :: String -> (Connection -> IO ()) -> IO ()
withConn dbName action = do
   conn <- open dbName
   action conn
   close conn
```

This function takes a `String`, which is the name of the database, and an action that takes a connection as an argument. The end result is an action of type `IO ()`. You've successfully made it possible to add users to the database from Haskell.

Quick check 41.2 Refactor `addUser` to use `withConn`.

QC 41.2 answer

```
addUser :: String -> IO ()
addUser userName = withConn "tools.db" $
                   \conn -> do
                     execute conn "INSERT INTO users (username) VALUES (?)"
                       (Only userName)
                     print "user added"
```

41.3.2 Creating checkouts

Another useful insert to perform is to create a `checkout`. A `checkout` requires both a `userId` and a `toolId`. The code for your `checkout` is similar to that of adding a user, but you need to pass in two values.

Listing 41.10 Checking out by adding the `toolId` and `userId` to `checkedout`

```
checkout :: Int -> Int -> IO ()
checkout userId toolId = withConn "tools.db" $
                          \conn -> do
                            execute conn
                              "INSERT INTO checkedout
                              (user_id,tool_id) VALUES (?,?)"
                              (userId,toolId)
```

Notice that `(userId,toolId)` is a plain tuple with no `Only` data constructor needed.

With `checkout` and `addUser`, you have the basis for many of the key operations you want your application to perform. You can test these actions, but you have no way of seeing whether your results worked without opening SQLite to see if the database has changed. In the next section, you'll look at reading data from your database and transforming it into your Haskell data types.

41.4 Reading data from the database and FromRow

The challenge when working with SQL data in Haskell is that you need an easy way to make instances of Haskell data types from raw data. To achieve this, the `sqlite-simple` library includes a type class called `FromRow`. Here's the definition of `FromRow`, which contains only one method you need to implement, `fromRow`.

Listing 41.11 The definition of the `FromRow` type class

```
class FromRow a where
   fromRow :: RowParser a
```

The `fromRow` method returns a `RowParser` of type `a`, where `a` is the same type as whatever type you're making an instance of `FromRow`. You won't directly use `fromRow`, but it will be used by functions to query your data. The result is that if you implement `FromRow`, you can easily transform queries into lists of your data types.

41.4.1 Making your data an instance of FromRow

Creating an instance of `FromRow` is similar to creating an instance of `FromJSON` in the previous lesson. You have to tell the `RowParser` how to construct your data types. The key part is a function from `SQLite.Simple` called `field`. The `field` function is used internally by `SQLite.Simple` to consume the data from a row and transform it into the values used by your type constructors. Here are the instances of `FromRow` for both `User` and `Tool`.

Listing 41.12 Making `User` and `Tool` instances of `FromRow`

```
instance FromRow User where
   fromRow = User <$> field
                  <*> field

instance FromRow Tool where
   fromRow = Tool <$> field
                  <*> field
                  <*> field
                  <*> field
                  <*> field
```

Now that `User` and `Tool` are both instances of `FromRow`, you can make queries against your database and translate them directly into lists of users and tools.

41.4.2 Listing users and tools

To query your data, you use two related functions: `query` and `query_` (notice the underscore). Looking at their type signatures, you can see the difference:

```
query :: (FromRow r, ToRow q) => Connection -> Query -> q -> IO [r]
query_ :: FromRow r => Connection -> Query -> IO [r]
```

The type signatures of these two functions are the same, except the underscore version takes one less argument. The `query` function assumes that you're passing in a query string and parameter for that query. The `query_` function with an underscore is for queries that take queries with no parameters as arguments. Also notice that `Query` is its own type. You've been treating your queries as strings, but this is all thanks to the `OverloadedStrings` extension, which is automatically translating for you.

Quick check 41.3 Why do you need two functions, query and query_?

You'll use these queries to print your users and tools. Here's a printUsers function; notice that you must specify the type you're querying.

Listing 41.13 Printing users from your database

```
printUsers :: IO ()
printUsers = withConn "tools.db" $
             \conn ->  do
               resp <- query_ conn "SELECT * FROM users;" :: IO [User]
               mapM_ print resp
```

The printUsers action also takes advantage of the fact that User is an instance of Show, displaying the user data as you expect. Now that you can print users, you can also test adding users:

```
GHCi> printUsers
1.)  willkurt
GHCi> addUser "test user"
"user added"
GHCi> printUsers
1.) willkurt
2.) test user
```

The next thing you want to do is print tools. The only added complication you have with tools is that you'd like to run several queries:

- List all of your tools
- List the checked-out tools
- List the available tools

To help you out, you'll write a printToolQuery function that takes a query and prints out the tools returned by that query. Here's the printTool query along with the code for the other queries' lists.

QC 41.3 answer Primarily because of the way Haskell handles types, Haskell doesn't support variable arguments. An alternative to making two functions is to use a Sum type that represents both sets of arguments and use pattern matching.

Listing 41.14 A generic way to run any queries of tools from your database

```
printToolQuery :: Query -> IO ()
printToolQuery q =  withConn "tools.db" $
                       \conn ->  do
                         resp <- query_ conn q :: IO [Tool]
                         mapM_ print resp


printTools :: IO ()
printTools =  printToolQuery "SELECT * FROM tools;"


printAvailable :: IO ()
printAvailable = printToolQuery $ mconcat [ "select * from tools "
                                          , "where id not in "
                                          , "(select tool_id from
                                          ➥checkedout);"]

printCheckedout :: IO ()
printCheckedout = printToolQuery $
                  mconcat [ "select * from tools "
                          , "where id in "
                          , "(select tool_id from checkedout);"]
```

In GHCi, you can test these actions as well as make sure that your `checkout` action from earlier works as expected:

```
GHCi> printTools
1.) hammer
description: hits stuff
last returned: 2017-01-01
times borrowed: 0

2.) saw
description: cuts stuff
last returned: 2017-01-01
times borrowed: 0

GHCi> checkout 1 2
GHCi> printCheckedOut
2.) saw
```

```
description: cuts stuff
last returned: 2017-01-01
times borrowed: 0
```

Two major steps are left until you can put together your project. You need to be able to check tools back in, and after those tools are back in, you need to update them. Because updating is next in your CRUD process, you'll look at updating your data.

41.5 Updating existing data

When a tool is checked back in, you want to do two updates. First, you want to increment its existing `timesBorrowed` by 1; second, you want to update the `lastReturned` date to the current date. This requires you to update an existing row in your database, which is the most complex step in your process if you want to ensure that you avoid errors.

The first thing you want to do is select a tool from your database by ID. Your `selectTool` function takes a `connect` and a `toolId` to look up the tool. It returns a rather complicated type: `IO (Maybe Tool)`. The `IO` indicates that your database operations always occur in an `IO` context. The inner `Maybe` type is used because it's possible to pass in an incorrect ID, resulting in an empty query. Here's the code for `selectTool`, along with a helper function `firstOrNothing`.

Listing 41.15 Safely selecting a `Tool` by ID

```
selectTool :: Connection -> Int -> IO (Maybe Tool)
selectTool conn toolId = do
   resp <- query conn
           "SELECT * FROM tools WHERE id = (?)"
           (Only toolId) :: IO [Tool]
   return $ firstOrNothing resp

firstOrNothing :: [a] -> Maybe a
firstOrNothing [] = Nothing
firstOrNothing (x:_) = Just x
```

The `firstOrNothing` function looks at the list of results returned by your query. If the list is empty, it returns `Nothing`; if you have results (presumably just one, because the ID is unique), it returns the first one.

After you have your tool, you need to update it. Getting the current day requires an `IO` action, so you'll assume that value is passed in to your function so you can keep your `updateTool` function pure. The `updateTool` function takes an existing tool and returns a new tool with an updated `lastReturned` date and `timesBorrowed` count, using record syntax (lesson 11).

Listing 41.16 `updateTool` updates your tool

```
updateTool :: Tool -> Day -> Tool
updateTool tool date = tool
   { lastReturned = date
   , timesBorrowed = 1 + timesBorrowed tool
   }
```

Next you need a way to insert your update of a `Maybe Tool`. Because the tool is a `Maybe Tool`, you want your code to update your table only if the `Maybe` value isn't `Nothing`. Your `updateOrWarn` action will tell you that the item isn't found if the value is `Nothing`; otherwise, it'll update the necessary fields in your database.

Listing 41.17 Safely updating your database

```
updateOrWarn :: Maybe Tool -> IO ()
updateOrWarn Nothing = print "id not found"
updateOrWarn (Just tool) =  withConn "tools.db" $
                            \conn -> do
                              let q = mconcat ["UPDATE TOOLS SET  "
                                              ,"lastReturned = ?,"
                                              ," timesBorrowed = ? "
                                              ,"WHERE ID = ?;"]

                              execute conn q (lastReturned tool
                                             , timesBorrowed tool
                                             , toolId tool)
                              print "tool updated"
```

Finally, you need to tie all of these steps together. Your final action, `updateToolTable`, takes a `toolId`, fetches the current date, and then performs the necessary steps to update the tool in the table.

Listing 41.18 `updateToolTable` **combines all the steps for updating the tool table**

```
updateToolTable :: Int -> IO ()
updateToolTable toolId = withConn "tools.db" $
                     \conn -> do
                       tool <- selectTool conn toolId
                       currentDay <- utctDay <$> getCurrentTime
                       let updatedTool = updateTool <$> tool
                                                    <*> pure currentDay
                       updateOrWarn updatedTool
```

The `updateToolTable` action allows you to safely update the tools table, and will inform you if an error occurs while updating the data. The final step you have to look at is checking an ite//m back in, which is the case of deleting a row from checkedout.

The ToRow type class

You can also use the `ToRow` type class. But `ToRow` is much less useful, because it transforms your data types into a tuple of values. As you can see from our examples of creating and updating values, you either don't have all the information you need (in the case of creating) or need only a specific subset. For reference, here's how to make `Tool` an instance of `ToRow` (note that you need to import `Data.Text` as `T`):

```
instance ToRow Tool where
   toRow tool = [ SQLInteger $ fromIntegral $ toolId tool
                , SQLText $ T.pack $ name tool
                , SQLText $ T.pack $ description tool
                , SQLText $ T.pack $  show $ lastReturned tool
                , SQLInteger $ fromIntegral $ timesBorrowed tool ]
```

The `SQLText` and `SQLInteger` constructors transform Haskell `Text` and `Integer` types to SQL data. In practice, you'll likely use `ToRow` much less often than `FromRow`. Still, it's good to know it exists.

41.6 Deleting data from your database

The final step of the CRUD process is deletion. Deleting your data is simple: you use the `execute` action just as you did when creating data. Your `checkin` action takes a `toolID` and deletes the row from the checkedout table. Because each tool can be checked out to only one person at time, the tool ID is all the information you need.

Listing 41.19 Checking in a tool with `checkin`

```
checkin :: Int -> IO ()
checkin toolId =  withConn "tools.db" $
                    \conn -> do
                      execute conn
                        "DELETE FROM checkedout WHERE tool_id = (?);"
                        (Only toolId)
```

As mentioned in the preceding section, you never want to check in a tool in isolation, but want to ensure that the tool's information is updated. Your final database action will be `checkinAndUpdate`, which calls `checkin` and then `updateToolTable`.

Listing 41.20 Making sure your tool is updated when it's checked in

```
checkinAndUpdate :: Int -> IO ()
checkinAndUpdate toolId = do
   checkin toolId
   updateToolTable toolId
```

At this point, you've seen every part of the CRUD process for working with a database when using Haskell. With all these basic tools in place, you can put together the rest of your command-line interface and check it out!

41.7 Putting it all together

You've written all the code you need for your database interaction. All you need now is to wrap these actions into a usable interface. Most of your database updates require a prompt from the user requesting either a username or an ID. Here are some `IO` actions that capture this behavior.

Listing 41.21 Organizing your database actions

```
promptAndAddUser :: IO ()
promptAndAddUser = do
   print "Enter new user name"
   userName <- getLine
   addUser userName


promptAndCheckout :: IO ()
promptAndCheckout = do
   print "Enter the id of the user"
   userId <- pure read <*> getLine
   print "Enter the id of the tool"
   toolId <- pure read <*> getLine
   checkout userId toolId

promptAndCheckin :: IO ()
promptAndCheckin = do
   print "enter the id of tool"
   toolId <- pure read <*> getLine
   checkinAndUpdate toolId
```

You can then bundle all of your actions, prompting the user into a single action that takes a command from the user and then performs that command. Notice that each of these commands, except `quit`, uses the >> operator (which performs an action, throws away the result, and performs the next) to call `main`. This allows your command-line interface to repeatedly prompt the user for more input until the user quits your program.

Listing 41.22 `performCommand` organizes all the commands the user can enter

```
performCommand :: String -> IO ()
performCommand command
   | command == "users" = printUsers >> main
   | command == "tools" = printTools >> main
   | command == "adduser" = promptAndAddUser >> main
   | command == "checkout" = promptAndCheckout >> main
   | command == "checkin" = promptAndCheckin >> main
   | command == "in" = printAvailable >> main
```

```
  | command == "out" = printCheckedout >> main
  | command == "quit" = print "bye!"
  | otherwise = print "Sorry command not found" >> main
```

Quick check 41.4 Why can't you use >>= instead of >>?

1. You can; it works fine.
2. >>= implies that `main` accepts an argument, which it doesn't.
3. >>= isn't a valid Haskell operator.

Finally, here's your revised `main`. You've been able to factor out most of the code you need into separate parts so your `main IO` action is minimal.

Listing 41.23 Your final `main IO` action

```
main :: IO ()
main = do
   print "Enter a command"
   command <- getLine
   performCommand command
```

The careful reader may notice that `performCommand` calls `main`, and `main` executes the `performCommand` action, leading to code that's recursive. In most languages, this would be a receipt for a stack overflow, but Haskell is smart about handling this. Haskell will notice that each function calls the other last, and is able to optimize this safely.

Now you can build your program and run it to test it out:

```
$ stack exec db-lesson-exe
"Enter a command"
users
1.)  willkurt
"Enter a command"
adduser
"Enter new user name"
```

QC 41.4 answer The answer is 2. When you use >>=, you're passing an argument in a context; the >> operator is used when you want to chain together actions and disregard their output.

```
test user
"user added"
"Enter a command"
tools
1.) hammer
 description: hits stuff
 last returned: 2017-01-01
 times borrowed: 0

2.) saw
 description: cuts stuff
 last returned: 2017-01-01
 times borrowed: 0

"Enter a command"
checkout
"Enter the id of the user"
1
"Enter the id of the tool"
2
"Enter a command"
out
2.) saw
 description: cuts stuff
 last returned: 2017-01-01
 times borrowed: 0

"Enter a command"
checkin
"enter the id of tool"
2
"tool updated"
"Enter a command"
in
1.) hammer
 description: hits stuff
 last returned: 2017-01-01
 times borrowed: 0
```

```
2.) saw
 description: cuts stuff
 last returned: 2017-02-26
 times borrowed: 1

"Enter a command"
quit
"bye!"
```

You've successfully implemented all the CRUD operations in Haskell, and created a useful tool that your friend can use to manage the tool-lending library.

Summary

In this lesson, our objective was to teach you how to make a simple database-driven application using `SQLite.Simple`. You were able to use the `FromRow` instance to make it easy for users to transform data from your SQLite3 database into Haskell types. You learned how to create, read, update, and delete data from a database through Haskell. In the end, you developed a simple application that allows you to perform a range of tasks related to managing a tool library. Let's see if you got this.

Q41.1 Create an `IO` action named `addTool`, like `addUser`, to add a tool to the database.

Q41.2 Add an `addtool` command that prompts the user for information and then adds the tool by using the `addTool` action from the preceding question.

LESSON 42

EFFICIENT, STATEFUL ARRAYS IN HASKELL

After reading lesson 42, you'll be able to

- Use the `UArray` type for efficient storage and retrieval
- Perform stateful computation on arrays with `STUArray`
- Treat properly encapsulated, stateful functions as pure functions

After finishing this book on Haskell, you get a call from a recruiter at GooMicroBook asking if you'd like to interview. You say you'd love to, and the recruiter mentions that there will be a coding interview in the programming language of your choice. "Any language I want?" you eagerly ask. The recruiter confirms that, yes, you can use any language. With delight, you say you'd like to do the interview in Haskell.

You get to your interview, and your interviewer walks in the room. She asks you to solve some algorithm questions on the whiteboard. After eating, breathing, and dreaming about Haskell for many months, you can hardly wait to show of your elite programming skills. She starts off with a common question: "Implement a linked list for me." You run up to the board and write this:

```
data MyList a = EmptyList | Cons a (MyList a)
```

To your secret pleasure, the interviewer seems a bit surprised when you say, "Done!" You go into a long rant explaining the virtues of Haskell, how powerful types are, and the value of pure functions. After listening to you patiently and kindly refraining from mentioning her PhD work in type theory, she tells you that she's impressed. "Okay then, since you've done such a good job on this one, I'll give you an easy question next." You're ready to show off even more Haskell; maybe you'll even use `Monad`! "All that I want you to do is implement a simple, boring, in-place bubble sort." Suddenly you realize that maybe Haskell wasn't the best choice for this interview.

Writing a bubble sort with Haskell has a few large issues. The first is that you've relied heavily on lists as your primary data structure, but they're not nearly as efficient as proper arrays for this type of problem. A much larger issue is the requirement that the sort be *in place*; You can't create a copy of your array. Nearly all the code you've written in this book relies on changing the state of a data structure the functional way: creating a new version of the structure and discarding the original. For the majority of problems, this is both reasonably efficient and easy to do. Sorting an array is one case where you absolutely need to modify the state of a data structure for reasons of efficiency.

Thankfully, if you read this lesson, you'll be prepared for this scenario. You're going to finish this book by tackling a problem that seems impossible in Haskell: efficient, in-place array algorithms. You'll learn about Haskell's strict (nonlazy) array type, `UArray`. Then you'll see that there's a context for performing mutation on an array by using the `STUArray` type. Finally, you'll put it all together to implement a bubble sort algorithm. Even though a bubble sort algorithm itself is the least efficient sorting algorithm, your code will run much faster than if you had written it using a list.

Consider this In many cases, using stateful mutation can lead to bugs in your code. But stateful mutation is essential to nearly all efficient array-based algorithms. The reason Haskell avoids stateful programs is that this makes it trivial to violate the principle of referential transparency: given the same inputs, a function will always return the same outputs.

But, even in object-oriented programming it's desirable and sometimes possible to have perfect encapsulation. Even though an object may perform stateful changes internally, the programmer never notices this, and the rules of referential transparency can be maintained. If you can use types to ensure that your stateful code is perfectly encapsulated, can you somehow safely use stateful code in your Haskell programs?

42.1 Creating efficient arrays in Haskell with the UArray type

You're facing three efficiency problems in your bubble-storing challenge:

- Lists are inherently slower than arrays for operations that involve looking up values.
- Lazy evaluation can cause major performance problems in practice.
- In-place sorting requires mutation (stateful programming).

The first two of these efficiencies can be solved by using the `UArray` type. In the next section, you'll go into detail about how the `UArray` type improves on these as well as learning basics of creating `UArray`s.

42.1.1 The inefficiencies of lazy lists

The first problem is that you need an array type. So far in this book, you've relied heavily on lists. But for problems such as sorting, lists are often extremely inefficient. One of the reasons for this inefficiency is that you can't directly access elements of a list. In unit 1, you learned about the `!!` operator for looking up an element in a list. If you create a large list, you can see just how poorly this lookup performs in practice.

Listing 42.1 An example of a reasonably large list of 10 million values

```
aLargeList :: [Int]
aLargeList = [1 .. 10000000]
```

You learned a while back that you can time functions in GHCi by using `:set +s`. By using this command, you can see how long it takes to look up the last element in your list:

```
GHCi> :set +s
GHCi> aLargeList !! 9999999
10000000
(0.05 secs, 460,064 bytes)
```

You can see that this took 0.05 seconds to look up, or 50 milliseconds. Although this isn't incredibly slow compared to an HTTP request, it's still a long time to look up an element.

You'll be using the type `UArray` on your arrays. For comparison, here's the equivalent-sized `UArray` (we'll explain building the array in the next section).

Listing 42.2 Your `UArray`, also containing 10 million values

```
aLargeArray :: UArray Int Int
aLargeArray = array (0,9999999) []
```

When you perform the same test in GHCi, using the `UArray` lookup operator `!`, you find it's essentially instantaneous:

```
GHCi> aLargeArray ! 9999999
0
(0.00 secs, 456,024 bytes)
```

The *U* in `UArray` stands for *unboxed*. Unboxed arrays don't use lazy evaluation (they use strict evaluation). You've seen this come up before in unit 4 in regards to both `Text` and `ByteString` types. Lazy evaluation, although powerful, is another frequent cause of inefficiency.

To explore the performance issues of lazy evaluation, let's look at a modified version of your `aLargeList`, `aLargeArrayList`.

Listing 42.3 Doubling the values in `aLargeList` impacts performance

```
aLargeListDoubled :: [Int]
aLargeListDoubled = map (*2) aLargeList
```

Now in GHCi (with `:set +s`), you can see what happens when you want to find the length of `aLargeListDoubled`:

```
GHCi> length aLargeListDoubled
10000000
(1.58 secs, 1,680,461,376 bytes)
```

Wow! It took 1.58 seconds to get the length of your list. Even more astonishing, it took 1.68 gigabytes of memory to perform this operation! The inherent inefficiencies in the list data structure don't explain this amazing use of system resources. You can demonstrate this further by running this exact code a second time in GHCi (in the same session):

```
GHCi> length aLargeListDoubled
10000000
(0.07 secs, 459,840 bytes)
```

To understand what's going on, you have to recall how lazy evaluation works. None of your computation on the list occurs until you absolutely need it. This includes generating the list in the first place. When you define `aLargeList`, Haskell stores the computations that you need to generate the list. When you multiply that list by 2 to create `aLargeListDoubled`, Haskell still hasn't evaluated anything. Finally, when you print out the length of the list, Haskell goes through and starts building the list and remembering that it needs to multiply each value. All of these computations Haskell plans to perform (technically called *thunks*) are stored in memory. For small lists, this isn't a notable hit to performance, but you can see how this affects performance on large lists. Given that 10 million characters isn't a particularly large amount of text, this is why `Data.Text` is strongly preferred over `String`.

The catch with using unboxed arrays is that they work only with primitive types: `Int`, `Char`, `Bool`, and `Double`. Haskell does offer a more general `Array` type that will work with any data the same way that `List` does, but `Array` is a lazy data structure. Our aim in this lesson is performance with classic computer science algorithms. For this purpose, `UArray` is definitely the data type to use. To use the `UArray` type, you'll import `Data.Array.Unboxed` to the top of your module. Additionally, if using stack, you need to add `array` to the list of `build-depends`.

42.1.2 Creating a UArray

As in most programming languages, when you create an array in Haskell, you have to specify its size. Unlike with most languages, you get to choose what your indices are! `UArray`s take two type parameters; the first is for the type of the index, and the second is for the type of the value. You have some flexibility in the type you can use for the index. You can use types that are members of `Enum` and `Bounded`. This means your index could be `Char` or `Int`, but not `Double` (not an instance of `Enum`), and not `Integer` (not an instance of `Bounded`). You could even have the index be of type `Bool`, but that would always be a two-element array. For the most part, you want your indices' `Int` types to be 0 to length –1. To create a `UArray`, you use the `array` function. The `array` function takes two arguments:

- The first is a pair of values in a tuple representing your lower and upper bounds for your indices.
- The second argument is a list of (index, value) pairs.

If you're missing an index in your pairs, Haskell will provide a default value. For `Int` types, this is `0`; and for `Bools`, it's `False`. Here's an example of creating a zero-indexed array of `Bools`. You're setting only a single value to `True`; the rest will default to `False`.

Listing 42.4 Creating a zero index array of Bool

```
zeroIndexArray :: UArray Int Bool
zeroIndexArray = array (0,9) [(3,True)]
```

You can look up values in your `UArray` by using the `!` operator (similar to the `!!` operator for lists). In GHCi, you can see that all of the values you didn't specify in the list of pairs are `False`:

```
GHCi> zeroIndexArray ! 5
False
GHCi> zeroIndexArray ! 3
True
```

If you do much mathematical computing in languages such as R or Matlab, you're used to using arrays indexed from 1. Most programming languages targeted toward mathematical computing use 1-indexed arrays, as this aligns more closely with conventions in mathematical notation. In Haskell, it's trivial to change your array indexing system by passing in a different pair for your bounds. Here's a 1-indexed array with all the `Bool`s set to `True`. You'll use your `zip` function combined with `cycle` to generate a list of value pairs that are all `True`.

Listing 42.5 An array indexed starting with 1

```
oneIndexArray :: UArray Int Bool
oneIndexArray = array (1,10) $ zip [1 .. 10] $ cycle [True]
```

As you can see, in GHCi all the values are set to `True` and your `UArray` starts at 1 and goes to 10:

```
GHCi> oneIndexArray ! 1
True
GHCi> oneIndexArray ! 10
True
```

Just as with most other programming languages, if you try to access an element outside your index bounds, you'll get an error:

```
GHCi> oneIndexArray ! 0
*** Exception: Ix{Int}.index: Index (0) out of range ((1,10))
```

Quick check 42.1 Create an array with the following signature:

```
qcArray :: UArray Int Bool
```

The array contains five elements indexed at 0 and the 2, and three elements are set to `True`.

42.1.3 Updating your UArray

Although accessing values in your `UArray` is great, you also need to be able to update it. The `UArray` can be updated like any functional data structure, by creating a copy of it with the appropriate value changes. Let's suppose you have an array representing the number of beans in four buckets.

Listing 42.6 A `UArray` representing beans in buckets

```
beansInBuckets :: UArray Int Int
beansInBuckets = array (0,3) []
```

Because you passed in an empty list of pairs for initial values, your `UArray` has been initialized to zeros:

```
GHCi> beansInBuckets ! 0
0
GHCi> beansInBuckets ! 2
0
```

Quick check 42.2 Rather than assume your values will be initialized to zeros, make sure of it.

QC 42.1 answer

```
qcArray :: UArray Int Bool
qcArray = array (0,4) [(1,True),(2,True)]
```

QC 42.2 answer

```
beansInBuckets' :: UArray Int Int
beansInBuckets' = array (0,3) $ zip [0 .. 3] $ cycle [0]
```

Now suppose you want to add five beans to bucket 1 and six beans to bucket 3 (with bucket 0 being your first bucket). You can do this by using the (//) operator. The first argument to (//) is your UArray, and the second argument is a new list of pairs. The result is a new UArray with the updated values.

Listing 42.7 Updating your UArray the functional way with //

```
updatedBiB :: UArray Int Int
updatedBiB = beansInBuckets // [(1,5),(3,6)]
```

You can see in GHCi that your values have been updated:

```
GHCi> updatedBiB ! 1
5
GHCi> updatedBiB ! 2
0
GHCi> updatedBiB ! 3
6
```

Next you want to add two beans to every bucket. It makes sense that you frequently want to update an existing value. To do this, you can use the accum function. This function takes a binary function, a UArray, and a list of values to apply the function to. Here's an example of adding two beans to every bucket:

```
GHCi> accum (+) updatedBiB $ zip [0 .. 3] $ cycle [2]
array (0,3) [(0,2),(1,7),(2,2),(3,8)]
```

You've solved one of the major problems with using lists for your data. With UArray, you can get efficient lookups as well as a more efficient data structure. But one glaring issue is still present. Nearly all truly efficient array-based algorithms are *in place*. Even bubble sort, which is the least efficient of the sorting algorithms, doesn't require you to use any new arrays. When you update an array in place, you don't have to have a second copy of the array to perform the update. But this is only possible because of an inherent statefulness of the array. When you used UArray, you were able to replicate an artificial sense of mutable state. For many examples, this is preferable to making changes to your data structure. But when you're using state specifically for efficiency reasons, this is a terrible solution.

Quick check 42.3 Try doubling the number of beans in each bucket.

42.2 Mutating state with STUArray

The vast majority of the time, Haskell forcing the programmer to remove statefulness from the code results in safer, more predictable code with roughly the same performance. This isn't true for most array algorithms. If Haskell had no way to mutate state in these cases, a wide range of essential algorithms would be off-limits in Haskell.

Haskell does have a solution to this problem. You'll be using a special type of `UArray` called an `STUArray`. The `STUArray` uses a more general type called `ST`. `ST` allows for stateful, nonlazy programming. In this lesson, you'll focus only on `STUArray`, but it's important to recognize that the solutions you present here for working with arrays can be extended to a larger class of stateful programs.

To use `STUArray`, you'll add the following imports:

```
import Data.Array.ST
import Control.Monad
import Control.Monad.ST
```

`STUArray` is an instance of `Monad`. In unit 5, you spent a lot of time looking at the family of type classes that include `Functor`, `Applicative`, and `Monad`. The aim of all of these type classes is to allow you to perform arbitrary computation within a context. You've seen a variety of examples of this throughout the book:

- `Maybe` types model the context of missing values.
- `List` types can be used to represent the context of nondeterministic computing.
- `IO` types allow you to separate stateful, error-prone I/O code from your pure functions.
- `Either` types provide a more detailed way to handle errors over `Maybe` types.

Like `IO`, `STUArray` allows you to perform computation normally forbidden in Haskell in a safe context. Just like `IO` actions, when working with `STUArrays`, you'll use do-notation to treat types in the `STUArray` context, just as if they were regular data.

QC 42.3 answer

```
accum (*) updateBib $ zip [0 .. 3] $ cycle [3]
```

The key power `STUArray` offers is the ability to change values in a `UArray` (see figure 42.1 for a visual explanation). This is the final efficiency gain you need in order to achieve efficiency on par with programming languages that allow state. By being able to change values in place, you can save tremendously on memory usage, and by not having to re-create a new copy of your data structure with each change, you can also save on time. This is the key to writing a bubble sort that's as efficient as you'd find in an algorithms text book.

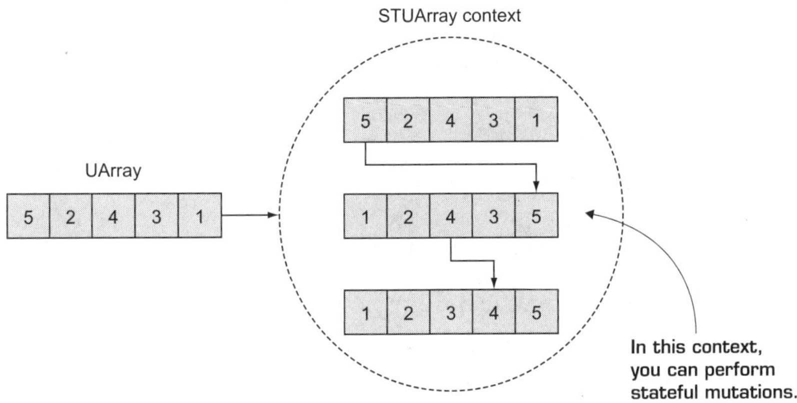

Figure 42.1 The `STUArray` is a context that allows for stateful mutations.

One important thing to understand about `STUArrays` and the `ST` type in general is that they aren't a hack that allows you to disregard all the functional purity you've worked so hard for. `STUArray` exists to allow you to perform stateful programming only when that statefulness is indistinguishable from pure code for the users of your functions. The vast majority of changes in data structures can be done with both reasonable efficiency and great safety, using the functional data structures you've used throughout the book.

You'll learn how to use `STUArray` by writing a function, called `listToSTUArray`, that takes a list of `Ints` and transforms that into an `STUArray`. In your first draft of `listToSTUArray`, you'll create an empty `STUArray` the size of your list. This is similar to initializing an empty array of a fixed size, only you'll do it in a monad. The `STUArray` type uses the `newArray` function, which takes a pair representing the bounds of the array as well as a value for initializing the array.

Listing 42.8 A first sketch of your `listToSTUArray` function

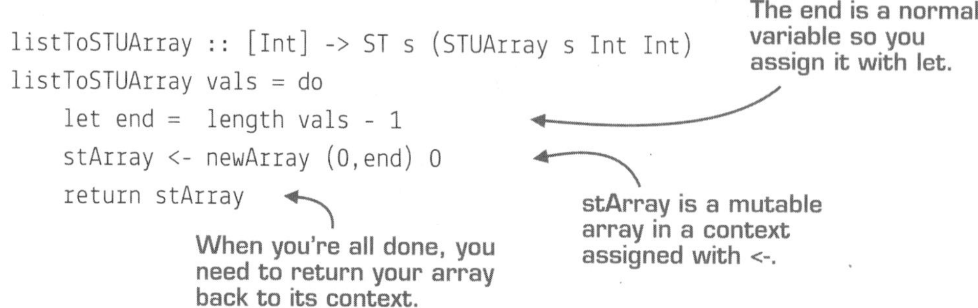
The end is a normal variable so you assign it with let.
stArray is a mutable array in a context assigned with <-.
When you're all done, you need to return your array back to its context.

```
listToSTUArray :: [Int] -> ST s (STUArray s Int Int)
listToSTUArray vals = do
    let end =  length vals - 1
    stArray <- newArray (0,end) 0
    return stArray
```

Next you want to add your loop, which you'll run through your list, and update your `stArray` value. You'll use `forM_` from `Control.Monad`. The `forM_` action takes your data and a function to apply to the data as arguments. This has the nice property of replicating a `for in` loop in languages such as Python.

To demonstrate how this replicates using a typical `for` loop, you'll use a list of indices and `(!!)` to look up values in your list. It'd be more efficient to zip these indices with the list values, but you want to replicate the feel of working in a more stateful language. The only thing left is for you to write the values from the list to your `stArray` value. For this, you'll use the `writeArray` function, which takes an `STUArray`, an index, and your value. The `writeArray` function performs a stateful mutation of your underlying array and doesn't create a copy of it.

Listing 42.9 The full code for copying a list to an `STUArray`

```
listToSTUArray :: [Int] -> ST s (STUArray s Int Int)
listToSTUArray vals = do
    let end =  length vals - 1
    myArray <- newArray (0,end) 0
    forM_ [0 .. end] $ \i -> do
      let val = vals !! i
      writeArray myArray i val
    return myArray
```

This forM_ action replicates a for loop in most languages.

Looking up val from a list isn't stateful, so it's assigned with a let.

Your writeArray function rewrites the data in your array.

With your `forM_` loop, you've written code that's similar to what you'd write in other stateful programming languages if you needed to.

If you load this in GHCi, you'll see that your code runs fine, except for one major problem:

```
GHCi> listToSTUArray [1,2,3]
<<ST action>>
```

Just as when you use the IO type, when using the ST type through STUArray, you end up with a program in a context. But unlike IO, there's no obvious way for you to show this stateful code. Thankfully, unlike IO, there's a way for you to take values out of a context when you're using STUArray.

42.3 Taking values out of the ST context

When you first learned about the IO type, you saw that it enabled you to keep your relatively dangerous IO code trapped in a context. Although STUArray is similar to IO, you're dealing with a much safer context. For starters, even though your code uses state, you're still upholding referential transparency. Every time you run listToSTUArray on the same input, you'll get exactly the same output. This brings up an important point about referential transparency and encapsulation in object-oriented programming languages. Encapsulation in OOP means that objects properly hide all of their implementation details from the user. Even in OOP, statefulness that breaks encapsulation is bad. The trouble is that OOP has no mechanism to enforce that state changes are property encapsulated. In your listToSTUArray code, because statefulness is contained in a context, you're forced to make sure your stateful code obeys encapsulation. Because STUArray is enforcing encapsulation, you're not constrained by the same limitations of IO. You can take values out of STUArray by using a function named runSTUArray (visualized in figure 42.2).

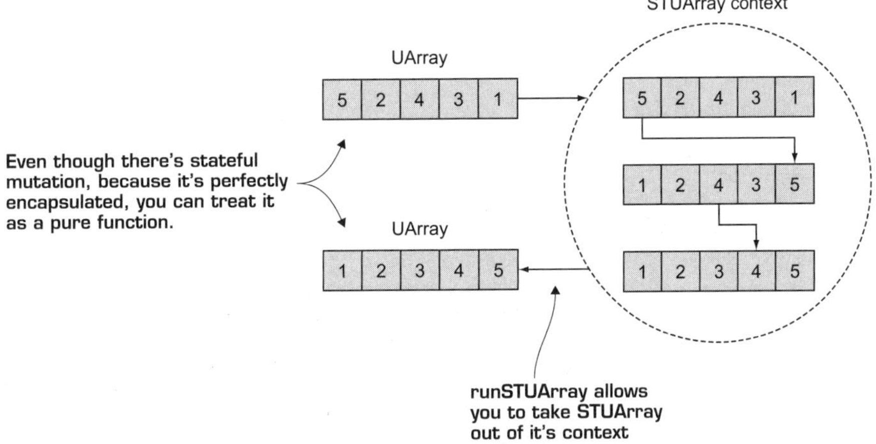

Figure 42.2 Unlike IO, you can take values out of the STUArray context.

The type signature of runSTUArray is as follows:

```
runSTUArray :: ST s (STUArray s i e) -> UArray i e
```

With runSTUArray, you can get the best of both worlds. You can keep your stateful code in a safe context, but still treat it as pure code. Here's a new function, listToUArray, that uses stateful programming but appears to be a pure function.

Listing 42.10 You can treat listToUArray as a pure function

```
listToUArray :: [Int] -> UArray Int Int
listToUArray vals = runSTUArray $ listToSTUArray vals
```

Now you can run the program in GHCi and get a meaningful result:

```
GHCi> listToUArray [1,2,3]
array (0,2) [(0,1),(1,2),(2,3)]
```

The important thing to realize is that using runSTUArray isn't cheating or allowing you to slip dangerous stateful code into your pure programs. Because STUArray forces you to maintain perfect encapsulation, you can leave the context of the STUArray without violating any of the core rules of functions introduced in lesson 2. Your code remains safe and predictable.

One thing worth noting is that it's common in Haskell to avoid writing an intermediary function such as listToSTUArray. Instead, you'd typically write listToUArray like this.

Listing 42.11 A common way of working with STUArrays and runSTUArray

```
listToUArray :: [Int] -> UArray Int Int
listToUArray vals = runSTUArray $ do
    let end =  length vals - 1
    myArray <- newArray (0,end) 0
    forM_ [0 .. end] $ \i -> do
        let val = vals !! i
        writeArray myArray i val
    return myArray
```

This version of listToUArray combines both of your function definitions into one.

The ST type

The ST type generalizes the behavior you see in STUArray. The STUArray type relies primarily on three actions: newArray, readArray, and writeArray. For the ST type, these are replaced with the more general functions: newSTRef, readSTRef, and writeSTRef. Likewise, instead of runSTUArray, you use runST. Here's a simple example of a swapST function that statefully swaps the values of two variables in a 2-tuple:

```
swapST :: (Int,Int) -> (Int,Int)
swapST (x,y) = runST $ do
    x' <- newSTRef x
    y' <- newSTRef y
    writeSTRef x' y
    writeSTRef y' x
    xfinal <- readSTRef x'
    yfinal <- readSTRef y'
    return (xfinal,yfinal)
```

Just as with STUArray, the primary purpose of all ST types is to allow you to implement perfectly encapsulated, stateful computation.

42.4 Implementing a bubble sort

You're finally ready to write your own version of a bubble sort in Haskell! In case you're not familiar with it, the bubble sort algorithm works as follows:

1. Start at the beginning of the array and compare a value to the value next to it.
2. If the original value is larger than the one next to it, swap them.
3. Repeat this until the largest value has "bubbled" to the end of the array.
4. Repeat this process with the $n - 1$ elements remaining in the array.

Figure 42.3 illustrates the algorithm.

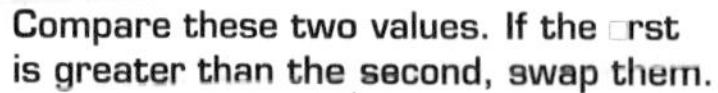

Compare these two values. If the first
is greater than the second, swap them.

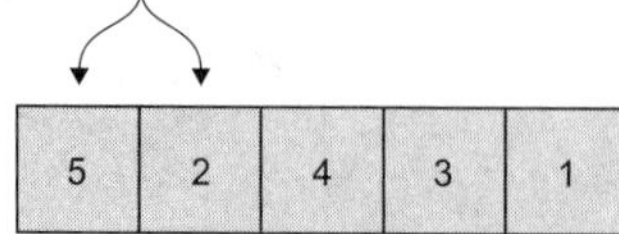

Repeat until you reach
the end of the array.

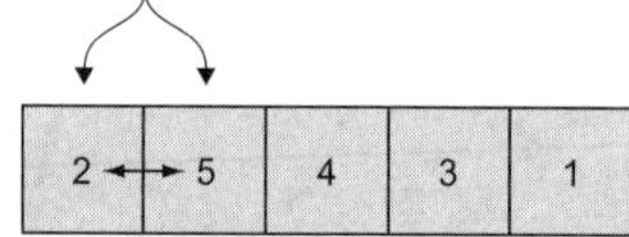

After you reach the end of the array, you know
that the largest value has "bubbled" to the top.

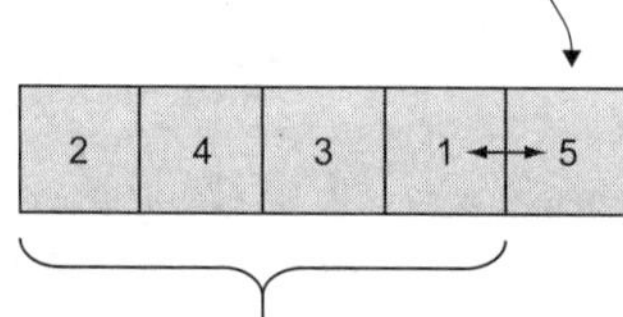

Now you just have to repeat
this process for the remaining
n–1 elements left in the array.

Figure 42.3 The bubble sort algorithm

You'll start with a `UArray` that you want to sort. You'll use the `listArray` function that's similar to the `listToUArry` function you wrote, but also takes a pair of bounds as input.

Listing 42.12 Sample data created using `listArray`

```
myData :: UArray Int Int
myData = listArray (0,5) [7,6,4,8,10,2]
```

Quick check 42.4 Use your `listToUArray` function to define `myData`.

QC 42.4 answer

```
myData' :: UArray Int Int
myData' = listToUArray [7,6,4,8,10,2]
```

To implement your `bubbleSort`, you need to introduce a few new functions. One thing you haven't done yet is use an existing `UArray` in the context of an `STUArray`. Just because you're in a context doesn't mean that you can treat `UArray` as though it were stateful. To do this, you use a function called `thaw`, which will unfreeze your `UArray` so you can work with it. You'll also use the `bounds` function, which gives you a pair representing the bounds of your array so you can figure out where it ends. `STUArray` has a function called `readArray` that reads a stateful value from an array. Finally, you'll use an interesting function named `when`, which works like an `if` without a `then` in most programming languages. Here's the implementation of `bubbleSort`.

Listing 42.13 Your implementation of `bubbleSort`

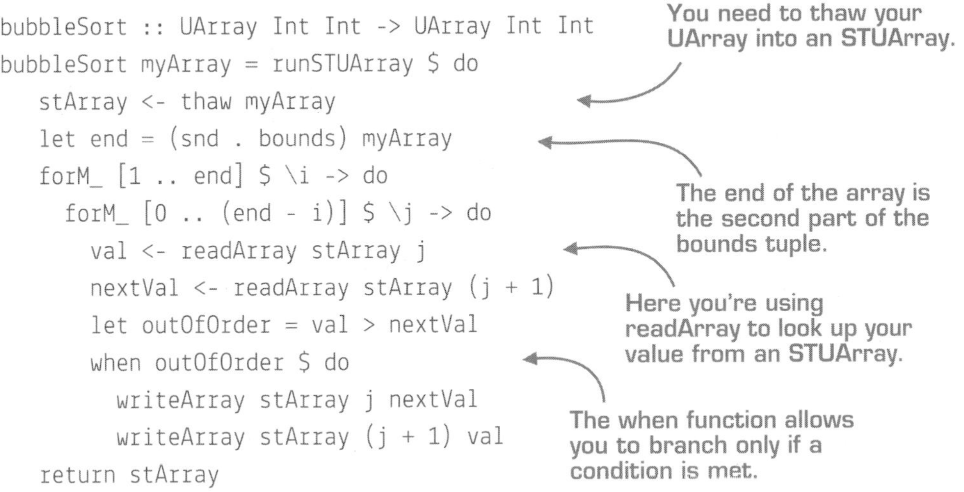

```
bubbleSort :: UArray Int Int -> UArray Int Int
bubbleSort myArray = runSTUArray $ do
   stArray <- thaw myArray
   let end = (snd . bounds) myArray
   forM_ [1 .. end] $ \i -> do
     forM_ [0 .. (end - i)] $ \j -> do
       val <- readArray stArray j
       nextVal <- readArray stArray (j + 1)
       let outOfOrder = val > nextVal
       when outOfOrder $ do
         writeArray stArray j nextVal
         writeArray stArray (j + 1) val
   return stArray
```

You need to thaw your UArray into an STUArray.
The end of the array is the second part of the bounds tuple.
Here you're using readArray to look up your value from an STUArray.
The when function allows you to branch only if a condition is met.

You can try out your `bubbleSort` function on your data:

```
GHCi> bubbleSort myData
array (0,5) [(0,2),(1,4),(2,6),(3,7),(4,8),(5,10)]
```

Now you have an imperative algorithm implemented in Haskell. The best part is that to do this, you didn't have to give up on any of the features that you've grown to love about Haskell. You've written a program that's efficient (well, for a bubble sort). At the same time, this code is predictable and obeys referential transparency.

Summary

In this lesson, our objective was to teach you how to write stateful, efficient algorithms in Haskell. You first learned about the `UArray` type, which allows for strictly evaluated arrays in Haskell. The downside of `UArray` is that you still have to treat state as you would for any other functional data structure. You then saw that `STUArray` allows you to perform stateful programming much the same way that `IO` types allow you to perform I/O programming. Because of the context of the STUArray, you're forced to maintain proper encapsulation. In practice, perfect encapsulation is the same as referential transparency. Therefore, you can transform your `STUArray` back into a regular `UArray`. This ultimately allows you to treat your stateful code as a pure function because it behaves like one. Let's see if you got this.

Q42.1 One of the most important operations in the implementation of a genetic algorithm is combining two arrays of Booleans through an operation called *crossover*. Crossover takes as input a pair of equal-sized arrays. Then a cutoff point is chosen, and the top and bottom are swapped. The final value is this new pair of arrays. Here's an illustration using lists and an example (using 1 for `True` and 0 for `False`):

```
([1,1,1,1,1],[0,0,0,0,0])
```

If you perform crossover at index 3, your result should be

```
[1,1,1,0,0]
```

Implement crossover where the result is a `UArray` but the crossover itself is performed using `STUArrays`.

Q42.2 Write a function that takes a `UArray Int Int` as an input. The input will have a mixture of zeros and other values. The function, `replaceZeros`, should return the array with all of the zeros replaced with the value –1.

Afterword

WHAT'S NEXT?

Undoubtedly, the greatest challenge in writing a Haskell book is determining the scope. The most wonderful and simultaneously terrifying part of Haskell is its seemingly unlimited number of topics to learn. Unfortunately, it's impossible to write a Haskell book without feeling that you've left out a great deal of interesting content.

The goal of this book has always been to provide a foundation for a solid understanding of both Haskell and functional programming in general. The good news is that if you've reached this point in the book, you have many options for taking your journey further. Even if you stop here, I'm confident that your view of software, programming, and computation in general has been expanded quite a bit. If you're interested in pursuing the topics in this book further, this afterword provides a few options of where to go next, depending on which direction interests you the most.

A deeper dive into Haskell

If you enjoyed unit 5 on `Functor`, `Applicative`, and `Monad`, the good news is that those topics are the tip of the Haskell iceberg. Many other type classes and topics in Haskell offer similar levels of interesting abstraction and new ways to think about programs. The best place to continue this is on the Typeclassopedia, which is part of the Haskell wiki (found at https://wiki.haskell.org/Typeclassopedia). One of the primary goals of this book is to equip you with a solid-enough understanding of Haskell's more abstract type classes that you could explore them on your own. The Typeclassopedia starts with the interesting type classes discussed in this book and then moves on to increasingly more powerful and abstract type classes.

One topic that we were unable to cover in this book is parallel and concurrent programming in Haskell. If you've done any work with parallel programming in a language such as C++, you know how tricky it can be to make sure state is maintained effectively when you have asynchronous computations being called. A major benefit of Haskell's obsession with pure functional programming is that it's much easier to parallelize Haskell code. A fantastic book by Simon Marlow, *Parallel and Concurrent Programming in Haskell* (O'Reilly Media, 2013), gives this topic the full coverage it deserves. Having completed this book, you should be able to easily jump in. Marlow's book is free to read online: http://chimera.labs.oreilly.com/books/1230000000929/index.html.

The biggest change in Haskell since I first learned the language is the amount of headway it has gained in becoming a "real" programming language. A growing number of software engineers are writing production code with Haskell. The stack build system, which is a relatively recent addition to Haskell, is evidence of this. A good place to start exploring packages and libraries for Haskell is on the Haskell-lang.org libraries page (https://haskell-lang.org/libraries). This page covers many of the essential packages and tools you can use for writing Haskell programs (and we've touched on many in this book).

More powerful type systems than Haskell?

If Haskell's powerful type system is what intrigued you the most about Haskell, you'll be happy to know that a few languages out there, based on Haskell, try to push the type envelope even further. Two interesting examples are Idris and Liquid Haskell. Both languages expand on Haskell's types by allowing even more detailed and powerful constraints on the types used in a program. Imagine if the compiler was able to warn you that `head` was a partial function, or you were able to specify the size of a list in your types. Both of these checks are beyond the power of Haskell's type system, but are possible in Liquid Haskell and Idris.

Idris—programming with dependent types

Idris is a programming language that allows for dependent types. Idris has first-class types in the same way Haskell has first-class functions, so types can be computed and manipulated in Idris the same way that you manipulate functions in Haskell. What sort of power does this provide? One of the problems in Haskell related to `foldl` is that although `foldl` is often more intuitive than `foldr`, `foldl` doesn't work on infinite lists. This, incidentally, makes `foldl` a partial function because you can't check whether a list is infinite, and infinite lists are a value the function is undefined on. You could solve this problem if you could guarantee that your lists were finite. This is beyond the power of Haskell's type system, but Idris's dependent types make it possible to specify that a list argument must be finite.

You can learn more about Idris by visiting the language's homepage (www.idris-lang.org/documentation/). Additionally, Manning has published a book on Idris by the creator of the language: *Type-Driven Development with Idris* by Edwin Brady (2017).

Liquid Haskell—provable types

Liquid Haskell expands on Haskell's type system by allowing you to use logical predicates with your types to ensure proper program behavior. These types are called *refinement types*. Like Idris, Liquid Haskell's type system works to eliminate partial functions through the type system. The constraints assumed on a program are checked at compile time. One example is that Liquid Haskell makes it possible to ensure that division by zero isn't possible at the type level. The amazing thing about this is that division by zero errors can be *caught when your code compiles*. The best place to learn more about Liquid Haskell is on the project's homepage (https://ucsd-progsys.github.io/liquidhaskell-blog/).

Other functional programming languages

Perhaps after reading through this book you've developed a love for functional programming but aren't quite sure that Haskell is the best language for you. There are a wide variety of mature, powerful functional programming languages that you can explore. Haskell is certainly the purest of these languages, but that can sometimes be a downside.

Functional programming languages broadly fall into two families: the Lisp family and the ML family. Haskell is a good representation of the ML type of functional programming languages, which usually use a similar type system (though each type system has its own unique features). The Lisp languages are generally dynamically typed and involve heavy use of parentheses and prefix operators. If you're interested in functional programming, I strongly recommend mastering both a Lisp family language and an ML family language. Although they share many commonalities, they're both different ways to think about programs.

Recommended programming languages in the Lisp family

The biggest shock to most newcomers to any Lisp language is the abundance of parentheses. Lisp represents all programs as trees of computation, and nested parentheses are a good way to represent these trees. The tree structure allows for sophisticated manipulation of programs as data. A hallmark of many Lisp languages is the idea of macros, which allows for the generation of code at compile type. This allows Lisp programmers to easily define their own syntax when necessary. Writing a custom domain-specific language (DSL) in a Lisp can often require just a few lines of code. The following are a couple of good options for exploring Lisp in greater depth.

Racket

The Racket programming language is the descendant of a long line of languages from the Scheme dialect of Lisp. It's probably the purest contemporary representation of the Lisp family and has amazing community support. Like Haskell, Racket has a relatively small commercial community compared to those who use the language to explore programming language theory. Despite its academic tendencies, the Racket community has done a great job making it easy to get started and learn Racket. You can learn more at the Racket website: https://racket-lang.org/.

Clojure

The Clojure programming language is by far the most commercially viable Lisp. Clojure sits on top of the Java Virtual Machine (JVM) and therefore has access to all Java libraries. A large community of practically minded, working software developers are using Clojure. If Lisp sounds interesting to you, but your primary interest is shipping code and getting things done, you'll be happy with the Clojure community. More information can be found on the Clojure page: https://clojure.org/.

Common Lisp

Although Common Lisp is unfortunately rather dated at this point, it's one of the most powerful programming languages ever created. Common Lisp is a language obsessed with abstracting out code as much as possible and creating, in my opinion, the most expressive programming language to date. The major downside is that it's difficult to use Common Lisp for practical applications today. If you study this language in depth, you'll fall tragically in love with it. A great intro to the language is Peter Seibel's *Practical Common Lisp* (Apress, 2005), which is available free online: www.gigamonkeys.com/book/.

Recommended programming languages in the ML family

Haskell belongs to the ML family of functional programming languages. The greatest defining features of ML languages are their powerful type systems. Haskell is arguably the most challenging of the ML family because of its combination of using lazy evaluation, enforcing pure functional programming, and relying heavily on abstract concepts such as monads. If you like most of what you learned in the book but feel that Haskell is just a bit too challenging to work with, you might find your new favorite language in this group. The ML family typically includes many languages that are as academic as Haskell, such as Miranda and Standard ML. I've excluded these in favor of the following more pragmatic alternatives.

F#

The F# programming language is an implementation of another ML variant (OCaml) for Microsoft's .NET programming environment. F# is a multiparadigm programming language with strong support for functional programming, as well as for object-oriented programming. If you're a .NET developer using a language such as C#, you'll likely find F# to be a great way to combine many of the things you enjoy about Haskell with the .NET ecosystem. Supported by Microsoft, F# has great documentation and a large variety of existing libraries and tools that will allow you to get a lot of practical work done. More can be learned from the F# homepage: http://fsharp.org/.

Scala

Like F#, Scala combines strong types, functional programming, and object-oriented programming. Scala runs on top of the JVM, and like Clojure, can readily make use of the vast number of libraries supported by that environment. Scala is a remarkably flexible language that allows you to write everything, from a less verbose form of Java, to code using monads and functors. Scala has a great community of developers and is probably your best bet if you'd like to do functional programming for a living. The tools and resources available for Scala are on par with any other industrial-strength programming language. You can learn more at the Scala site: www.scala-lang.org.

Elm and PureScript

Elm (http://elm-lang.org/) and PureScript (www.purescript.org) are distinct programming languages that offer the same goal: creating a language resembling Haskell that can be compiled to JavaScript. The Elm programming language is focused on creating JavaScript user interfaces using functional programming. The Elm website has a wide variety of great examples to get you started. PureScript (not to be confused with TypeScript) is focused on making a Haskell-like language that compiles to JavaScript. PureScript is similar to Haskell in syntax and usage and should be fairly easy to get started with, now that you've completed this book.

Appendix

ANSWERS TO END-OF-LESSON EXERCISES

The beautiful thing about code is that there are no wrong answers as long as you get the right results. The answers to the exercises shown here should be viewed as simply one possible solution to the problem. Especially in Haskell, there are many paths to the correct solution; if you have an alternative answer that gives the correct results, that's the correct solution.

Unit 1

Lesson 2

Q2.1

```
inc x = x + 1
double x = x*2
square x = x^2
```

Q2.2

```
ex3 n = if n `mod` 2 == 0
        then n - 2
        else 3*n+1
```

Q2.3

```
ifEven n = if even n
           then n - 2
           else 3 * n + 1
```

Lesson 3

Q3.1

```
simple = (\x -> x)
makeChange = (\owed given ->
                if given - owed > 0
                then given - owed
                else 0)
```

Q3.2

```
inc = (\x -> x+1)
double = (\x -> x*2)
square = (\x -> x^2)

counter x = (\x -> x + 1)
            ((\x -> x + 1)
             ((\x -> x) x))
```

Lesson 4

Q4.1 Note—if the results are equal, you need to compare first names:

```
compareLastNames name1 name2 = if result == EQ
                               then compare (fst name1) (fst name2)
                               else result
  where result = compare (snd name1) (snd name2)
```

Q4.2 And the new DC office:

```
dcOffice name = nameText ++ " PO Box 1337 - Washington DC, 20001"
  where nameText = (fst name) ++ " " ++ (snd name) ++ ", Esq."

getLocationFunction location = case location of
  "ny" -> nyOffice
  "sf" -> sfOffice
  "reno" -> renoOffice
  "dc" -> dcOffice
  _ -> (\name -> (fst name) ++ " " ++ (snd name))
```

Lesson 5

Q5.1

```
ifEven myFunction x = if even x
                      then myFunction x
                      else x

inc n = n + 1
double n = n*2
square n = n^2

ifEvenInc = ifEven inc
ifEvenDouble = ifEven double
ifEvenSquare = ifEven square
```

Q5.2

```
binaryPartialApplication binaryFunc arg = (\x -> binaryFunc arg x)
```

Here's an example:

```
takeFromFour = binaryPartialApplication (-) 4
```

Lesson 6

Q6.1

```
repeat n = cycle [n]
```

Q6.2

```
subseq start end myList = take difference (drop start myList)
  where difference = end - start
```

Q6.3

```
inFirstHalf val myList = val 'elem' firstHalf
  where midpoint = (length myList) 'div' 2
        firstHalf = take midpoint myList
```

Lesson 7

Q7.1

```
myTail [] = []
myTail (_:xs) = xs
```

Q7.2

```
myGCD a 0 = a
myGCD a b = myGCD b (a 'mod' b)
```

Lesson 8

Q8.1

```
myReverse [] = []
myReverse (x:[]) = [x]
myReverse (x:xs) = (myReverse xs) ++ [x]
```

Q8.2

```
fastFib _ _ 0 = 0
fastFib _ _ 1 = 1
fastFib _ _ 2 = 1
fastFib x y 3 = x + y
fastFib x y c = fastFib (x + y) x (c - 1)
```

Note that you can use a function to hide the fact that you always start with `1 1`:

```
fib n = fastFib 1 1 n
```

Lesson 9

Q9.1

```
myElem val myList = (length filteredList) /= 0
  where filteredList = filter (== val) myList
```

Q9.2

```
isPalindrome text = processedText == reverse processedText
   where noSpaces = filter (/= ' ') text
         processedText = map toLower noSpaces
```

Q9.3

```
harmonic n = sum (take n seriesValues)
  where seriesPairs = zip (cycle [1.0])  [1.0,2.0 .. ]
        seriesValues = map
                       (\pair -> (fst pair)/(snd pair))
                       seriesPairs
```

Unit 2

Lesson 11

Q11.1

```
filter :: (a -> Bool) -> [a] -> [a]
```

If you look at map, you can see there are two differences:

```
map :: (a -> b) -> [a] -> [b]
```

First is that the function passed into filter must return a Bool.
Second is that map can transform the type of the list, whereas filter can't.

Q11.2 For tail, you can return the empty list if the list is empty:

```
safeTail :: [a] -> [a]
safeTail [] = []
safeTail (x:xs) = xs
```

You can't do the same for head, because there's no sane default value for an element. You can't return an empty list, because an empty list is the same type as the elements of the list. See lesson 37 for a more detailed discussion of this topic.

Q11.3

```
myFoldl :: (a -> b -> a) -> a -> [b] -> a
myFoldl f init [] = init
myFoldl f init (x:xs) = myFoldl f newInit xs
  where newInit = f init x
```

Lesson 12

Q12.1 You can make this much easier by reusing canDonateTo:

```
donorFor :: Patient -> Patient -> Bool
donorFor p1 p2 = canDonateTo (bloodType p1) (bloodType p2)
```

Q12.2 You add this helper function to display sex:

```
showSex Male = "Male"
showSex Female = "Female"

patientSummary :: Patient -> String
patientSummary patient = "**************\n" ++
                         "Sex: " ++ showSex (sex patient) ++ "\n" ++
```

```
"Age: " ++ show (age patient) ++ "\n" ++
"Height: " ++ show (height patient) ++ " in.\n" ++
"Weight: " ++ show (weight patient) ++ " lbs.\n" ++
"Blood Type: " ++ showBloodType (bloodType patient) ++
"\n**************\n"
```

Lesson 13

Q13.1 If you look at the type classes that each belongs to, you get a good sense of your answer.

For `Word`:

```
instance Bounded Word
instance Enum Word
instance Eq Word
instance Integral Word
instance Num Word
instance Ord Word
instance Read Word
instance Real Word
instance Show Word
```

For `Int`:

```
instance Bounded Int
instance Enum Int
instance Eq Int
instance Integral Int
instance Num Int
instance Ord Int
instance Read Int
instance Real Int
instance Show Int
```

You can see that they share identical type classes. The best guess would be that `Word` has different bounds than `Int`. If you look at `maxBound`, you can see that `Word` is larger than `Int`:

```
GHCi> maxBound :: Word
18446744073709551615
GHCi> maxBound :: Int
9223372036854775807
```

But Word also has minBound of 0, whereas Int is much lower:

```
GHCi> minBound :: Word
0
GHCi> minBound :: Int
-9223372036854775808
```

So as you might have guessed, Word is an Int that takes on only positive values—essentially an unsigned Int.

Q13.2 You can see the difference if you try inc and succ on the maxBound of Int:

```
GHCi> inc maxBound :: Int
-9223372036854775808
GHCi> succ maxBound :: Int
*** Exception: Prelude.Enum.succ{Int}: tried to take 'succ' of maxBound
```

Because there's no true successor to a Bounded type, succ throws an error. The inc function just rotates you back to the beginning.

Q13.3

```
cycleSucc :: (Bounded a, Enum a, Eq a) => a -> a
cycleSucc n = if n == maxBound
              then minBound
              else succ n
```

Lesson 14

Q14.1 Suppose you have a type like this:

```
data Number = One | Two | Three deriving Enum
```

Now you can use fromEnum to convert this into an Int.
This makes implementing Eq easy as well as Ord:

```
instance Eq Number where
  (==) num1 num2 = (fromEnum num1) == (fromEnum num2)

instance Ord Number where
  compare num1 num2 = compare (fromEnum num1) (fromEnum num2)
```

Q14.2

```
data FiveSidedDie = Side1 | Side2 | Side3 | Side4 |
➥Side5 deriving (Enum, Eq, Show)

class (Eq a, Enum a) => Die a where
```

```
  roll :: Int -> a

instance Die FiveSidedDie where
  roll n = toEnum (n `mod` 5)
```

Unit 3

Lesson 16

Q16.1

```
data Pamphlet = Pamphlet {
  pamphletTitle :: String,
  description :: String,
  contact :: String
  }

data StoreItem = BookItem Book
               | RecordItem VinylRecord
               | ToyItem CollectibleToy
               | PamphletItem Pamphlet
```

Now you need to add another pattern for `price`:

```
price :: StoreItem -> Double
price (BookItem book) = bookPrice book
price (RecordItem record) = recordPrice record
price (ToyItem toy) = toyPrice toy
price (PamphletItem _) = 0.0
```

Q16.2

```
type Radius = Double
type Height = Double
type Width = Double

data Shape = Circle Radius
           | Square Height
           | Rectangle Height Width deriving Show

perimeter :: Shape -> Double
perimeter (Circle r) = 2*pi*r
perimeter (Square h) = 4*h
```

```
perimeter (Rectangle h w) = 2*h + 2*w

area :: Shape -> Double
area (Circle r) = pi*r^2
area (Square h)  = h^2
area (Rectangle h w) = h*w
```

Lesson 17

Q17.1

```
data Color = Red |
   Yellow |
   Blue |
   Green |
   Purple |
   Orange |
   Brown |
   Clear deriving (Show,Eq)

instance Semigroup Color where
   (<>) Clear any = any
   (<>) any Clear = any
   (<>) Red Blue = Purple
   (<>) Blue Red = Purple
   (<>) Yellow Blue = Green
   (<>) Blue Yellow = Green
   (<>) Yellow Red = Orange
   (<>) Red Yellow = Orange
   (<>) a b | a == b = a
            | all (`elem` [Red,Blue,Purple]) [a,b] = Purple
            | all (`elem` [Blue,Yellow,Green]) [a,b] = Green
            | all (`elem` [Red,Yellow,Orange]) [a,b] = Orange
            | otherwise = Brown

instance Monoid Color where
   mempty = Clear
   mappend col1 col2 = col1 <> col2
```

Q17.2

```
data  Events = Events [String]
data  Probs = Probs [Double]

combineEvents :: Events -> Events -> Events
combineEvents (Events e1) (Events e2) = Events (cartCombine combiner e1 e2)
  where combiner = (\x y -> mconcat [x,"-",y])

instance Semigroup Events where
  (<>) = combineEvents

instance Monoid Events where
  mappend = (<>)
  mempty = Events []

combineProbs :: Probs -> Probs -> Probs
combineProbs (Probs p1) (Probs p2) = Probs (cartCombine (*) p1 p2)

instance Semigroup Probs where
  (<>) = combineProbs

instance Monoid Probs where
  mappend = (<>)
  mempty = Probs []
```

Lesson 18

Q18.1

```
boxMap :: (a -> b) -> Box a -> Box b
boxMap func (Box val) = Box (func val)

tripleMap :: (a -> b) -> Triple a -> Triple b
tripleMap func (Triple v1 v2 v3) = Triple (func v1) (func v2) (func v3)
```

Q18.2 The trick is that `Organ` needs to be of type `Ord` to be a key for a `Map`.

You add `enum` to easily build a list of all organs:

```
data Organ = Heart | Brain | Kidney | Spleen deriving (Show, Eq, Ord, Enum)

values :: [Organ]
values = map snd (Map.toList organCatalog)
```

Now you have a list of all organs:

```
allOrgans :: [Organ]
allOrgans = [Heart .. Spleen]
```

Then count those organs:

```
organCounts :: [Int]
organCounts = map countOrgan allOrgans
  where countOrgan = (\organ ->
                      (length . filter (== organ)) values)
```

Now build your organ inventory:

```
organInventory :: Map.Map Organ Int
organInventory = Map.fromList (zip allOrgans organCounts)
```

Lesson 19

Q19.1

```
data Organ = Heart | Brain | Kidney | Spleen deriving (Show, Eq)

sampleResults :: [Maybe Organ]
sampleResults = [(Just Brain),Nothing,Nothing,(Just Spleen)]

emptyDrawers :: [Maybe Organ] -> Int
emptyDrawers contents = (length . filter isNothing) contents
```

Q19.2

```
maybeMap :: (a -> b) -> Maybe a -> Maybe b
maybeMap func Nothing = Nothing
maybeMap func (Just val) = Just (func val)
```

Unit 4

Lesson 21

Q21.1

```
helloPerson :: String -> String
helloPerson name = "Hello" ++ " " ++ name ++ "!"

sampleMap :: Map.Map Int String
sampleMap = Map.fromList [(1,"Will")]

mainMaybe :: Maybe String
mainMaybe = do
   name <- Map.lookup 1 sampleMap
   let statement = helloPerson name
   return statement
```

Q21.2

```
fib 0 = 0
fib 1 = 1
fib 2 = 1
fib n = fib (n-1) + fib (n - 2)

main :: IO ()
main = do
  putStrLn "enter a number"
  number <- getLine
  let value = fib (read number)
  putStrLn (show value)
```

Lesson 22

Q22.1 Remember that lazy I/O lets you treat your input like a list:

```
sampleInput :: [String]
sampleInput = ["21","+","123"]
```

This function isn't perfect, but the aim is just to get familiar with lazy I/O:

```
calc :: [String] -> Int
calc (val1:"+":val2:rest) = read val1 + read val2
calc (val1:"*":val2:rest) = read val1 * read val2

main :: IO ()
main = do
  userInput <- getContents
  let values = lines userInput
  print (calc values)
```

Q22.2

```
quotes :: [String]
quotes = ["quote 1"
         ,"quote 2"
         ,"quote 3"
         ,"quote 4"
         ,"quote 5"]

lookupQuote :: [String] -> [String]
lookupQuote [] = []
```

```
lookupQuote ("n":xs) = []
lookupQuote (x:xs) = quote : (lookupQuote xs)
  where quote = quotes !! (read x - 1)

main :: IO ()
main = do
  userInput <- getContents
  mapM_ putStrLn (lookupQuote  (lines userInput))
```

Lesson 23

Q23.1

```
import qualified Data.Text as T
import qualified Data.Text.IO as TIO

helloPerson :: T.Text -> T.Text
helloPerson name = mconcat [ "Hello "
                           , name
                           , "!"]

main :: IO ()
main = do
  TIO.putStrLn "Hello! What's your name?"
  name <- TIO.getLine
  let statement = helloPerson name
  TIO.putStrLn statement
```

Q23.2

```
import qualified Data.Text.Lazy as T
import qualified Data.Text.Lazy.IO as TIO

toInts :: T.Text -> [Int]
toInts = map (read . T.unpack) . T.lines

main :: IO ()
main = do
  userInput <- TIO.getContents
  let numbers = toInts userInput
  TIO.putStrLn ((T.pack . show . sum) numbers)
```

Lesson 24

Q24.1

```
import System.IO
import System.Environment
import qualified Data.Text as T
import qualified Data.Text.IO as TI

main :: IO ()
main = do
  args <- getArgs
  let source =  args !! 0
  let dest = args !! 1
  input <- TI.readFile source
  TI.writeFile dest input
```

Q24.2

```
import System.IO
import System.Environment
import qualified Data.Text as T
import qualified Data.Text.IO as TI

main :: IO ()
main = do
  args <- getArgs
  let fileName = head args
  input <- TI.readFile fileName
  TI.writeFile fileName (T.toUpper input)
```

Lesson 25

Q25.1

```
import System.IO
import System.Environment
import qualified Data.Text as T
import qualified Data.ByteString as B
import qualified Data.Text.Encoding as E

main :: IO ()
main = do
```

```
  args <- getArgs
  let source =  args !! 0
  input <- B.readFile source
  putStrLn "Bytes:"
  print (B.length input)
  putStrLn "Characters:"
  print ((T.length . E.decodeUtf8) input)
```

Q25.2

```
reverseSection :: Int -> Int -> BC.ByteString -> BC.ByteString
reverseSection start size bytes = mconcat [before,changed,after]
  where (before,rest) = BC.splitAt start bytes
        (target,after) = BC.splitAt size rest
        changed =  BC.reverse target

randomReverseBytes :: BC.ByteString -> IO BC.ByteString
randomReverseBytes bytes = do
  let sectionSize = 25
  let bytesLength = BC.length bytes
  start <- randomRIO (0,(bytesLength - sectionSize))
  return (reverseSection start sectionSize bytes)
```

Unit 5

Lesson 27

QC27.1

```
data Box a = Box a deriving Show

instance Functor Box where
   fmap func (Box val)  = Box (func val)
```

QC27.2

```
myBox :: Box Int
myBox = Box 1

unwrap :: Box a -> a
unwrap (Box val) = val
```

QC27.3

```
printCost :: Maybe Double -> IO()
printCost Nothing = putStrLn "item not found"
printCost (Just cost)= print cost

main :: IO ()
main = do
  putStrLn "enter a part number"
  partNo <- getLine
  let part = Map.lookup (read partNo) partsDB
  printCost (cost <$> part)
```

Lesson 28

Q28.1 Unlike `haversineMaybe`, you can't use pattern matching to get your values, so you have to use familiar do-notation if you don't use `<*>`:

```
haversineIO :: IO LatLong -> IO LatLong -> IO Double
haversineIO ioVal1 ioVal2 = do
   val1 <- ioVal1
   val2 <- ioVal2
   let dist = haversine val1 val2
   return dist
```

Q28.2

```
haversineIO :: IO LatLong -> IO LatLong -> IO Double
haversineIO ioVal1 ioVal2 =  haversine <$> ioVal1 <*> ioVal2
```

Q28.3

```
printCost :: Maybe Double -> IO()
printCost Nothing = putStrLn "missing item"
printCost (Just cost)= print cost

main :: IO ()
main = do
  putStrLn "enter a part number 1"
  partNo1 <- getLine
  putStrLn "enter a part number 2"
  partNo2 <- getLine
  let part1 = Map.lookup (read partNo1) partsDB
  let part2 = Map.lookup (read partNo2) partsDB
```

```
let cheapest = min <$> (cost <$> part1) <*> (cost <$> part2)
printCost cheapest
```

Lesson 29

Q29.1

```
allFmap :: Applicative f => (a -> b) -> f a -> f b
allFmap func app = (pure func) <*> app
```

Q29.2

```
example :: Int
example = (*) ((+) 2 4) 6

exampleMaybe :: Maybe Int
exampleMaybe = pure (*) <*> (pure (+) <*> pure 2 <*> pure 4) <*> pure 6
```

Q29.3

```
startingBeer :: [Int]
startingBeer = [6,12]

remainingBeer :: [Int]
remainingBeer = (\count -> count - 4) <$> startingBeer

guests :: [Int]
guests = [2,3]

totalPeople :: [Int]
totalPeople = (+ 2) <$> guests

beersPerGuest :: [Int]
beersPerGuest = [3,4]

totalBeersNeeded :: [Int]
totalBeersNeeded = (pure (*)) <*>  beersPerGuest <*> totalPeople

beersToPurchase :: [Int]
beersToPurchase = (pure (-)) <*> totalBeersNeeded  <*> remainingBeer
```

Lesson30

Q30.1

```
allFmapM :: Monad m => (a -> b) -> m a -> m b
allFmapM func val = val >>= (\x -> return (func x))
```

Q30.2

```
allApp :: Monad m => m (a -> b) -> m a -> m b
allApp func val = func >>= (\f -> val >>= (\x -> return (f x)) )
```

Q30.3

```
bind :: Maybe a -> (a -> Maybe b) -> Maybe b
bind Nothing _ = Nothing
bind (Just val) func = func val
```

Lesson 31

Q31.1 Now that you've done this once, you'll never again forget how useful do-notation is!

```
main :: IO ()
main = putStrLn "What is the size of pizza 1" >>
       getLine >>=
       (\size1 ->
         putStrLn "What is the cost of pizza 1" >>
         getLine >>=
         (\cost1 ->
           putStrLn "What is the size of pizza 2" >>
           getLine >>=
           (\size2 ->
             putStrLn "What is the cost of pizza 2" >>
             getLine >>=
             (\cost2 ->
               (\pizza1 ->
                 (\pizza2 ->
                   (\betterPizza ->
                     putStrLn (describePizza betterPizza):
                   ) (comparePizzas pizza1 pizza2)
                 )(read size2,read cost2)
               )(read size1, read cost1)
             ))))
```

Q31.2

```
listMain :: [String]
listMain = do
```

```
   size1 <- [10,12,17]
   cost1 <- [12.0,15.0,20.0]
   size2 <- [10,11,18]
   cost2 <- [13.0,14.0,21.0]
   let pizza1 = (size1,cost1)
   let pizza2 = (size2,cost2)
   let betterPizza = comparePizzas pizza1 pizza2
   return (describePizza betterPizza)
```

Q31.3

```
monadMain :: Monad m => m Double -> m Double
          -> m Double -> m Double -> m String
monadMain s1 c1 s2 c2 = do
   size1 <- s1
   cost1 <- c1
   size2 <- s2
   cost2 <- c2
   let pizza1 = (size1,cost1)
   let pizza2 = (size2,cost2)
   let betterPizza = comparePizzas pizza1 pizza2
   return (describePizza betterPizza)
```

Lesson 32

Q32.1

```
monthEnds :: [Int]
monthEnds = [31,28,31,30,31,30,31,31,30,31,30,31]

dates :: [Int] -> [Int]
dates ends = [date| end <- ends, date <- [1 ..end ] ]
```

Q32.2

```
datesDo :: [Int] -> [Int]
datesDo ends = do
   end <- ends
   date <- [1 .. end]
   return date

datesMonad :: [Int] -> [Int]
datesMonad ends  =  ends >>=
```

```
(\end ->
  [1 .. end] >>=
    (\date -> return date))
```

Unit 6

The exercises in unit 6 consist of refactoring code into multiple files. This takes up too much space for an appendix, and the exercises aren't so much about being correct as about manually walking through the steps covered in each lesson.

Unit 7

Lesson 38

Q38.1 Make a helper function here:

```
allDigits :: String -> Bool
allDigits val = all (== True) (map isDigit val)

addStrInts :: String -> String -> Either Int String
addStrInts val1 val2 | allDigits val1 && allDigits val2 =
                                            Left (read val1 +
                                                  read val2)
                     | not (allDigits val1 || allDigits val2) =
                                              Right "both args invalid"
                     | not (allDigits val1) = Right "first arg invalid"
                     | otherwise = Right "second arg invalid"
```

Q38.2

```
safeSucc :: (Enum a, Bounded a, Eq a) => a -> Maybe a
safeSucc n = if n == maxBound
             then Nothing
             else Just (succ n)

safeTail :: [a] -> [a]
safeTail [] = []
safeTail (x:xs) = xs

safeLast :: [a] -> Either a String
safeLast [] = Right "empty list"
safeLast xs =  safeLast' 10000 xs
```

You know that the empty list isn't possible, because only `safeLast` will call this function, and it already checks for the empty list:

```
safeLast' :: Int -> [a] -> Either a String
safeLast' 0 _ = Right "List exceeds safe bound"
safeLast' _ (x:[]) = Left x
safeLast' n (x:xs) = safeLast' (n - 1) xs
```

Lesson 39

Q39.1

```
buildRequestNOSSL :: BC.ByteString -> BC.ByteString
                  -> BC.ByteString -> BC.ByteString -> Request
buildRequestNOSSL token host method path  = setRequestMethod method
                                  $ setRequestHost host
                                  $ setRequestHeader "token" [token]
                                  $ setRequestSecure False
                                  $ setRequestPort 80
                                  $ setRequestPath path
                                  $ defaultRequest
```

Q39.2 Note that you also need to add `http-types` to your project and import `Network.HTTP.Types.Status`:

```
main :: IO ()
main = do
  response <- httpLBS request
  let status = getResponseStatusCode response
  if status == 200
    then do
         print "saving request to file"
         let jsonBody = getResponseBody response
         L.writeFile "data.json" jsonBody
    else print $ statusMessage $ getResponseStatus response
```

Lesson 40

QC40.1

```
instance ToJSON NOAAResult where
   toJSON (NOAAResult uid mindate maxdate name datacoverage resultId) =
```

```
    object ["uid" .= uid
           ,"mindate" .= mindate
           ,"maxdate" .= maxdate
           ,"name" .= name
           ,"datacoverage" .= datacoverage
           ,"id" .= resultId]

instance ToJSON Resultset

instance ToJSON Metadata

instance ToJSON NOAAResponse
```

QC 40.2

```
data IntList = EmptyList | Cons Int IntList deriving (Show,Generic)

instance ToJSON IntList
instance FromJSON IntList
```

Lesson 41

Q41.1

```
addTool :: String -> String -> IO ()
addTool toolName toolDesc  = withConn "tools.db" $
                  \conn -> do
                    execute conn (mconcat ["INSERT INTO tools
                                          ,"(name,description "
                                          ,",timesBorrowed)"
                                          ,"VALUES (?,?,?)"])
                      (toolName,toolDesc,(0 :: Int))
                    print "tool added"
```

Q41.2

```
promptAndAddTool :: IO ()
promptAndAddTool = do
   print "Enter tool name"
   toolName <- getLine
   print "Enter tool description"
   toolDesc <- getLine
   addTool toolName toolDesc
```

```
performCommand :: String -> IO ()
performCommand command
   | command == "users" = printUsers >> main
   | command == "tools" = printTools >> main
   | command == "adduser" = promptAndAddUser >> main
   | command == "checkout" = promptAndCheckout >> main
   | command == "checkin" = promptAndCheckin >> main
   | command == "in" = printAvailable >> main
   | command == "out" = printCheckedout >> main
   | command == "quit" = print "bye!"
   | command == "addtool" = promptAndAddTool >> main
   | otherwise = print "Sorry command not found" >> main
```

Lesson 42

Q42.1

```
crossOver :: (UArray Int Int ,UArray Int Int) -> Int -> UArray Int Int
crossOver (a1,a2) crossOverPt = runSTUArray $ do
  st1 <- thaw a1
  let end = (snd . bounds) a1
  forM_ [crossOverPt .. end] $ \i -> do
    writeArray st1 i $ a2 ! i
  return st1
```

Q42.2

```
replaceZeros :: UArray Int Int -> UArray Int Int
replaceZeros array = runSTUArray $ do
  starray <- thaw array
  let end = (snd . bounds) array
  let count = 0
  forM_ [0 .. end] $ \i -> do
    val <- readArray starray i
    when (val == 0) $ do
      writeArray starray i (-1)
  return starray
```

INDEX

Symbols

Numerics

A

RELATED MANNING TITLES

Get Programming in F#
A guide for .NET developers
by Isaac Abraham

ISBN: 9781617293993
592 pages, $44.99
February 2018

Functional Programming in Scala
by Paul Chiusano and Runar Bjarnason

ISBN: 9781617290657
320 pages, $44.99
September 2014

Type-Driven Development with Idris
by Edwin Brady

ISBN: 9781617293023
480 pages, $49.99
March 2017

Functional Programming in Java
How functional techniques improve your Java programs
by Pierre-Yves Saumont

ISBN: 9781617292736
472 pages, $49.99
January 2017

For ordering information go to www.manning.com